OPERATING SYSTEMS PRINCIPLES

OPERATING SYSTEMS PRINCIPLES

SECOND EDITION

Stanley A. Kurzban
Thomas S. Heines
Anthony P. Sayers

VNR VAN NOSTRAND REINHOLD COMPANY
New York

Copyright © 1984 by Van Nostrand Reinhold Company Inc.

Library of Congress Catalog Card Number: 83-10274
ISBN: 0-442-25734-1

Manufactured in the United States of America

Published by Van Nostrand Reinhold Company Inc.
115 Fifth Avenue
New York, New York 10003

Van Nostrand Reinhold Company Limited
Molly Millars Lane
Wokingham, Berkshire RG11 2PY, England

Van Nostrand Reinhold
480 La Trobe Street
Melbourne, Victoria 3000, Australia

Macmillan of Canada
Division of Canada Publishing Corporation
164 Commander Boulevard
Agincourt, Ontario M1S 3C7, Canada

15 14 13 12 11 10 9 8 7 6 5 4 3

Library of Congress Cataloging in Publication Data

Kurzban, Stanley A.
   Operating systems principles.

   Bibliography: p.
   Includes index.
   1. Operating systems (Computers) I. Heines, Thomas S.
(Thomas Samuel), 1927–   II. Sayers, Anthony P.
III. Title.
QA76.6.K874   1984   001.64'2   83-10274
ISBN 0-442-25734-1

THE VAN NOSTRAND REINHOLD DATA PROCESSING SERIES

Edited by Ned Chapin, Ph.D.

IMS Programming Techniques: A Guide to Using DL/1
Dan Kapp and Joseph L. Leben

Reducing COBOL Complexity Through Structured Programming
Carma L. McClure

Composite/Structured Design
Glenford J. Myers

Reliable Software Through Composite Design
Glenford J. Myers

Top-Down Structured Programming Techniques
Clement L. McGowen and John R. Kelly

Operating Systems Principles
Stanley Kurzban, T.S. Heines and A.P. Sayers

Microcomputer Handbook
Charles J. Sippl

Strategic Planning of Management Information Systems
Paul Siegel

Flowcharts
Ned Chapin

Introduction to Artificial Intelligence
Philip C. Jackson, Jr.

Computers and Management for Business
Douglas A. Colbert

Operating Systems Survey
Anthony P. Sayers

Management of Information Technology: Case Studies
Elizabeth B. Adams

Compiler Techniques
Bary W. Pollack

Documentation Manual
J. Van Duyn

Preface to First Edition

This book is an introduction to the concepts and technology of computer operating systems and is intended for use by students taking a first course in operating systems theory. Typical of the courses for which this book would be appropriate are the "undergraduate course of operating systems principles" described by the COSINE Committee on Education of the National Academy of Engineering's Commission on Education [COS71] and the Course 14 of the ACM's "Curriculum 68" [ACM68]. This book is also of value to those in management, procuring, project planning, and the like, who may become involved in the development, modification, or use of an operating system.

It is assumed that the reader has some familiarity with the elements of computer architecture, an assembly language, and one or more higher-level languages, and has, in addition, some experience in the use of an operating system.

The material in this book should enable readers to understand the function and design of any operating system they might encounter. They should be able to participate in the design, implementation, or modification of an operating system after learning the specifics of a given project.

The style of the book is tutorial; there are many examples and exercises. Abundant references direct the reader to more detailed studies of particular subjects.

For the purposes of this book, an operating system includes supervisory and file-management routines, utility programs, and processors for the system's control languages. Compilers are discussed only insofar as their characteristics are affected by their host operating system.

This book covers the concepts of all operating systems in current use. Since the authors have the greatest familiarity with the IBM 360/370 Operating System(s), more examples are taken from these systems than from any other; however, the concepts in the book are by no means limited to those systems.

Preface to the
Second Edition

A measure of the aptness of this book's title is the extent to which its topics, "Principles," apply to operating systems as they evolve. We hope the reader agrees that the past seven years give evidence of the wisdom with which our title and topics were chosen.

While principles endure, emphasis may not. Many have observed that vast fortunes depend on operating systems' attributes, particularly their reliability and security. So it is that these topics receive increased attention in the present edition. This is especially true of the latter topic, one whose importance many failed to appreciate in 1975.

Another area growing in significance is distributed processing. Accordingly, the present edition devotes more attention to the movement of data and requests for service into and out of the system. On the other hand, various developments, including enhancements to the computers on which operating systems run, have modified the roles of queuing theory and compiler design, leading us to omit these topics that properly deserve separate books of their own rather than the cursory treatment we can afford them in the present context.

References to features and facilities that conserve space in main storage or optimize placement of files on secondary storage are retained despite the fact that reduced costs per unit and improved use of multiprogramming techniques have rendered some of these obsolete in the contexts of some systems.

The successors of operating systems developed for IBM's System/360 and System/370 computers now run on many other computers as well. To avoid confusion, we continue to refer to the older families of computers.

Stan Kurzban
Tom Heines

Contents

1
Introduction

The term "operating system" came into widespread use in the late 1950s. Sayers [Say71] defines an operating system as "a set of programs and routines which guide a computer in the performance of its tasks and assist the programs (and programmers) with certain supporting functions." This definition is accurate and useful, but by no means the only one. The American National Standard definition is: "Software which controls the execution of computer programs and which may provide scheduling, debugging, input/output control, accounting, compilation, storage assignment, data management, and related services." This definition, while similar to Sayers', seems too restrictive and too dependent on other terms which themselves are jargon and require definition.

We can expand Sayers' definition by naming the supporting functions provided or the programs assisted. Alternatively, we may make reference to current practices in the computer industry by defining operating systems as "that programming which is provided by the vendor of a computing system as an integral part of the product he markets." This, of course, yields an incomplete and imprecise definition which varies with vendors and computers.

Let us, then, accept Sayers' definition of an operating system with some qualifying remarks. Some authorities would restrict the term "operating system" to a set of programs which creates an apparent computing system as comprehensive as the original hardware system, but simpler and easier to use. For our purposes, however, those programs which are peripheral to the computing system, but vital to the effective use of the system and of potential value to all those who use the system, are included. Examples of such programs are utilities (for example, file-copying programs, sorts, and listing programs), spooling[1] programs, and routines for managing networks of computers. Language processing programs — assemblers, compilers, and interpreters — are considered here only insofar as they are influenced by the characteristics of particular operating systems.

Having defined our subject, we next consider how operating systems have evolved to their current level of sophistication. We then discuss the purposes

---

[1] Spooling, from simultaneous peripheral operations on-line, is the processing of data between a device designed for communication with people (a printer or card punch, for example) and an intermediate storage device (such as a disk or magnetic tape device).

served by operating systems, their constituent parts, some programming techniques used in their development, and the influence of computers upon the operating systems which support them. These topics will lay the foundation needed for more detailed study of operating systems.

1.1 HISTORICAL PERSPECTIVE

The development of operating systems has been marked by two different types of progress: evolution and retrenchment. Within generations of computers, evolution has dominated, with successive advances occurring in response to problems successively encountered. The problems often arose as a result of earlier advances, a phenomenon Marine [Mar70], in another context, attributes to "the engineering mentality," the way of thinking which insists upon solving every problem individually without regard for related problems or side effects. Such an approach, despite its seeming inadequacy, yields prompt solutions to problems, a requirement in the fast-advancing field of electronic computing. This type of development has fortunately been reinforced by retrenchment, more comprehensive advances, which consolidated earlier technological gains. These advances have most often coincided with the introduction of radically different computers, but also at times, for combinations of less than obvious reasons, occurred in the absence of hardware innovation. Radically new operating systems, not truly revolutionary, but significantly innovative, have permitted the consolidation of earlier advances and the development of integrated sets of new programs which provide totally new facilities.

Before there was an operating system, there were computers. With little or no accompanying programming, the computer was a very complex tool, difficult for even its designers to use efficiently. Systems with one-card loaders and primitive assemblers could be of use to those with the patience and analytical skill needed to break a problem down to a succession of additions, divisions, etc., provided someone well acquainted with the computer could write input/output (I/O) routines for them. But some systems developed prior to 1955 lacked even an assembler. They had to be programmed in octal or decimal, with the programmers supplying operation codes and branch locations by themselves. The addition of a single instruction near the beginning of a program meant the relocation (and repunching) of perhaps thousands of addresses, or patching — the addition of code at the end of a program and the replacement of an existing instruction by a branch to the new code. The new code had to begin with the replaced instruction, and end with a branch back to the location following the replacement. A program with many patches was not only inefficient, but also very difficult to debug.

The users of these primitive systems normally operated the computer personally. The absence of both aids for debugging and established operating procedures made this necessary. No third party could have known how to interrogate and modify storage in response to an unexpected condition or a bug. No one but the programmer could distinguish a loop from normal computation or determine from patterns of lights that a new reel of magnetic tape should be mounted.

Monitors

The first problem to be solved by a systems program, that is, one which performed no work specifically requested by any user, was, naturally enough, that of accomplishing transitions between users' programs. This was a serious problem. Many jobs required more time for preparation than for execution. *Monitors* such as the one developed in the late 1950s by programmers at General Motors and North American Aviation for the IBM 704 [Ros69a] accomplished job-to-job transition and invoked other programs which facilitated use of the computer — an assembler, a loader, a FORTRAN compiler, and a dump.

Monitors soon were developed to accept and produce reels of magnetic tape in lieu of card decks and printed listings, respectively. The tapes could be processed by a less expensive (peripheral) computer used only for that purpose. This relieved the principal (central) computer of the burden of dealing with slower devices. Jobs to be run under the monitors were restricted as to what they could do, making job set-up so simple that it was possible for operators to replace the programmers at the computer. Procedures could be varied, but the variations permitted were well-defined and within the operators' capabilities.

With the appropriation by the monitor of magnetic tape drives for specialized use, restrictions had to be placed upon programmers' use of I/O devices. Note that this is a typical example of a problem caused by a solution. This problem was a fortunate one, however, inasmuch as it led to the development of I/O subroutines. These greatly simplified programmers' views of I/O operations. Since these routines were used very frequently, they were stored in *libraries* on magnetic tape as object (executable or binary), rather than source (character string), code. This led in turn to the more extensive use of libraries of programs in this more efficient format.

Since such programs had to be used by almost all of the system's programmers, it became necessary to permit their loading at various locations in main storage to meet the constraints of many varied main programs. The relocatable *loader* could modify the routines as they were loaded from libraries, to reflect the locations selected for them.

Other innovations which appeared in the late 1950s included *directories* for program libraries to facilitate sequential searching, *overlay* mechanisms to permit the serial use of given storage locations by a sequence of routines, and a system *log* wherein accounting data could be recorded by the monitor.

Executives

The monitor of the late 1950s became an *executive* in the early 1960s. (This term had also been used earlier.) The executive was designed to facilitate efficient use of the channels and interruption mechanisms which were then becoming available. These permitted computational processing to occur simultaneously with I/O operations. The completion of an I/O operation caused an interruption of processing. Processing could be resumed after the successful completion of the I/O operation had been noted somewhere or something had been done about an unsuccessful operation. The complexity involved was best dealt with by a single group of programmers whose executive could then make other programmers' jobs easier.

Supervisors

As executives became *supervisors,* they performed more functions of general necessity, but troublesome complexity. They also became permanently resident in main storage, giving the term "system overhead" a spatial dimension as well as a temporal one. Most of the supervisor's routines were useful to most users of the system, but *all* users had to tolerate the presence of *all* the routines in main storage at *all* times.

With the problem of usability solved, the problem of integrity appeared; that is, since almost any reasonably intelligent person could now program a computer, many who might better not have, did. And when they did, they effected unintentional modifications of the supervisor, rendering it inoperable. So it was that protection mechanisms, such as registers for bounding addessing capability and locks for restricting access to sensitive data, were developed.

The IBM 7040/7090 family of computers was a focus for much of the evolutionary and nonevolutionary work of the early 1960s. IBM produced IBSYS [IBM6] with its IBJOB monitor and IOCS (Input/Output Control System) in 1963. In 1962-1965 Project MAC at MIT produced the Compatible Time-Sharing System (CTSS, language-compatible with FMS, the FORTRAN Monitor System) [Cri65], a system which *swapped* users' programs between main and secondary storage at intervals called *time slices.* Significant work was also done at the University of Michigan [Mic63], Yale [Yal63], and IBM's research laboratory at Yorktown Heights, New York, among other places. These systems consolidated earlier advances and opened new avenues of progress. All of the systems, but most notably IBSYS, went through significant periods of evolution, but nevertheless represented milestones in the development of operating systems at their inception.

Operating Systems

The IBM System/360 Operating System (OS/360) [Mea66], which supported the System/360 series of computers, ushered in the present era of operating systems.

While many facilities of existing operating systems (checkpoint/restart, time-sharing, and even simple multiprogramming) were lacking in OS/360 when it was first released in 1965, that system was truly a new species [Ros67]. It is well represented in the material which follows, and is therefore not described further at this point. Still more recent landmark systems are MULTICS (*multiplexed information and computing service*) [Cor65] and IBM's TSS/360 and OS/VS [IBM7]. Descriptions of these are also deferred.

The history of operating systems is not exclusively American. The ATLAS system [Kil67], developed in England by Ferranti, Limited, and Manchester University, seems to have been "years ahead of its time." The GEORGE systems [Cut70], developed by International Computers, Limited, (ICL), are also noteworthy and the THE System [Dij68b], developed by Dijkstra at the University of Eindhoven, the Netherlands, has contributed as much as any other to the theory of systems programming.

An excellent survey of the history of operating systems [Ros69a] is the source for much of the foregoing. The first two papers of [Rose67] cover the same ground and related subjects. See also [Kat73]. More detailed views of individual systems are best gleaned from the references cited.

1.2 GOALS OF OPERATING SYSTEMS

Operating systems are intended to facilitate efficient use of computers. They provide a convenient interface to hide from programmers the complexity of the bare computing systems. They manage the resources of computing systems so that the resources are optimally used. They permit the accounting for individuals' use of resources. They make it possible for programs to be impervious to minor malfunctions or the unavailability of one out of many similar resources, for example, one magnetic tape drive out of ten that might be attached to a computer. They protect users' programs and data from accidental or malicious destruction, theft, or unauthorized disclosure to other users. To do this effectively, they provide the same protection for themselves. And they can even give computing systems the appearance of being much larger than they really are, via so-called "virtual" resources.

Some of the terms we use, because they have special meanings in our context, require definitions. These are supplied in the following list of attributes of operating systems:

1. Usability — the property of being easy to use; appearing to have been designed for the user's convenience.
2. Generality — the property of being useful in many ways; the system does all and only what the set of all of its users want it to do.
3. Efficiency — the property of functioning quickly; the system makes optimum use of the resources at its disposal.

4. Visibility — the property of revealing to users all they must know to take maximum advantage of the system.
5. Flexibility — adaptability to a specific environment; the system's behavior can be suited to its tasks.
6. Opacity (commonly called "transparency" in defiance of that word's normal meaning) — the property of allowing users to remain unaware of all details they need not know, all that lies beneath the interface provided by the system.
7. Security — the property of protecting data from unauthorized access, whether malicious or accidental.
8. Integrity — the property of protecting itself and users from damage or any other ill effect of others' errors or malice.
9. Capacity — the property of lacking unnecessary limitations.
10. Reliability — the property of appearing to fail as rarely as possible.
11. Availability — the property of providing as much function as much of the time as possible.
12. Serviceability (or maintainability) — the property of being easily and quickly repaired.
13. Extensibility — the property of accepting additions and modifications with maximum ease.

The definitions of the attributes in our list contain few terms that restrict their applicability to operating systems. The designers of any product might do well to consult the list in doing their work.

All of these characteristics contribute to the broader goals of an operating system: to permit people to accomplish meaningful tasks more easily and less expensively than would otherwise be possible. The attributes we have listed may be seen as subgoals which contribute in more or less obvious ways to the principal objectives of ease of use and efficiency, in the more general sense of the latter term.

The most obvious accomplishment of an operating system is its presentation to the user of an interface much easier to use than that of the computing system itself. This is not so much true with respect to computational processing, where the assembler stands between the user and the computer. But it is true with respect to the peripheral, yet vital, processing incidental to computation.

Before data can be processed, it must be communicated. The operating system permits programmers to code simple READ and WRITE statements, although the computer itself requires much more precise direction. To process data efficiently, one must manage resources. The operating system needs only statements concerning requirements for types of resources. The selection of specific resources is handled by the system. In general, the operating system permits users to express their requirements in terms meaningful to them, instead of in the language specific to some conglomeration of circuits and registers.

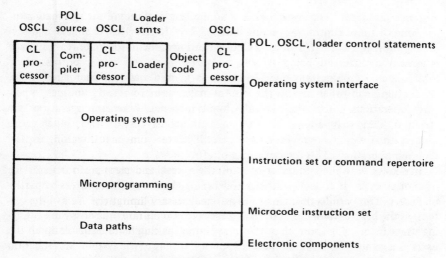

Figure 1.1. Levels of Interface for a Compile/Load/Go Job.

This simplification may be seen as an interface of a level higher than that of the computer itself. A higher-level language such as COBOL, FORTRAN, or PL/1 can be perceived as a still higher level of interface, one provided by a compiler. The compiler, in turn, is written to the interface of the operating system, the same interface at which the compiler's output, the object program, executes. This notion of levels of interface is graphically illustrated in Figure 1.1, where the operating system's control language (OSCL) is seen as another language. In the case of the OSCL, the language used for communicating with the operating system, the language processor is probably not properly called a compiler. But the analogy has substantial validity.

The facilities offered by an operating system are dictated by the generality of their usefulness. All useful programs must obtain data and produce data. I/O routines are therefore of general usefulness. For this reason, they are included in operating systems. Languages intended for use in scientific computation are likely to include a square-root function because it is of general use to scientists. But many operating systems are used extensively for nonscientific processing, and so do not have square-root facilities. Such a facility would not be of sufficient use to a sufficient portion of the using population to justify the cost of its implementation. Operating systems are not immune to economic principles: a product's value must exceed the cost of its production. This defines the bounds of generality.

An operating system is designed to serve not only its individual users, but also, more importantly, the totality of all its users as a group. One way it accomplishes the latter objective is by coordinating the users' utilization of the system's resources. The resources of a computing system are many: main storage, one or more central processing units (CPUs), I/O devices, channels, and secondary storage media. Whenever a CPU is waiting for work or main storage space is unused, a resource is being wasted. An operating system tries to process users' jobs in such combinations and sequences as to maximize the use of resources. By spooling and other means, the system makes use of unused resources to perform operations before they are absolutely required. When the operations are required, they may appear to occur instantaneously or, at least, much more quickly than would otherwise be the case. Thus less time is lost waiting for the required operation. This is an example of efficiency.

In dealing with the system's resources, the operating system performs a service of another type. It collects statistics concerning the use of the resources by particular users. This permits the manager of an installation to charge the users of the system on the basis of their use of it. This serves the community of users by discouraging users from using more than they need, thus making more available to all the users as a group. These data on use also permit tuning of the system, modification of parameters of the system, and even its configuration, to tailor the system to the requirements of its users. The provision of these data is visibility. The consequent tuning illustrates flexibility.

In providing a high level of interface, the operating system shields its users from more than just the computer's complexity. They are also protected from its variability. Since they may ask for *a* tape drive rather than *that* tape drive, they need not be aware that *that* tape drive is unavailable due to preventive maintenance. In fact, the tape drive they are given to use *may* be superior (for example, with respect to the density of the data on the recording medium) to the one they were expecting. It may even be a disk drive! The point is that by creating a new interface, the operating system can continue to function without apparent change, even if the interface to which it is written changes substantially. Just as a higher-level language may be machine-independent, so an operating system may be independent of many of the characteristics of the computing system beneath it. This is opacity. (It is in the sense that users "see" the tape drive "through" the system that some mistake opacity for "transparency.")

Operating systems exploit inventions that make it possible to restrict access to certain facilities and storage locations. An operating system may require that a user know a certain password or be authorized in some prescribed manner before he is granted certain privileges. These privileges might include the right to execute I/O instructions directly rather than through the system's I/O routines, the right to modify or destroy certain data files, or the right to read from certain main or secondary storage locations. Thus, the system can protect data and programs from unauthorized use or destruction. This applies not only to malicious misuse, where users try to circumvent the system's regulations for their own nefarious purposes, but also to accidents whereby valuable data might unintentionally be destroyed or exposed to view by unauthorized persons. These are all aspects of security.

The value of protection is greatest to the operating system's own resources, for if the system itself were not secure, the mechanisms it uses to protect others would be vulnerable. Self-defense is more a requirement than a right of operating systems.

The isolation provided by protection mechanisms also contributes to the integrity of the high-level interface of the operating system. Only because these mechanisms exist can users be sure that apparent errors in their own programs are not really due to the action of some other user.

An operating system may expand the apparent storage capacity of a computing system. Through a technique called virtual storage, discussed in Chapter 4, users may be led to believe that the main storage space of the system is much larger than it really is. This deception is accomplished by the system's dynamic mapping of portions of a large virtual address-space into a small real one. At any instant of time, all critical portions of the virtual space needed for the execution of the current instruction are mapped into real main-storage locations.

The operating system always provides the only interface its users see. The actual computer is hidden by it. There is no reason that an operating system could not simulate virtual disks, virtual tape drives, virtual CPUs, and so forth, by techniques analogous to those which implement virtual storage. The extent to which this has been done is discussed in subsequent chapters. It can be stated here, however, that few systems go beyond virtual storage, that is, linearly addressable storage, in extending their effective capacity.

RAS Characteristics

The value of an operating system may be measured by its success in meeting its objectives. Particular objectives, as we explain below, may be stated with reference to the general goals of operating systems described above. Our goals, treated here as a group because they are not realized through distinct functions of the system, are reliability, availability, and serviceability, sometimes referred to as *RAS characteristics*.

Simply stated, a reliable system is one which rarely permits the effects of malfunctions in either hardware or software to be visible at the users' interfaces. (If errors rarely occur, so much the better, but this is not a realistic condition.) Jobs are not aborted unnecessarily, data are not lost, and erroneous results are not produced. A reliable system is not a lucky accident, but the intentional product of careful development.

An available system is one which continues to function despite the failure or absence of one or more of its components. Continued functioning may be degraded to the extent that resources have been lost, but no total interruption of service should occur unless it is completely unavoidable. An available system anticipates failure and is prepared to cope with its consequences.

A serviceable system is one which facilitates the repair of failing components. Those responsible for repair are given as much assistance as possible in the detection of errors and the diagnosis of their causes. Failing components can be isolated so as to suffer no unwanted interference from the rest of the system, yet they can be interrogated and modified easily with the system's assistance. A serviceable system takes proper cognizance of the roles of each of its components.

An extensible system is one that has been so thoughtfully designed that one can add unanticipated function to it with a minimum of effort, because plausible options have not been foreclosed by unnecessarily restrictive implementation.

The 13 qualities of a good operating system, as given above, are the reasons for which operating systems are developed and the criteria by which they can be evaluated. Note that other lists have been proposed [Neu69, Abe73]. Many of Neumann's items are encompassed by our usability.

The manner in which detailed objectives are formulated for specific operating systems is discussed in Chapter 7. In Chapters 2 through 6, the relationships between the functions and goals of operating systems are illuminated.

1.3 COMPONENTS OF OPERATING SYSTEMS

The Component Scheme

There are many schemes for dividing operating systems into their components. We have chosen for its simplicity a scheme with two divisions. Most schemes [Say71, Dij68b], which divide systems into many categories, tend to be a further breakdown of the two parts in our scheme. With the inclusion of the proper functions in each of the two divisions, a two-division scheme should be as useful as a more extensive subdivision and easier to comprehend.

The two main parts of an operating system, then, are: (1) the supervisor, or management component, and (2) the support component. The management component is responsible for regulating the activities of the data processing system, and the support component, or support services, is responsible for ensuring that those activities can occur. The latter component helps the user to maintain the data, the system, the programs, and the installation. The support function may be regarded as the maintenance function of the operating system.

We formally define these two divisions as follows: The supervisory, or *management component* is that set of operating system functions which dynamically controls the total data-processing-system environment. The *support component* is the set of operating system functions which maintains and supports the programs and data of the user and the operating system.

Table 1.1. Components of Operating Systems.

A. MANAGEMENT COMPONENT — The operating system
functions which control the system.

Function	Description
1. Job management	Allocation of those resources which can be requested prior to the execution of programs; job scheduling.
2. Task management	Dynamic supervision of those resources which cannot be requested prior to program submission, other than input/output devices: timer, main storage, CPU time, and so on; also error recovery.
3. Data management	Allocation of auxiliary storage below the file level, and the supervision of all input/output routines and activities, including interfaces for users; also space management, access methods or channel programs, buffer management, and error recovery.

B. SUPPORT COMPONENT — The functions which support the
management component or provide aids for the user.

Function	Description
1. Application program management aids	Aids for the user in the maintenance of his programs.
2. Compilers and interfaces	High-level language capability for the operating system user.
3. Management support functions	Accounting aids, access control, record keeping, simulation programs, checkpoint/restart.
4. Utilities/loader	Listing programs, editing programs, loaders, sorts.

We shall examine these two operating system components in the order in which they were introduced. Readers should refer to Table 1.1 as they proceed in order to keep the overall structure of an operating system and its parts in perspective.

The Management Component

There are three management functions: (1) job management, (2) task management, and (3) data management. The dynamic controlling portions of an operating system are divided into these three broad functional areas.

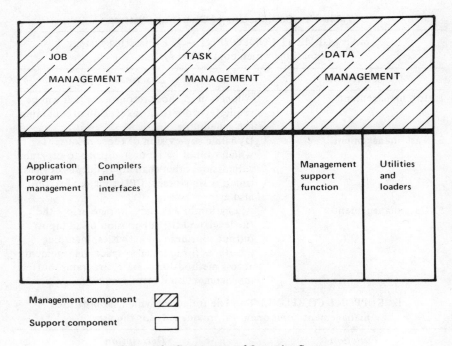

Figure 1.2. Components of Operating Systems.

Job Management. Job Management is the set of routines which together act to effect the allocation of those resources which can be requested prior to the actual initiation of the user's program(s) within the central processing unit. Among these resources are main storage, files, the programs to be executed, and a preferred position on the input queue, for those systems which use a job queue; in addition, the user may also request the allocation of I/O devices, specific or nonspecific secondary storage volumes, and a particular execution priority for his job when it does begin execution (although priority is actually assigned and can usually be overridden by task management).

We now introduce two definitions. A *job* is the smallest unit of work that can be presented to the computing system by the user. (A logically similar definition calls a job the smallest unit of work that can be presented for accounting purposes.) A *job step* is also a unit of work, but whereas a job can be presented to the computing system as an entity, a job step cannot. It is a logical subdivision of a job. It exists to allow the user to group logically order-dependent computing operations into a single unit. It allows the user to prevent a program from executing in the event of a failure in a necessary previous operation.

An example of the use of a job with multiple steps is the COMPILE/LOAD/ GO type of job. The object program produced by such a job should not be executed (GO step) unless it has been successfully edited and loaded; also, it should not be loaded unless it has been successfully compiled. The last two job steps are dependent upon the preceding step(s): they should not be executed if the previous step fails. If we did not have the job step available to us, then we would nevertheless have to have some scheme of logically tying successive programs together. The job/job-step method is a natural way to do this.

The job/job-step relationship is both a traditional and a logically sound method of accomplishing the grouping of programs into logically interdependent groups when necessary. It should also be noted that no job step can be submitted to the computing system unless it is part of a job. Jobs containing only a single step are not only permitted, but they are also the only way to get a single operation into the system — as part of a job.

Now that a job and a job step have been defined, it is appropriate to continue our discussion of job management. Again, job management accomplishes the allocation of those resources, such as files and devices, which are obtained prior to the execution of the program(s) by the system. These requests are made through the use of an operating system and an operating system control language (OSCL). Every operating system must permit users to communicate with the system when they submit work to it. The OSCL is the relevant medium when the user wants to request system resources for allocation to programs. In addition to being a vehicle for requests, it must permit the user to do three other things: (1) give a unique name to the unit of work being presented to the system, (2) specify the particular program to be executed within each job step, and (3) define the I/O units and files which are needed by the job. Note that the latter two items may also be considered resources in some sense.

Job management routines read and interpret the OSCL statements and make the necessary allocations of resources available from the system. The OSCL is used to request the resources, and job management fills the requests stated by the user through the language.

Another function of job management mentioned above is that of requesting a preferred place on the job queue, on those operating systems which use such a queue. A job queue is an area in external storage which contains records of the various jobs that have been presented to the computing system. Users may submit many jobs to the system through an input device, for example, a terminal or card reader. If the OSCL processor is not interactive, the OSCL text is then placed by the job management routines in an area of auxiliary storage, typically a direct-access storage device, which has been reserved for the purpose. An interactive processor does not do this until the user directs it to do so.

In a typical multiprogramming system, four job steps might be executing concurrently. These would be steps from four separate jobs. If 15 jobs have been submitted to the system, 11 jobs remain on the job queue while the first four jobs execute. In some operating systems, the jobs are then admitted to execution on the system one at a time, in the order of their submission, as a job within the system completes execution. In other systems, the positions of jobs in the queue (their priorities or classes) can be altered even after they have been placed on the job queue. In either case, the job queue serves as a buffer between the user's input device, which is typically a low-speed device, and the computing system. When resources become available (as they are released by terminating jobs), the computing system is not forced to wait for the very slow input of jobs from a card reader. They are already waiting on a high-speed external storage device for their turns in the system.

Task Management. The next major operating system management function to be discussed is *task management,* which may be defined as the dynamic supervision of those resources, exclusive of input-output devices, which cannot be requested prior to program execution. Examples of these resources are the system timer, main storage in excess of some orginal allotment, CPU time (and with it, control of the user's portion of the computing system), and certain control functions which the operating system reserves for itself. Another part of task management is some error recovery, again exclusive of input-output processing. The operating system contains recovery routines for many kinds of errors and malfunctions, both of hardware and of software.

A *task* is the smallest unit of work that can actively contend for system resources. If the distinction between a task and a job or job step is unclear, the reader should remember that a job and a job step are externally defined units of work; that is, they are presented to the computing system by the user. A task, on the other hand, is an internal unit of work. It is *created* by the operating system as a job step is accepted by the system. Once a job step comes into the system, a specific program is requested from the system's libraries of programs and is brought into main storage for execution. Once it is actually residing in main storage and has begun to execute, it is then on a system queue as a task (or process).

The task is the entity within the operating system which vies with other similar entities on the queue of tasks for resources, especially control of the central processor. The operating system periodically searches through its queue of tasks to determine which task is to receive control of the CPU. These tasks within the operating system are usually arranged in some sort of order by priority, so that at the time the system checks its task queue, the highest priority ready task (one not awaiting the completion of some event) is given control. It retains control until it requests a resource which cannot be immediately provided, such as an input-output service. It is then placed into a wait state (that is, it will not be executed) until the request can be satisfied.

When a task goes into a wait state for the completion of a resource request, the next highest priority task on the queue of tasks is given control, and this process continues until all tasks in the system are waiting for events; at this time the entire system is effectively in a wait state, until a task is once again

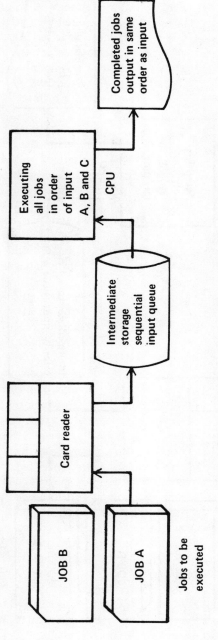

Figure 1.3. Sequential Scheduler. Jobs execute as they are presented to the system.

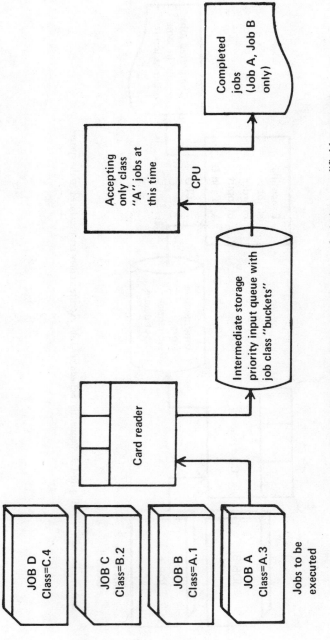

Figure I.4. Priority Scheduler. Jobs execute by class and priority as specified by program.

ready to resume processing. Typically, the top-priority tasks in an operating system are tasks which are not part of any individual user program, for example, the task monitoring the operator's console, the dispatching task, which in turn passes control of the central processor to other tasks, system error recovery tasks, and certain other operating system functions which we examine later. These supervisory tasks are quite naturally of a higher priority than those tasks they are supervising, such as users' programs executing within the system.

Data Management. The third major management function is *data management,* the dynamic supervision of input/output activities. In addition, data management routines handle the allocation of external storage below the file and device levels, provide user interfaces with the system during input-output operations, and allow for error recovery during these operations. (Allocation at the file and device level is usually handled by the OSCL processor during its resource allocation activity.)

An integral part of data management, which allows for the dynamic supervision previously mentioned, is performed by its *access methods,* routines which build standard channel programs. These channel programs are real programs directed to the hardware channel instead of the central processor. They instruct the channel to perform various operations which are then performed independently of the programs being executed within the central processor. The user merely requests a complete input-output operation of the operating system. An access method of the operating system extracts a standard channel program and sees that it is ultimately sent to the channel for execution.

The data management function of the operating system then ensures that the input operation or output operation is initiated and provides the user task with a buffer, an area in main storage for the information to reside on the way in or out of main storage as the input-output operation progresses. Buffers provide a means of obtaining I/O overlap, described in greater detail below, so that the main system is not tied down to the slower speed of the input-output devices on the system; more than one buffer can be processed simultaneously by channels while the central processor proceeds independently.

Error recovery for input/output devices consists for the most part of retry routines. The device is instructed by a data management routine to retry an operation some predetermined number of times. If the condition is corrected before the number of retries is reached, the error was temporary and the task requesting the operation is not affected. On the other hand, if the number of allowed retries is reached and the error has not been corrected, the system can categorize the error as a permanent or unrecoverable I/O error and begin to terminate the affected task unless the user has taken steps to include recovery routines within the program. The user's own recovery routines might try requesting that the system perform the entire I/O operation over again, including the system error routines; might attempt to replace the record in error with a dummy record; or, if permitted, might add coding within the system's error recovery routines.

Another aspect of the data management function is buffer management. An I/O operation typically causes the following sequence of events to occur: The operating system causes a section of main storage to be reserved to hold the data entering or leaving the CPU; this area is called a buffer. The I/O operation, for example, the reading of a card, is then initiated. As the first card is read by the card reader, the data on the card are transferred through the channel to the buffer area in main storage.

The program then operates on the data in the buffer at the same time that the next I/O operation is initiated, thus producing I/O overlap. It should be noted that the buffer area is typically the size of a physical record, not necessarily the same length as a logical record. A very common technique is to combine two or more logical records into a block. This saves both I/O time and physical space on the external storage medium. This technique is discussed in Chapter 5, Data Management.

The Support Component

The *support component* of an operating system includes the following functions: (1) application program maintenance aids, (2) compiler interfaces, (3) management support functions, and (4) utilities, linkage editors/loaders, and sort/merge programs.

Application Program Maintenance. Application program maintenance is another function of the system. Users maintain their own application programs, but the system normally includes routines to facilitate the user's maintenance effort. Subcomponents of this system function might be library maintenance aids, load module generators, and utility programs which allow modification of programs' instructions in main storage or auxiliary storage.

Library maintenance includes the ability for the user to build and maintain files with source code, object code, and accompanying control language on auxiliary storage. These files enable the user to simplify application program maintenance by reducing the amount of redundant writing, card keypunching, and so on, needed to maintain programs.

The load module generator, called a linkage editor in IBM systems, is used to place executable modules on auxiliary storage for easy retrieval. These modules can be accessed for making changes, again reducing the amount of keypunching and deck handling necessary for program maintenance.

Compilers and Their Interfaces. Compilers and their interfaces are commonly provided and maintained with operating systems. Operating systems handle compilers in different ways. As an example, some manufacturers offer compilers as integral parts of their operating systems while others do not. Some provide numerous compilers at no extra charge, while others provide only one or two, such as those for COBOL and FORTRAN, and still others provide none.

Some vendors (for example, IBM) treat the compiler as a standard problem program (as opposed to a system program), while others (for example, Honeywell) provide for the use of some of the operating system's executive functions which are not open to the normal problem program, such as the use of system files and communications tables.

Other systems provide libraries of subroutines for the use of the compilers during the compilation phase, or for the use of the resulting object modules during actual program execution. Also commonly provided is the ability of the object program to invoke system utilities without going through another job step. Examples are COBOL invoking the system's sort/merge utilities, and FORTRAN invoking the system's main-storage print routines.

Management Support Functions. Management support functions allow management to account for the activities within the system, both for purposes of charging the individual user of the operating system, and for purposes of improving the efficiency of the system by tuning the system for optimum performance.

These support services can include such functions as: support of new equipment that the user might wish to use, system simulators, system measurement programs or devices (such as IBM's System Measurement Instrument), accounting routines, special management utilities for main storage or auxiliary storage, System Management Facility (IBM), dump programs, and some checkpoint/restart routines.

System administrators (programmers employed by the firm using the system) might find the system measurement utilities useful in determining the charge to a given user for his use of the system. They can use, for example, the elapsed time or the CPU time given by the system as a basis for charging for the system's use. These statistics are given to the operating system's user as part of its management support function.

Another use of the management support routines can be noted in the case of the storage dump program. The application programmers can use dumps for debugging programs as they write them; the systems programmer can use the dump to find the cause of irregularities in the operation of the system; those who maintain the system can use the dump in fixing the system when it malfunctions. All of these uses of the dumps produced by the system can aid the manager of the user's data-processing facility in his job of maintaining a smoothly functioning system.

Utilities and Loader. Utilities are provided by the operating system so that the user can accomplish certain commonly needed tasks with a minimum of difficulty. Examples of utilities are: file move; file copy; sort; merge; volume formatting; cataloging; auxiliary-storage space allocation; file generation; listings of various files, system tables, catalogs, and members of libraries; and diverse types of data editing.

The linkage editor and loader are the routines which actually perform the binding function in the operating system environment. Until a source program is compiled, it is no more than a collection of high-level source statements. After compilation a program becomes a collection of machine (-readable) language statements. The linkage editor/loader binds the statements into executable modules by resolving some symbols to addresses while indicating all undefined address references within the module. The module then can be assigned a main-storage reference point at program load time via the use of a base register or its equivalent, which is loaded with this main-storage reference address for the duration of the program's residence in the system.

1.4 OPERATING SYSTEM DESIGN TECHNIQUES

The programming techniques used in operating systems differ in two respects from those found in many applications programs. First, the operating system programmers must have access to all the machine features and all the peripheral devices to be referenced by the operating system. This means that they see detail that many application programmers never see. Second, they must maintain data structures which describe their system. Some of the usual techniques for this are discussed below. The use of pointers from one data record to another is considered. Another technique discussed is hash addressing, which uses the value of a data item to find its address.

Data Structures

An operating system needs to maintain many kinds of information on tasks, devices, data locations, space allocations, and so forth. The programmer of an operating system must have ready access to all this information. The operating system further must maintain dynamically changing data in queues, stacks, and other types of structures implying an ordering or a priority. A major technique used in organizing the information in operating system programs is the use of pointers which establish the desired relationships between the data elements. Knuth [Knu68] discusses this topic in detail.

One of the most common serving disciplines for establishing the priority of an item is first come, first served — the priority of an item is determined by its arrival time. A queue, or waiting line, can be used to represent this relationship. Items are added to the queue at one end and removed from the other. A simple way to maintain a queue is to put the identification of the arriving items in an array (see Figure 1.5). To avoid having to move each item in the array every

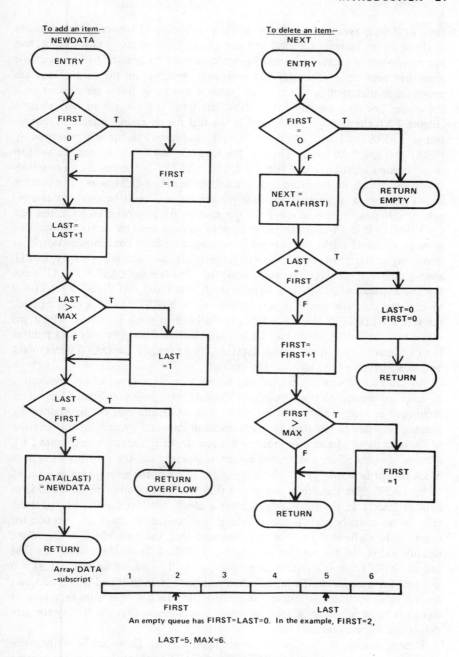

To add an item—
NEWDATA

To delete an item—
NEXT

Array DATA
-subscript

An empty queue has FIRST=LAST=0. In the example, FIRST=2,

LAST=5, MAX=6.

Figure 1.5. Maintaining a Queue in an Array.

time an item is removed, one uses pointers consisting of subscripts or addresses in the array to indicate the first and last items. To eliminate wasting space, one can reuse vacated locations by starting again at word 1 when the highest available word has been used. This imposes a circular structure on the data. There are problems in maintaining this type of queue if too many items are present or if the queue becomes empty. In the flow chart for the routine to add an item (Figure 1.5), the test for FIRST = 0 is the test for an empty queue. A true result sets FIRST = 1 and LAST = 1, because the empty queue is represented by FIRST = 0 and LAST = 0. The test for LAST > MAX is a test for the need to reuse vacated locations. The test for LAST = FIRST is the test for an overflow condition, which results from trying to add an item to a full queue. The routine shows generation of an error message. Other actions might be required as a result of overflow in special cases. In the routine for removing an item, the test for FIRST = 0 is a test for trying to remove an item from an empty queue. The message returned might be regarded as indicating an error condition or simply as answering a request to see if the queue is empty. If the queue is not empty, FIRST always points to the data item to be removed. The test for LAST = FIRST is the test for a queue with only one item in it. A true result sets FIRST = LAST = 0 to indicate that the queue is now empty. After FIRST has been incremented, the test for FIRST > MAX is a test for the need to reuse locations. The items present in the DATA array may be the information desired or may be a pointer to or address of data in a different location. For example, the DATA items might be disk addresses of the information desired.

An alternative way of maintaining access to various types of information is to make the pointer to the data part of the data item itself (see Figure 1.6). This technique is commonly called list processing. A queue can be maintained by keeping pointers to the first and last blocks of data and by keeping the location of the next block at a known location in each block. In the example (Figure 1.6), a block consists of six contiguous words of storage, and the address of the next block is kept in word 6. New items are added to the queue after the block pointed to by LAST. The last block contains a 0 in word 6 as well as having its address kept in LAST. In the routine for adding a block, the test for FIRST = 0 is the test for an initially empty queue, which requires special handling. No test for overflow is performed because it is assumed that the new block to be added already exists. In the routine for removing a block from the queue, the first test for FIRST = 0 is a test for an empty queue. The second test for FIRST = 0 is a test for a queue which initially had only one item in it and which becomes empty as a result of executing the routine. In the use of queues to represent elements requiring some service, an empty queue means that the facility for providing that service becomes idle.

Priority queues are required for many applications. These can be easily maintained by making vectors out of FIRST and LAST so that elements representing

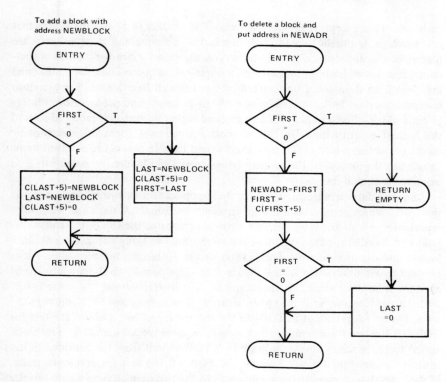

C(X) means contents of word with address X. FIRST and LAST have addresses of the corresponding blocks. Word six has the successor address. Last block has word six equal zero. An empty queue has FIRST = LAST = 0.

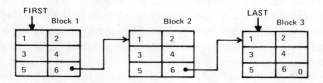

Figure 1.6. Maintaining a Queue by Pointers.

each priority are kept as separate queues. The advantage of this method is that no search is required to add new items. Items having the same priority are placed in the appropriate queue and within the priority are handled on a first-come, first-served basis. Alternatively, a single linked queue could be maintained into which an item could be inserted on the basis of its priority. The insertion operations would be facilitated by using both successor and predecessor pointers in each block. The advantage of this method is that no search is required to find the highest priority item. In this method, arrival time might or might not be used to establish priority. Some method would have to be used to position items having equal priority, or the priority computation would have to assign a unique priority for each item.

Another data arrangement which finds application in operating systems is the stack, which represents a last-in, first-out discipline. A stack can be readily represented by an array by keeping a single pointer to the top of the stack. No pointer is needed for the bottom of the stack, since an array naturally contains a lowest address or subscript. The pointer or list processing techniques may also be used to maintain a stack (see Figure 1.7). The pointer to the predecessor of an item is kept in word 3 in the example. The lowest item in the stack is on' with no predecessor, so 0 is kept in word 3. The only accessible element in th stack has its address kept in TOP. In the routine for adding a block, the test for TOP = 0 is a test for an empty stack, which requires special handling. The block added to the stack is always indicated by TOP on exit from the routine. In the routine for deleting a block, the test for TOP = 0 is a test for an empty stack. If the stack is not empty, the predecessor to the top item is always raised to the top. An important use of a stack in an operating system is to provide the data manipulation necessary for recursive procedures, those which call themselves. In this application, the parameters for a procedure must be saved when a new level of the procedure is activated and restored when a lower level of the procedure is reactivated. Another application of a stack in an operating system is for language analysis. The processor for the operating system control language might well use a stack.

The possibilities for establishing relationships between various kinds of data by means of pointers are very great. The information contained in an operating system may be regarded as a large data structure with pointers between the elements linking the whole structure together. A limited example of this is given by the task control block described in Appendix C. The task control block may be regarded as the representation of a task or independent unit of work in IBM operating systems for System/370. The task control block is itself kept as part of a priority queue by the pointer to the next task control block. Most of the fields in the task control block are addresses of other control blocks representing resources needed by the task. These other control blocks may also be linked into queues or other data structures. Both one-way and two-way pointers are used,

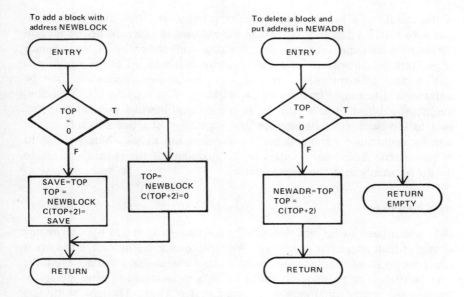

To add a block with
address NEWBLOCK

To delete a block and
put address in NEWADR

C(X) means contents of word with address X. TOP has address of stack top.
Word three has address of next lower block or predecessor. The lowest block
has word three equal zero. An empty stack has TOP=0.

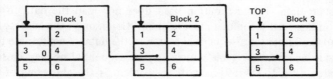

Figure 1.7. Maintaining a Stack with Pointers.

and some of the other control blocks point back to the task control block in a
circular fashion. The use of two-way pointers, also called double chaining, requires more data space and more processing than the use of one-way pointers.
The extra structure indicated by the two-way pointers sometimes improves
efficiency, and the redundancy sometimes aids in debugging and error recovery.
The net effect is a very large data structure whose central organization is effected
through the task control block queue. Wulf [Wul74] has extended this concept
by considering the system control blocks as defined objects and by providing
functions for accessing these objects. All accesses, including those by system
modules, would be made only by the standard functions.

Searching of operating system lists is frequently required, despite the extensive use of pointers. An example might be the search required to insert an element

in the middle of a list formed in order of priority. A search might also be required to match a data field other than the one used to order the list. A sequential search is convenient for short lists. Starting at one end of the list, the sequence of pointers is followed until the search condition is satisfied or the search fails.

If a more efficient search method is required, more information must be maintained than simple pointers to the neighbors of an item in a list. Typically, the list would have to be sorted. In an environment in which pointers are being used to represent data relationships, the imposition of a tree structure on the data by maintaining more pointers is convenient and allows a binary search to be performed. Additional pointers to the midpoint of the remaining items in the list essentially form the tree structure.

Hash Addressing

Data which need to be retrieved rapidly are frequently stored by a technique known as hash addressing or hashing. With this technique, the data or the key is converted to an address by some function, thus eliminating a search to find the data location. The technique is useful for data to be stored in main storage or direct-access secondary storage or combinations of these. The hash addressing technique may be regarded as a programmed version of an associative memory, in which data may be retrieved by its value. The function must have the property that it maps the data into some fixed region of storage set aside for storage of the particular data. If the function used does not map the data to a unique address, some special technique must be used. Commonly, the address is used as the beginning address for a sequential search of the data. An alternate technique is to provide an overflow table which may be sequential or may be sorted for binary search [Pri71, Dod69]. Another problem is the clustering of the table entries around certain addresses. This effect can be alleviated by the use of nonlinear functions for address calculation [Bel70a, Bel70b, Mau68, Rad70]. An experimental study [Lum71b] of eight methods on large files showed that the simple division/remainder or modular division method is one of the best. In this method, each item in the table is represented by a subscript ranging from one to the maximum number of items in the table. The key of an item to be added is divided by the number of items in the table, and the remainder is taken as the subscript of the item to be added.

The reason for queuing items requiring service is to see that the service facilities remain active despite the unpredictable nature of the arrival times of items requiring service. The queue also serves as a list of items requiring a particular service. Each resource in a system has a separate queue. An item should not be placed in a queue unless it actually requires the service facility related to the queue. Separate lists may be kept for items which do not presently require any resource. The queue should not be used for items in a system whose resource demands are completely predictable or for items that cannot wait for a resource.

1.5 RELATIONSHIPS WITH HARDWARE

There are two basic kinds of main-storage organizations in computers: *word-oriented* and *byte-oriented* also known as *fixed* and *variable word length,* respectively. The basic difference between the two is one of addressing capability. The byte-oriented machine is capable of addressing each individual character position in main storage. In this instance we are equating each character position with a byte (six or eight bits per byte is the norm for the majority of computers). On the other hand, a word-oriented machine cannot easily, if at all, address individual character positions in main storage. It must instead address a larger portion of main storage which is called a word.

The various manufacturers assign different multiples of character-positions, or bytes, to make up a word. For example IBM System/370 computers assign 4 bytes to a word. This means that a word is 32 bits long in that computer family, since IBM uses the 8-bit EBCDIC (Extended Binary Coded Decimal Interchange Code) in its architecture. On the other hand, the Honeywell (HIS) 6000 series uses a 36-bit word. If HIS uses a 6-bit code in their architecture, then this means that with an additional 4 bits per word these computers can fit 6 characters into a word instead of 4.

The effect of this difference in architecture in relation to operating systems is largely one of application. Since word-oriented machines such as the HIS/GE 600 series can access only *words* directly, and not individual character positions, it becomes rather expensive in terms of machine cycles and general efficiency to address or modify individual characters within that word. This means that applications which require extensive manipulation of individual characters are not particularly well suited to a word-oriented machine.

On the other hand, byte-oriented machines will typically require more CPU resources to manipulate data on the field level than on the individual-character level, so that applications which require manipulation of data longer than a byte, such as mathematical operations requiring precision to many decimal places are not as easily performed on a byte-oriented machine as they are on a word machine, which not only addresses but also manipulates data on a multicharacter level.

Until recently there was a generally accepted "rule of thumb" that commercial applications, which typically require extensive manipulating of individual characters, are best done on a byte-oriented machine, while scientific applications are best done on a word-oriented machine. See Figure 1.8.

In recent years, however, the distinction between the two kinds of machines has become rather cloudy, with the introduction of the variable-word hybrid

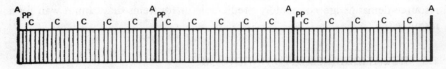

Word-oriented architecture.   Main storage points marked A are addressable;
                              from one A point to another is a word. Points
                              marked C are the delimiters of individual six-bit
                              characters. Bits marked PP are used for parity.
                              Individual characters are not directly addressable.

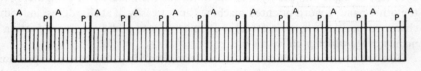

Byte–oriented architecture.   Main storage points marked A are addressable;
                             from one A point to another is a byte (character).
                             Bits marked P are used for parity. Individual
                             bytes each must be addressed directly. Multiple
                             character groups are not addressable.

Figure 1.8. Byte-oriented and Word-oriented Architectures.

computer. This hybrid allows the user to vary the size of words to fit his needs. Another device is the use of fast indirect addressing instructions, such as the HIS 6000 series uses. The indirect addressing technique also allows the user to use more easily the individual character positions in a word-oriented machine.

The operating system must be concerned with the application of the hardware. If the machine is word-oriented, the operating system may be constructed as a primarily mathematical system, with a less extensive data manipulation capability. The operating system in a byte-oriented machine, conversely, might be more data oriented, with much more emphasis on data handling and manipulation for the predominantly commercial user.

In terms of system design, the first thing one must decide is whether the operating system is to reside in a word-oriented machine or in a byte-oriented machine, which is a very important question. It should be remembered, however, that the distinction between "commercial" byte-oriented and "scientific" word-oriented computers is gradually disappearing.

The next question concerns the microcoded machine: Modern computers are actually made to perform by the use of the medium of microcode. The hardware physically exists in its frames and packages without the possibility of use until an instruction set is built into it; hardware alone is not sufficient for the operation of a computer. The computer must be told how its circuits are to be used to effect the various instructions that might be given to it by the programs that operate within the computer. This is accomplished by the use of microcode. Microcode is the highest level of programming in a computer, or the lowest, depending on how you view it. It is the set of programs which instructs the hardware how to react to machine-language instructions given to it. The microcode is typically "read-only." In other words, it is permanently resident within the computer; it cannot be changed in any manner available to users, as opposed to the normal computer programs, which can modify themselves or be modified. The microcode is manufactured along with the hardware and it is read into the hardware when the computing system is first started up. Once into the internal registers and control storage in the computer, the microcode defines a standard instruction set. This instruction set is now the sum total of the instructions which the computer can be given by a regular program such as an operating system or a user program executing with an operating system. The instruction set being contained on the microcode is, of course, more volatile than the hardware; it can be altered by the manufacturer to modify the instruction set and thus cause a computer to perform as though it were a different kind of computer.

In terms of operating system design, this means that the manufacturer could supply an operating system based on the type of machine that the microcode is emulating. For example, an operating system oriented toward scientific applications with more powerful mathematical instructions available to it, such as vector manipulation capabilities, could be supplied for the user of word-oriented microcode, while an information system could be built into the operating system to be used on byte-oriented microcode. See Figure 1.9.

Another consideration is whether the system is going to have a virtual storage scheme or a standard real storage scheme. If a virtual storage scheme is chosen, a decision must be made as to the kind of scheme it will be. This affects both the hardware and software, of course, since the address translation must be incorporated into both if a virtual storage system is to be used (virtual storage concepts and types are discussed at length later in this book).

As a final point, designers as a rule have counted on the disparity between CPU and I/O speeds to provide them with built-in "overhead time" which they can use while waiting for necessary operating system functions to be performed; the users waiting for an event — for example, an output operation on tape — do not mind, since they have to wait anyway. With modern device and channel speeds, however, particularly in the direct-access devices, there is less wait time per I/O operation in which to perform these functions while enjoying control of the computing system. The designer of a modern operating system is instead obliged to perform these functions concurrently with the user, stretching the operating system function being performed over *several* event waits. This introduces a greater possible error range, since there is a greater possibility of interaction with other events. When the problem is solved, however, the resultant operating sys-

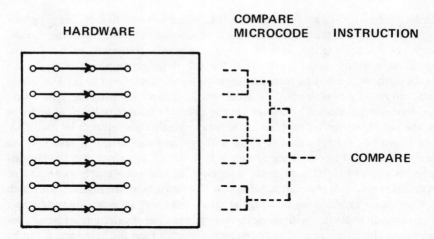

A. Individual hardware circuits and a logical representation of the compare microcode prior to its loading into the system.

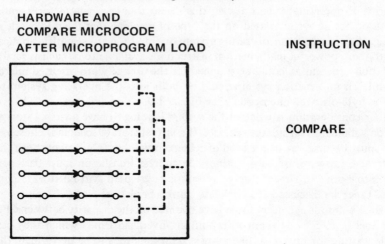

B. The combination of hardware and microcode after microcode loading. The individual hardware circuits are now logically combined in such a way as to allow the execution of the compare instruction.

Figure 1.9. Microcode and Hardware Interaction.

tem should be more efficient, since there will be less supervisory-event wait time for the user.

QUESTIONS

1. Place these terms in chronological (historical) order: executive, monitor, operating system, supervisor.
2. Place these problems in the historical order in which they were solved:
   a. Protection of the system.
   b. Spooling.
   c. Overlapping I/O with computing.
   d. Assembly.
   e. Program relocation.
   f. Job-to-job transition.
3. Describe some improvements that might be made in a computing system which would have an impact on programmers were it not for operating systems.
4. Rank the operating systems described below in order of the number of different facilities you would expect each to provide:
   a. An airline reservation system.
   b. A system dedicated to solving n simultaneous equations in n unknowns.
   c. A system for accounting, engineering, and scientific applications at General Motors.
   d. A system for all the business applications of a large brokerage firm.
   e. A system for Ajax Corner Grocery.
   Justify your rankings with at least one new facility for each system judged to be more complex than its predecessors on your list.
5. Assume that a potential user of an operating system lists the 13 qualities of good systems in order of their value to him; that is, if security is above efficiency in his list, he would be generous in permitting the system to expend resources to assure security. Prepare the lists that might be made by these organizations:
   a. The Central Intelligence Agency.
   b. North Carolina University.
   c. Standard Oil of New Jersey.
   d. Corner Grocery, Inc.
   e. National Aeronautics and Space Administration.
   f. Federal Aviation Authority.
   g. Internal Revenue Service.

PROBLEM

1. Assume that a control block consists of 20 words of data. Use the pointer or list processing methods described in the text to do the following:
   a. Add sufficient words to this control block that it can be a part of: (1) a queue, (2) two queues, (3) a queue and a stack, (4) a priority queue with priority in word 6.

b. Prepare flow charts for routines to perform the following functions for each of the four cases specified in (a): (1) add a block to a queue or stack, (2) delete a block from a queue or stack, (3) search for a block with a specified value in word 12, (4) sort into increasing order based on the value in word 11. Do any of the above require new pointers to be defined?

c. Implement the routines as FORTRAN subroutines.

2
Types of Operating Systems

There have been many schemes proposed for the classification of operating systems. Among classification criteria have been the following; the organization of main storage; the amount of multiprogramming allowed; the kind of secondary storage device used by the system for its work areas; the functional or application areas in which the system is to be used; and the basic design of their processes. For example, is a system to be categorized because it has four or five major functions which operate in parallel, or because it is designed in a layered approach, where the innermost layer is the highest-priority level and the various outer layers have successively lower priorities, such as the MULTICS system?

For the purposes of this book we have decided to divide operating systems into five types: (1) serial batch processing, (2) simple multiprogramming, (3) complex multiprogramming, (4) multiprocessing systems, and (5) real-time systems.

Among all the various schemes of classification, this is merely another which may or may not be unique and certainly will not be favored by all readers. It is our contention, however, that there is no "right way" of classifying operating systems. The best that can be hoped for is a reasonable classification for purposes of discussion.

This is so because of the large degree of overlap between various categories of operating systems. Many operating systems will combine many of the functions of data processing which our classification scheme might ascribe to a particular type of operating system. In other words, examining a specific operating system, the reader might find elements of as many as three or four of our classifications of types of operating systems within one actual operating system. Bearing in mind that this somewhat arbitrary classification scheme is intended as a vehicle for discussion, let us begin with the first type of system, the serial batch processing system.

2.1 SERIAL BATCH PROCESSING SYSTEMS

The serial batch processing system is characterized by the fact that only one user's program may be executing within the computing system at a given time.

There is no possibility of multiprogramming or time sharing. Only one program is operating and that one program, once initiated, must continue to its completion before the next program can begin.

The reason that operating systems exist which allow only serial batch processing is that many of the services discussed in Chapter 3 are also useful to the batch users whose programs are not executing as part of a multiprogramming environment. For instance, if they use an operating system which assists in the input/output (I/O) or data management portion of their programming, they need only ask for a particular I/O event to take place. They do not have to build a channel program and do not have to form buffers; they do not have to account for the time between the start and completion of an I/O event. Instead they merely say in their program that they would like to access a certain area on an I/O medium and then the operating system handles the event for them.

In much the same manner, users might have use for hardware interfaces that the operating system can provide. For example, they may not wish to do the programming necessary to accept input from a remote terminal. Given an operating system, the user is required only to accept a requested record from a remote keyboard, as opposed to a card reader, without having to provide channel programs, error recovery, and the rest. An operating system provides this service through its interfaces with the I/O hardware.

Another very important service is provided by the language processors, such as those for FORTRAN, COBOL, PL/1, ALGOL, and SNOBOL. If the operating system designer has provided these compilers for the application programmer to use, then all the programmer need do is load his source program into the operating system; the compiler processes the source program and prepares it for binding. Again, if users did not have an operating system, with all its services, they would be required to write their own compiler and to handle all of the I/O programming associated with the compilation, including the utility file usage, and so on, in the conversion of the source listing to the final machine-language instructions which are required. Part of the value of a high-level language is that the users do not need to be intimately familiar with the various instructions that computer offers at the machine-language level. They use a high-level language that is fairly similar to the English language or scientific notation with which they are familiar. The compiler ultimately readies their programs for binding in a relatively short time compared to the time required to write in machine language. Operating systems provide this service for the user.

The operating system normally provides certain utilities for the user which obviate the development of too many housekeeping routines, which can become expensive. Examples of utilities' functions are file maintenance, program maintenance, sort and merge, direct-access-device space maintenance, and initializing tape and direct-access volumes. In short, utilities do whatever is necessary in the installation to allow normal programming without user-written programs to take care of each minor maintenance chore. Most operating systems do provide these utilities, and this is another reason the user might want to use a serial batch processing system, particularly on a smaller computer.

Job accounting is another important function that an operating system can perform for the user. Job accounting tells the manager of the computer how

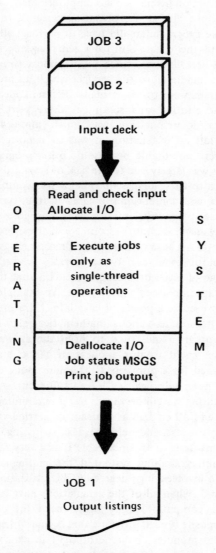

Figure 2.1. Serial Batch System Operation.

much CPU time and how much of the system's resources are chargeable to each user. The job accounting can help determine the users' bills and also inform supervisory personnel in the installation exactly how much computing power is both used and needed.

It appears that these operating system services do indeed make it worthwhile for the average serial (nonmultiprogramming) batch processing user to install and use an operating system on his particular computer. Many of the second generation computers did not always use operating systems, for example, the IBM 1401 system, and the programmers did have to perform all of these services for themselves. This kept the installation from achieving any great degree of standardization in most installations, since programmers were left to their own devices as to how to handle all of the services which his program required. In a given installation, there were often as many different ideas on how to handle input/output, job accounting, and so on, as there were programmers in the installation. Program documentation was much more difficult to develop; when programmers left an installation, it was soon noticed that the programs they had written were not usable because no other programmer knew how to maintain them. This was largely due to the lack of standards in the installation.

An advantage of a serial system is that, being less complex, it is not liable to develop the deadlock and contention problems of other types of systems. Since there is only one user of the system at a given time, there is no possibility of multiple programs wanting the same resource and therefore causing the system to go into a wait state because of deadlock. Since there is but one user, there can be no contention for resources between users.

Another advantage of serial processing systems is that they allow a machine to be dedicated to a specific use at a given time. An example of this is a computing system which is used as a powerful calculator. If a program is designed to accept the input variables to various mathematical algorithms which can be performed by this program and then to print the answers on a printer, the operating system dedicated to this application can operate more efficiently because it can be tuned for a primarily CPU-bound mode of operation, that is, one where the CPU never idles waiting for an I/O event. A system such as this would have less operating system overhead; I/O programming is not important to the user of this system, other than as a means of getting values into the system for this equations to process, and neither is task switching, since this function is also unneeded by this user. It is conceivable that a very large system could be formulated as a uniprogramming system if the mathematics involved in the programming were to involve a high degree of CPU utilization.

On the other hand, when all of the calculations have been completed, then another user of the computer facility might need the computing system to process a directly opposite type of program, that is, one which is highly I/O-bound. The operating system modules could be brought in which handle I/O and the operating systems modules which handle heavy mathematical requirements could also be moved from the system to an external program library. This scheme would allow various kinds of users to use a total system. A serial-batch-oriented system, if used properly, is a most efficacious way to provide these services.

On the other hand, a multiprogramming system, which might well have both CPU-bound and I/O-bound jobs executing concurrently, must have many of its routines resident in main storage to operate efficiently. This means the operating system itself requires more main storage during multiprogramming and that means more overhead costs. It is probable that a measurement of the total throughput of the system would show that a pair of programs might have taken longer to execute while executing concurrently than the same pair of programs in a serial-batching environment run consecutively.

In certain cases, particularly a dedicated communication-oriented system with very high usage, it might be the case that trying to introduce multiprogramming into the system results first in the degradation of the system's teleprocessing function because of increased system overhead or some user interference. Second, there could be a marked increase in the amount of time it takes to execute the batch programs over that required to execute batch programs in a telecommunications-oriented system. A user whose system is overloaded by active users of communications equipment might install a separate system. A smaller processor might serve to anticipate peak demands.

With some special exceptions, a serial processing system is basically a remnant of the second generation of computers. The current state of the art seems to point toward more and more multiprogramming, even in relatively small systems, such as the PDP-8 and the XDS SIGMA 7. This allows the users to take advantage of the high disparity between CPU and I/O times. The serial batch system is an excellent choice for the small user just beginning to use computers. For most users, however, the move toward complex multiprogramming seems to be inevitable.

2.2 SIMPLE MULTIPROGRAMMING SYSTEMS

Introduction

Multiprogramming systems, whether simple or complex, have a common characteristic — concurrency; that is, more than one process can be executing within the same computing system at the same time. This is not to say that simultaneous operation is possible; parallel processing can only occur where there is a possibility of more than one instruction being executed at the same time, such as in a multiprocessing computing system. In concurrent multiprogramming operating systems, however, contending programs may very easily be in the midst of execution at the same time as they alternately use the instruction processor. Each program, or process, will have its own portion of the total system's resources as required. It is up to the operating system itself to determine which of the concurrently executing programs is at a point where it is not fully utilizing the instruction processor and therefore to allow another program to use it.

Resource Contention

I/O Overlap. The basic rationale behind multiprogramming is that a given computer program, if it performs any significant amount of I/O activity, does not fully utilize the computer due to the disparity in speed between the I/O units and the central processor. This difference in speed is generally in excess of 1000 to 1. The central processor operates in a micro- or even nanosecond (10^{-6}, 10^{-9} s) range while I/O devices typically operate in a millisecond (10^{-3} s) range. Since the machine is obviously capable of doing up to thousands of operations in the central processor while waiting for the completion of a single requested I/O event, it follows that one way to use the system efficiently is to allow another program to be executing while the first program is waiting. This is the principle of concurrency.

There are two views on multiprogramming. The most commonly held view is that given the fact that I/O activity is slow in relation to the central processor activity, it follows that the larger the disparity between the two, the more concurrent processes should be executing in order to ensure that the total computing system be in the wait state, and thus not fully using its processing resources, as little as possible. Most operating systems are designed on this premise.

There is, however, the differing view that if the I/O processing could be made more efficient, then fewer programs would need to be executed concurrently because there would be less wait time. An interesting example of this kind of design is seen in the VS2 Release 2 Operating System (MVS) developed by IBM. That system, following this philosophy, uses various devices and schemes to make I/O operations as efficient as possible. There is less system wait time, often in spite of fewer programs executing concurrently. It is particularly interesting that at the same time it is using this principle, the system still allows even more users to enter the system concurrently than its predecessor operating systems did. Although this approach is a workable one, it is not as yet widely used. The first approach, depending on the disparity in speed between I/O and central processor to allow and demand more concurrency to utilize wait time, is much the more widely used approach.

The basic scheme used in most systems, then, is based on the premise of allowing a large number of concurrent programs to use the system and yet prevent their interference with one another.

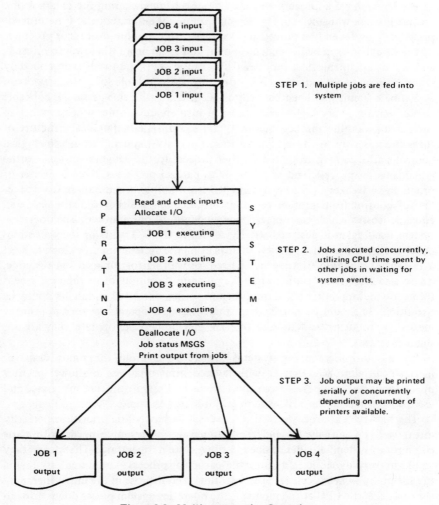

Figure 2.2. Multiprogramming Operation.

Hierarchy or Equality: The Questions of Processes and Tasking. In order to prevent interference, the operating system must have a logical relationship among all concurrent processes such that one cannot interfere with another. This design is commonly implemented in one of two ways: either the processes can be regarded as equals, such that each process operates as if it were in its own computer and does not depend on another process within the system, or else the various processes within the operating system are related in a hierarchical order.

In the hierarchical approach, an initial process begins, causing the creation of a second process which is logically dependent upon it and inferior to it in terms of priority. This dependent process in turn may create another process or processes which would in turn be dependent upon it and again be a little lower in priority, and so on out to the final process. This "onion skin" approach is described by Dijkstra in a paper on the THE operating system [Dij68b]. Most work on operating systems had been basically in accordance with this particular concept: that of having a very high-level process in turn create another process, which in turn creates another process below it, and so on. The hierarchical structure of these processes in turn results in a stronger operating system through the logical control paths coming from the mother process to the daughter process to the granddaughter process, and so forth. With parallel processes, there is danger of producing a weaker operating system structure simply because there is a weaker line of control from mother to daughter process, since they are all considered equal processes which can operate independently of one another. The operating system itself again is designed strictly to utilize the I/O waits or the wait states produced by some other activity, such as using the system timer or clock to start a task after a period of time has passed, or waiting for some shared resource. These also imply wait states; while the program is waiting for its time increment to expire before initiating a subprogram, other unrelated programs could be executing. It should be noted, then, that while I/O operations are the primary means of producing wait time so that another process can operate, they are not the only means.

Some multiprogramming systems are designed using the onion skin, or hierarchical, approach, that is, with layered skins of lower and lower priority processes as one progresses from the nucleus and out to the various service and user processes, as in the THE system [Dij68b] for example.

The hierarchical processes will not necessarily have static priorities; a priority might well be initially set and then altered as the resource needs within the computing system are determined during system operation. Therefore, they would be very dynamic in nature. If a particular process — even one very low in the hierarchy — needs central processor time, and if those in the upper hierarchy are not using the CPU at the moment, the operating system passes down through the hierarchy and finally gives the execution of the CPU to the particular process in question, even though it has a lower priority. This can result in fairly significant overhead; however, with proper communication between the various levels of hierarchy, it is not necessarily unbearable.

A nonhierarchical approach is to create all, or most, processes as equal, as in IBM's OS/360, and to bring those needed into the computer at the same time, when the system is first loaded into the computer. Once in, however, there must then be a means of establishing a priority structure among them. This is ordinarily a static priority such that I/O-bound tasks such as the console task would have the highest priority; just below them would be the priority of the dispatcher (the process within the operating system which is responsible for allocating computer time among all contending processes below it, whether the users' or the operating system's tasks), followed by other system processes; the user's tasks would then follow in their assigned priorities. It would probably be preferable to have the error recovery process prioritized above the dispatcher or scheduler, since all tasks may have to be stopped while the system corrects a major error. If the scheduler is allowed to function while the system is trying to recover from an error, then the system could get into a wait state rather easily. Alternatively, certain lower-priority processes can be run disabled (allowing no interrupts to be processed), which in effect gives a task top priority when it does begin to execute. The user must be informed that there is a problem, after which the error recovery process should be given control of the system to correct the malfunction. If it succeeds, then control can pass back to the scheduler, which can then resume its normal function of managing resources.

Static priority seems to be a workable compromise between equal processes and the tree-structured hierarchy. If an operating system is written for a specific application, however, rather than a general application range, it may be more efficient if one or the other extreme were to be followed more closely. There is no need to make a specialized application-oriented system have all of the capabilities of a more generalized full-function operating system.

Main Storage. Since the operating system must prioritize the processes or tasks executing within the system as far as their allocation of CPU time is concerned it would seem that there is a similar requirement for other shared resources within a system. Main storage, whether in a real or virtual storage system, must still be allocated in a multiprogramming environment to each of the contending tasks.

In order to allocate main storage, there must be an overall sharing scheme or organization of main (or virtual) storage. This is discussed at length in Chapter 4, but, briefly, the schemes in general use involve fixed partitions and variable partitions.

Fixed partitions are used in schemes in which all available storage is organized into predefined fixed regions. Each program, as it is loaded into the system for execution, is placed in a partition of sufficient size to hold it. Examples of the fixed-storage scheme are the HIS Mod 4, IBM DOS, and PDP TSS/8 operating systems.

Variable partitions or regions are more often used in the larger computers; the salient feature of these memory organizations is that they allow for *dynamic* allocation as needed in order to load a program. All use some sort of specification by the user, normally in the operating system control language (OSCL), to determine the amount of storage required for the program. The size of the storage requirement is then used to allocate the appropriate main storage to the program.

Devices and Files. Since multiple users often have requirements for the same I/O device or data file, a multiprogramming system must provide the service of device and file allocation. Only one program can use an I/O device at a time, unless it is an auxiliary storage device; an auxiliary storage device has multiple files and can allow multiple users, one for each file, unless the system allows shared file usage, normally on a read-only basis.

A device is requested through OSCL or the operator's console. The operating system looks at its various tables of devices and determines whether it can allocate a device to a requestor if it is not already in use, or else causes the requestor to wait if another user has already been allocated the device. The same rule holds true for files, again excepting shared use.

If the system did not allocate I/O devices, then concurrent processing of the same file by two programs might occur, which could lead to disastrous results. Not only could users' data be altered by other users, but also the system's data could be compromised. In order to have multiprogramming, one must have the operating system supervise devices and files.

Spooling

Another function which is required before multiprogramming can occur effectively is that of spooling. Spooling is the use of secondary storage, usually direct access, as intermediate storage for system input and output. This should not be confused with input and output from the individual programs, such as data-card input and tape output, since a program uses these data whether it executes in a serial batch system or a multiprogramming system. The *system's* input and output is the subject of spooling.

System input is exemplified by OSCL (JCL in OS/360 is an example), while anything going through the system's output writer is system output. Generally speaking, direct output is program output, through one of the devices allocated to the program by the system prior to job execution. The output writer, on the other hand, is not allocated to the program but rather prints the data contained in spool files which are created and maintained by the system and used by the user program, usually when the job has run to completion. See Figure 2.3.

This intermediate storage frees the system from excessive I/O wait time, since the spool data can be printed by the system's output writer while the next job is in execution. The direct-access devices are about 1000 or more times slower than the CPU; this is enough of a speed discrepancy to allow multiprogramming. Card I/O is even slower, requiring as much as 300 milliseconds per operation, which is another factor of 10 in terms of CPU-I/O speed disparity. This is clearly excessive, and the spooling function helps to neutralize it.

Spooling need not be considered a merely mechanical function or one restricted to a single computing system. These points are made by the Job Entry Subsystems

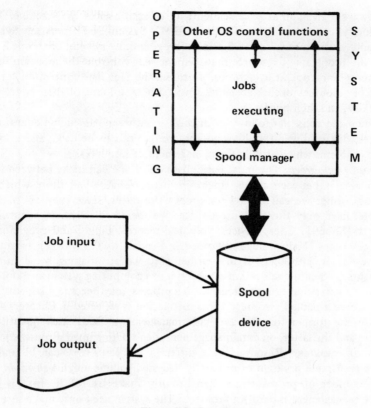

Figure 2.3. Spooling.

(JES2 and JES3) of operating systems that run on System/370 computers. [IBM4] These perform sophisticated operations, including syntactical verification, scheduling, and routing through networks, on streams of operating system input as they process input files embedded in them. More on these subjects appears in the next section and elsewhere below.

Design Considerations

Abernathy et al. [Abe73] are the authors of a survey of design goals for operating systems. The survey is extensive and delves particularly into the conflicts between design goals. We present some of their salient design considerations.

Management of Resources. In the early days of computers, management of resources was no problem. Computers had storage, devices, and files, of course, but they were given all at once sequentially to each user of the machine. Even the primary control program (PCP) of IBM's System/360 Operating System, admittedly a throwback in 1965 as a uniprogramming system, contended with few of the problems of resource management that confront the most ambitious of contemporary operating systems. In these, the fact that contention for and sharing of resources occurs accounts for a sizable amount of their code, their complexity, and their bugs.

In the paragraphs that follow, we distinguish between named and quantitative resources, discuss the different ways that resources can be used, and examine specific problems which arise in the management of resources.

Types of resources. The most basic distinction one can make between types of resources is between those which are distinguishable and those which are not. The former we call *named resources.* The latter, since they are indistinguishable, have only the attribute of size. We therefore call them *quantitative resources* [Sho69]. Files, devices, volumes, records, tables, and programs are named resources. Main storage and processing capability (CPU time), are quantitative resources, although, in the former case we are making some implicit assumptions. When the relocation capabilities of a computing system are limited, a section of main storage, once allocated to a process, may become distinguishable and therefore a named resource. (This distinction is reflected in Chapters 4 and 5, where the former, on job and task management, deals with quantitative resources and the latter, on data management, deals with named resources.)

Uses of resources. Resources also differ in the ways they can be and are used. A reentrable program or a directly accessed volume may be *sharable;* that is, any number of processes can concurrently make use of it. In this case, resource management is hardly a problem. The system need only make sure that the resource is available to all.

A resource may be *serially reusable.* Some (self-reinitializing) programs, main storage, files, and data in a data base can have this attribute. Only a finite number of processes, usually one, can use such a resource at one time, but any number can use it sequentially, one after another. Resources of this type, serially reusable resources (SRRs), are the ones most frequently the subject of study, and deservedly so, as their management is most complex and their use most frequent and vital.

A resource is *consumable* [Hol72] if it can be used only once and then no longer exists. CPU time is clearly such a resource. Its allocation is a matter of some concern because it is needed, it is finite in supply, and contention for it certainly exists. It has been the subject of considerable study, as we observe in Section 2.4, but is somehow more tractable than serially reusable resources.

Resource management. In looking more closely at the problems of resource management, we consider deadlock and blocking, the conditions we seek to avoid; and optimization, our goal within the constraints imposed by our wish to avoid deadlock and blocking.

Holt [Hol72] lists 18 references in which deadlock receives significant attention. Havender [Hav68] dealt with specific resources in the context of an operating system, OS/360. Collier [Col68] took a more general approach, but Haberman [Hab69] is generally considered the landmark paper in the field. The earliest work, terminology, and formal representation of resource contention are due to Dijkstra [Dij68b]. Our presentation of the subject follows Coffman [Cof71] and Holt [Hol72] most closely.

Deadlock exists when n processes each have exclusive control of at least one resource required by another and require (that is, cannot proceed without and are waiting for) one resource exclusively controlled by another, and cannot be made to relinquish control of a relevant resource. Among other terms used to describe this condition are *deadly embrace* and *circular wait*. The latter term is apt because it has been shown, for example, in [Col68], that n processes are deadlocked if there exist n orderings p_i, $1 \leqslant i \leqslant n$, of the n processes such that p_i has exclusive control of a resource required by p_{i+1} for $1 \leqslant i \leqslant n - 1$ and p_n has exclusive control of a resource requested by p_1. Thus, the p_i form a circle or, in terms of graph theory, a circuit, cycle, or directed loop.

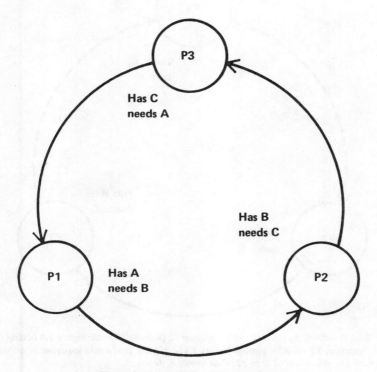

Figure 2.4. Deadlock, or Circular Wait.

Deadlock can be avoided, prevented, detected, or ignored. *Avoidance* means that no allocation is allowed to begin if, taken together with inevitable allocations, it may cause deadlock. *Prevention* implies that processes are not permitted to behave in ways which make deadlock possible. Prevention involves prohibiting a process from starting if it may cause deadlock as a result of the resource acquisition it is known to be anticipating. Avoidance involves prohibiting a process from continuing to run as programmed due to its interaction (through contention for resources) with other processes. The halted process may wait and try to resume later, aware that the system might terminate its execution, or it may terminate itself, presumably undoing any effect that may, if left as it is, compromise the integrity of some data. *Detection* occurs when deadlocks are permitted and recognized. *Ignorance* is the most prevalent approach to deadlock and should require no definition.

Deadlock can be avoided only if the resource requirements of processes are known before the processes are scheduled. Techniques for the avoidance of

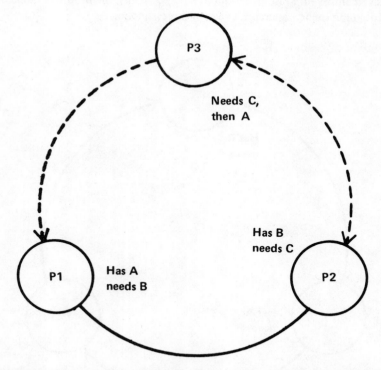

Figure 2.5. Deadlock Avoidance. If P3 is given C, the condition of Figure 2.4 occurs (deadlock). Therefore, P2 must be given C before P3 is. We say that a safe sequence of allocations begins with the allocation of C to P2, thus avoiding deadlock.

deadlock were first described in [Hab69] and developed further in [Sho70], [Heb70] and [Fon71]. Deadlock avoidance involves the determination of *safe sequences* in which demands for resources can be satisfied. [Kos73] has recently cast new light on the adequacy of various techniques using semaphores [Hab69] and Petri nets [Pat70] for avoiding deadlock. The costs of the algorithms necessary for deadlock avoidance are discussed best in [Hol71b].

Avoidance is impossible in many of the environments where deadlock is encountered simply because processes take fundamentally irreversible actions prior to determining the full extents of their requirements for resources. Note that were this not the case, each request for a new resource could be treated as the termination of a process and the acquisition of the resource as the inception of a new one, heir to all the resources of the one being terminated. This cannot be done if failure to acquire the resource must imply the termination of a process which leaves something half-done, that is, neither fully done due to the completion of the process as originally defined, nor undone by reversing all the process' acts to the point of termination (backout).

When avoidance is not impossible, it is usually impractical due to the high ratio of its cost to its value.

Prevention of deadlock is succinctly described in [Hav68]. Deadlock can be said to be prevented in a context if and only if one of the following holds:

1. Each process must request all of the resources it requires simultaneously.
2. Each process must relinquish all held resources when making a request for resources (possibly including reacquisition, *but not retention,* of resources previously held).
3. An ordering r_i is imposed on all resources such that a process can request a resource r_i if and only if it holds no resource r_j such that $j > i$.

Prevention of deadlock is possible only in restricted environments. While alternative 2 above may not seem very restrictive at first glance, by substituting the phrase "terminal session" for the word "process," we quickly perceive its intolerability. The substitution is justified, even when data from a data base are our only resources, if we recognize the unitary nature of the typical terminal session involving a series of queries, a single but complex transaction, and so on.

Detection of deadlock poses problems similar in nature and scope to avoidance. The costs of proposed algorithms are discussed in [Hol71b]. Once a deadlock is detected, only the abortion of one or more of the processes involved or, at least, the retraction of a resource from a process, can provide relief. [Hol71b] describes a relatively efficient algorithm for the detection of deadlock in a system where all resources are reusable. Breaking a deadlock by aborting one of the offending processes is usually done at the discretion of the operator. While it places the burden of responsibility (unfairly) on the operator's shoulders, it is the most widely used method for recovery from deadlocks.

To end the discussion on deadlock, we note that it is one of the biggest problems in the design of operating systems, and the hardest one to solve. No existing operational multiprogramming system in general use has been able to solve the problem completely. Frailey [Fra73] examined the problem and outlined a promising approach towards a solution. For hierarchical systems, Howard [How73] suggests a mixed approach concentrating on four main resources, concluding that most deadlock situations are resolved by attacking these four potential deadlocks.

It is the infrequency of deadlock that makes ignorance of it an attractive alternative in many cases. No other course of action, as pointed out in [Hol72], requires so little of a system's time or space. The cost of an actual undetected deadlock is difficult to assess and so to compare with the cost of alternative strategies.

Blocking [Hol71] is a phenomenon similar to deadlock and many of our comments apply to both. Blocking occurs when a process cannot proceed because each of *n* other processes alternately acquires a resource which the blocked process needs. This topic deserves mention here, but little else.

The goal of resource management, then, is to optimize allocation of resources with respect to avoidance of deadlock and blocking and some notion of throughput. The latter objective is treated in our discussion of process scheduling.

The Auxiliary Storage Medium. The deadlock problem, although a major problem in operating systems design, is not the only one. Another major design question is that of the I/O medium used as the basis for the operating system. Most modern operating systems are based on direct-access devices as the primary I/O facility that the operating system uses for temporary storage and in some cases pseudo-main storage (virtual storage systems), depending on the type of operating system. An occasional operating system may be designed primarily for sequential processing, such as tape operating systems, in which case magnetic tape serves as the system temporary storage area (IBM TOS). If an operating system is sufficiently generalized, it can handle both direct-access devices and tapes with more or less equal ease. The various kinds of I/O which may be encountered by the user of this operating system play a very large part in its design. As an example, the input-output supervisor modules must be able to handle the various kinds of I/O media. In a general operating system this can include the CRTs, tapes, disks, remote terminals, even microfilm, as well as the unit record (UR) equipment, such as card readers and printers.

The design of the operating system is somewhat dependent on the I/O devices. If there is a combination of slow and fast I/O devices, it may affect the operating system strategy in terms of how to handle I/O wait time. If an operating system is primarily punched-card oriented, the designer of the operating system is assured that most I/O times will be very long in proportion to the CPU speed because of the slowness inherent in a card reader. On the other hand, if the operating system experiences fairly heavy direct-access usage, then due to the speed of such direct-access devices as drums and magnetic disks the data transfer rate is very high; the system designers must realize that they do not have the luxury of as many instructions in which to accomplish a particular internal operating system process as they would have had if they were using a card reader. They may have to break their process up into very small modules that execute in the shorter time allowed by a faster direct-access device.

Error Recovery. Error recovery is another major area of concern in an operating system, particularly multiprogramming systems. If there is an error in a serial system, it goes into a wait state. Normally the operator can easily determine what has happened to the system. The error usually has occurred in the user program, or else a permanent I/O error has occurred. In a multiprogramming operating system, one must consider the interaction among the programs concurrently executing throughout the system, together with the added operating system function necessary to handle this interaction. The general complexity of the multiprogramming system makes error recovery more difficult to design. One must be able to recover from errors while affecting each of the multiprogramming users as little as possible.

Communication. Another consideration in designing an operating system is the idea of communications and cooperation among the various components of the operating system. Whether we have the hierarchical type of operating system structure or the equal process concept, we still need to have means of communication between the various processes. Many of the actions called for within the operating system, particularly multiprogramming operating systems, require that two or more processes interact with each other. An example of this is the data management module interacting with an error recovery module in the event of an I/O error. This communication, also sometimes called process interaction [Dij68a], can range from the semaphores mentioned above to the mere sharing of data.

Another possibility is that of passing messages between two processes rather than sharing data, with processes working on a message to the exclusion of the other. One process might pass the word to the other process that it has stopped using a resource and allow the other one to start using the resource. Some systems pass these messages through what are called ports, or mailboxes [Sev72]. The mailboxes are temporary recipients of messages. There are two actions involved: one in passing from one process to a mailbox, and one in passing from a mailbox to another process. This results in a greater use of main storage, whereas the semaphore scheme does not, since it is acting only upon a single small place in main storage. Each scheme has its own positive attributes. The passing of data probably allows for more parallelism; in other words, processes can handle resources simultaneously as long as each one is informed of the usage, whereas with a semaphore, one process is absolutely restricted from using a resource until another process is through with it.

Another way of communicating between processes in queuing, where the requests for particular resources are put into a list. This could be considered a special form of a mailbox approach, the mailboxes being positions in the list. The order of their use would depend on whether a first-in-first-out (FIFO), last-in-first-out (LIFO), or push-down-stack scheme is used. The operating system controls these mailboxes so that the various users receive their particular use of the resource when they are authorized to do so.

2.3 COMPLEX MULTIPROGRAMMING

The distinction between simple and complex multiprogramming systems is largely an artificial one. In general, a complex multiprogramming system is distinguished by having, in addition to all of those attributes listed in the preceding section, one or more of the following facilities: (1) a scheduler which uses priority queuing and promotion, in conjunction with a spooled job queue on a secondary storage device, (2) time slicing, or (3) time sharing. We discuss each of the three facilities below.

The Priority Scheduler

The priority scheduler works in conjunction with a direct-access spool file called a job queue. The job queue is basically composed of either compressed OSCL data by job, or else the card images of all OSCL that has been presented to the operating system for eventual execution. This OSCL is placed on the job queue file so that each job remains an entity and occupies its own unique place in the job queue.

At this point it may seem to the reader that the job queue is really only an instance of a spooling file discussed in Section 2.2; however, with the priority scheduler, we see an additional capability called the job class. This is implemented by the subdividing of the input spool file (job queue). Each subdivision corresponds to a job class (for example, classes A through O are used in IBM systems which are based on OS/360). Each job is assigned to a class when it enters the system, either by the user through a parameter, or by the system through default values. The size of the individual job class is variable within the job queue spool file: each class uses as much of the total job queue file as it needs.

The IBM scheduler further allows priorities to be set on jobs within a job class, so that each job is placed in its particular spool area (job class) in order of assigned job priority, instead of first-in-first-out (FIFO); however, if two jobs of the same priority are presented to the system, then the FIFO rule applies between these jobs.

In some cases, such as IBM's JES2 and UNIVAC EXEC-8, we see the additional concept of priority aging. In this case, as a job is kept within a job queue while waiting for some resource, the priority of the job is raised until the system is forced to accept it and allocate the resource. This aging also occurs in conjunction with deadline scheduling as in EXEC-8 and VS2 Release 2. As the deadline for a job's completion nears, the operating system ages the priority of a job upwards until the system accepts the job and executes it.

Once the job is read into the system, the job queue priority may (as in IBM/MVT) or may not (as in IBM/MFT) be used in determining the internal or dispatching priority for task management purposes. This internal scheduling is discussed at length in Section 4.5.

Time Slicing

Time slicing is a form of internal scheduling. The time-slicing facility is found in many complex multiprogramming systems; it is also called round-robin scheduling [Ham73]. In time slicing, the various users, once in the system, do not *have* to relinquish their place in storage to another job that is waiting for it, as in a swapping system. In time slicing, the operating system will take the concurrent users, or a portion thereof, and put them into a time-slice group such that each of the users is allocated a certain amount of time in the system. This has the effect of allowing users to be very I/O-bound or very CPU-bound without affecting their slices. In either case, they still get their maximum time slices. For example, the highest priority program operating in the system will be given control of the central processor, whether there has been an I/O request from the highest priority or not.

The second highest priority program then executes until its allotted time slice (say, 300 milliseconds) ends, as the highest did. At this time, the third highest priority user in the system is given control, and so on.

Some operating systems use the time-slice method as well as the conventional interrupt-driven method. Given the fact that a low-priority program has 300 milliseconds, to continue the use of the example, and an interrupt occurs within the system, the priority tables are searched and the highest-priority ready task is given control of the system. When this program goes into a wait state, the next highest priority task gains control. In this hybrid system, the time-slice algorithm does not override the normal interrupt-driven scheduler, but rather augments it so that a user is guaranteed to begin his time slice in a regular rotation among the users. Once a task gets a slice, it has control of the central processor at least until an interrupt is received by the system, at which time the highest-priority ready task again receives control. This hybrid time slicing is basically a compromise, and does at least guarantee some time in control of the central processor for each user in the time-slice group.

Time Sharing

Time sharing is another complex multiprogramming facility found in wide use. Some systems which implement time sharing are HIS GECOS and IBM MVT/TSO, which are essentially general multiprogramming systems which also offer time sharing, as do the UNIVAC EXEC-8, Burroughs MCP, and PDP-8 TSS. IBM's TSS is an example of a system designed exclusively for time sharing, as is CTSS from the MIT MAC project.

Time sharing accomplishes two things: (1) It allows more users to contend for system resources, which may reduce the idle (nonproductive) time on the CPU drastically, by as much as 40%. Even though there is more overhead involved with more users, a central processor may go from 60 to 90% utilization, so that even if the overhead increases by 10%, the effective CPU utilization is still obviously increased by the use of time sharing. (2) If interactivity with terminal users is the goal of an installation, then time sharing is a good choice to consider; it allows many more users to gain increased responsiveness. However, if batch throughput is still the prime consideration in the installation, then time slicing/remote job entry (conversational or not) should be reviewed by the installation. Time sharing will reduce response time at the terminal, but often at the expense of batch throughput time; time slicing can give some improvement in response time without affecting too adversely the batch throughput.

The main difference between time slicing and time sharing is that time slicing is a scheduling technique used in implementing time-sharing operating systems.

Time sharing can also be implemented in a serial scheduling system, such as the PDP-8 TSS-8 operating system, so that rather than one job running all the way through to completion and the next job then being brought in, each program is permitted to operate for a certain length of time, for example, 400 milliseconds, after which it is swapped out to secondary storage. The next program is brought in and operates for a similar length of time, and so on until the first program again executes.

When time sharing is used with a complex multiprogramming system, this cyclic awarding of the control of the central processor is still done. However, the CPU is controlled by a time-sharing monitor program, which gains control of the CPU and then allocates its portion of the CPU time among its time-sharing users. The time-sharing region, an area of main storage occupied intermittently by several jobs, enjoys favored consideration for control, but also allows concurrent batch (or background) processing.

A time-sharing region may have as many as 30 users, and these users contend for the resources of the entire computing system in effect as daughter tasks of the main time-sharing task, which in turn might be only one of many tasks operating in the system. We might see three time-sharing tasks, which in turn might be only three of many tasks operating in the system. We might see three time-sharing regions and five batch regions all on the same system on a large machine. The time-sharing region ordinarily will have a subdispatching capability, in which the time-sharing region receives control of the CPU as a function of its internal or dispatching priority. Once it has control of the central processor, its 30 users would be considered to determine which one was to get control of the CPU while the time-sharing region itself owned the CPU. Since time-sharing users are normally in a wait state much of the time, 30 is not a particularly large number of time-sharing users. (When users sit at time-sharing terminals they are not communicating with a CPU while they type. They communicate with the main system only when they press the ENTER key, when the entire line they typed is transmitted into the system. Typing a line might take a minute and it might take less than a second to transmit the entire line to the central processor.)

To summarize, we have seen three facets found in complex multiprogramming systems, either singly or in combination: (1) the job queue/priority scheduler facility, (2) time slicing and (3) time sharing; these are all means of making a general multiprogramming system more useful to a system user.

2.4 MULTIPROCESSING SYSTEMS

We define multiprocessing as the execution of 2 to n instructions in parallel on 2 to n central processors in a single computing system. We differ from Baer [Bae73], who would insist that our 2 to n instructions be contained within 2 to n portions of a single program, and for two reasons: (1) Our more general definition is fairly widely accepted, and (2) Our definition allows us to construct a continuum of multiprocessing systems ranging from tightly coupled through very loosely coupled systems. We preface a discussion of that continuum with the definition of *multiprogramming* (as opposed to multiprocessing) in order to avoid confusion: multiprogramming is the concurrent interleaved execution of programs in a *single* central processor.

Tightly Coupled Systems

Tightly coupled systems (see Figure 2.6) are computing systems which have more than one CPU sharing common main storage through a hardware link. Baer [Bae73] defines four distinct kinds of tightly coupled systems: (1) homogeneous multiprocessors, composed of multiple identical CPUs; (2) nonhomogeneous multiprocessors, in which the arithmetic and logical unit (ALU) is a set of special-purpose functional units; (3) array processors, composed of a set of identical processors (called processing elements, or PEs) acting synchronously under control of a common broadcast unit; and (4) pipeline processors, systems

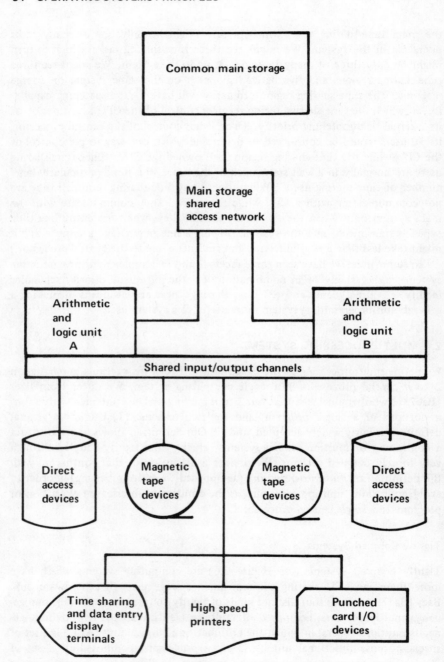

Figure 2.6. Tightly Coupled Multiprocessing Network (Dual Processor).

in which the CPU has the capability of performing operations on streams (vectors) of operands. For the discussion of multiprocessing we employ his classification scheme.

Homogeneous Multiprocessors. The homogeneous type of multiprocessor is implemented in varying configurations with respect to CPU-main storage pairing. In the first type the memories and processors are connected by a cross-bar (matrix) switching system. This kind of system configuration is employed in the Burroughs 6700 series. The central concern in this kind of configuration is the switching. Each pairing of storage to processor is accomplished by switching and the waiting request must be queued, either by the hardware or by the operating system.

The second kind of homogeneous configuration is the multiple bus. In this scheme, the CPUs share a common path to each particular memory. The operating system or hardware must prevent two processors from operating in the same storage simultaneously. CDC 3600, IBM 360/67, UNIVAC 1108 and MULTICS are examples of these multiprocessors, the last being an operating system built for the HIS/GE 600 series.

The third kind of homogeneous multiprocessor is the shared bus. In this system a single bus is the interface between all processors and main storage. The operating system can control the use of this bus by time sharing the contending processors for access to memory. The CDC 6600, IBM MP65 (360) and 158MP and 168MP (370) are examples of this configuration.

The significance for the operating system in these homogeneous multiprocessors is rather limited in the first two cases, since hardware handles most of the interaction between the processors and main storage. The operating system for the most part can be a multiprogramming operating system with a few adjustments for MP (multiprocessing) operation. The third configuration, with the shared bus, on the other hand, requires that the operating system employ a number of system locks to prevent unauthorized use of storage by the wrong processor. The shoulder tap is an example of this; one processor checks with the other processor through the operating system, and when it is determined that a particular portion of common storage is available and the shared bus is free, the requesting CPU can proceed. See Figure 2.6 for an illustration of tightly coupled multiprocessing. The main advantage of the shared-bus configuration is that it is less costly to use. The disadvantage is that there is more delay in accessing common storage because of contention for the shared bus.

Nonhomogeneous Multiprocessors. The nonhomogeneous multiprocessors are so classified because of the special-purpose processors in the computing unit, which are actually CPUs in their own right. These multiprocessors are typically equipped with "look-ahead" hardware, which scans the instruction stream in advance and can schedule multiple instructions into separate functional units.

This allows parallel processing of sequential instructions. The operating system in this kind of computing system must be designed with time interdependencies in mind — one instruction could finish executing before an instruction previous to it in the same program, and in fact within the same arithmetic expression, can finish. The operating system should check for this after an interruption in the event of the failure of the equivalent hardware checking circuit. Examples of nonhomogeneous multiprocessors are the IBM 360/91 and the CDC 6600 and 7600 series. In addition, the CDC 6500 has dual central control processors to pair with its special-purpose processors, all using the SCOPE operating system.

Array Processors. Array processors are designed primarily as scientific application machines, since they are used most effectively for manipulation of ordered sets of data. One control processor directs the parallel performance of an instruction in a number of processing elements. Vector manipulations and related mathematics are particularly suited for this kind of multiprocessor. The operating system involved will probably not be particularly biased toward I/O operations, but rather the opposite; scientific CPU-bound applications are very well suited for this design, an example of which is the Illiac IV and its operating system.

Pipeline Processors. The so-called "pipeline" processors can operate directly on vector streams. The operating system should allow the handling of such powerful instructions as average and dot products, and use this capability to advantage; the bias of the operating system should again be toward scientific applications. The CDC STAR (STring ARray)-100 computer is a pipeline computer.

To assess tightly coupled multiprocessors in general terms, we may say that for scientific applications the array processor and pipeline designs can be well utilized, since they were designed for the purpose, and their throughput is significantly greater than an equivalent conventional computer. Baer [Bae73] gives ample proof of this statement.

On the other hand, tightly coupled multiprocessors being used in business (I/O and data manipulation) applications are normally of the shared-bus type of homogeneous design; because of the amount of storage access-path contention and related operating system overhead, such as the shoulder tap (to the extent that one processor goes into an event wait condition until the other processor has finished with a needed resource and so notified the first), the performance of the multiprocessing system will be somewhat lower than that of two equivalent uniprocessors running the same job stream. The saving advantage is that of system availability.

There will be at least full functional availability if one of the processors fails. On-line systems, for example a reservation system, must have 100% functional capability. The operating system must be designed with this in mind.

Loosely Coupled Systems

The loosely coupled systems do not closely interact as tightly coupled systems do. They share communication — for example, common direct-access volumes, link edited programs, and the like. They often use messages as the only control that a processor might exercise; the processor sends a message and the operator in the distant computer room sees this message and reacts accordingly; or software in one system communicates with the software in the other system to request shared resources. The distinguishing characteristic is that there is no direct control of the resources of one processor by the other(s). A loosely coupled network has, because of its physically separate processors and control programs, only the hardware function of communicating between one another to be responsible for. The tightly coupled multiprocessor has better throughput due to the direct resource control enjoyed by the processors.

The loosely coupled type provides the user with convenient multiprocessing capability. The two simple processors need only be linked by telephonic land lines or a channel-to-channel connection. It is still the case that one is the master and one is the slave. The master basically makes the decisions and does much of the processing, while the slave handles the I/O as necessary. The loosely coupled network operates on the basic assumption that as long as there are two computers, each self-contained, there might just as well be lines of communication between the two, so that instead of working at odds with each other because of shared files and the like, rather they work on a common set of programs that need to be executed.

The loosely coupled network might well have a common job stream or set of processes that must be accomplished, instead of having a problem between the two processors because they are totally separate and thereby possibly duplicating work. We instead have the processors bound by a relationship, that of master to slave. One processor is always the master, the other processor is always the slave, as might be the case in tightly coupled networks. The result is having one computer doing the scheduling of I/O requirements or requests, and the other doing all the heavy computing required for the particular job set. One computer shows that it needs to be involved with the I/O, the other is involved with the heavy processing. There may be complex dependencies among jobs. It may be necessary to prevent one job from running until another has been completed or unless another has been completed successfully. JES3, for example, [IBM4] permits the expression of, and enforces, such restrictions. JES2 and JES3, for example, make it possible for one of the two or more computers involved to handle the I/O while the other handles processing of the data. Typically there is a large computer scheduled to do the raw computing for the various jobs, and a small computer handling the I/O requirements of all jobs. Even though there are separate control programs for each computer, means are found to differentiate between the two broad types of tasks required of each computer in a loosely coupled network. On the one hand we have the I/O handler, and on the other we have the basic computing processor, each communicating with the other. If two computers are used in conjunction in this manner, it normally leads to a more efficient total utilization of the entire system.

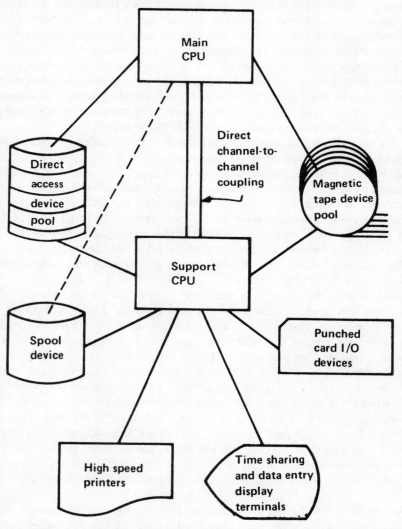

Figure 2.7. Loosely Coupled Multiprocessing Network (Two CPUs). Dotted line illustrates possible spooling device operation.

The control program on one or more processors is primarily concerned with the I/O requests of the total system; the remaining computer is charged with the responsibility of all major computing tasks. In this manner, because of the reduced requirement for generalized operating systems within one or the other computers, it is possible to find a distinct reduction in the total amount of main storage required and processor overhead incurred by the operating system on each computer.

The main drawback is the fact that given one computer primarily I/O-oriented and the other primarily computing-oriented, additional code becomes necessary to handle the interface between the two. Very typically both of the loosely coupled systems share a common direct-access facility. One of the loosely coupled network processors requests programs from this facility that are required to handle its particular assigned function, such as I/O or raw computing. For many users, the multiprocessor is a better way of utilizing multiple computers within a given installation than the traditional way of having multiple generalized computing systems within the same installation.

Virtual Machine Systems

We include operating systems and hardware which allow multiple virtual machines in this chapter, since they do appear to the user as though there are multiple central processors in the system, even though in reality there is only one central processor; the virtual CPUs that the users see are actually simulations of CPUs by the main operating system, which is in turn monitoring the progress of separate operating systems executing on their virtual CPUs. These virtual machine operating systems require a hardware system which includes relocation (dynamic address translation) capability.

A virtual machine takes the concept of multiprogramming one logical step further. Instead of having one operating system with many partitions or regions for the various users, we use a hardware system that has virtual machine capability, load a virtual machine monitor operating system (one which is primarily concerned with addressing translation), and install multiple virtual machines on it. An example of this is the IBM CP/67 operating system used on the 360/67 computer, which has a capability of multiple virtual machines within one hardware configuration. Another example is the virtual machine facility used on the IBM 370 series (VM/370), which is a direct descendant of the earlier CP/67 system. The basic scheme behind either the CP/67 or the VM/370 system is that instead of having an operating system and CPU for each user, we can let all execute within the same machine. The difference between this scheme and a true multiprocessing system is that instructions on the various virtual systems are performed concurrently and *not* in parallel, as in a multiprocessing system.

In one real machine we can find several operating systems in execution: OS, DOS, VS1, and several smaller conversational monitor systems (CMS), which are primarily used for interactive computing by a time-sharing type of user. When all users are active, the system does indeed seem to be a sort of multiprocessor.

Within a single machine using a single operating system, the system performs all services required by the users. When the operating system has sufficient resources to perform these services, the user can have his program execute, along with others in the system. On the other hand, the VM or CP/67 monitor systems not only have to see that the operating systems performing under them perform all services for the users, but additionally must translate the virtual I/O commands and virtual storage address references within each of the virtual machines. A virtual machine is a complete simulated computing system with an apparent (virtual) main-storage address range from 0 to whatever the maximum address permitted by the simulated computer's addressing mechanism is. The user's operating system is resident within the virtual memory allowed the individual virtual machine. The virtual machine allows each user to have his own dedicated machine; he does not encounter interference from the programs of other users, but the performance of any of the virtual machines cannot be as good as the performance of the equivalent real machine would be, due to the increased overhead in the virtual address translations.

2.5 REAL-TIME SYSTEMS

Types of Real-Time Systems

There are two types of real-time systems, systems which interact with their environments to perform work: the process control system and the process monitor system. The process control system will take analog or digital sensor input, analyze it, and then cause an action to occur which changes the process which it is controlling. This can be thought of as a servomechanism, or feedback loop, which has been designed as an integral part of the computer. The process monitor type of system does not affect the process that it is monitoring but merely reports on it; it too accepts both analog and digital input data.

This particular kind of data processing is becoming more and more prevalent in industry, and as the requirement for automated processing continues to increase (particularly in the fields of environmental monitoring, such as water-pollution monitoring, sewage-effluent control, and microscopic assembly processes), it will become a major sector of the data processing industry. Although the programming on these systems is now unfamiliar to many of the people in the computing industry it is an area of endeavor that will enjoy more and more attention as the industry evolves.

Among the operating system considerations related to the real-time systems are: (1) management of analog data, (2) integration of real-time applications into normal multiprogramming operating systems which also process normal batch work in other partitions or regions, and (3) increased need for reliability, since the applications involved can affect lives (air traffic control), production in a factory, or a multimillion-dollar facility, such as an oil pipeline. Indeed, a users' group for digital control systems [Smi70] advocates a reliability factor of 99.95%, which is equivalent to just four hours down time per *year*.

Before discussing these considerations, we discuss examples of real-time systems. The first kind of system that we consider is the process control system. The inputs are normally sensors of some sort: an air pollution device, a blood-analysis device in a clinical laboratory, or a device to measure oil flow in a pipeline. These sensor devices provide input to the central processor, where there is a control program which fields these sensory interrupts and then submits them to another program, which once it has received notice of the interrupts, issues the appropriate actions for output I/O devices to take.

An example is the oil pipeline. Sensors are placed at strategic points along the line, perhaps every three miles or so; they measure the rate of oil flow past that particular point. As oil flow increases or decreases, the sensors send this information at regular intervals to the central processor, which in turn feeds the interrupt information to another program. This program will analyze the information, determine the action required, and then send an I/O command through the operating system to another device which actively regulates the oil flow at a point prior to the detecting sensor so that the oil in that portion of the pipeline speeds up or slows down as appropriate. This ensures a constant oil flow throughout the pipeline. Instead of the expensive alternative of assigning numerous people the task of monitoring the flow and making the appropriate adjustments, one inexpensive system alone can monitor an entire pipeline.

In a similar manner, many cities are installing traffic control systems where sensors count the traffic rates past key intersections; if the traffic flow becomes too heavy at a given intersection the appropriate traffic lights in the vicinity are changed so that they facilitate traffic flow away from that intersection, and thereby handle the increased volume of traffic. This scheme has greatly reduced the severity of rush-hour traffic jams. These are examples of process control systems.

Related to these, but functionally somewhat different from them, are the sensor-based systems which monitor processes but do not necessarily control them. An example of this can be found in a laboratory in a hospital, where a basic automation tool is the blood analyzer unit which takes a given sample of a patient's blood from a test tube, breaks it up into eight or more streams, and then puts each of the individual streams of this sample through various chemical tests to determine the chemical composition of the blood. After the blood-analyzing machine has analyzed the blood and has determined the various chemical constituents and the relative amounts of each in this particular patient's blood, the results are fed into a sensor-based computer. Instead of regulation of a process, however, the computer in this kind of system merely records the results of the process, displaying the test results on a printer (which a regular computing system is often unable to do because it cannot accept analog input) or passing the results to a regular computer located in another part of the hospital through transmission lines. In the latter case, the data are first converted by the sensor-based computer to digital data, of a form suitable for that particular operating system and computer. To carry this example somewhat further, let us assume a blood analyzer actually puts out a waveform on a plotting device. If the analyzer is used by itself, the only output that the pathologist has is a wave graph from the plotting machine. A sensor-based system can take the analog waveform, accept it as input, convert it to digital form, put it in a format acceptable to a regular batch computer, and transmit it so that the batch computer can finally put out the various reports which provide the test results that the pathologist needs. Another kind of laboratory system has the sensor-based computer put out its own reports instead of passing the converted data to a batch machine.

We see that the sensor-based computer can accept analog input and change it to digital output for the use of another computer, or it can write reports in direct-output fashion for the user. It is still an operating system because it is in fact a control program, albeit within a sensor-based computer that handles input/output interrupts.

Input/Output Considerations

Analog input presents some difficulties for the system programmer. Analog input is data presented in a format different from that of digital data, since it consists of continuously variable voltage as opposed to the several discrete voltage levels of a digital computer. The system designer normally resorts to an analog to digital (A-D) conversion device, which monitors the analog data and converts it to digital data on the basis of wave magnitude, frequency change or some other electrical property. Figure 2.8 gives an example of such a conversion.

After conversion, the programmer is still faced with the problem of signal duration. In pure digital systems, the signal is either on or off. The system programmer and designer do not have to concern themselves with the duration of the signal. The programmer of an analog system, on the other hand, must worry about the length of signal as well as its presence when he develops his I/O channel program, with respect to the instruction set used by the application programmer. To be sure, the application programmer has the main burden in terms of I/O activities, but the system designer must get the data to the application programmer in as easily usable a format as possible.

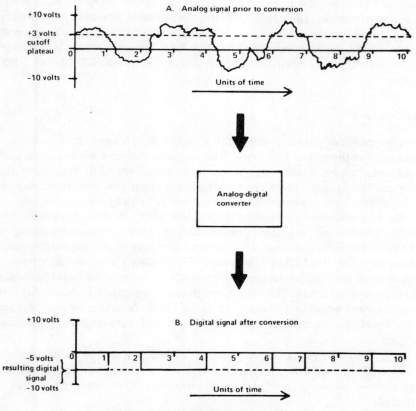

Figure 2.8. Analog-Digital Conversion.

Integration

Once the data formatting and transmittal problem is solved, the real-time operating systems designer is often faced with the problem of designing a generalized system which allows real-time programs to operate in the foreground (highest-priority) region while processing non-real-time programs in the background (lower-priority) regions.

The real-time job requires instantaneous response to abnormal conditions. The priority of these abnormal interrupts from real-time I/O must be high enough to allow the job to gain immediate control of the system resources as required. On the other extreme, the system must not devote too great a portion of its resources to the real-time job during normal activity, or the non-real-time applications will suffer. This problem can be resolved by the use of a special interrupt level for the emergency condition, or else by giving the real-time job the highest system dispatching priority, with normal interrupt handling code being as brief as possible so as to diminish system overhead, or by some combination of the two schemes. The IBM 1800 MPX operating system is an example of integrated programming for real-time systems, as are the XDS Sigma 2 RBM systems.

Reliability

Another problem in real-time systems is reliability. This problem is particularly important as the system gets larger. The very large real-time systems, such as the FAA uses for air traffic control, are more concerned with availability than efficient throughput. These large systems often have two complete computers built into the total system, with one being included strictly for backup.

An issue involved in the maintenance of availability in real-time systems is the "fail-safe or fail-soft" question. In a fail-safe environment, the system is designed so that there are at least two of all hardware components, so that in the event of component failure a backup component is immediately pressed into service. In this kind of system, one design criterion is to ensure that total system capability is available at all times. The system programmer is mainly concerned with error detection and immediate component substitution. In case of error the failing component will be isolated from the system and its substitute immediately utilized.

In a fail-*soft* system, however, there are not necessarily substitute units available for noncritical components, and the system is allowed to run in a functionally complete but performance-degraded state until repairs can be effected.

Both the FAA systems and the NASA systems for use in space programs have certain functions which are of a fail-safe design and others of a fail-soft design (naturally, the less critical functions). This is because the fail-soft design is less expensive to implement. Walther [Wal73] discusses these considerations as incorporated in the Sperry-Rand UNIVAC ARTS III operating system. The IBM 9020, used for air traffic control, is another such system.

Although real-time systems are as yet a relatively small part of the computing milieu, there is an increased importance being placed on them as technology advances to a point where human monitoring of resources is too limited to be effective.

QUESTIONS

1. Give three reasons why a serial batch processing system is often the best system for a specialized use.

2. Give an example of a serial scheduling system which has also had time sharing included in it.
3. What is the principle behind multiprogramming? State two views on the best way to implement it, with examples of the use of each view.
4. Tell whether the listed resources can be (a) named or quantitative or both; and (b) sharable, serially reusable, consumable, or some combination of these:
   i. Main storage.
   ii. Programs.
   iii. Files.
   iv. Use of a central processor.
   v. Devices.
   vi. Volumes.
   vii. Tables in storage.
5. Of the three kinds of homogeneous multiprocessing systems, which is of the most interest to operating system designers, and why? Give examples of each of the three kinds of homogeneous multiprocessors.
6. Discuss the problem encountered in handling analog data in real-time systems. What does signal duration mean to the real-time system designer in particular?

PROBLEMS

1. A computer system has devices with the following characteristics:

Card reader		1000 cards/minute
Printer		1000 lines/minute
Disk:	average access time/record	0.05 second
	data transfer rate	500,000 bytes/second
Tape:	start time/record	0.01 second
	data transfer rate	50,000 bytes/second

Two kinds of jobs are processed by this system:

	Student Jobs	Production Jobs
Card input	200 cards/job	50 cards/job
Printing	500 lines/job	5000 lines/job
Disk records	100/job, 400 bytes per record	1000/job, 800 bytes per record
Tape records	none	500/job, 8000 bytes per record
CPU	1 min/job	2 min/job

One day's work consists of 300 student jobs and 25 production jobs. Assume serial processing in which only one resource is active at any time. For this system and work load, calculate:
a. The utilization of all resources during the time the system is running.
b. The total time to finish the day's work.
c. The throughput in jobs per hour while the system is running.

2. A computer system has resources CPU, IOP1, and IOP2. Two identical programs are active in this system. They make demands on the resources in the following order:

Resource	Time (milliseconds)
CPU	60
IOP1	90
CPU	20
IOP2	80

The programs each repeat this cycle continuously. The CPU is interruptible, but IOP1 and IOP2 are not. Any priority scheme can be used to get efficient utilization of the resources. After the system has been operating for a long period of time, so that any start-up irregularities may be disregarded, compute: (a) the utilization of each resource, and (b) the average wait time per cycle. Display graphically the sequence of events for each active program. In addition, compute the resource utilization if these programs were run by a serial processing system.

3. A computer system has a central processor (CPU) and an input/output processor (IOP) and runs three programs with the following usage (in milliseconds) of these resources:

	P1	P2	P3
CPU	180	10	10
IOP	20	20	90

Each program starts with a CPU period and then alternates IOP and CPU usage. The job mix is such that 2 cycles of P1 are run for 8 cycles of P2 and 5 cycles of P3. Devise a priority rule that will maximize resource utilization when all three program types are run simultaneously in a multiprogramming mode. Compute the utilizations of the CPU and IOP and the total cycle time required to process this job mix. Compare the results with those obtained with serial processing.

3
Operating System Services

The activities of an operating system can be studied by examining the nature of its relationships with the computer and with the user programs present in the computer. The operating system is an intermediary between the user programs and the computer and is supposed to make the computer more readily usable. The operating system provides its users with a variety of well-defined services, which may be requested by the user by specifying the proper parameters. Some of the services are provided by the control program itself, and others are provided by programs which must execute under the supervision of the control program, as user programs do. The nature of the services provided and the methods for specifying these services are discussed in this chapter for the following categories:

1. Hardware interfaces.
2. Input/output services.
3. Error recovery.
4. Language processors.
5. Utilities.
6. Accounting for resource usage.
7. Access control.

3.1 HARDWARE INTERFACES

The operating system must be able to control all the machine features that it is to use. Interfaces must be present which allow control information to be passed from the operating system to the machine and status information to be passed from the machine to the operating system. The nature of some of these interfaces is discussed. For the most part, these interfaces are not known in detail to the user programs. The topics to be discussed include the initial program loading procedure, by which the nucleus is loaded into a computer; the processor status indicators, which contain information on the current state of an executing program; the instruction set, which the machine executes; the privileged instructions, which restrict access to some system functions; interrupts, which allow communication between independent processes; storage protection, which permits multiple users to be present in main storage; relocation, which allows programs to be placed anywhere in main storage; and timers, which allow the operating system to provide timing services.

Initial Program Loading

When a computer is manufactured, its main storage contains no instructions or data. It is incapable of executing any commands because none are there to be executed. Some provision has to be made to insert and execute instructions which will at least allow the reading of further instructions and data. This process is known as initial program loading or bootstrapping.

One of the simplest methods for doing initial program loading is making it a manual operation. For example, a PDP-8 minicomputer has a switch register whose bits may be set by toggle switches on the control panel. The switch register may be set to control a storage address for program loading and then to insert a particular bit pattern at that location by using manual control switches. Seventeen instructions are inserted this way. The computer is then started at the beginning of these instructions, which constitute a program for accepting data and instructions from the console. The usual first task done by this program is to read a more efficient and longer binary loader program, which can process the system software.

The inclusion of a manual operation such as described above would be incompatible with a modern operating system. It is too time-consuming and subject to error to be useful as a routine procedure. The usual practice is to have some form of hardware aid so that the program loading commands may be entered from a console. The initial program may then be loaded from a secondary storage device.

For example, the System/360 may keep three initial program loading records on the system residence disk volume on track 0 of cylinder 0. Utility programs (IEHDASDR or IBCDASDI) can be used to place the initial program loading records there. A hardware feature simulates a READ to insert 24 bytes from the first record at absolute address 0. These bytes are the initial program loading program status word and two channel command words which cause the computer to read the second record and transfer to it. The second record then causes reading of the third record, which is the actual text of the desired initial program. This program then does the following steps:

1. Determines which nucleus is to be used.
2. Loads general and floating-point registers.
3. Determines the size of main storage and clears it to zero.
4. Locates the nucleus on a secondary storage device, calculates its size, and assigns addresses to its control sections.

5. Relocates itself above the region where the nucleus is to be loaded.
6. Reads in the nucleus initialization program and the nucleus control sections.
7. Transfers to the nucleus initialization program to complete the specification of optional features.

Processor Status Indicators

The central processor state must be capable of being stored to enable switching the central processor from one program to another. Usually the state desired is the one the central processor is in between instructions. Thus, many of the special internal hardware registers used in implementing the machine instructions need not be saved. The ordinary registers (general registers, floating-point registers, index registers, accumulators, and so on) which are referenced by the machine instructions must be saved and restored when tasks are suspended and then activated again. A user program has the responsibility for saving and restoring its own registers when it uses subroutines. To facilitate the use of program modules from different language processors, it is desirable to establish a standard method for saving and restoring registers. The operating system has to be responsible for saving and restoring registers when it switches its attention from one program to another as well as when it calls its own subroutines. However, the operating system must not expect that register contents will be restored when it receives control from a user program, because then it would not be secure from error by a user program.

Additional information on the state of the system must also be kept. To allow convenient suspension and restoring of programs, this information is frequently kept in a relatively compact area. Some of the terms used for these data are:

1. Program status word — IBM System/360 and System/370.
2. Processor state register — UNIVAC 1106/1108.
3. Program status doubleword — XDS Sigma 6/9.

The program status word for the IBM/360 includes fields for the instruction address, condition code, interrupt masks, storage protection key, interrupt code, instruction length code, and problem and wait states.

The IBM System/370 actually has two forms of the program status word, for basic control mode and for extended control mode. The program status word for the basic control mode is about the same as that for the System/360. The program status word for extended control mode is modified by removing channel masks, interrupt code, and instruction length code to control registers. Bits are added for program event recording, translation mode, and program status word format. In the IBM System/370, control registers which contain system status information are used in addition to the program status word to describe the processor state. This additional status information reflects the system complexity and the need of the operating system for a more precise indication of the processor state than is provided by the program status word. Some of the kinds of information kept in these state indicators are:

1. Program location or address.
2. Storage protection indication and key.
3. Interrupt classes allowed and codes generated.
4. Supervisor state/problem state indication.
5. Indicators of execution modes — instruction type, instruction length, coding convention, and the like.
6. Wait state/running state indication.
7. Emulation or compatibility indicators.
8. Base register indicators.

The actual data required are very machine-dependent and also are dependent on the needs of the operating system.

An attempt has been made to systematize the description of a processor state by Bell and Newell [Bel71], who use a system they call ISP for specifying processor states and for comparing the state descriptions of different processors. The ISP System conceives of the computer as being constructed from various elements such as registers, processors, and memory. The size in bits of these elements and the permitted transitions among them are described. The formats of instructions and data in terms of bit patterns are also part of the ISP System. The operations performed on data or on other instructions are specified for each instruction. Diagrams of the sequencing of operations during instruction execution complete the ISP conception of a computer.

Instruction Set

Computers respond to a set of binary number codes which are referred to as their machine instructions. These instructions may be executed directly by the central processor of the computer when they are present in main storage. The instruction may be regarded as an interface between the programmer and the machine. The requirements that the operating system places on the instruction set include the ability to control all the hardware features of the computer. Most of the special requirements for operating system programming result in privileged instructions, discussed below. In the IBM System/370, one of the few nonprivileged instructions that has particular significance to systems programming is the Test-and-Set instruction. This instruction tests a byte to see if the first bit is 0 and sets the byte to all 1's. The testing and setting operations are not separable, so no other program can modify the byte in question between testing and setting. The condition code indicates the test result. This instruction allows sharing of a resource by using one byte as a flag byte to control access to the resource by competing processes. The resource is indicated to be available or unavailable by 1 or 0 in the flag byte's first bit.

Privileged Instructions

In a modern computer, certain instructions are reserved for use by the supervisor of the operating system. These privileged instructions typically fall into the following categories:

1. Instructions which alter the processor state.
2. Instructions which implement storage protection.
3. Instructions which are used for maintenance.
4. Instructions which operate the input/output devices.
5. Instructions which set the system auxiliaries, such as the clock.
6. Instructions which communicate between processors.

Unauthorized users are not allowed to use these instructions, which are concerned with overall system management, with protection of system integrity, or with system and user security. An attempt by a user program to use a privileged instruction usually generates an interrupt. The central processor can recognize by hardware whether the system can execute the privileged instructions. Some of the terms used to indicate the distinction and the location of the indication are:

1. Supervisor state/problem state (IBM) − located in the program status word.
2. Control state/normal state (Burroughs) − located in the control state flip-flop.
3. Master mode/slave mode (XDS) − located in the program status double-word.
4. Monitor state/program state (CDC) − located in a mode flip-flop.
5. Privileged state/nonprivileged state (SEL).
6. Executive mode/guard mode (UNIVAC) − located in the processor state register.

Instructions are provided to switch from one state to the other. For example, in the IBM System/370 a supervisor call (SVC) instruction is used to generate an interrupt which notifies the supervisor that service is required. A code in this instruction also identifies the service desired. The supervisor uses a load program status word (LPSW) privileged instruction to return to the problem state. The SVC instruction may also be used by the supervisor to generate an interrupt for services it may require from other supervisor modules.

The number of distinct states of privilege need not be limited to two. PDP computers [DEC2] have three states — kernel, supervisor, and problem — while IBM's 8100 [IBM37] has eight. Of particular interest is the notion of a "kernel" state. A kernel [Ame79] is something relatively small and hard, well-protected. So it is with an operating system's kernel. The kernel is that portion of an operating system whose flawless functioning is most vital. If, for example, every access is mediated by a kernel and the correct operation of the kernel can be certified, then one can be confident that impermissible access never occurs. This is a component of the notion of security, as it applies to operating systems. More is made of this in sections on security and access control below.

Interrupts

The interrupt is a vital feature which allows operations on various devices to go on in parallel and asynchronously and still be able to notify the supervisor that its services are needed. The interrupt is also used to notify the supervisor that some improper or invalid operation has been attempted or that a malfunction has occurred. The interrupt causes the central processor to stop execution on its current activity and to jump to one of a few fixed locations. Processor-state information may be saved automatically by hardware devices or it may be done by software after the jump. The number of locations provided for the jump varies widely from machine to machine, as does the amount of additional status information stored in storage registers on the cause of the interrupt or the nature of the services desired.

The simplest kind of interrupt processing occurs in a PDP-8, which has only one interrupt class, which causes a jump to absolute address 1 and stores the current program location address at absolute address 0. To determine the cause of the interrupt, the program must interrogate hardware flags on all the devices which might have caused the interrupt. Separate instructions are provided for each device to test its status. Instructions are provided to turn the interrupt facility on and off. Further interrupts must frequently be prevented to allow queues and status information to be completely manipulated in response to an existing interrupt.

A more complex interrupt structure is provided by the UNIVAC 1108. Twenty-seven different kinds of interrupts are recognized and each causes jumping to a separate fixed location as well as storing the processor-state register contents in index register 0. By this means, a separate routine may be entered directly by each of the 27 kinds of interrupts. Additional fixed storage locations are provided to store status information on input/output devices. A tabulation of the interrupt classes is given in Table 3.1.

The IBM System/370 uses a somewhat different method for interrupt identification and processing. Six classes of interrupt are provided:

1. External — used by outside devices or CPUs to request service.
2. Supervisor Call — used by a program to request service.
3. Program — used when the hardware detects improper program conditions.
4. Machine Check — used when the hardware detects a machine error.
5. Input/Output — used by peripheral devices to request service.
6. Restart — used to respond to the restart key on the console.

Table 3.1. UNIVAC 1108 Interrupt Classes [UNI3].

Decimal Address	Fixed Assignment
136	Power Loss Interrupt
137	ESI Access Control Word Parity Error Interrupt
138	ISI Access Control Word Parity Error Interrupt
139	I/O Data Parity Error Interrupt
143	Day Clock Interrupt
144	ISI Input Monitor Interrupt
145	ISI Output Monitor Interrupt
146	ISI Function Monitor Interrupt
147	ISI External Interrupt
148	ESI Input Monitor Interrupt
149	ESI Output Monitor Interrupt
151	ESI External Interrupt
153	Real Time Clock Interrupt
154	Interprocessor Interrupt #0
155	Interprocessor Interrupt #1
157	Main Storage Parity Error Interrupt (MEM 2)
158	Main Storage Parity Error Interrupt (MEM 3)
159	Main Storage Parity Error Interrupt (MEM 4)
160	Control Register Parity Error Interrupt
161	Illegal Instruction Interrupt
162	Executive Return Interrupt
163	Guard Mode/Storage Limits Protection Fault Interrupt
164	Test and Set Interrupt
165	Floating-Point Characteristic Underflow Interrupt
166	Floating-Point Characteristic Overflow Interrupt
167	Divide Fault Interrupt
Largest address in machine	Main Storage Parity Error Interrupt (MEM 1)

Additional information on the nature of the interrupt is conveyed to the operating system in various ways. External interrupts cause bits in the program status word to be set for manual and timer interrupts. Additional data may be obtained from signal-in lines connected to the hardware. Supervisor call interrupts occur as the result of an SVC instruction. The nature of the service desired is indicated by an eight-bit code in the instruction which is transferred to the program status word by execution of the instruction. Further information on supervisor services is usually provided by loading registers or memory locations by a predefined convention. Program interrupts cause a code to be stored in the program status word. The various kinds of program interrupts and their codes are listed in Table 3.2. Further status information for machine checks is provided by automatic storage of system data at fixed locations and calling of an internal diagnostic procedure. An input/output interrupt causes a channel status word to be stored at a fixed location to provide more information on the cause of the interrupt. The device and channel are identified by code placed in the program status word or control registers.

Table 3.2. IBM System/370 Program Interrupt Classes [IBM16].

Type	Code	Cause
Operation	1	Instruction code illegal or not installed.
Privileged operation	2	Attempt by a problem program to use a privileged instruction.
Execute	3	Attempt by an execute instruction to do another execute instruction.
Protection	4	Storage protection violation.
Addressing	5	Generated address outside memory.
Specification	6	Improper boundary alignment.
Data	7	Improper code to be processed by this type instruction.
Fixed point overflow	8	Fixed point number too large.
Fixed point divide	9	Result of fixed point division too large.
Decimal overflow	A	Decimal number too large.
Decimal divide	B	Result of decimal division too large.
Exponent overflow	C	Floating point exponent too large.
Exponent underflow	D	Floating point exponent too small.
Significance	E	Floating point fraction is zero.
Floating point divide	F	Floating point division by zero.
Segment translation	10	Current segment not in segment table.
Page translation	11	Current page not in page table.
Translation specification	12	Invalid address translation.
Special operation	13	Set system mask instruction during extended mode.
Monitor	40	Result of monitor call instruction.
Program event	80	Event specified control registers 9–11.

The facility in System/360 for allowing or preventing interrupts is implemented by a number of mask bits contained in the program status word. Separate mask bits are used for input/output interrupts on each channel, for external interrupts, for machine check interrupts, and for some program interrupts. An interrupt is prevented or allowed by setting the appropriate mask bit to 0 or 1. All the mask bits except those for program interrupts can be changed only by privileged instructions. In System/370, more masks in control registers are provided for particular conditions, and the masks in the program status word govern only the overall class of interrupt. For example, all input/output interrupts are controlled by a mask in the program status word and interrupts for each channel are controlled by masks in control registers. Both masks must be set to 1 to allow interrupts on a particular channel. A priority scheme controls the order in which simultaneous interrupts remain pending (in the absence of machine check interrupts) until recognized.

Storage Protection

One of the key features needed in a computer to enable concurrent processing of several tasks is the ability to protect the main storage area assigned to one program from being altered by another program. If this feature is provided, then several programs can exist concurrently in main storage and not interfere with one another. The basic protection required is prevention of modifying another program's main storage area. A further degree of protection may be provided by preventing a program from reading data in another program's main storage area, but this is necessary only for security considerations. Usually, supervisory programs can operate anywhere in storage. To accomplish this, the storage protection must have the capability of being turned on and off. For storage protection to be effective, the generated address for every storage access must be inspected and checked to see if it is valid for the type of protection being used. While it is possible to accomplish this action by software, the effect on operating speed is likely to be drastic because of the amount of checking to be done. Thus, storage protection is usually accomplished by hardware.

A UNIVAC 1108 accomplishes storage protection at three levels. In open mode, intended for executive programs, no storage protection is in effect. In privileged mode, intended for well-checked-out programs, such as executive subroutines, protection against writing out-of-bounds is provided. In user programs, protection against reading from, writing to, and jumping to improper locations is provided. The storage boundaries are kept in a storage limits register, which is loaded by the executive routine just prior to activating a particular program. The storage limits register contains upper and lower addresses for instructions and for data and may be loaded only by a privileged instruction. An improper storage reference generates an interrupt.

An IBM System/360 accomplishes storage protection by a somewhat different means. Each block of 2048 bytes of storage has a multi-bit storage protection key associated with it. Four bits of the storage protection key are used to define 16 regions, each with a unique key. A fifth bit is used to indicate whether fetch protection is also to be provided. The storage protection key is checked against four bits of the program status word. If the program status word has all four of these bits equal to 0, any protection key is considered to be matched. This mode of operation is normally associated with supervisor programs and allows access to any region in storage. If the four bits of the program status word do not match the storage protection key for the address being referenced, a program interrupt is generated. A similar form of protection against storage accesses by the input/output operations conducted by channels is provided by keeping the protection key in the four high-order bits of the channel address word or channel status word as appropriate. The storage protection keys can be set only by privileged instructions. In a System/370, the storage protection key is extended to seven bits. One of the two additional bits is a reference bit, which is set to 1 each time any location within the 2048-byte block is referenced. The other is a change bit, which is set to 1 each time any location within the 2048-byte block is modified. These bits are used for main storage management when dynamic address translation is being used.

Storage protection in the original MULTICS system was provided by a combination of hardware and software. The access rights of users were maintained in the directory described in Chapter 5 on program library management. A system of protection rings was established to allow users and the supervisor to control access rights to program segments under their control. Conceptually, protection rings are a series of concentric circles, as illustrated in Figure 3.1. A user is associated with a particular level and may reference freely other levels with higher numbers. Only restricted access is granted to lower levels and checking of access rights is done in such cases [Gra68]. Each supervisor program operates in ring 0 or 1, and user programs normally initiate operation in ring 4. This leaves rings 2 and 3 for users to establish protected areas. Also, rings 5, 6 and 7 can be established by users as free areas, which cannot then harm the user's program in ring 4, as described by Schroeder [Sch72].

The implementation of the rings by hardware is also described by Schroeder. The access rights for a segment are kept in three 3-bit registers which define the ring limits as follows:

0 to R1	Range of rings from which writing may be done
0 to R2	Range of rings from which reading may be done
R1 to R3	Range of rings from which executing may be done
R2 + 1 to R3	Range of rings from which a downward transfer may be made to controlled points in the lower ring

with $0 \leqslant R1 \leqslant R2 \leqslant R3 \leqslant 7$

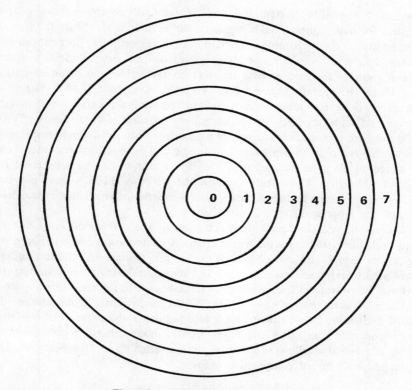

Figure 3.1. MULTICS Protection Rings.

In addition, flags associated with a segment may be set to prevent any reading, writing, or execution. For example, a data area should never be executed by users, regardless of their access rights.

Relocation

Two hardware features used to implement relocation are base registers and address translation. Both these features allow deferring the calculation of actual addresses until a program is executed and allow a program to be located anywhere in storage.

The contents of a base register are added to an address field in an instruction to generate the actual address used to reference storage. Thus, a program can be assembled with addresses calculated relative to its beginning or other arbitrary points, with the expectation that the base address will be added at execution time. Several methods are used to establish the base register contents in commercial computers. The IBM System/360 and System/370 computers use general registers for base registers, index registers, and accumulators. Since the general registers are accessible to programmers it is their responsibility to establish and change their contents. The operating system has no way to identify which general registers are used as base registers, so that relocation of an executing program by the operating system is not possible. As a result, the roll-out/roll-in feature of these computers is restricted to removing a program to secondary storage and reloading back to the same place in main storage. The UNIVAC 1108 has base register fields as part of a processor-state register, whose contents can be changed only by a privileged instruction. The base register contents can be added to all generated addresses, or the addition may be suppressed for indirect addressing. These features allow the UNIVAC 1108 to have program relocation performed by the operating system supervisor, which may dynamically relocate any program during execution.

Address translation defers the calculation of the real main-storage address until each instruction is actually executed. A distinction is made between the logical, or virtual, address space seen by the programmer and the real address space used to reference main storage. The address translation hardware features perform the conversion from the logical address space to the real address space.

The address translation used in IBM OS/VS1 for System/370 conceives of the virtual address as being broken down into segments and pages. The complete address, including any base and index register modifications, is generated as a 24-bit address, thus allowing a virtual address space up to 16 megabytes. The 24-bit address is then decomposed as follows:

1. Bits 0-7 are regarded as segment numbers, so that there are 256 segments of 64K (65,536) bytes each. (1K=1024)
2. Bits 8-12 are regarded as page numbers, so that there are 32 pages per segment.
3. Bits 13-23 are regarded as displacements within a page, so that there are 2K bytes per page.

OS/VS2 uses 4K pages with only 16 pages per segment. Control register 0 uses two bits to record the page size. The segment number is used to establish a location in a segment table, which contains the location of a page table for that segment. The page number is used to establish a location in the page table, which contains the location on entry in a page frame table for that page and an indication of whether that page is in real storage. The page frame table contains an entry for each real page and identifies the program name, the segment and page number, and the availability of the page. All these tables allow the real address to be calculated from the virtual address or provide an indication that the desired page is not present in real main storage. The address calculations based on the tables are done in addition to normal address calculations, and slow down instruction execution significantly even though done by hardware. A small associative memory is used to speed up the process by looking up recently used addresses directly, or a translation look-aside buffer is used to speed up the translation for recently used addresses.

A different view of addressing is used in MULTICS, as described by Schroeder [Sch72], and in its derivative CLICS [Cla71]. The segment is the primary unit of logical memory space. Each address consists of a pair of numbers, a segment number and a word number within the segment. The descriptor defined for a segmented memory on the HIS 645 allows for 256K segments, each consisting of up to 256K words. The user accesses segments symbolically, and the directory establishes a connection between the symbols and the corresponding segment number. The directory is also used to record access rights of users, as described in Chapter 5 in the section on program library management. A user can reference any segment symbolically, and one of the design considerations in MULTICS was to make the linkage as efficient as possible, at least after the first reference to a name. A known-segment table is used to record the segment number of a segment, once a directory search has established a legitimate connection.

To support the segmentation in MULTICS, a series of tables is used to access segments. Since MULTICS is also paged, page tables provide a translation from the logical address space to the real address space. The tables are linked together as follows to reference word i of segment s:

1. A descriptor base register (DBR) points to the page table for the descriptor segment (DS) table.
2. An entry in the page table for DS points to the DS.
3. The DS contains a segment descriptor word (SDW) for each segment known to a process.
4. The SDW for segment s points to the page table for segment s.
5. An entry in the page table for segment s points to the page containing word i of segment s.

The pointers used in these tables refer to real storage addresses, so that if a storage reference is made to a page which is not present in main storage, a page fault is generated to allow a paging supervisor routine to retrieve the necessary page from secondary storage.

Timers

An operating system needs access to timing service for many reasons. At the least, time information is required for the accounting records which keep track of resource usage. A more vital part is played by timing services in providing time-sharing or time-slicing service. The timing service is frequently provided by storing a binary number in memory and allowing programs to interrogate this location to ascertain the time. The time interval at which this location is incremented (or decremented) determines the resolution of the timer, and the total number of bits used for timing determines the cycle, the largest time interval that can be measured. In many cases it is desirable to let the timer generate an interrupt periodically or at programmed times to allow the operating system to respond to time-dependent factors. A time-of-day clock is also useful in sequencing of events and in recording events.

The UNIVAC 1108 provides several timing services. Interval timing is provided by an 18-bit counter which is decremented every 200 microseconds. The cycle for this clock is thus about 52 seconds. This clock is loaded with an initial value by a privileged instruction and generates an interrupt when it reaches zero. A day clock is provided to maintain a standard time. This time is used for accounting and file control. It is changed every 600 milliseconds and automatically generates an interrupt every 6 seconds unless disabled by the operator. Timing service is requested by a problem program by operating system services DATE$, TDATE$, and TIME$ (see Table 3.3).

An IBM System/360 has a 24-bit timer which is updated every 16 milliseconds (for 60-Hz line frequency). The timer is decremented by 5, so that it appears to be updated every 3 milliseconds. The cycle is about 15 hours. The value in storage where the time is located may be fetched by any program, but the more usual way of providing timing service is by system macros such as TIME, STIMER, and TTIMER. The IBM System/370 has a similar timer which is actually updated every 3 milliseconds. The System/370 also has a time-of-day clock, which is 52 bits long and is incremented every microsecond. This provides a very accurate clock with a cycle of 143 years. The clock may be set by a privileged instruction, which is further protected by a manual switch on the console. A nonprivileged machine instruction allows any assembly-language program to obtain the clock value.

In a multiprogramming environment, timing services are usually provided to each user. Since it is impractical to provide each user with a separate hardware timer, the supervisor can access the hardware timer and give the user the appearance of having a separate timer. This can be done by queuing the requests for interval timing according to the expiration time of the interval. On each timer interrupt, the head of the queue is removed and the time remaining for other queued requests can be updated. A queued request is delayed if the requesting process is forced to wait. One problem with this procedure arises in time-critical routines for interrupt handling. The need to execute these routines rapidly may delay updating of the timer, so that inaccurate timing may result. This problem is especially acute in systems which are heavily I/O-bound or which use paging.

3.2 INPUT/OUTPUT SERVICES

The provision of input/output services by the operating system constitutes one of its most important duties. There are several reasons for this:

1. The amount of detailed programming to operate devices and the degree of machine dependence of the programming require much technical knowledge.
2. The management of the parallel operation of several input/output devices and the central processor is a complex process, particularly with asynchronous operation.
3. The gross speed and access time difference between the input/output devices and the central processor is difficult to cope with on a casual basis.

In order to develop the idea of input/output services more fully, we discuss a relatively simple computer, the PDP-8, and some of the concepts of input/output programming are developed in terms of the facilities available on this computer [DEC4]. The teletype console is used in the examples as the input device and the output device.

When the teletype keyboard is struck, the code for the character is sent to an input hardware buffer. While the hardware buffer is being filled, a flag (a hardware switch whose status can be tested by an instruction) is lowered (set to 0) until the buffer is full, and then it is raised (set to 1). Another instruction transfers data from the input hardware buffer to the accumulator, from which normal computer instructions operate.

Output is similar. A separate output buffer and output instructions are used to print characters. A teletype unit does not automatically print like a typewriter, so printing must be separately programmed.

The simplest type of programming involves merely stalling by repeated testing of a flag until the flag is raised. This type of programming is illustrated in Figure 3.2, which shows a routine to accept one character from the keyboard into the accumulator and echo that character by printing it. Only one stalling routine need be included for both the input and output operations, since they operate at similar speeds. During the period of time that the input flag is being tested, no productive computing is being done. The teletype unit works at about 10 characters per second and the processor takes about 3 microseconds per instruction. The computer could have executed about 30,000 instructions during the period of time to transmit one character, and this amount of computation is wasted by the repeated testing of the keyboard flag. If the character being entered at the keyboard is not needed immediately, other computation can be done such that the testing of the keyboard flag is done only occasionally. This

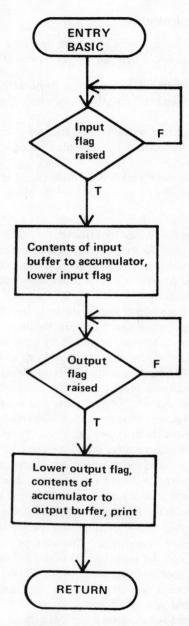

Figure 3.2. Flow Chart for Basic Input/Output Programming of PDP-8. The input and output flags are raised by hardware to indicate that the device is ready.

involves difficult programming and constant attention to the timing of both the input/output device and the instructions.

A better method of input/output programming uses interrupts. Instructions are provided for turning an interrupt facility on and off. The previous example was assumed to be programmed with the interrupt turned off. When the interrupt facility is turned on, the raising of any peripheral-device flag causes an interrupt, which in turn causes storing of the program counter at absolute address 0 and a jump to absolute address 1. The interrupt also turns off the interrupt facility. A routine to accept characters and print characters using the interrupt facility is shown in Figure 3.3. When an interrupt procedure is being used, the interrupts occur at unpredictable times. Thus, the state of the computer must be saved at the beginning of the interrupt handling procedure and restored at the end. This amounts to saving and restoring of the accumulator and link register.

The flags of each device must be checked to determine which device caused the interrupt. In Figure 3.3, only the teletype unit is assumed to be connected, so if neither flag from this unit is raised, an error has occurred. The first flag to be found raised causes a transfer to a routine which takes appropriate action. For a keyboard flag, the character in the hardware buffer is transferred to the accumulator and then stored in storage. The routine must also do some form of storage management to place the stored characters at known locations so they can be retrieved by the program. For a printer flag, a character is loaded into the accumulator from a storage location and then transferred to the output hardware buffer for printing. If both flags are raised, only the first one will be effective, and the second one will be processed on a later interrupt. The last action of the interrupt handling routine is to turn the interrupt facility back on to enable further interrupts. A pending interrupt is not taken until another instruction has been executed, in order to allow a return jump to the calling program before the return address is modified.

If more devices are connected, the testing sequence for flags raised is longer. A problem arises with some high-speed devices because the interrupt must be processed and the data transferred before a certain time has elapsed. If this is not done in time, the data will be lost, overwritten by the next data coming in. Thus, the testing of the high-speed-device flags should be done before the testing of the low-speed-device flags. In addition, the portion of the interrupt handling routine for handling low-speed devices must be made interruptible so it can defer handling of data from a low-speed device if interrupted by a high-speed device. Another difference from the previous routine is that the program location counter stored at absolute address 0 must be saved and restored to maintain the correct return address. Typically, a stack would be used to store the program counter and the registers, so that the last program to be interrupted would be the first to be returned to. By proper sequencing of the flag testing and by allowing some of the interrupt handling routines to be interruptible, one

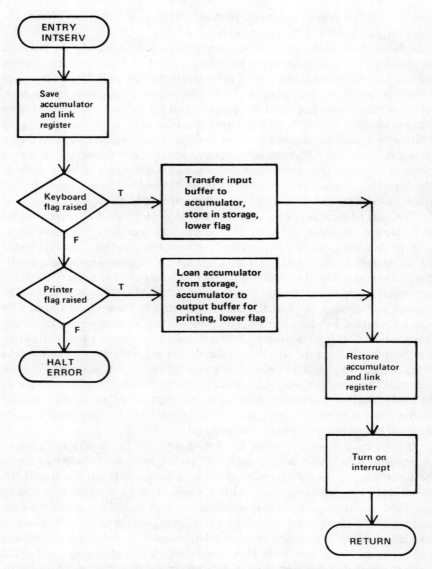

Figure 3.3. Flow Chart for Input/Output Programming of PDP-8 Using Interrupt.

can satisfy a variety of time constraints. An implementation of these concepts is shown by the flow chart in Figure 3.4, which adds a tape unit to the system. Control information placed in the tape control unit by the tape interrupt handling routine determines whether reading, writing, or other action is to be taken. The interrupt facility is off during the entire routine for tape interrupt handling. The interrupt is turned on for keyboard or printer interrupt handling. It must be turned off again while the routine is restoring system status information to maintain this information correctly as a unit.

When a large amount of data is to be transferred by a high-speed device, the repeated saving and restoring of status information and the transfer of data through the accumulator may interfere with the data transfer. To accommodate high-speed devices, the PDP-8 has still another input/output capability, referred to as a data-break or cycle-stealing facility. This facility allows the central processor to suspend operation for either one memory cycle or three and transfer data from a hardware buffer in the device to the computer memory without further action by the central processor. Information in the device control unit or the computer storage specifies the number of words to be transferred. The device control unit reduces the word count by one and increases the storage address by one each time the cycle-stealing operation is performed. Thus, a block of data containing many storage words can be transferred without attention from the program or the central processor. A device flag can be raised to indicate the end of data transfer. This flag may be tested under program control or it may be used to cause an interrupt to be handled by an interrupt handling routine similar to those already discussed. A much larger amount of data can be transferred this way than by passing each word of data through the accumulator. Since data are not transferred under program control, the program and the interrupt handling routine should be written so as not to access a storage area during data transfer. This will typically mean that some sort of status flag must be kept in the program to prevent access to data while they are in the process of being transferred.

We have seen the development of input/output routines from the very simplest routines, which simply make the whole computer wait while data transfer occurs, to quite complex routines, which allow considerable parallel operation of the input/output devices and the central processor. The hardware devices to accomplish this are the interrupt and the data-break or cycle-stealing facilities. The data-break or cycle-stealing facility also implies a device control unit capable of doing simple computation such as manipulating status information contained in registers.

The IBM System/360 and System/370 provide a method for doing input/output operations different from the method just described. A more complex functional representation of the hardware is used, and different methods are employed to define the desired operations and return the status information.

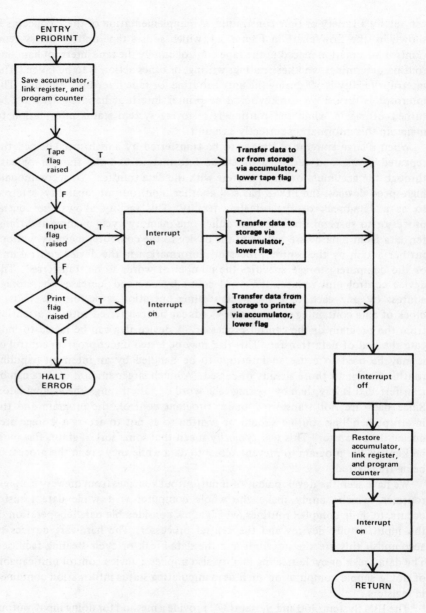

Figure 3.4. Software Priority Interrupt for Input/Output Programming of PDP-8.

The hardware for input/output operations is divided functionally or logically into the following elements:

1. Devices — the actual machines which contain data and transmit or receive them.

2. Control units — which provide a data path from device to channel or the reverse, provide logical facilities to operate the device, and convert data from device coding to that required by the channel or the reverse; from the standpoint of the interface with the operating system, the device and control unit are essentially a single element, since neither is effective without the other.

3. Channels — independent processors which decode instructions and contain logical and storage facilities; they communicate between memory and control units and do most of the detail work for input/output operations.

4. Main storage — the ultimate recipient of data for input or the source for output: status information is also placed in main storage.

5. Central processor — which issues privileged instructions to initiate, test, or stop input/output operations.

Three kinds of channels are distinguished: (1) byte multiplexor channel, (2) selector channel, and (3) block multiplexor channel. A byte multiplexor channel is intended for use with slow devices such as card readers and printers. The single channel is shared by transmitting data first from one device then from another, usually one byte at a time. The device is said to be connected via a subchannel. A selector channel is connected to just one device at a time and is intended for high-speed data transmission from drum, disk, and tape devices. A byte multiplexor channel can be made to function like a selector channel, and is then said to be operating in burst mode. Only one data transfer at a time can be accommodated on a selector channel. A block multiplexor channel is intended for high-speed devices, but it alternates transmitting whole blocks of data from several devices.

Between different models of these computers, the actual physical separation of the above functions varies considerably. In some cases, all five of the above elements are separate, physically identifiable units, and the elements operate in parallel with each other. Sometimes, the channels and the central processor share facilities by interleaving their operations. Thus, the input/output operations and computing operations compete with each other and interfere with each other. In other cases, the integrated file adapter combines control unit, channel, and central processor, so that these elements are all competing for the use of the computer hardware facilities. The storage for the integrated file adapter is also in the same storage as that used for programs, although it is not program addressable.

Despite these model-to-model differences, which have a great deal to do with the evaluation of the physical performance of the devices, the input/output interface between the operating system and the devices is kept the same. The interface may be broken down into three categories: (1) machine instructions, (2) channel instructions, and (3) status information.

The machine instructions for input/output operations are quite simple. They consist of seven privileged instructions:

1. START I/O – initiates an operation on the device whose hardware address is specified in the instruction by a channel program whose address in memory is given by the channel address word.
2. START I/O, FAST RELEASE (System/370 only) – same as Start I/O except used for a block multiplex channel; it then initiates I/O on a subchannel.
3. TEST I/O – the state of the channel and device whose addresses are contained in the instruction is used to set the condition code of the program status word and may also cause the channel status word to be stored.
4. HALT I/O – stops operation on the device and channel whose hardware address is contained in the instruction and may cause the channel status word to be stored.
5. HALT DEVICE (System/370 only) – stops operation on a particular device on a multiplexed channel.
6. TEST CHANNEL – indicates channel status in the condition code of the program status word.
7. STORE CHANNEL ID (System/370 only) – indicates the type of channel and points to error recovery data.

The channel instructions consist of one or more channel command words (CCW) located in the computer main storage. The channel uses these instructions to control the actual input/output operation. The channel command word contains: (1) a command code to indicate the operation desired, (2) a data address in storage, (3) control flags, and (4) a byte count.

Six control flags are used to indicate special handling of the channel instruction. The functions controlled are:

1. Data chaining – which allows the use of data address fields from several channel command words, so that a single input/output operation may reference data in several noncontiguous main storage areas.
2. Command chaining – which permits execution of channel command words from sequential main storage doublewords.
3. Length suppression – which controls the indication of incorrect length records.

4. Skip — which allows the channel to receive data from a device and not transmit it to main storage.
5. Program interrupt — which generates an input/output interrupt to notify the central processor of the partial completion of an input/output operation.
6. Indirect addressing — which allows the channel to obtain data addresses of 2048-byte blocks from the address indicated by the channel command word.

The use of the various flags allows relatively complex data-transfer operations with one input/output operation. The data chaining facility allows scatter-reading, which takes a single record from a device and places it in two or more noncontiguous main storage areas, and gather-writing, which takes data from two or more noncontiguous main storage areas and combines it into a single record. The skipping facility additionally allows portions of a record to be skipped on reading. These facilities can reduce the number of input/output operations needed. The indirect addressing facility can be used to improve efficiency of paging operations by allowing a record to be placed in noncontiguous blocks in main storage. The program interrupt facility can be used to allocate main storage dynamically during input/output operations.

Six general kinds of channel command codes are used:

1. WRITE — initiates data transfer to an output device.
2. READ — initiates data transfer from an input device.
3. READ BACKWARD — initiates data transfer from an input device whose mechanism is moving backward (magnetic tape).
4. CONTROL — initiates movement of a device mechanism, such as SEEK for a direct-access device or REWIND for a tape.
5. SENSE — causes status information to placed in main storage on six kinds of exceptional conditions: command reject, intervention required, parity error, equipment check, data check, and overrun.
6. TRANSFER IN CHANNEL — specifies the address of the next channel command.

Modification of additional bits allows specification of various operations which are device-dependent and quite specialized.

Status information is given to the channel by the channel address word and received back by the channel status word and the program status word. The channel address word contains the storage protection key and the address of the first channel command word in a new channel program. The channel status word is used to indicate device status and reasons for interrupts to the input/output program. The channel status word gives the following data: (1) storage protection key, (2) current channel command word address, (3) status bits to indicate device and channel conditions, and (4) residual byte count for the current channel command word. Additional status information may be placed in the program status word for certain kinds of conditions to identify the channel and device causing an interrupt. The status information obtained by using the SENSE command contains much more detail and is typically used for diagnosis or error recovery. To initiate an input/output operation, the following general sequence is used:

1. The program issues a START I/O command, which indicates the device, after placing the protection key and channel program address in the channel address word.
2. The channel uses the data from step 1 to start executing the channel program, which executes asynchronously from the program in the central processor.
3. The device performs the operations specified by the channel.
4. When a device reaches the end of an operation or the channel reaches the end of a channel program, this condition is indicated to the program by an interrupt and by storing relevant data in the channel status word and program status word. Error conditions or busy devices may modify the sequence of events and the nature of the status information transmitted. The program can then take appropriate action.

Input/Output Supervisor. The complex nature of the routines and the need for use of privileged instructions indicate that the input/output operations are best handled by control program routines. Thus, the program referred to above is part of the supervisor and is called the input/output supervisor. Other portions of the supervisor also use the input/output supervisor to do input/output operations, even though their privileged status does not require them to do so. Typical user programs request input/output operations to be performed by the operating system by setting up certain control blocks and then using a supervisor call to initiate action. These requests are described in Chapter 5 under the topic of accessing techniques.

The input/output supervisor as used for IBM System/360 or System/370 [IBM25] operating systems contains all actual machine instructions for input/output operations. The input/output supervisor also schedules input/output operations on the various devices, maintains queues for requests for devices which are busy, handles termination of input/output events, and reacts to error conditions on input/output devices.

The input/output supervisor requires that the following data areas be available as input:

1. Input/Output Block — created by the requestor as the primary communication region to supply the input/output supervisor with addresses of the other data provided and of the channel program and to receive status and sense data.
2. Event Control Block — created by the requestor to indicate status of input/output events by the input/output supervisor.
3. Data Control Block — created by the requestor to specify the attributes of a file.
4. Data Extent Block — created by the supervisor when a file is opened and used to indicate the physical location and attributes of a file.
5. Unit Control Block — created during system generation for each device to describe the device, to associate an address with it, and to record its status.
6. Device Table — created during system generation to point to optional routines.
7. Channel Program — created by the requestor to direct the channel activity.

Given the above data areas, the input/output supervisor validates the input data by checking some or all of the following: (1) protection key, (2) consistency of pointers between input output block, data extent block and data control block, (3) boundary alignment of channel program and event control block, and (4) direct access seek address within region specified in data extent block. If the input data are valid, the input/output supervisor can process the request.

Each request to the input/output supervisor is represented by a request queue element, which is obtained from a list of available blocks of main storage for these elements. The request queue element, which contains the addresses of other control blocks related to the request, is formed whether the necessary device is available or not. The status of the device is kept in the unit control block. If the device needed is not available, the request queue element is placed in a queue for that device. The queue position can be based on:

1. Arrival time, that is, new arrivals are placed at the end of the line (FIFO).
2. Priority of the requesting task.
3. Seek address (for a direct-access device), to minimize the number and length of seeks.

The queuing discipline is chosen at system generation time. A request can be removed from the queue when the device becomes available.

When the device is available, a channel which connects to the device must also be available. The channel availability is ascertained with a TEST CHANNEL instruction for selector channels and block multiplexor channels. The byte multiplexor channel is not tested because the condition code will indicate that it is available if any subchannel is available. The condition code returned from the START I/O instruction is used to test the byte multiplexor channel availability. In some cases, there may be more than one path to a device, so that several channels will need to be tested. If the channel is not available, the request must be queued.

When the device and channel are available, an input/output operation can be begun. The activities performed are somewhat different for unit record, magnetic tape, and direct-access devices. The address of the requestor's channel program is presented to the input/output supervisor in the input/output block. For unit record devices, the address of the channel program is transferred to the channel address word, and execution of a START I/O instruction initiates the channel operations. For magnetic tape devices, a MODE SET channel command word is constructed by the input/output supervisor to specify density, recording mode, parity, and so on, from information in the data extent block. This is followed by a TRANSFER IN CHANNEL command which points to the requestor's channel program. The channel address word is made to point to the MODE SET command, and execution of a START I/O instruction begins the channel program. For direct-access devices, the input/output supervisor constructs all channel command words involving SEEK operations. Some direct-access devices (2314) require two SEEKs, one to position the mechanism and another to reset the control unit address to the correct value. Other devices (3330) only require one SEEK, as the channel can be detached during the seek and then return to the channel program. In either case, the SEEK commands are followed by a SET FILE MASK channel command word, which prevents further seeks, and by a TRANSFER IN CHANNEL to the beginning of the requestor's channel program. A START I/O instruction initiates the channel program. For all kinds of devices, the condition code is tested to verify that the operation has started, and the unit control block is flagged to record the device status as busy.

The end of an input/output operation causes an interrupt to allow the input/output supervisor to verify successful completion or to analyze the cause for an incomplete operation. The channel status word and the program status word provide the necessary information in either case. If the operation was completed successfully, the event control block is flagged, the channel status word contents are moved to the input/output block, and the request queue element for the operation is freed. If an error condition is found, error analysis routines are called. A completed operation allows the starting of a new operation for the device or channel from the requests kept in the respective queues. If no operation can be started, the device or channel is marked as being idle.

The input/output supervisor for OS/VS must also provide facilities to handle channel programs in a virtual storage environment. Channel programs must be translated from virtual addresses to real addresses, because the channels do not use the address translation feature of System/370. Page fixes are applied to the control blocks and buffers for the duration of the operation being performed. Finally, the real address in the channel status word must be translated to a virtual address when the input/output operation is complete, before placing the contents in the input/output block.

The error routines in the input/output supervisor allow the operation to be restarted a predetermined number of times for each kind of device, if analysis of the error condition indicates that this would be an appropriate action. The input/output block is flagged to notify the requestor of error conditions. A SENSE channel command word is used to obtain further information on the source of the error. Some errors, for example a card-reader jam, require that the operator perform manual corrections. If these activities do not allow successful completion of the requested operation, the operation is considered to have a permanent error and attempts to complete it are abandoned, with an indication to the requestor in the input/output block.

The centralization implied by the provision of an input/output supervisor in IBM systems results to some extent from the architecture and capabilities of the central processor and channels in the System/370 computers. One alternative arrangement is provided in the CDC CYBER 70 or CDC 6600 computers and the SCOPE operating systems provided for them [CDC2, CDC3]. These computers have the capability of having one or two central processors connected to central main storage and 10 to 20 peripheral processors, each having its own 4K-word main storage. The peripheral processors have a relatively complete instruction set which includes arithmetic, logical, branching, and data movement instructions. They also have instructions which transfer data to and from the central main storage and which interrupt the central processor. One of the peripheral processors holds a monitor which directs all the system activities and which contains communication areas for all the other peripheral processors [Ohl69]. Some monitor functions are also executed by the central processor. The remainder of the peripheral processors serve to control input/output activities. The relatively large instruction set in the peripheral processors allows them to act quite independently in doing the input/output activities, thus decentralizing the input/output functions to a great extent. Each routine resident in a peripheral processor receives its direction from the communication region of the monitor, which is responsible for the overall scheduling of input/output operations but not for the details.

3.3 ERROR RECOVERY

There are three general types of errors which can occur within a computing system: (1) User programming errors are errors committed by the user in his application programming and are of two kinds. The first kind is the violation of system architecture and/or programming restrictions; the second is the misuse of system resources, primarily I/O, which occurs when programmers do not violate system rules, but do misuse the system in such a way that they get unexpected or wrong results. (2) System programming errors are software errors in the operating system. These errors are either direct errors, which are actual malfunctions in an operating system's routine(s), or indirect errors, which are caused by one module interacting with another in such a way that the resultant error was not foreseeable until the two modules were executed concurrently. (3) Hardware errors are actual malfunctions of the computing system hardware. These are caused either by bad system or circuit design or by actual failure of a hardware component.

The operating system contributes many of the methods of recovery from these errors: (1) invoking and monitoring much of the hardware retry capability, (2) supplying its own error handling routines, both for hardware and software, and (3) providing a checkpoint/restart capability.

User Programming Errors

The operating system must anticipate the possibility of user programming errors. The greatest concern of the operating system designer is normally that of prevention of accidental (and, occasionally, deliberate) violation of systems architecture and/or operating system or other-user address space. The system normally will utilize some sort of storage protection feature; for example, in IBM systems with one address space, it is a storage-protect flag byte, which is set to a unique value for the life of the user program. This unique flag byte value is assigned to the main storage which has been allocated to the program. Any attempt by the program to write to main storage not assigned to the program will encounter a different value of the storage-protect flag. A similar statement applies to attempts to read from or branch to fetch-protected storage. The operating system must eventually inform the user that the program has violated storage protection conventions and either terminate the user's program or else make provisions for a recovery attempt by the user program. The choice of termination or recovery will depend on the circumstances causing the violation.

On the other hand, if the size of a program exceeds the initial main storage allocation for the program, then the condition normally becomes apparent when a program is loaded into main storage, or else at the time a called subroutine is dynamically invoked during execution of the program. The storage violation is noted when a program or subroutine is brought into a program's assigned storage. In this event, the system, particularly if it dynamically allocates storage should attempt to make more main storage available for the program to use. If the operating system can do this, the storage-protect violation can be discounted and user program processing can continue. An example of this kind of error is seen when a program, while executing, creates another task which extends beyond assigned main storage for that program. In systems with virtual storage, the address space allocated to a user can be made large enough to preclude this type of error in most cases. Additionally, in systems with multiple virtual machines capability, the user is limited only to the entire address space allocated to his entire virtual computing system. In both cases, however, the user is still constrained by the size of the address space, however large.

The system is protected against violation in another important way: the reservation of certain operations for the supervisor's exclusive use. These operations are normally of the type that could modify main storage without regard to storage-protect considerations or could affect other system-wide resources shared by all users. Access to system information tables on a read-only basis is often permitted to user programs, but access to current status information is normally reserved for the supervisor.

The operating system must normally provide these reserved services on a request basis to user programs, but the user programs themselves cannot be permitted to perform reserved functions, because the operating system could then lose the correct status of a given resource, which it must have in order to allocate the resource in proper condition for user programs.

In the event of a violation attempt by a user program, the operating system ordinarily aborts or terminates the job immediately — the system itself must remain inviolate.

The other main concern of the operating system must be the possible misuse of system resources by the user program. This occurs when the user program tries to avail itself of system resources concerning which it has or uses erroneous information. This could result in adulteration of the resource. This occurs most often in the course of I/O processing.

The user program, for example, might tell the operating system that it is going to perform a write operation in file A. It describes file A to the operating system as a disk file, having a block length attribute of 5 records, and a record length attribute of 120 characters. The actual attributes of the file show that it does indeed have 120 characters per record, but the blocks are only three records long.

The operating system can correct an error for the programmer, terminate the program, or provide an exit to a routine that the user has already included in the system to correct such errors. If the operating system corrects the error, the user programmer has no control over the error; perhaps the program assumes a block of 600 characters, to continue using our example, and cannot properly handle 360-character blocks. This could eventually result in the file being irretrievably damaged, particularly in our I/O write operation.

Conversely, it can be validly argued that if the operating system allows users to correct their own errors completely, it is running a rather serious risk: if the user makes an error in the original instance, then can the accuracy of error handling routines be assumed? We rather doubt it. The operating system should not take the risk of error compounding error, especially with file resources that are shared among the users of the system. A possible exception to this argument might be allowed if the operating system has the ability to examine error recovery routines supplied by the user to see if they do in fact reverse the process causing the error. "Reverse" here is used in the sense outlined by Bjork and Davies [Bjo72], where all transformations of data done by the errant process are truly inverted. This inversion is also termed "backing out" and can be used on either the user level or the system programming level.

Finally, the program can be abnormally terminated. If this happens, the user may very well be denied the opportunity of making a simple correction of his error which, if allowed, could result in savings of considerable computer time. This time savings could be extremely important, particularly in the kind of program which uses data entered from many sources and does heavy computation on the data. An example could be the gathering of data from many physics laboratories covering a particular nuclear reaction. These empirical data are to be examined and interpolated to see if they fit a hypothesis being tested. It would be most unfortunate if the entire program were to be terminated after many hours of processing on the system because of the unusual format of data which were received from a distant laboratory.

It would appear, then, that we are locked on the tines of a trilemma:

1. If the user corrects the error, the system lacks complete control of its resources.
2. If the system corrects the error, the users lack control over their allocated resources.
3. If the task is terminated, neither user nor system lacks control (the program and be rerun), but much CPU time can be wasted; also, the user process may have been irreversible and unrecoverable at the time of termination, with resultant partial or total loss of the resource being acted upon.

The solution to the problem lies in one of two approaches. The first is an arbitrary choice of one of the three schemes applied consistently throughout the system. The second is most commonly employed, that of a compromise among the three possibilities. One such compromise used in many operating systems, such as IBM OS and VS, UNIVAC EXEC-8, CDC SCOPE, and Burroughs MCP, is that of having errors involving shared system resources corrected by the system, while errors involving user resources can either end programs or be user-corrected, depending on the type of error encountered and the decision of the user to invoke an error routine.

It should be noted that this discussion applies to the misuse of system resources only; upon actual violations of system architecture, such as storage protect or privileged operation, an interruption occurs and the operating system may abort the job. IBM OS/VS HIS GECOS, and UNIVAC EXEC-8 allow users' routines, if present, to process many program exceptions as desired.

System Programming Errors

For the most part, system programming errors call for the same considerations that were discussed for user programming errors. In addition, system programming is susceptible to certain additional errors, those of interactive processes. An error of this kind can, of course, occur in the user programs as well as system programs, since both use the same instruction set (excepting privileged instructions). However, from an operating system viewpoint, this error is not as important in user programs as the errors discussed above.

For this discussion, let us define interactive processes at the user programming level as being concurrent within the same user storage-protect region or user address space. On the system programming level, each interactive process is in a unique storage-protect region or address space. Together they belong in the system programming category. Together these processes can cause the system to deadlock. System deadlock is discussed at length in another section, but the fact remains that avoidance is the key error recovery method for this situation. In the absence of avoidance of deadlock by system software, the contending programs can often be determined, and one of them can be cancelled, either by the operating system (which would require the checking of additional flags and significant overhead therein — Dijkstra's semaphores [Dij68a], or some similar deadlock detector), else by the operator at the system console after detecting the deadlock.

In either event, this kind of error is serious, since the entire system is often forced into a wait state until the contending programs resolve their problem. Although system or operator cancellation of a program may be distasteful to the user involved, it should be remembered that a prolonged system deadlock is a much less satisfactory alternative. In any event, prevention and avoidance of deadlocks are very costly; probably intolerably so. Exceptions to this cost trade-off are found by some real-time systems users, who may even have written their own deadlock handling routines because of their requirement for total system availability.

What can the operating system designer do to counteract software errors, by either user or system? One of the likeliest paths is software engineering, the use of some programming techniques which have recently been adopted by operating system designers. These techniques, notably top-down programming and structured programming (as espoused by Dijkstra [Dij68b] and others) may well result in a more error-free logic flow in all programs. The techniques have proven fairly effective in *reducing the incidence* of software errors. This is the most preferable sort of error handling: preventing the occurrence of the errors. The other main course of action to be followed is that of *reducing the impact* of the errors when they *do* occur. This can be done using the following methods:

1. Error recovery by "backing out" of the error, which will have all volatile resources restored to their original state.
2. Checkpoint/restart, in which a program stores all volatile data (both in the program and in its associated files) at predetermined points in the program. In the event of error, the affected program merely starts over from the last checkpoint. This can often be done either automatically by the system or through operator control.
3. Rerunning the job — the most obvious, but on balance probably the most expensive method to choose.
4. Ledgering — the keeping of a ledger of all transactions with either a list of volatile values before and/or after each transaction or a set of reversing algorithms to be invoked which will reverse the error-resultant data to original state. Bjork [Bjo72] touches on this.

A warm start, or system restart, may simply be the application of Method 2 or Method 3 to every job in the system at the time its functioning was interrupted.

Hardware Error Recovery

The same objectives apply to hardware error recovery as to software: (1) reduce the incidence of errors, and (2) reduce the impact of errors when they do occur. From the operating system point of view, the system must be notified of both the occurrence of hardware errors and the recovery or nonrecovery from them. There is little that the operating system itself can do about hardware errors except to notify the operator of their occurrence, giving as much information as possible while doing so, and then trying the failing instruction again if possible, if the hardware was unable to do so through hardware retry circuitry.

In the case of I/O hardware errors, an operating system can do one other thing: switch the errant operation to another device or channel path as required and retry the operation. The operator is also notified of this action and asked to take steps to isolate the offending device or path from further use until it is repaired. IBM's MVS-XA automates much of the procedure.

In summary, the operating system can do much to assist in the recovery from errors, both hardware and software, but the best recovery is the prevention of them to begin with.

3.4 LANGUAGE PROCESSORS

Language processors are programs included with all operating systems to provide the programmer with the ability to generate machine code for the computer. The processors range from assemblers, which provide the ability to specify one machine instruction from one assembly-language instruction, to high-level language compilers or interpreters, which may generate many machine instructions or activate large built-in subprograms with a single high-level language statement.

The major tasks performed by language processors are:

1. Associate symbols with machine addresses.
2. Produce machine code to perform the specified operations.
3. Connect the program to the operating system for necessary services.
4. Prepare an executable version of the program in main storage or create a file containing auxiliary information for later execution.

The writing of language processors is a large subject. Several excellent books are available to describe the techniques [Gri71, McKn70]. In what follows, we attempt to discuss only those aspects of language processors in which the relationships with the rest of the operating system are significant: (1) language processor characteristics, (2) executable program characteristics, and (3) interface between user programs and operating system services.

Language Processor Characteristics

In some sense, a language processor can be regarded by the operating system as just another user program. The characteristics that make it exceptional are that it is a service program likely to be used by many people, and that for most of these people the direct output of the language processor (the machine-language program) has no intrinsic interest. As a service program, a language processor may be granted certain privileges normally regarded as under the exclusive control of the supervisor. Thus, a language processor might, for reasons of efficiency, do the following:

1. Directly modify tables used for communication between it and the supervisor.
2. Assume special job-control conventions, such as having the supervisor perform some initialization and place control information directly in the language processor tables.
3. Use special files and access methods or use ordinary files and methods in an irregular way.

4. Use a special library not available to programs in general.
5. Perform services such as opening and closing files for itself.

When a language processor performs these activities for itself, the precise boundary between the supervisor and the language processor becomes hard to define. The language processor might even run in the supervisor state to do some of these activities. From the standpoint of the user of the language processor, this boundary has no particular significance as long as the combination works properly. From the standpoint of systems programmers who are writing the supervisor and the compiler, the precise boundary and the conventions followed should be well defined, so that the programming tasks may be well defined.

One method for providing this kind of special access to the supervisor is provided in OS/VS by the ability to call exit routines. Exit routines are special portions of user programs which are called by supervisor routines so that a user may do special processing related to supervisor functions. They run in problem state and return control to the supervisor when completed. As an example, the OPEN routine can call an exit routine supplied by a user program to do user label processing and to specify file attributes not specified in the three normal places — the data control block, the DD statement, and the file label. In effect, the exit routine provides well-defined, but irregular, access to the supervisor routines. This type of access can be used by compilers to do the special processing referred to above, which normal users would not ordinarily do.

Language processors have a number of other characteristics in common which set them apart from user programs. Language processors tend to be large programs. Frequently, overlay techniques have been used to program them to conserve storage. Secondary storage is also used often for saving the source file for subsequent passes, for storing work or scratch files, and for writing the output file. A language processor in a multiprogramming or time-sharing system could be in demand by more than one user at a time. A reentrable program is frequently provided in preference to providing each user with a separate copy.

Language processors may be classified by the number of passes they make over the source code. A one-pass processor can be used to give fast processing and minimize the use of secondary storage. Since most programming languages allow locations to be referenced symbolically before they are defined, a one-pass processor must necessarily employ some form of fix-up or going-back to modify code previously generated. The XPL compiler is a one-pass compiler [McKn70]. A two-pass processor allows symbolic references to be defined in the first pass over the source code, and machine code to be generated on the second pass. A two-pass arrangement is quite feasible for an assembler, and many compilers use it whenever little optimizing is to be done. The UNIVAC FORTRAN V compiler [UNI3] uses six passes, as follows:

1. Transforms source code into internal format and constructs files and tables.
2. Deals with storage assignment for variables and analyzes loops.
3. Does arithmetic code and index register optimization.
4. Does loop optimization.
5. Completes storage assignment and code generation.
6. Produces relocatable binary code file and edits output.

The IBM PL/1 compiler [IBM29] divides the processing into the following logical phases, which have the same approximate significance as a pass defined as above.

1. Compile time processor — reads text and modifies text according to compile-time processing specified.
2. Read in — checks syntax and removes comments and extra blanks.
3. Dictionary — replaces character representations by coded references.
4. Pretranslator — prepares the text for translation and generates statements for some implied features.
5. Translator — converts the source to triples of operators and operands.
6. Aggregates — does array and structure mapping and checking or provides object code for this purpose.
7. Optimization — reorders the triples if optimization is requested.
8. Psuedo-code — converts the triples to a version similar to machine code.
9. Storage allocation — sets up "dope vectors" and code for dynamic allocation.
10. Register allocation — allocates actual registers for symbolic register references.
11. Final assembly — completes machine code.
12. Error editor — diagnostic message processing.

The logical phases are further broken down into as many as 117 physical phases, which may or may not represent repeated source passes and which may not all be used for any particular compilation. The PL/1 compiler is set up to use a storage partition as small as 44,374 bytes. When the main storage has all been used, secondary storage is provided automatically. Larger storage areas permit more processing to be done before secondary storage is used.

Executable Program Characteristics

The output produced by a language processor is ultimately the executable program. Sometimes, intermediate forms of the program are produced for combining with other programs or for executing later.

Most operating systems of any generality assume that the programs produced are segmented and relocatable. Because of this, some form of binding program is part of the operating system. This program — variously called a binder, a loader, or a linkage editor — typically converts relative addresses to absolute ones, gathers program segments together, and supplies program segments from system libraries. The binding process is discussed further in Section 3.5 and in Chapter 6. Thus, a program usually passes through a language processor and a binding program before loading for execution.

A program is relocatable if it can be loaded anywhere in main storage for execution. Part of the relocatability may be achieved by hardware aids, such as base registers whose contents are included in all generated addresses from instructions. If the base registers are not accessible to user programs, dynamic relocation by the supervisor is possible even after a program has started to execute, and relocation can be a supervisor function. The user-accessible base registers in the System/360 and 370 computers allow a program to be relocated at the time it is loaded, but not after it has started to execute. The addition of the dynamic address translation facility to the System/370 allows the actual program pages to be relocated at instruction execution time, but the programmer's view via OS/VS is that the program is being statically relocated in virtual storage. Relocatability may also be aided by software. Absolute addresses in main storage of locations in the program or of the locations of other programs, i.e. address constants, cannot be determined until the program is loaded and all program segments have been given definite addresses. To allow the adjustment of such address constants, the language processor must record the location of any values to be adjusted and the change to be made to that value. This information must be kept with the program until it has been loaded and the adjustment made.

Programming languages allow defining symbols, which may be local to portions of a program, which may be global throughout the program, or which may be external. The external symbols of a program allow it to be combined with other programs and are usually all the symbols that retain their identity after the language processor has completed its work. The language processor must associate the external symbols with their locations in the program and save this information along with program text and relocation information.

The OS/VS language processor outputs are called object modules. All the language processors use the same object module format. The object module consists of the binary program text, the external symbol table, and relocation information, and thus provides a complete representation of a relocatable program suitable for loading. The details of the object module records are discussed in section 3.5, which deals with the linking together and loading of object modules into executable programs.

The usability attributes of a program also influence the way it can be treated by the operating system. Some of the usability attributes which have been defined are:

1. Nonreusable — applied to a program that modifies its instructions or data.
2. Serially reusable — applied to a program that initializes itself, although its instructions and data may be modified during execution.
3. Reentrable — applied to a program that does not modify its instructions.

The operating system must be able to recognize these attributes, that is, they must be stored along with the program file. To conserve storage and to reduce input/output activity, it is desirable to allow more than one user to execute a copy of a program. However, if a program is nonreusable, each user must have a new copy, even if the same main storage area is used. Serially reusable programs allow only one user at a time to execute a program, so that multiple use requests must be queued by the system to maintain proper use. Reentrable programs can be used by more than one user at the same time. To keep storage protection active, the reentrable code and any constant data can be kept in a read-only area of the supervisor so that no user can modify them. A data area for each user can be kept in the user's main storage area, so that other users cannot modify it. To avoid keeping inactive programs in storage, a use count must be maintained for programs with multiple users. When the use count is zero, the storage can be used for other purposes if desired.

Interfaces Between User Programs and Operating System Services

The ability of the programmer of a language to invoke the facilities of the operating system during execution of his program varies a great deal from language to language and even among various implementations of what is nominally the same language. The nature of the operating system should not be apparent to the user of a language processor. To a certain point this can be accomplished. However, it is naive to think that programmers of a high-level language can make the best use of the operating system facilities provided unless they understand the nature of these services and the way they are being implemented. As an example, users of a virtual storage system for their FORTRAN programs are partly relieved of considering the size of their programs. They may find out that they pay an intolerable penalty in time and in I/O activity if they do not understand the paging mechanism being used to provide the service.

Many high-level languages are designed to be machine-independent. Anyone who has ever tried to transfer a program from one machine to another knows that true machine-independence or portability is rarely attained, even with strictly computational programs. Despite standards, each compiler seems to have slightly different ways of regarding the program statements, and special functions or statements are frequently provided. In the relationship with the operating system, the question of machine-independence becomes even more important. One of the goals of an operating system is to provide convenient access to the hardware of a particular machine. The desire to provide machine-independence then conflicts directly with the desire to provide the machine services to the programmer of a high-level language. One is faced with either limiting the language capability to provide machine-independence or making the machine features available with language statements that are special. Different compiler writers regard this conflict in different ways, and the usual result is that virtually no program in a high-level language is completely transferable from one machine to another. The style of program writing also influences the ability to transfer a program from one machine to another. A frequent source of this problem is the different word sizes in different machines. A programmer who tries to pack data efficiently on one machine finds he has exceeded the word capacity on another machine.

The services of an operating system can be invoked in several ways:

1. By an explicit statement in the language used for programming, such as a READ or WRITE in FORTRAN.
2. By the job control language statements accompanying the program, such as the EXEC or DD statements of OS/VS.
3. By default or by an implied request, such as storage protection or file opening in a FORTRAN program.

Most operating systems are programmed in assembly language. For this reason, complete access to operating system services is usually available to assembly language programmers. In OS/VS, supervisor services are provided through the use of macroinstructions, macros. For many of these services, the actual providing of the service is done by code located in the supervisor. The macro provides communication areas and an SVC instruction to notify the supervisor that a particular kind of service is desired. An exception to this arrangement is provided by the Burroughs systems [BUR2, BUR4], which use only high-level languages for system programming. The UNIVAC 1100 OS [UNI1] provides the assembly language programmer with services by executive requests. A summary of the executive requests is given in Table 3.3 to illustrate the scope of the services provided. These services are invoked by loading necessary parameters into registers and by following that by an executive request instruction with one of the indicated operands.

Table 3.3. Summary of Operating System Services Provided by UNIVAC 1100 OS[UNI1].

Activity registration	Register activity (FORK$)
	Timed activity registration (TFORK$)
	Timed wait (TWAIT$)
	Activity wait (AWAIT$)
	Activity naming (NAME$)
	Activity activation (ACT$)
	Activity deactivation (DACT$)
	Activity deletion (ADLT$)
Termination	Normal exit (EXIT$)
	Abnormal exit (ABORT$)
	Error exit (ERR$)
File supervision	Buffer pool expansion (BJOIN$)
	Buffer pool setup (BPOOL$)
	Communications buffer pool removal (CGET$)
	Communications buffer pool addition (CADD$)
	Communications buffer pool setup (CPOOL$)
	Directory item retrieval (DITEM$)
	Facility determination (FACIL$)
	Tape reel number set initialization (TINTL$)
	Tape swapping (TSWAP$)
Real Time	Enter real time status (RT$)
	Leave real time status (NRT$)
Reentrable Routines	Enter reentrable routine (LINK$)
	Return from reentrable routine (ULINK$)
Dynamic Facilities	Request additional core (MCORE$)
	Release unneeded core (LCORE$)
	Interpret control statements (CSF$)
Input/Output Requests (only major requests shown)	Initiate I/O and return (IO$)
	Initiate I/O and return on completion (IOW$)
	Initiate I/O and exit, give interrupt handler control on completion (IOXI$)

Table 3.3 (Cont.)

Input/Output Requests (Cont.)	Initiate I/O and return, interrupt on completion (IOI$)
	Initiate I/O, give interrupt handler control on completion, and return (IOWI$)
	Wait for completion of specific I/O request (WAIT$)
	Wait for completion of any I/O request (WANY$)
Symbiont Control	System initiated print file (PRINT$)
	System initiated punch file (PUNCH$)
	Read control stream (READ$)
Checkpoint/Restart	Save run status (CKPT$)
	Begin at a checkpoint (RSTRT$)
Miscellaneous	Reduce interrupt priority (UNLCK$)
	Recover option letters (OPT$)
	Return date (DATE$)
	Return time (TIME$)
	Read program control table (PCT$)
	Snapshot dump (SNAP$)
	Set condition word (SETC$)
	Retrieve condition word (COND$)
	Load a program segment (LOAD$)

The IBM PL/1 compiler also presents virtually all the services of OS/VS to the programmer, who has the following services available through specific commands in the language:

1. Use of most of the access methods provided by the system.
2. Specification of file structure parameters.
3. File opening, closing, and disposition.
4. Dynamic storage allocation and release.
5. Special condition or exception handling.
6. Generation of reentrant code.
7. Sorting.
8. Creation of multiple tasks and subtasks.

Thus, a PL/1 programmer may specify virtually any kind of service. In this sense, PL/1 could be a suitable language for writing operating system programs, although efficiency considerations might counter the convenience and documentation value of this approach. The MULTICS system at MIT was coded in PL/1. The more recent CLICS system at MIT was coded in a special language similar to PL/1, with more well-defined properties [Cla71]. The applicability of languages for systems programming is discussed further in Chapter 7.

In a similar way, the ALGOL variant ESPOL [BUR6], used by the Burroughs Corporation for their systems programming, has specific reference to system routines for interrupt handling, process activation and suspension, timing, event monitoring, resource control, and access to the hardware stack. ESPOL also has a queue as a data structure to facilitate programming system routines. Because of these features, this language is used for programming the Burroughs MCP. Access to these features is necessary, since machine or assembly language programming is not normally done on this company's machines. In a more nearly typical ALGOL language implementation, the user is more isolated from the facilities of the operating system. The ALGOL language intrinsically has a capacity to allocate storage dynamically by the block structure and by recursive procedures. The original ALGOL specification did not even specify input/output statements, although all actual implementations necessarily do so.

The COBOL language has excellent access to operating system facilities for input/output defined as part of the language. If the appropriate devices are available, the COBOL language permits processing of sequential, indexed sequential, and random-access files. It further allows the programmer to specify record and block formats and characteristics in some detail. Some instructions for device control are also available. A SORT instruction allows files to be sorted on any desired field.

As a language, FORTRAN provides few operating system services to its users by explicit statements in the language. The only services directly requested by FORTRAN language statements are those concerned with input or output. FORTRAN programs use static virtual storage allocation and so storage management techniques are not provided to the FORTRAN programmer. A programmer must manage storage within the program by reusing or redefining the data areas. FORTRAN programs can be put into an overlay structure in IBM systems, but the linkage editor must be used to do it. The storage management provided by OS/VS segmentation and paging are not seen by the FORTRAN programmer. Many of the operating system services provided to FORTRAN programmers must be specified by the job control language. For example, in IBM FORTRAN, the programmer must specify sequential file attributes by the DCB parameter of a DD statement in the job control language for the program. In effect, this means that the programmer must go outside the language to access operating system services.

The programs produced by the IBM FORTRAN compilers use a run-time library to interact with the operating system. The run-time library consists of two types of subroutines: computational or mathematical subroutines, and

Table 3.4. FORTRAN G Run-Time Library for Operating System Interface [IBM28].

Function	Name
I/O Subroutines	
1. I/O operations and data area	IHCFCOMH
2. Sequential access I/O data management interface	IHCFIOSH
3. Direct access I/O data management interface	IHCDIOSE
4. Namelist	IHCNAMEL
5. Formatted and namelist data conversion	IHCFCVTH
6. Unit assignment table	IHCUATBL
Error Handling Subroutines	
7. Source statement compiler detected error handling	IHCIBERH
8. Terminal error message and diagnostic traceback	IHCTRCH
9. Error handling and message generation	IHCERRM
10. Error option table	IHCUOPT
11. Error option handling	IHCFOPT
12. Program interrupt handling	IHCFINTH
13. Boundary alignment	IHCADJST
14. Abnormal termination interception	IHCSTAE
Miscellaneous Program Services	
15. Test for divide check interrupt	IHCFDVCH
16. Test for overflow/underflow interrupt	IHCFOVER
17. Simulate and test sense lights	IHCSLIT
18. Terminate execution	IHCFEXIT
19. Dump main storage data areas	IHCFDUMP
20. Produce debugging information	IHCDBUG

subroutines to interact with the operating systems. These are listed in Table 3.4. The advantage of breaking down the interface to the operating system into subroutines is that only those routines actually called need be loaded.

The executing program calls the computational subroutines and some of the interface subroutines (for example, IHCFCOMH). Most of the other interface subroutines are called only by other interface subroutines (for example, IHCFCOMH calls IHCFIOSH), but a few may be called either way (for example, IHCDIOSE is called either by the executing program or by IHCFCOMH). These calling relationships are summarized in Table 3.5 for the I/O routines. Ultimately, the I/O is performed by the standard access methods for sequential and direct access. Another group of routines in Table 3.4 is related to error handling. These routines write error messages and allow prescribed numbers of various errors before terminating the job. An extended error handling option provides the programmer with the ability to control the number of each category of error and

Table 3.5. FORTRAN G Run-Time Library I/O Subroutine Relationships
[IBM28].

Calling Program	Called Program	Service Performed
User code	IHCDIOSE	Handle DEFINE FILE
	IHCNAMEL	Handle NAMELIST READ/WRITE
	IHCFCOMH	Handle other I/O Statements
IHCFCOMH	IHCFCVTH	Formatted data conversion
	IHCDIOSE	Interpret direct-access I/O requests
	IHCFIOSH	Interpret sequential I/O requests
	Supervisor	Send console messages
IHCNAMEL	IHCFCVTH	Namelist data conversion
	IHCFIOSH	Interpret sequential I/O requests
IHCDIOSE	Supervisor	Direct-access I/O
	Supervisor	Sequential I/O (Initialization)
IHCFIOSH	Supervisor	Sequential I/O

the action to be taken when an error is identified. The remaining routines in Table 3.4 provide program services primarily concerned with debugging.

3.5 UTILITIES

A utility program may be defined as a complete program which performs a specific function related to the use of an operating system. Typically, the operating system supplier provides a number of utility programs to go with the system. A utility program may be operated under the supervision of the operating system control program just as any other program, or it may be a stand-alone program. The modules which make up the operating system and the language processors (see Section 3.4) are not normally considered utility programs. Utility programs provide access to the operating system facilities without the user's having to consider all the details of the system. A particular function to be accomplished, such as deleting a file, might sometimes be done by the control program, at other times by a utility program, and at still other times by a user-written routine. As a result, classifying a particular program as a utility program might sometimes be difficult. This is not considered to be a serious problem, because the only reason for classifying programs this way is to discuss together a group of programs with somewhat similar objectives.

Some of the functions which may be done by utility programs are:

1. Linking and loading of segmented programs.
2. Sorting and merging of files.
3. Maintaining operating system facilities.
4. Maintaining files.

5. Initializing and maintaining secondary storage devices.
6. Assisting debugging.
7. Examining of accounting data.

The function of linking and loading may be broken down into several subfunctions:

1. Gathering together all the modules from compiler output, from user object module input, and from libraries.
2. Resolving external references between modules.
3. Constructing a program module for loading.
4. Constructing programs with overlay structure.
5. Detecting and diagnosing errors.
6. Loading the program.

When these subfunctions are done, relative to execution of the program, varies widely. Some of them may be done by separate utility programs and others by the control program. Not all need to be done.

IBM provides two utility programs in OS/VS for doing linking and loading, namely the loader and the linkage editor. In addition, a program fetch routine is included as a part of the control program. The output from all IBM language processors is in the form of object modules, which contain the program text and related external symbol and relocation information. The object modules may be written on a secondary storage file or kept in main storage. The linkage editor takes object modules as a portion of its primary input and produces load modules as its output. The remainder of the linkage editor input may be load modules produced from previous execution of the linkage editor. External references are resolved to the extent possible and desired by the programmer. Considerable facilities for editing the output are provided by the linkage editor. A further discussion of the linkage editor is provided in Chapter 6 in the context of symbol binding. The linkage editor writes the load modules on secondary storage in a partitioned file (see Section 5.2). The program fetch routine takes load modules as its input and produces a copy of the program text in main storage ready to execute with address constant relocation performed. The loader combines some of the functions of the linkage editor and the program fetch routine by taking object modules and load modules as input and producing an executable copy of the program text in main storage with all address constants adjusted for relocation. The loader cannot save a program for execution at a later time. It does not allow much editing and cannot produce a program with an overlay structure.

The details of loader processing can be considered in more detail by examining the loader parameters, by considering the data flow and files used, and by

Table 3.6. Loader Parameters [IBM2].

Parameters[1]	Action Taken or Meaning
MAP	A map of external names and the corresponding absolute addresses is produced.
RES	After the primary input from SYSLIN has been processed, the link pack area queue is searched before the search of SYSLIB.
CALL	After the primary input from SYSLIN has been processed and any processing implied by the RES parameter has been completed, SYSLIB is searched to resolve external references.
LET	Execution of the program is attempted even if some errors are found.
PRINT	Messages are printed on SYSPRINT.
TERM	Messages are printed on SYSTERM.
SIZE=number	Specifies an amount of virtual storage to be used by the loader.
EP=name	Specifies an entry point for the loaded program.
NAME=name	Specifies a name to identify the loaded program.

[1] The opposite action for each of the parameters, except the last three, will be taken if the parameter is preceded by NO; for example, NOMAP means a map is not produced.

examining the action taken by the loader with the various kinds of data records used as its input. The parameters which control the loader processing are summarized in Table 3.6. These parameters may be specified by the PARM field of the EXEC statement which invokes the loader. The parameters control the listing of loader output, the extent to which libraries are to be searched, and a few attributes (name and entry point) of the loaded program.

The data flow in the loader is illustrated in Figure 3.5. The primary input file is the SYSLIN file, which may contain object or load modules. The entire SYSLIN file is used to place executable program text in storage and resolve external references to the extent possible. If some external references remain unresolved, several options still exist:

1. The link pack area can be searched to see if any of the desired modules are resident in main storage; specified via the RES parameter.
2. Program libraries in the SYSLIB file can be searched to see if any of the desired modules are present; specified via the CALL parameter.

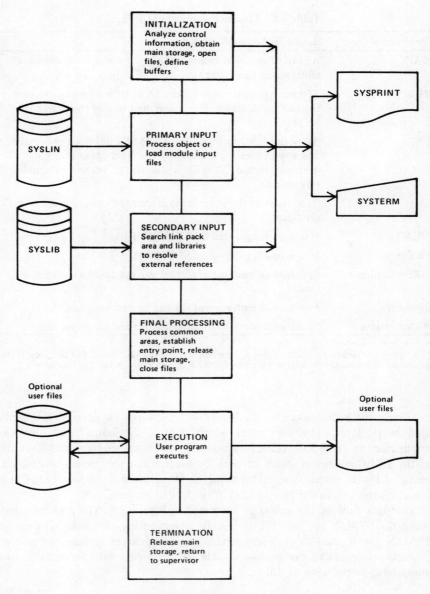

Figure 3.5. Loader Data Flow.

3. Execution of the program with external references undefined can be attempted; specified via the LET parameter. This situation might arise if a module is to be loaded dynamically during program execution or if a call to the missing module is known to be bypassed. Execution of a program with a missing module is occasionally necessary during debugging.

If output has been requested the SYSPRINT file is used for that purpose. The SYSTEM file contains the same information as the SYSPRINT file and is provided for routing the output to a time-sharing terminal if that option is being used. When the program has been loaded, the loader branches to it, just as to a subroutine. The loader executes and then returns control to the loader, which terminates its execution and returns to the supervisor.

All the IBM language processors use a common format for object modules, so that combining object modules from different language processors is simplified and a single version of the loader and of the linkage editor will handle the output of all language processors. Combining of object modules produced by the FORTRAN and COBOL compilers with those produced by the assembler is quite feasible, provided the conventions for register usage and parameter list passing are followed by the assembly language programmer. Combining PL/1 object modules with those produced by the assembler is also possible, but detailed knowledge of the PL/1 data structures and storage management routines is necessary for the assembly language programmer.

An object module may contain one or more control sections. A control section is the basic unit of a relocatable program and must be manipulated as a unit by the loader program. An OS/VS object module consists of several types of records:

1. SYM — special symbol tale for program testing; not used by the loader.
2. ESD — external symbols dictionary; contains symbol names and relative addresses.
3. TXT — text; contains binary program image.
4. RLD — relocation dictionary; contains location of symbol to be relocated and what relocation is to be performed on it.
5. END — physically last in object deck; may contain entry point and processor identification data.
6. MOD — contains location in storage of object modules already in storage.

The external symbols (ESD) are further broken down as follows:

1. SD — control section definition by CSECT, START, or subprogram names.
2. LD — label definition by ENTRY.

3. ER — external reference; defined by EXTERNAL, by a V-type address constant, or by a CALL.
4. PC — private code; defined by an unnamed CSECT or START.
5. CM — named or blank common; defined by COM or COMMON.
6. PR — pseudo-register; defined by DXD.
7. WX — weak external reference; an external reference which must not be resolved by a search of the SYSLIB file.

Similar records are also present in load modules, although the record formats are quite different. A load module may have been constructed from more than one object module, in which case a combined external symbols dictionary (CESD) is used in place of the ESD. The entry point symbols in a load module are called LR symbols, which differ from LD symbols in a minor way.

The loader processes the object modules and load modules one at a time. The ESD records are used to construct a CESD for the program to be loaded. The CESD consists primarily of symbols and their corresponding absolute addresses.

The LD and LR symbols in the input become LR symbols in the CESD. The PC symbols are transferred directly to the CESD so that each region of unnamed code will be in a unique location. For each other external symbol in the input, the symbol is resolved by searching the CESD to see if the name is already entered. If the name is not found in the CESD, it is entered there. In addition, LR symbols are chained to their corresponding SD symbols. A symbol is considered to be defined by its occurrence in (1) an SD, LD, CM, PR, or LR; (2) a private library; or (3) the automatic call library contained in SYSLIB. Sometimes, an external reference cannot be resolved because it is defined in a later input module. The records for unresolved external references are chained to the CESD entry for processing when the symbol is defined later. If there are multiple occurrences of SD symbols, the first occurrence is used. Multiple occurrences of CM symbols are processed by recording the length of the larger common section in the CESD. A match between CM and SD symbols becomes and SD in the CESD with the length of the longer of the two inputs.

The TXT records are read into buffers. The correct main storage location for these records is always available when the corresponding ESD records have already been processed (or an error condition exists). After a check to make sure there is enough room, the TXT records are moved to their correct main storage location.

The RLD records are used to do the relocation adjustments to the text already present in main storage for any symbols that have been defined. The RLD records for undefined symbols are saved so that the relocation may be done when the symbol is defined. The END record indicates the end of a module and may also be used to establish an entry point for the loaded program.

The loader goes through all the object modules in the primary input SYSLIN and then attempts to resolve external references by searching the library SYSLIB. When processing has been completed, each ER or WX symbol reference must match a corresponding symbol definition or there will be an unresolved external reference. Unless the parameters have been used to designate otherwise, an unresolved external reference is considered to be an error.

A sort/merge utility routine is usually provided, particularly with operating systems to be used for commercial or administrative applications. Typically, the generality and flexibility of the sort/merge utility routine is considered to be one of its most important attributes. Some of the criteria which may be used to evaluate a sort/merge utility are:

1. Ability to handle data on any form of recording medium, such as card, tape, disk, or drum.
2. Ability to process records of any size and format and containing keys of any size and location.
3. Ability to handle any number of input/output devices.
4. Ability to handle a sorting problem of any size by an efficient method.
5. Ability to use any access method in the scope of the operating system.
6. Ability to use efficiently all the resources available to a particular problem.
7. Ability to be used alone or in combination with another program.
8. Ability to use any desired collating sequence.
9. Ability to combine the sorting and merging operations in any desired combination and for any number of devices.
10. Ability to choose the sorting algorithm to match characteristics of the data, such as partial order.
11. Ability to process list data by pointer manipulation rather than data movement.

These criteria frequently conflict, so that the number and kind of features available vary in practice.

Many sorting methods are available and choosing a method to use is a difficult and complex task. For large sorting problems, particularly those that involve the use of secondary storage, the choice of a sorting method may have major economic consequences. The balancing of the manipulations required by the sorting algorithm, the speed of the central processor, the amount of main storage available, and the speed and number of secondary storage devices of various kinds may require that a utility for sorting and merging offer the user a choice of methods. Martin [Mar71] has reviewed many of the methods and has an excellent bibliography.

The strategies involved in large sorting problems can be briefly summarized as follows:

1. The records to be sorted are brought into as large an area of main storage as can be allocated to the problem.
2. A sorting algorithm, usually one utilizing the random-access capability of main storage, forms the records into sorted strings of records.
3. The sorted strings are written to secondary storage on at least two devices.
4. Steps 1-3 are repeated until the entire input file has been processed.
5. The sorted strings are merged from the secondary storage devices. For k devices, the sorted string length is multiplied by k each time they are merged.
6. The merged strings are written to secondary storage on at least two devices.
7. Steps 5 and 6 are repeated until the entire file has been merged into a single sorted string of records.

The internal sorting methods used in the sorting algorithm may be classified as quadratic, logarithmic, or linear according to the relationship between the number of items in the file to be sorted and the number of operations to be performed. Examples of typical algorithms of the three types are:

1. Quadratic — bubble sort, in which an out-of-sequence record is exchanged with its neighbors until it is in sequence.
2. Logarithmic — binary-insertion sort, in which a record is added to an existing sorted list by a binary search.
3. Linear — address calculation, in which the hash addressing technique described in Chapter 1 is used to calculate the position of a record in the sorted list.

The more efficient logarithmic and linear methods are more difficult to program and may reduce the amount of main storage available for records because of a larger program and because of areas needed for pointers to the records. The choice of an algorithm is also dependent on the use to be made of the sorted file and on its structure. A file, such as one to be printed, must be physically sequentially organized and so the complete records must be placed in order. For other purposes, the records must merely be logically sorted, and a sorted index to the records is adequate.

The order in which the successive distributions and merges are done as steps 5 and 6 of the overall sorting strategy leads to a number of recognized techniques:

1. Balanced merge — Half of the available devices serve as input for merges. The other half of the devices are used to receive the sorted strings after merging.
2. Polyphase merge — All but one of the available devices serve as input for merges, and the other device receives the output. When one of the input devices becomes empty, it starts receiving output, and the former output device is used for input. This method is most effective if the initial distribution is unequal and the numbers of records on each device are generalized Fibonacci numbers.
3. Oscillating merge — The distribution and merging are intermingled. One device contains the input, one device is empty, and single sorted strings are distributed to the other devices. The distributed strings are merged before further distribution occurs. This method requires devices with the capability of reading backwards to be effective.

Some analyses of the effectiveness of various sorting methods are available [Flo69, Mar71]. Although the address calculation sort is very effective, the function used to calculate the addresses may depend on the data. Consequently, it is not used much, and logarithmic methods are widely used. Of the various merging strategies for tape sorts, the polyphase merge is faster than the oscillating merge for fewer than six tape drives. The oscillating sort is faster for six or more drives, but requires tape drives that can reverse quickly and read backward [Flo69]. The relationship of a sort/merge utility with the rest of the operating system is relatively straightforward. The ability to use all the input/output access methods is a major requirement of a sort/merge utility, so that all types of files can be used as input. Frequently, there is a need to use the sort/merge utility both as a program by itself or as a subroutine of another program (requirement 7 above). In this case, the operating system needs to have very carefully defined conventions regarding the way programs are called the data locations are transmitted.

To give an idea of the scope of the operating system functions which can be performed by utility programs, we give a summary of the OS/VS utility programs supplied by IBM in Table 3.7. Most of these programs can execute as separate job steps under the operating system. Used this way, the utility programs operate on normal OS/VS files supplied as input and produce normal OS/VS files as output, without the intervention or control of any other program. Alternatively, these same utility programs may be invoked by a problem program through the use of a CALL, LINK, or ATTACH macro. Invoked this second way, the utility programs are effectively used as subroutines and may also process data areas in the invoking program. Use of the utility programs by the programs produced by a language processor is also made simple by this second method. The language processor merely needs to set up the proper parameter

Table 3.7. Summary of IBM Utility Programs and Service Aids for OS/VS.

Name	Use
IEHPROGM	Scratch or rename a file or a partitioned file member, catalog or uncatalog a file, maintain file index names and generations.
IEHMOVE	Move or copy a sequential, direct, or partitioned file, unload a partitioned file to magnetic tape and reload it to a direct-access volume.
IEHLIST	List the catalog of a file, the directory of a partitioned file, or the table of contents of a disk volume.
IEHINITT	Put standard labels on magnetic tapes.
IEHIOSUP	Update tables for the supervisor call library.
IEHDASDR	For direct-access device, check tracks and assign alternate tracks, prepare a volume for use, dump back-up copies to magnetic tape, and restore volumes from back-up copies.
IEBCOPY	Copy, compress, expand, or reallocate space for a partitioned file on a direct-access device.
IEBGENER	Copy sequential file or a partitioned file member to a variety of devices, produce a partitioned file from sequential input, change records by editing or reblocking, and place user labels on sequential files.
IEBCOMPR	Verify all or part of sequential or partitioned files by comparing logical records.
IEBPTPCH	Print or punch all or part of a sequential or partitioned file, a directory of a partitioned file, or an edited sequential or partitioned file.
IEBUPDTE	Add, delete, replace, or copy records or members of sequential or partitioned files, sequence number a file, produce a partitioned file from sequential input.
IEBISAM	For an indexed sequential file on a direct-access volume, copy to another location, convert to sequential output, print out the contents, transfer sequential input to the file.
IEBEDIT	Produce a file containing job and job-step data for future execution.
IEBUPDAT	Add, delete, replace, or copy records or members of a partitioned file, number or renumber records.
IEBDG	Provide test data to aid debugging.
IBCDASDI	Initialize direct-access volumes and assign alternate tracks.
IBCDMPRS	Dump a direct-access volume to magnetic tape or to another direct-access volume, and restore a direct-access volume from the dumped volume.

Table 3.7. (Cont.)

Name	Use
IEHATLAS	Recover data from defective tracks on direct-access volumes and assign alternate tracks.
IFCDIPOO	Initialize a data set for the system log.
IFCEREPO	Print the system log.
IMCJQDMP	Print the job queue as a stand-alone program.
IMCOSJQD	Print the job queue under the operating system.
IMBLIST	Print object modules and load modules.
IMBMDMAP	Map load modules.
GTF	Trace certain system events.
IMDPRDMP	Print dumps, time-sharing swapping data, and GTF trace data.
IMAPTFLE	Apply temporary program fixes to the operating system and generate job control to do so.
IMDSADMP	Dump main storage as a stand-alone program.
IMASPZAP	Replace instructions or data in a load module.
IEBIMAGE	Create modules for use in advanced printing applications.
IDCAMS	Manipulate VSAM catalogs and data sets.
IAPAP100	Check out direct access storage drives.
ICAPRTBL	Exploit printers' unique features.
IEBTCRIN	Read data from tape cartridges.
IFHSTATR	Print records of tape errors [IBM33].

list to utilize the utility programs in the program which it is producing. A few of the programs (IMCJQDMP and IMDSADMP) operate as stand-alone programs which are not entered into the computer via the job stream. These programs, which produce dumps of main storage, are useful for detecting operating system problems in that they do not use the operating system and, therefore, do not disturb the data being dumped. These programs must be initiated by operations at the console.

The functions performed by these IBM utility programs may be roughly classified by the kind of operations they do:

1. System utilities (IEH...) — maintain control information about data sets without modifying the data sets.
2. Data set utilities (IEB...) — work with the information contained in data sets by coping, modifying, or comparing logical records inside the data sets.

3. Independent utilities (IBC...) — operate outside the operating system to prepare and maintain direct-access volumes.
4. Service aids (the other names) — for debugging and repairing system and application programs; used for formatting and printing hexadecimal data, and for modifying existing programs or data by changing the information in hexadecimal form.

To illustrate the kind of programming involved in these utility programs, the IEBGENER program we discuss in more detail. The input to IEBGENER is essentially sequential, although the program will also allow the use of one member of a partitioned data set. The output may be a sequential data set or a partitioned data set. For the latter case, the directory for the partitioned data set must also be constructed. The data flow for IEBGENER is given in Fig. 3.6. The control statements are entered on SYSIN and the diagnostic messages are output in SYSPRINT. The data sets SYSUT1 (input) and SYSUT2 (output)

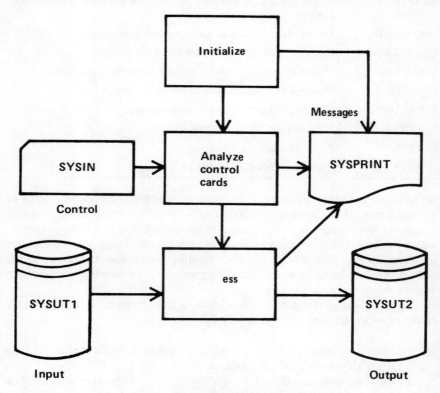

Figure 3.6. IEBGENER Data Flow.

are shown as being on disk. If the data sets have sequential organization, they may also be on tape, cards, printer, or any sequential device. A partitioned data set must reside on a direct access device, due to IBM operating system conventions. The IEBGENER has an overlay structure, so that the processing portion and the control card analysis portion occupy the same area in storage.

Several kinds of control statements are provided to the user of IEBGENER to allow modification of the transmission of input to output:

1. GENERATE – is required if the output is partitioned, if editing is to be done, or if user routines are provided. The parameters supplied control the table sizes required for processing.
2. EXITS – specifies user exits, which are user-written routines called by IEBGENER at various points. User exits can be set up to process input header labels, output header labels, input trailer labels, and output trailer labels. They may also be used to create output record keys to handle input/output device errors, to edit the records before processing by IEBGENER, and to record user totals in the output records.
3. LABELS – controls whether user labels are to be treated as data or ignored.
4. MEMBER – specifies member names of an output partitioned data set. Omitting these statements means the output is sequential.
5. RECORD – identifies groups of records to be processed identically and supplies editing information for that group.

If no control statements are supplied, IEBGENER copies a sequential data set from input to output.

A simplified flow chart showing the processing done by IEBGENER is given in Fig. 3.7 for the case of processing sequential input and output without user exits or spanned records. The processing is very straightforward. The control statement records are read and processed in their entirety, and the information is stored in tables. Following this, records are read from SYSUT1, edited, and written on SYSUT2. A basic access method is used, and blocking and unblocking are done by IEBGENER. There is certainly nothing complicated about the program, although many details have been omitted from the flow chart. Actually, IEBGENER uses both basic and queued access methods and uses different numbers of buffers and work areas depending on the nature of the records being processed. The complete flow chart has a great many more branches to it for the processing, but the logic remains much the same.

The real value of a program like IEBGENER is that it has already been programmed and tested. It may be used without concern for all the coding detail necessary to do the logically simple but lengthy operations. The arguments for having a program like this are much the same as the arguments for having a

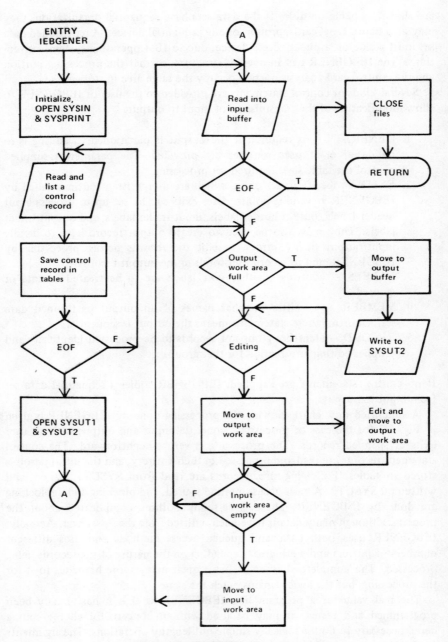

Figure 3.7. IEBGENER Flow Chart.

high-level programming language. Users can control a large program with a relatively small programming effort. They may have to pay for the generality and convenience by having a larger or slower program than they might otherwise code, but they will generally be finished more quickly. The utility programs greatly enhance the usability of an operating system by providing simplified access to the components of the operating system and to the files contained in it.

Not all utility programs are necessarily provided by the computer or operating system supplier. Utility programs may be obtained from a number of commercial sources. An installation can write its own utilities for commonly used operations or for operations that no available programs can perform.

3.6 ACCOUNTING FOR RESOURCE USAGE

The use of a computer represents consumption of valuable resources. To use these resources effectively, one must keep records on their usage by different individuals. Some of the reasons for keeping these records are:

1. To restrict access to the system to legitimate users with valid accounts, a security function.
2. To charge the users for their computing activities.
3. To inform users of the status and progress of their programs.
4. To provide data for job scheduling by the operations staff.
5. To provide data for resource allocation during execution.
6. To assist in repair and maintenance activities.
7. To analyze overall system performance.
8. To plan future systems which may meet the needs of actual users.

The size and nature of the records required depends on the relative importance of the above criteria and also on the environment provided by the computer, its peripheral equipment, and its software.

The simplest case occurs when a single user requires the whole system. A simple record of time used can serve as the basis for charging the user. Very simple records on resource usage can serve both for management of present systems and planning future ones. For example, if an installation has six tape drives and two of them are never used, it benefits neither user nor installation manager to have these devices present. Simple records on usage can support a decision to reduce the number. A problem arises even in this simple system for users who need no tape drives. Should they be charged for their costs? The answer to this question depends on the nature of the operation.

If the service is being provided commercially, the users are free to select any computing service they wish and the computer manager is free to charge the user any price users are willing to pay. Under these circumstances, charging for equipment not used is irrelevant because users are not really concerned with any breakdown of the cost they pay for service. If the service is being provided by an in-house computer, the computer manager may have a monopoly and tend to price the computer services so that the cost of all equipment available is prorated in some way to all users. The user is likely to be very concerned about the fairness and accuracy of the pricing method under these circumstances. With this kind of concern, the extent of the records on usage will be of great interest to the user.

The problem for an in-house operation is further complicated by a variety of choices regarding cost allocation. In its simplest terms, the computer operation may be regarded either as a cost center which contributes to general overhead or as a profit center which is expected to be productive like any other profit center of an operation. Neither alternative is completely satisfactory. The cost center approach tends to make the users regard the service as a free resource, and the profit center approach may deprive the computer manager of control over the elements which lead to the operation's profit. Motivating the managers of the various elements of the organization is very important in deciding on an approach.

The question of recording resource usage becomes much more complex when a multiprogramming system is being used because: (1) activities may be going on in parallel, (2) several users may be active at once, and (3) some resources may be shared while others are required exclusively. The resources used and the amount of their usage may depend on the work of the other users and their demands on the computer system. A result of this is that a particular program may not always use the same resources even if it is repeated exactly. One reason for the variability is that there is a cost associated with switching from one user to another. The frequency of switching will vary with the job mix present. This cost can be regarded as a multiprogramming overhead cost. Another more difficult problem arises from one job interfering with the resources for another. An obvious example is extra seeks required of a movable head disk unit as it retrieves records alternately for one job and a different job whose data are stored in a different location on the same disk volume. The question of who should pay for idle resources also becomes very complex for a multiprogramming system. Because of these considerations, the recordkeeping requirements for a multiprogramming system are likely to be extensive.

Cost allocation for a multiprogramming system is a difficult, controversial problem. The controversy arises because users of computer services tend to feel the price they pay for a given program or unit of work should be fixed. In fact, the resources required to run a given program in a multiprogramming environment vary according to criteria not under the control of the purchaser. One answer [Tay71] is to leave the pricing variable and let it be a management function to price the services rendered according to policies which reflect the cost of the resources and their value to the user. A more common approach is to work out some technical solution to the problem of resource usage and develop an algorithm to allow computer recording and billing. The productive time that the resources are used may enter into the calculation, so that the degradation of service due to multiprogramming is estimated [Ret72]. Thus, when users are ready to use resources, but the operating system prevents this, they are not charged for use of the resources. This approach can account for wait time, but it cannot account for degradation of performance caused by interference between jobs.

Actual pricing policies used for service depend largely on the nature of the service provided [Sel70]. Some possible strategies include:

1. Charges are based on some standard transaction. The nature of the transactions is fixed and the resource usage is predictable or negligible.
2. Charges are based on usage of resources whose cost and whose value to the user is known. The resource usage is variable and unpredictable. The resource usage is a major portion of the costs.
3. A flat rate is charged for access to the system. The resources available are relatively fixed, as in a dedicated single-language system, and the service does not depend on the number of users.

To help even out the load on the facilities, variation of the price of the services with time is frequently practiced. Thus, service during the day on normal workdays commands a higher price than night or weekend service.

The problem of accounting for usage of virtual resources is even more troublesome. A program in virtual storage is actually partly in real main storage and partly in real secondary storage. The users of the virtual storage system have no control over the amount of the real resources they are using or over the amount of overhead caused by paging their programs in and out. If users are to be charged for his usage of real resources, then frequent recording of usage and its attendant overhead are necessary. If users are to be charged for his usage of virtual resources, then they may be paying for resources that they are not actually using at all. No universal solution is possible. Each installation and its users have to evaluate the alternatives to arrive at some compromise between the accuracy of accounting for resource usage and the cost of doing the accounting.

The resources for which records may need to be kept are:

1. Main storage.
2. Central processor.
3. I/O devices and control units.
4. Channels.
5. Recording media, such as tape, disk, drum, or cards.
6. Software.

Typically, both time and quantity records would be significant data to establish resource usage. The nature of this information is such that it is best acquired and recorded by the operating system. Supplementary records on extra personnel services required for keypunching, debugging, and so forth, could be kept with the data, but would not likely be acquired by the operating system. Software resources may include proprietary programs and the operating system itself. The recognition that the operating system is a resource which benefits the user is helpful in making cost allocations [Sny69].

The data needed for system evaluation are likely to be more voluminous than those needed for some of the other purposes for keeping accounting records. Persons analyzing system performance are likely to be as interested in the reasons for resource usage as in actual usage figures. For this reason, they are likely to be interested in direct data on idle resources, which would normally only be obtained by inference. They are also likely to need data on specific equipment behavior, such as frequency of disk seeks. For system evaluation, the data must represent the entire state of the system at a particular time. The totality of usage determines overall system performance and the service provided to each user. The question of system performance evaluation is covered in Chapter 7.

As an illustration of the type of data recorded, the MTS system at the University of Michigan records information [Boe70] in two files. The first file is maintained for each valid user identification and contains current and maximum amounts of the following quantities:

1. Terminal time.
2. CPU time.
3. Actual storage integral.
4. File space in use.
5. File space integral.
6. Dollars spent.
7. Number of times signed on.
8. Number of batch runs.
9. Number of cards read.
10. Number of cards punched.
11. Number of lines printed.
12. Number of pages printed.

The second file contains an entry for each session the user has with the system and contains the above data for that session. The first file is used primarily to control access to the system and the second file is used primarily for billing and reporting to the user.

As an example of a more comprehensive data gathering system, the System Management Facilities (SMF) provided by IBM for System/360 and System/370 [IBM27] can be used to record data for accounting purposes as well as for system performance evaluations. It may be used with any version of the system. To facilitate use of the information collected, SMF provides six control program exits to allow processing of the data collected or to perform any other desired computations.

Four categories of records are kept and written by SMF to appropriate data sets. These records contain:

1. Information on the system and on the use of input/output devices.
2. Information describing the activity of data sets.
3. Information on the space available on direct-access volumes.
4. Information on how each job or job step used the system resources.

There are 63 types of records which fall in these four categories. Brief record descriptions are given in Table 3.8. Which records are written on the SMF data set may be determined at initial program loading (IPL) by specification of several parameters or by a default list established in SYS1.PARMLIB before the first IPL.

The six control program exits are provided to allow processing of SMF data during execution and to add additional records to the SMF data set if an installation so desires. These routines are called by the job scheduler and will add to the system overhead time each time they are used. The exit routines are:

1. Job Validation — called by job management before interpreting each JCL statement; allows user to cancel the job.
2. Job Initiation — called by initiator/terminator when a job on the input queue is selected for initiation; allows user to cancel the job.
3. Step Initiation — called by initiator/terminator just before job step is started but before allocation; allows user to cancel step or job.
4. SYSOUT Limit — called by I/O Supervisor when the number of logical records written exceeds the number specified by the user; allows user to cancel the job or continue processing with a new limit.
5. Termination — called by initiator/terminator at the end of every job and job step; allows user to cancel job and specify whether an SMF record is to be written.
6. Time Limit — called by timer interrupt handler whenever the job time limit, step time limit, or job-wait time limit is exceeded; allows user to decide whether to cancel or continue job.

Table 3.8. SMF Record Types for IBM System/370 [IBM27].

Record Name	Record Type	When Written	Contents
IPL	0	System Init. after IPL	Amount of main storage; SMF options
Dump Header	2	Begin DUMP SMF data to tape	Standard header
Dump Trailer	3	End DUMP SMF data to tape	Standard header
Step Termination	4	After job step termination	Time started and ended; CPU time; main storage used; device used
Job Termination	5	After job termination	Time started and ended; in reader input device type and class
Output Writer	6	End of SYSOUT processing	Writer activity information
Data Lost	7	When SMF data is available	Count of SMF records not written
I/O Configuration	8	System Init. after IPL	Device descriptions
VARY ONLINE	9	On operator command	Device added
Allocation Recovery	10	Allocation recovery	Device allocation
VARY OFFLINE	11	On operator command	Device removed
INPUT or RDBACK Data Set Activity	14	When data set is closed or processed by EOV	Data set information
OUTPUT, UPDAT INOUT, or OUTIN Data Set Activity	15	When data set is closed or processed by EOV	Data set information
Sort/Merge Statistics	16	During sorting	Parameters of the sort
Scratch Data Set Status	17	When data set is scratched	Data set name and volumes

Table 3.8. (Cont.)

Record Name	Record Type	When Written	Contents
Rename Data Set Status	18	When data set is renamed	Old and new data set names and volumes
Direct Access Volume	19	IPL, HALT EOD, SWITCH SMF, or when volume is demounted	Volume information on unallocated space and alternate tracks
Job Commencement	20	Job Init.	Misc. job and account data
ESV	21	When tape volume is demounted	Error statistics
Configuration	22	IPL or VARY of a CPU component	Command and system
SMF Status	23	At requested intervals	SMF data set description
JES3 Device Allocation	25	Allocation	Allocation's description
Job Purge	26	All output of a job complete	Job's description
Start TS	30	On START TS command	Time-sharing procedures information
TIOC	31	When terminal input/output controller is called	I/O Control Information
Driver	32	When driver init. is called	Time-sharing user information
TS-Step Termination	34	Step Termination by LOGOFF	Similar to type 4
Logoff	35	Job termination by LOGOFF	Similar to type 5
Dynamic DD	40	Deallocation	Dynamic allocation information
JES Start	43	JES startup	Procedure's description

Table 3.8. (Cont.)

Record Name	Record Type	When Written	Contents
JES Stop	45	JES cessation	Circumstances of stop
JES SIGNON	47	Connection	Connection's description
JES SIGNOFF	48	Disconnection	Disconnection's details
JES Integrity	49	Wrong password	Details of error
VTAM Tuning	50	At requested intervals	VTAM statistics
JES2 LOGON	52	LOGON to JES2	LOGON's description
JES2 LOGOFF	53	LOGOFF of JES2	LOGOFF's description
JES2 Integrity	54	Wrong password	Details of error
JES2 Network SIGNON	55	Connection	Connection's description
JES2 Network Integrity	56	Wrong password	Details of error
JES Net Output	57	Send output	Sending's description
JES2 Network SIGNOFF	58	Disconnection	Disconnection's details
VSAM Volume Record	60	Volume update	Update's description
VSAM Catalog Update	61	Catalog update	Update's description
VSAM OPEN	62	VSAM OPEN	OPEN's description
VSAM Definition	63	VSAM data set definition	Definition's description
VSAM Status	64	VSAM EOV	Status of data set
VSAM Catalog Delete	65	Catalog delete	Deletion's description
VSAM Catalog Alter	66	Catalog alter	Alteration's description
VSAM Catalog Entry Delete	67	Entry delete	Deletion's description

Table 3.8. (Cont.)

Record Name	Record Type	When Written	Contents
VSAM Catalog Entry Rename	68	Entry rename	Renaming's description
VSAM Space Operation	69	Space operation	Operation's description
CPU Activity	70	At requested intervals	Wait time and status
Paging Activity	71	At requested intervals	Paging statistics
Workload Activity	72	At requested intervals	Statistics on RMF performance groups
Channel Activity	73	On request	Channel statistics
Device Activity	74	On request	Device statistics
Page/Swap DS Activity	75	At requested intervals	Paging data set statistics
Trace Activity	76	At requested intervals	Tracing statistics
Enqueue Activity	77	At requested intervals	Resource contention statistics
Monitored Activity	79	At requested intervals	As for 71–77, as monitored
RACF Processing	80	Access request	Request's description and processing
RACF Initialization	81	Start RACF	Startup's description
Security (Cryptography)	82	Operation	Operation's description
System Status	90	IPL and SET	Command's description

The actions indicated above are accomplished by setting the return code. The routines may contain coding to do other computation as desired. The SMF also writes job step and job time messages in the system message data set for each job. The user referred to in the exit routine descriptions is typically the installation management rather than the individual programmer.

3.7 ACCESS CONTROL

Users of operating systems may wish to control who has access to their data. They may wish to allow some people to read their data, but not to modify them, and others to do either. The system must provide the needed function and some measure of assurance that the function is effectively performed. The assurance is called system integrity and is discussed in Section 4.5. The present discussion is restricted to the function of access control itself.

Access control is typically discussed in terms of files of data, but protection of files would be of little use were the data from the files not also protected in main storage. Programs are themselves data and subject to the same type of protection. Supervisory services, such as the updating of a file directory, must also be protected. Finally, access to physical resources, such as space on secondary storage media, must be controlled for effective accounting and to prevent users from monopolizing resources to the extent that they prevent others from getting what they need to get their work done.

Approaches to Access Control

There are two fundamental approaches [Kur82b] to access control. One can focus on the resources themselves and permit access only to individuals who have demonstrated in some way that they are authorized to effect the type of access they request. Alternatively, one can focus on individuals and, once they have established their identities in the course of a series of interactions with the system, grant or deny their requests for access in accordance with information the system has about what accesses are authorized. The latter approach is far superior, for reasons given below, but our discussion begins with the former and older approach.

In the simplest form of resource-oriented access control, each distinct privilege is associated with a protecting mechanism, typically a password. Anyone who can supply the password to the system is granted the associated privilege, for example, reading the payroll file. Each user must remember one password for each authorized privilege, each user must supply one password for each privilege requested during a series of interactions with the system, and each password is known, shared, by each user who has the associated privilege.

It is possible to enhance the resource-oriented approach by letting resources be aggregated, grouped, so that fewer passwords are needed, but this does not mitigate the approach's fundamental disadvantages.

In an individual-oriented approach, users, when they initiate a series of interactions with the system, do something that establishes their identities. The task may be the provision of a password or a physical object, such as a magnetically inscribed plastic card, or it may be an act that permits some sort of physical analysis, say fingerprint reading or signature analysis. These alternatives to passwords apply also to the resource-oriented approach, but are too clumsy or time-consuming to be of practical value in that case. Once the user's identity is established to the system's, (the installation's management's) satisfaction, the user need no longer be concerned about access control. The system appears to "know" what the user may do, and, indeed, it does.

The individual-oriented approach has a number of advantages:

1. Users need perform but one security-related activity, verification of their identities, for each series of interactions with the system, not one per needed resource. Users unduly burdened by security-related demands may become antagonists of the system, and enemies of the enterprise.
2. When authority must be withdrawn from one of a number of users, it is not necessary to inform all of the other users of a new password, an exposure-prone activity at best, as well as a burdensome one.
3. Because no secret information is shared, if an unauthorized individual is found to have learned a password, the person whose secret became known can be positively identified and held accountable.
4. Each individual need remember only one password.

Either approach described above may underlie any of a number of policies for control of access. While policies are established by management, operating systems must supply the structures that permit the implementation of those policies, so it is appropriate to discuss them here [Fer81].

A policy may be based on a notion of the (hierarchical) level of sensitivity of a resource. Perhaps the best-known categories used for such a level-based policy are Top Secret, Secret, Confidential, and Unclassified. People may be permitted to read data whose classification is equal to or less than their own (security clearance). Users may be permitted to modify data whose classification is less than or equal to or lower than their own but, because uncontrolled, *de facto*, downgrading of information's classification must be prevented, no lower than that of the most sensitive data read during the current process. The last-described restriction is called the Star Property because of its statement in a footnote designated by an asterisk, a star, in a widely used report.

Resources may be categorized nonhierarchically either in addition to or instead of hierarchically. Categories might be Weapons, Deployment, Military Intelligence Nuclear Research, Electronic Battlefield, Communications, and the like. A single item of data might be in more than one category if, for example, it concerns the deployment of a weapon. Then a user might need access to data in both categories to gain access to the item. More simply, resources may be grouped because they all relate to one project or one department rather than to one category of object.

Policies may group individuals as well as resources. All bank tellers or all system operators may share a set of access rights by virtue of their membership in that group.

Supplementing or replacing any or all of the schemes described above may be what is called discretionary, because it depends on individuals discretion rather than on established criteria, access control, also referred to as need-to-know. In such a scheme, an authorized individual grants a specific privilege to a specific user.

An operating system must facilitate implementation, use, and, importantly, administration of whatever access control policies management may wish to employ.

Implementation of Access Control

The control of access to sensitive resources involves function invoked each time a user requests access and, if individual-oriented access control is employed, function invoked when permission to access a resource is granted or revoked.

Access can most easily be controlled if an operating system contains a single program that implements all the needed functions and that program is invoked each time a request for access to a sensitive resource is made. Also, the mediation of every request is most easily ensured if a single program effects every access to resources of each defined type. For example, all data in files might be accessed only via a file management system, all directories of files through a directory manager, etc. Each resource manager might invoke a single access control program, like the Resource Access Control Facility (RACF) [IBM34] of IBM's MVS, for example, to process each request. The request is either granted or denied as indicated by the access control program.

The emphasis in the preceding paragraph on single programs has several motivations. First, if only one program manages each type of resource, one need only consider, modify, or verify one program to be assured that every access to the resource protected is processed properly, that is, that protection is effectively provided. Second, if only one program effects access control, one need only provide access control function in that program, not redundantly in many different programs. That produces a saving in development resources as well as improved reliability, because only one set of functions must be debugged and maintained.

In the case of individual-oriented access control, the access control program must do more than merely accept an identifier for a resource and request an associated indicator of authorization, such as a password, from the user. The program now needs to ascertain the identities of both resource and user and to determine whether access of the requested type, for example, read or modify, is authorized. To do this, it must consult data provided by authorized administrators of the system. The needed information is a function, type of access permitted, of two variables, resource name and user name. Think of a two-dimensional array, each column, say, representing a resource and each row representing a user. One should expect that most values in the array would indicate that no access is permitted. The array is therefore called a sparse matrix, one with few nonzero entries. Such a matrix can be stored efficiently only if zeroes need not be represented explicitly. One therefore chooses to store only the rows and their nonzero entries or the columns and their nonzero entries. If the users are associated with their authorities, the scheme is said to be ticket-based or capability-based, each authority being a ticket or capability. If the capability is supported by special function of the underlying computer system, one has a capability-based system, an appealing concept treated in more detail in Section 4.1 below. If resources are associated with their authorized accessors, the scheme is resource-based. In either case, a resource may represent a set of many user-perceived resources and a user may represent a set of grouped users. Identifying a user as a member of a specific group or a resource as a member of a specific set becomes a separate function of the access control program.

Efficiency can be gained by using algorithms that obviate searches of an array. For example, users may be permitted any sort of access to all resources whose names begin with their identifiers. Names of departments or projects could be used just as well.

When systems are interconnected, complications arise. Interesting questions, not pursued here, include:

1. Can a system be the accessor, in the eyes of the system in which a resource is stored?
2. Can a user's identity be securely transmitted from one system to another?
3. Should authorization data be stored in the system with the data, the user' system, or a central system?
4. What protocols are needed to protect the integrity of authorization data and resources transmitted among systems?

Auditing Access

It is not enough to provide efficient, effective, and easy-to-use facilities that can be used to control access to resources. Auditors must be able to learn what is happening in the system and to assure themselves that activities are controlled [And81] and consistent with management's directives. It is therefore necessary to provide for the logging of all access control activity and for the processing of logs to make their contents usefully available to auditors [Kur80].

It must be possible to obtain selective logging, say of all denied requests for access or all requests for access to the most sensitive files. The log should contain the names of accessors and resources and also the time and type of access, the program used, the port through which the user entered the system, and whatever other data an auditor might request.

More data must be collected because they might be useful than an auditor would routinely want to see each day. It must be possible for auditors to select from all collected data only those items they wish printed for scrutiny. Random selection might be employed for sampling of otherwise unexceptional data on the chance that some irregularity will be uncovered by unanticipated means. The chance of discovery by such unpredictable surveillance may be enough to discourage wrongdoing. Selection might rely on frequency or hour of access or entry through a little-used port such as a terminal at a remote location. Those who make logging and data-reducing functions available cannot safely rule out any algorithm for selection of data.

Related Function

Access control is but one function that contributes to the security provided by an operating system. Related topics discussed below are system integrity, resistance to tampering with or circumvention of access control function; cryptography, hiding of the meaning of data when physical access cannot be prevented; and techniques of identification, how the identity of a user can be determined with an acceptable degree of cost in terms of development, storage, and elapsed time and certainty in terms of false rejections and false acceptances.

PROBLEMS

1. Combine the two IBM System/370 object modules given below into a loaded program with an initial address of 1000 (all numerical values are given in hexadecimal). Report the resulting storage contents and the addresses assigned to all external symbols in the two modules. Each relocated item is four bytes long.

Module 1	ESD	Symbol	Type	Address
		A	SD	0
		B	LD	8
		X	ER	—
		Y	ER	—
	TXT	Address = 0		Length = 10

00 00 00 04 00 00 00 00 00 00 00 00 00 00 00 00

RLD	Symbol	Sign	Address
	A	+	0
	A	−	4
	X	+	4
	X	+	8
	X	−	C
	Y	+	C

Module 2

ESD	Symbol	Type	Address
	X	SD	0
	Y	LD	4
	A	ER	−
	B	ER	−

TXT   Address = 0   Length = 10

00 00 00 00 00 00 00 00 00 00 00 00 00 00 00 00

RLD	Symbol	Sign	Address
	X	+	C
	A	+	0
	A	−	8
	A	−	C
	B	+	4
	B	+	8
	B	+	C

2. Use the same two object modules from the previous problem to produce a relocatable object module. The output module should contain all necessary external symbols and relocation information. Can the output be simpler if it is never necessary to recover the two control sections A and X separately again?

3. Assemble the following program (without using a computer) and give the contents of the ESD, TXT, and RLD records. Include the RLD only where necessary to make the whole module relocatable as a unit.

```
PGM          CSECT
             EXTRN             MORE
             ENTRY             HERE
             USING             PGM,15
             L                 12,ADATA
             BC                15,0(14)
ADATA        DC                A(DATA)
AADATA       DC                A(ADATA)
DATA         DC                A(DATA-PGM)
```

HERE	DC	A(MORE-PGM)
	DS	4F
VQ	DC	V(Q)
	DC	A(MORE-DATA)
	DC	A(HERE)
	END	PGM

ESD	Symbol	Type	Address

TXT	Address =		Length =

RLD	Symbol	Sign	Address

4. The following hardware features in an IBM System/360 computer permit the operating system to provide services to the users of the system. Describe the services provided by the system when each hardware feature is present and describe the difficulty in providing operating system services if the feature were absent.
   a. Channels.
   b. I/O interrupts.
   c. Storage protection.
   d. Supervisor state.
   e. External interrupt.
   f. SVC interrupt.

5. Discuss the means by which program relocation is implemented in an IBM System/360 computer. Discuss which portions of relocation are handled by hardware and which by software. Identify which parts of relocation are handled at assembly time, program loading time, and execution time. Develop a system by which programs in this computer could be dynamically relocated after they had begun to execute.

6. Prepare a loading program by going through the steps outlined below and reporting on each step. In addition to the obvious results, also indicate any considerations that led you to make any choices you made for optional parts of the problem.
   a. Obtain the format of the file produced by one or more of the language processors for your computer. This file will consist of program code plus additional data on external symbols used in the program, on program segmentation, and on the location of any relocatable code.
   b. Prepare a flow chart for converting the file produced by the language processor into an executable program loaded in main storage. A two-pass arrangement is natural for this routine. Pass 1 serves to decide where segments are placed in storage, and pass 2 does any relocation necessary. Branching to the entry point of the loaded

program will cause it to be executed. Assume that all the necessary input to your program is in one file and that no libraries need to be searched.

c. Prepare some programs to be processed by a language processor to produce the files necessary to test the loading routine. These programs should be written to cause execution of all the branches of the loading program, including those which detect and react to erroneous input data.

d. Select a language in which to write your loading program. For the purposes of this problem, the efficiency of the loading program is not as important as its logical arrangement. Note, however, that some high-level languages may be very clumsy for doing this type of programming because of their limited facilities for manipulation of arbitrary binary data.

e. Implement and test the loading program as outlined above.

7. Modify the loading program of the previous problem so that it acts as a linker rather than a loader, that is, so that the result is still a relocatable program and is written out as a file rather than being executed immediately. What changes are necessary in the flow chart? What additional decisions need to be made about the results produced by the linker? What advantages are there to using a linker compared to a loader?

8. Make up some matrices showing authorized access and show how these would be represented by lists and by tickets. Discuss the relative merits of each approach using your matrices to illustrate your points.

4
Job and Task Management

4.1 GENERAL

This chapter deals with the principles of job and task management, which are two of the three functions of the operating system management component. The third, data management, is the subject of the next chapter. In this section of the chapter, the first two functions are considered in a discussion of the various activities of each.

In the section on addressed storage, the various principles of storage management are examined. A separate section on virtual storage management principles follows. The fourth section is about data storage principles and the last two sections are discussions of processes, or tasks, and job scheduling. The resources under discussion in this context are quantitative rather than named. The reader may wish to review the distinction, made in Section 2.1 above. Named resources are discussed in the next chapter.

Before investigating the job and task management functions, let us review the definitions of job and task. A job is the smallest unit of work that can be presented to the computing system by a user. It cannot enter the system until it is defined, either through the medium of the operating system control language (OSCL) or else directly by the operator through console communication. The GECOS system uses former means, while IBM DOS can either accept OSCL from the card reader or be provided the information by the operator.

In either case, we can break a job down into subdivisions called steps. A job may consist of a number of steps or it may consist of one step. As an example we can have a job consisting of a compile step, a load step, and a go step (execution). A single unit of work, the job, is thus reduced into three subunits — the steps. One reason for this division into steps is to allow for the variations in real storage requirements between the parts of the job; a compilation might well require more main storage than the loading or execution of the resultant program. With a step scheme a job can release some of its main storage after the compile phase of the job is completed.

Another use of the job/step scheme is to facilitate conditional program execution; if the compile step has several errors due to coding mistakes, then the programmer will not want the program to be executed. Condition checks can be used on the load and go steps for the successful completion of the compile step. If compilation is erroneous, the system can abort the job. The operating system programmer should in any event provide for conditional program execution, and the job/step scheme is an excellent way to satisfy this requirement.

The task, on the other hand, is not user-submitted. The task is created by the operating system in response to OSCL; the OSCL tells the operating system that a program will need certain system resources when it begins execution. The definition of a task is: the smallest unit of work that can contend for system resources. Once a program specified in an OSCL job step is loaded and begins execution, it is a task. Multitasking is the situation encountered when a given executing program causes a subtask of itself to be created. With these definitions we can begin discussing job and task management.

Job Management

Job management can be viewed as the arranging of the computer environment prior to program execution. After the system schedules the job and its turn for execution arrives, the appropriate amount of storage is reserved for the job, which has requested a certain amount of storage either through OSCL or by operating system default values. Any I/O device or file allocations are also done by the job management function. Accounting information is gathered for later use by either system or user accounting routines. Keeping this list of job management activities in mind, let us examine each of them, with the exception of job scheduling, which is discussed in another section of the chapter.

Communications with the system occur through the medium of OSCL. There are three main kinds of statements: the job statement, the execute or step statement, and a device or file allocation request statement. The operating system normally requires each of them when a job is presented to the system (unless the job does no I/O, in which case no device allocation statement may be necessary for execution). These OSCL statements are normally examined by an interpreter routine, which checks for any errors in syntax. The job is terminated before execution if an error is serious enough to be potentially confusing to the system.

The job statement defines the job to the system; such requests as priority, main storage, CPU time, and output routing requests may be present on the job statement, as well as user accounting information.

The execute statement tells the operating system which program to bring in from the program library file for execution; it may also have parameters (requests) similar to those in the job statement, as well as information usable by the program at execution time.

The device allocation request statement will contain such requests as the file name, the device type (optionally, the specific device address), the file status (for example, new or old), the direct-access space requirement if applicable, and the volume identifier, specifying the disk pack or tape reel which is required.

The operator can communicate with the system through the control console and make requests for many of these same resources. Request options are not as varied or as powerful as those of OSCL, but are useful in many situations.

The operating system designer must be extremely careful in the resource allocation area because of the strong possibility of deadlock; file allocation in particular is a danger area [Bjo72]. See above.

I/O resource allocation in job management occurs on three levels. The device level is the level at which an entire device is allocated to a program, whether on an exclusive basis or on a shared basis (with other users in the system). At this level, a program can be awarded control over an I/O device for the entire duration of the program, while others might be forced to wait for the device until the first program is through with it.

The second level of allocation is the file level. This can be an existing file or the space required for a new file and its subsequent formation. These first two levels are very prevalent among modern operating systems, while the third level, the subfile level, is now in use on IBM's virtual systems. In this level, the system maintains a large space for all system users, who in turn are allocated space within this space as necessary. This prevents much of the direct-access space fragmentation prevalent when individual user files are used. See Figure 4.1.

The OSCL and operator job initialization commands, when a job is submitted through console commands, are taken into the system by a reader module. This module is either in an operating system program library and brought into the system and executed as needed, or else is resident in main storage.

In either event, the reader module is charged with the responsibility of (1) handling the channel programming necessary to exercise the system input reader, and (2) interpreting the OSCL that is read and rejecting OSCL with improper syntax or inconsistent specifications; in the case of systems with spooling, the OSCL is (3) passed to the input job queue on a direct-access device. Once the OSCL is on the spool file, the scheduler takes it over, which may be in actual card image format or may be in the form of various tables containing the appropriate data which have been gleaned from the OSCL.

In the case of remote job entry (RJE), the first responsibility changes from I/O programming for the input reader to I/O programming for a remote terminal, which can range from a CPU to a printer/keyboard device. The basic difference between RJE and normal reader operation is that one is local and the other is remote. Functionally they are the same; the operating system considers the RJE terminal to be an input reader that happens to be talking across a telephone line.

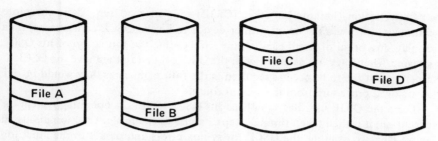

A. Traditional file placement on direct-access devices. Four files on up to four devices, each requiring individual system resources when it is accessed.

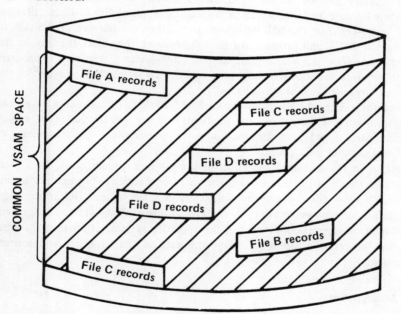

B. Enlarged view of single, direct-access device, showing IBM VSAM scheme. The common VSAM data space contains records from the equivalents of the four files in A above. The common data location allows sharing of system resources during concurrent file accesses.

Figure 4.1. VSAM Structure.

Conversational remote job entry (CRJE) adds another step. Users at remote terminals can use a keyboard/printer device to key in OSCL card images, then display any or all of them back at any time during the formation of his OSCL stream. When they are satisfied with the OSCL, they can then save the OSCL as a permanent file to be used as required in the future, much as they would invoke a cataloged procedure from the system console.

Once the CRJE user has submitted his OSCL file to the operating system for execution, it is then taken through steps 2 and 3 of the reader function discussed above (that is, examine the OSCL for syntax errors and pass it to the input job queue).

A cataloged procedure contains OSCL statements which have been stored in a system library created for this purpose. The system programmer stores the procedure because it is a job which has widespread applicability in the installation. If this job's OSCL is available to system users, they are relieved of the task of creating the OSCL and program for the job. Instead, they can either invoke the procedure itself, which will contain all necessary device allocation and program execution cards for the particular job, or in many cases they can invoke the procedure from the operator's console.

Once the procedure has been invoked and the OSCL statements have been brought into the system from the procedure library, the reader module then exercises parts 2 and 3 of its function — the syntax check and the passing of OSCL to the input job queue.

Finally, in the accounting portion of the job management area, the system collects user accounting information such as user identification, execution time involved, elapsed time, paging information if applicable, and I/O device usage information, and passes the data to the accounting routines in the management component or support component of the operating system. It provides information that makes it possible to charge the user on the basis of the resources consumed.

Task Management

The task management function of the operating system is charged with the dynamic allocation of the system resources used by an executing program, whether user or system routines. Task management must handle the initialization of programs; recovery management in the case of errors; resource management, including queues; dynamic storage; the system timer and clock; and task dispatching.

The first part of task management that a program sees as it enters the system is the task initiation process. In order for a program to be executed it must be initiated. Initiation is the means by which a program in a program library is loaded into main storage, the binding process is completed, the appropriate control blocks and register storage areas are formed, the appropriate resources are allocated, and the program can then begin execution as a task. In a multiprogramming operating system, the program begins execution after it is initially dispatched.

During initialization the program requires certain resources from the system, the most important of which is main storage. The operating system must get most information about program execution requirements from the OSCL, whether explicitly or by default in the absence of specific parameters. For example, a set of OSCL statements for a job could request 150K bytes of storage on the job or execution statement for a given program, or the operating system could have had a default value of 150K bytes specified as a default value at system generation (Sysgen) time by the system programmer in the installation. (Sysgen is the process by which the system programmer specifies the eventual characteristics for his installation's operating system-to-be.)

In addition to an initial main storage allocation, some operating systems allow users to request and be dynamically allocated additional main storage for their programs as required. IBM OS and VS as well as HIS GECOS allow this additional allocation, while CDC SCOPE 3 does not.

Another resource which a program may require is the system timer. This can be used by programs for such things as program execution time limiting, or starting some new process either after a specified interval or at a specific time (deadline scheduling), for example, in the UNIVAC 1108 EXEC-8 operating system.

Finally the program, now a task, needs one additional resource in order to be initiated: the CPU itself. This is discussed below; the first time a task gets control is really a special case of the more general function of task dispatching.

Resource management is the part of task management which controls the dynamic resources in the system. The needs of the individual programs executing in a multiprogramming environment, which is where resource management becomes important, must be balanced against the needs of the total system and its throughput for the active set of batch programs flowing through the system in a given time increment; if the system is a time-sharing system, the same trade-off must be considered by the system programmer, but instead of throughput the response time for the terminal users might be the prime consideration.

The operating system must be designed so that the entire computing system will be utilized as much as possible while still providing reasonable performance to the individual users, whether batch or interactive or both. There is a compelling economic reason for this requirement: as technology progresses and hardware becomes less expensive (per throughput/hour) the cost of the hardware assumes a proportionately smaller share of the data processing budget.

Conversely, the cost of programming is a greater portion of the data-processing budget, so that the productivity of the programmer becomes ever more important.

The more efficient the system, the greater the productivity of the programming staff. In the past, it was often the case that added function was as important as efficiency in operating system design; the trend is now toward greater utilization of the hardware, as exemplified by the popularity of virtual storage systems, which are increasing productivity [Parm72].

One of the prime vehicles used in resource management is the queue. The queue can be implemented with many different algorithms, such as FIFO (first-in-first-out); LIFO (last-in-first-out); push-down stack, in which the most recent requestor will get first chance at the resource (this queue is used by the CDC SCOPE 3 dispatcher); or prioritized, in which the request from the highest-priority task will obtain the subject resource, commonly used in task dispatching.

Each segment is placed in the queue by means of the creation of a cell within the operating system consisting of at least an address where the resource is to be delivered, and another address pointing to the next requestor in the queue. As a request is satisfied, the queue cell associated with that request is erased after the cell pointed to by it is moved to the top of the list.

Dynamic storage, the system timer, the overlay supervisor, and the task dispatcher, which allocates the CPU resource itself, are all examples of queue-driven resources, and are all managed using one of the various algorithms mentioned above. See Figure 4.2.

The dispatcher is worthy of special note, since it is so central to the operation of the system. There are various kinds of dispatchers using various queue management techniques. The first kind is found in serial tasking systems such as IBM OS/PCP and the SEL 810 operating system; in this kind of operating system there is no dispatching queue — execution of jobs is done one at a time and when a program starts it automatically gains control of the CPU by virtue of starting and keeps it until execution is complete. The only queuing that is done is manipulation of the job stream prior to entry of the job into the system. This can be done by the operator.

In multiprogramming systems, there is a rich variety of dispatching schemes. The simplest is a linear dispatcher of the static type, which automatically assigns dispatching priorities to executing tasks based on the partition of main storage they happen to get loaded into; partition 1 might have the highest priority, partition n the lowest. IBM MFT and HIS Mod 4 operating systems use this principle. One shortcoming is that a high-priority partition might have a long-running program executing in it, so that an emergency job could not get the highest priority until that job is completed.

A slightly more flexible scheme is called a variable dispatcher, another type of linear system, in which the OSCL user or operator can affect the priority of the job somewhat because there are fixed partitions on which to base a static priority scheme. Instead, a job statement can contain a priority parameter which the system can use to raise or lower the use priority as required (examples are IBM OS/MVT and CDC MASTER).

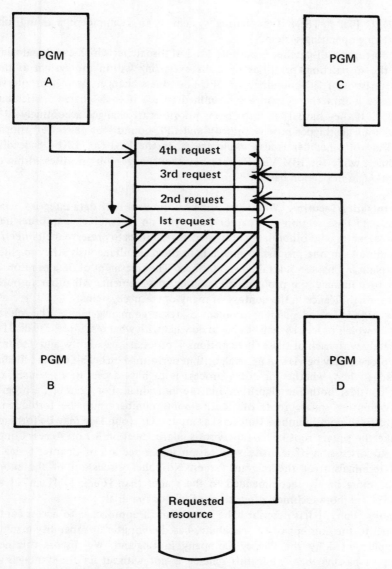

Figure 4.2. FIFO (First-In-First-Out) Resource Queue. The first request receives the desired resource when it becomes available. Any remaining requests move to the front of the queue.

Yet a third linear dispatcher is the round-robin or time-slicing dispatcher. The programs receive control of the CPU on a regular basis for a system-generated time interval, after which the next program gets control, and so on until all users have had a turn, at which time control is passed to the start of the list again.

The DEC PDP-8 TSS-8 time-sharing system is an example of a round-robin dispatching operating system.

The heuristic dispatcher is another kind of dispatcher which can dynamically alter the dispatching priorities of tasks executing within the system as their characteristics of I/O-boundness or CPU-boundness change. At regular intervals the tasks within the system are examined to see if their characteristics have changed. If they have, their dispatching priorities are changed accordingly: I/O-bound jobs get higher relative priority and CPU-bound jobs get lower priority. This kind of scheduler is also implemented in the UNIVAC EXEC-8 deadline scheduler, while the IBM VS2 Release 1 system changes job priorities within the system on an inspection basis.

Data Integrity/Security. While our principal discussion of data integrity occurs in the data base section of Chapter 5, a word on the subject is in order here. Records, tables, and other data are treated as resources to preserve their *integrity*. Were more than one process to manipulate them simultaneously, they might, as we explain in Chapter 5, attain invalid values. The treatment of data as resources tends to dominate the problem of resource management. All other resources pale to insignificance in the context of many operating systems.

Security is an independent problem of resource management. The relevant issue is: which processes shall be able to do what with what resources. We deal first separately with each of these three notions — processes, capability, and resources.

A process may be viewed as an algorithm performed on behalf of an individual. To judge, then, whether or not a process is to have access to a resource, one must consider both the algorithm and the individual. For example, a program for computing square roots of floating-point numbers may be forbidden to receive fixed-point numbers (integers) as inputs. Or, John Doe may be forbidden to take the square root of his supervisor's salary. Section 3.7 on Access Control and our discussion of identity verification in the section of Chapter 5 dealing with terminals treat the relevant issues. No fuller discussion of the subject can be more highly recommended to the reader than [Fer81]. [Lam71] and [Gra68] are more technical discussions of related material.

Fabry [Fab73] has described the succession of approaches to access control that led to the concept of the capability-based computer or capability machine, as implemented by the Plessey Company in England. We discuss this next, noting in passing that, while this scheme is not without its disadvantages and other schemes are more prevalent in the literature as well as in actual computers, capability machines seem to be such natural evolutionary successors to, say, the Rice computer [Ili62] and machines of Burroughs, GE/HIS, and IBM, that we treat the others as variations thereof. Our entire discussion of capability machines is based on [Fab73].

A *capability* is something like an address constant, but is used as the sole means of addressing a resource. Access to the resource can therefore be restricted to those who have the matching capability. Here again, a resource is not merely data, but may also be any other sort of addressed object defined by the system. A capability can be formed by the system only when an object is created or when an existing capability is copied. Only the system can ever create a capability. Capabilities are separated from other data either by being tagged, that is, uniquely identified as such wherever they appear, or by being permitted to reside only in places reserved for only that purpose.

With a capability machine, only the creator of an object and those to whom he gives a copy of the associated capability can ever access the object. The problems of identity and subversive programs do not vanish in such a machine, but [Lam71] and [Fab73] are among the works which can give the student an idea of the problems that do. In particular, lists of individuals and what they are authorized to do or lists of objects and the individuals authorized to perform given functions on them do not have to be maintained. Also, one need not worry about the idle formation of addresses in either main or virtual storage, as this is impossible. (We see below that segmentation shares this advantage.) On the other hand, how one withdraws authorization in a capability machine is unclear, since capabilities are easily copied and stashed, and much needless overhead is obviously entailed when security is not a concern.

Disadvantages notwithstanding, capabilities offer advantages in terms of reliability and security, topics of rapidly increasing concern. The first commercially prominent capability-based machine is IBM's System/38 [IBM38]. Conventional virtual storage systems represent a step backward from capability machines. Such systems offer the security of closed address spaces, as discussed in Section 4.2, but addressing must involve (page and/or segment) tables unique to particular process. Shared objects must be separately addressable in the space of each sharer.

Where capabilities are not used for the protection of files, a separate mechanism must be employed, as described in Section 3.7. It is also necessary to ensure that the protection provided cannot be subverted or circumvented. The extent to which a system does this is called its (system) integrity [McP74]. This entails the protection of data on secondary storage, the protection of the process that mediates access and its code and data, and the protection of accessed data in primary storage. All of these require, in turn, the protection of the system against unauthorized modification. The following sections on storage management lay the groundwork for the subsequent discussion of system integrity.

The remaining part of task management, error recovery, is discussed above, in Chapter 3. Thus, we move on to the next topic, addressed storage.

4.2 MANAGEMENT OF ADDRESSED STORAGE (REAL)

Addressed storage is the main and virtual storage of an operating system. It is distinguished from named storage in that the latter (persistent files) exists between instances of use of the system. For this reason, they must be identified by the individuals using the system and are therefore given names, symbolic identifiers meaningful to and expressible by people. Once the person is no longer involved in the progress of work, the system has no need of names as such. Numeric identifiers, addresses, carry less redundancy and are therefore more efficient from the system's point of view. In studying addressed storage, then, we are looking at the data as they are seen by processes. Named storage contains data which may at any point in time be of no interest to any defined process.

In managing addressed data, we are interested in making the most efficient use of the relevant resources, where efficiency is measured in terms of throughput or response time, the amount of meaningful, defined work accomplished by the system within some interval of time. This goal applies to all the discussions of this chapter and should be borne in mind throughout, even if it is not restated as often as it might be.

In pursuing this goal, the system takes as subgoals the utilization of the individual resources which contribute to the realization of addressed storage. At a minimum, these are main storage and the processing and storage space consumed by the execution of the processes which effect the management of addressed storage. In a virtual storage system, a paging device and the channel and control unit which connect it to the rest of the system are also involved, as well as additional storage devices, disks, and their connective equipment.

Another subgoal might be utilization of the central processor(s). The larger the number of processes resident in main storage, the larger the number of processes actively contending for the central processor(s), and, consequently, the greater the probability that there will always be at least one process ready to use each central processor at all times that is, that no processor is ever idle. This perfection is, in practice, rarely obtained.

Maximizing the number of processes concurrently served helps in the realization of another goal as important in most systems as throughput: concurrently serving with acceptable response time a maximal number of interactive users of the system. An *interactive user* is an individual who uses the system by conducting a dialog with it. Such a user typically sits at a terminal and communicates via a command language. More is said of interactive use in Chapters 2, 5, and 6. _Response time_ is the amount of time that elapses between the entry of a full command by an interactive user and the completion of the system's response thereto.

The problems of managing addressed storage vary greatly from system to system. Basically, where hardware mechanisms for relocation of addresses do not alleviate the problem, fragmentation is a prime concern. If quantities of storage of randomly varying amounts were to be acquired and released by processes at randomly varying points in time, a map of storage might soon resemble a Swiss cheese, available storage being the holes. This is inefficient utilization of storage. The notions of page, segment, partition, and region, all discussed below, are used to prevent or contain fragmentation.

Security, discussed in the preceding section, is another concern of addressed storage management. The clearing of released storage is one mechanism directed at this problem. Protection of storage by fetch and store keys is another, and segmentation of storage into separate address spaces still another, both hardware-assisted.

In managing addressed storage, there are several aspects of the task we must consider. We must concern ourselves with what the system places in main storage and what it excludes from main storage. We can never ignore the effects of particular hardware design, especially mechanisms for address relocation, on what we do. We must also consider the magnitude and the topological and performance attributes of the media with which we are working.

The constraint of limited main storage is a real one. Development programmers must spend much time and energy considering how much of the operating system they can include in the resident nucleus and how much they must call as needed from a program library on a secondary storage device. The trade-off is as follows: "How much is the proposed function worth if it will be resident? Is the increased performance to be gained by leaving the function resident worth the increased main storage overhead?" Naturally, the storage constraint is a difficult programming problem, which may explain the popularity of virtual storage systems.

In the pages that follow, we look at ways of preventing fragmentation that apply to systems without virtual storage. We next (Section 4.3) look at techniques of address relocation and some implementations of virtual storage. Then we focus on strategies associated with the implementation of virtual storage and conclude with a discussion of shared storage.

Storage Utilization

We discuss here three strategies applicable to systems without virtual storage. The first kind of storage utilization strategy involves having the entire storage area of the computer available to a single user program. The other two strategies are used in multiprogramming operating systems. The operating systems take up some of the main storage in the computing system for themselves. The remainder of the main storage can be allocated to user programs in one of two ways, either with partitions of fixed sizes or with regions of variable size. The fixed partition strategy simply utilizes the fact that a given operating system nucleus will take up a relatively small portion of the total main storage in the system.

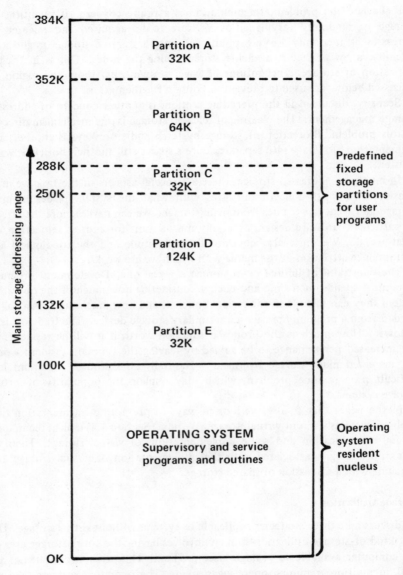

Figure 4.3. Fixed Partition Main Storage Structure.

The remainder of the main storage is divided into finite fixed areas of main storage for multiple user programs. The fixed partition concept is a very workable concept, but it tends to waste main storage; a program that requires about 30,000 (30K) bytes may be loaded into a partition of some 96K bytes. Once a

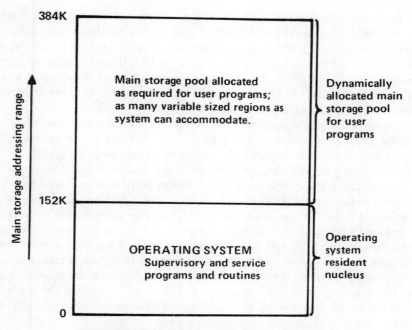

Figure 4.4. Variable Region Main Storage Structure.

program is in a partition, the remainder of the storage not used by the program within that partition is unused until a program that is large enough to use all the main storage in that partition is brought in. This is called intra-partition fragmentation.

The fixed partition method of allocating main storage is an uncomplicated storage management scheme. The variable region method allows a user program to acquire dynamically as much of the main storage remaining outside of the operating system nucleus as it needs. This can be done either automatically or through the use of job control statements. With the variable region concept, intra-partition fragmentation tends to be reduced when programmers request only as much of the main storage as they need, and no more. After a request for 30K bytes is read into the computer, a region of 30K bytes is allocated to that program instead of 96K bytes. The program is loaded into that 30K-byte region and begins execution. The remaining 66K-byte storage area is available for another pro' am's use, whereas in a fixed partition storage management scheme, 96K - 32K = 66K might be wasted. On the other hand, the disadvantage of a variable region type of storage management is that it is much more complex and requires more of the central processor's time and of main storage space to do the dynamic allocation of main storage for the various programs as they enter and leave the system.

Fragmentation remains a problem in the variable region method. If a region of 20K bytes is released by a terminating program and that region is bounded by regions occupied by long-running programs which are not subject to compaction (see below), the freed region remains unused until a sufficiently small program is available to occupy that space. Fragmentation of this sort is typical of a class of problems discussed in Margolin [Mar71] and elsewhere. They are susceptible to convincing mathematical analysis.

The variable region concept seems to work better in a larger computer because it usually has considerably more storage capacity and can absorb the increased main storage overhead required by a variable region operating system. As an example, IBM's OS/MVT system typically might require 150K for the operating system's exclusive use, whereas OS/MFT system might require only 70K or 80K of main storage for the exclusive use of the operating system, albeit only some fraction of this difference is accounted for by storage management routines. In a small machine of 256K total main storage, the 150K system requires too much main storage overhead to be meaningfully considered for use. It reduces the available main storage to a point where the dynamic allocation of main storage is not feasible, because there is not enough storage remaining outside of the operating system to be used efficiently. We find in practice that the larger the main storage on a computing system, the more benefits are realized through the use of a variable region type of operating system.

Relocatability

Both of these types of systems, the fixed partition and the variable region, require that a program be relocatable, that is, the program must not have absolute main storage addresses assigned within itself until after it has been loaded into a partition or a region. The reason for this is that as the programs come into the system, it must be possible to load them into any one of the partitions or, in the case of the variable region system, nearly any location in main storage. If absolute addresses are assigned to the programs prior to their being loaded into the system, one does not have the ability to place the programs in any part of main storage. Multiprogramming still may be possible without relocatability (for example, IBM's DOS system), but it requires much more maintenance on the part of the system and/or application programmer and limits the ease of use of the multiprogramming system in question. The basic mechanism that permits relocatability is the base register. A program references all locations within itself in terms of the base register address; that is, a program has an assigned base register and when the program is loaded, the register is loaded with the address of the main storage location marking the beginning of the program. Once the program is loaded into the main storage and that address is placed into the base register, all instructions within the program that reference a main storage address within the program's area actually reference some offset from that base register. This is the basic scheme that gives a program the attribute of relocatability. (Address constants are a separate topic; see Section 6.1.)

A programmer may wish to write a program that obtains during its time of execution space in main storage above and beyond that allocated to it originally. This may be because only during execution will the size of the needed space be known or because the program is to be used recursively (see Sections 5.6 and 6.1). A system might provide such functions as IBM calls GETMAIN and FREEMAIN for this purpose. Managing such space, *within* regions or partitions, is a rather straightforward task, but one with many variables. Storage space may be shared by all users or local to either a single user or the system or even a subsystem that supports a number of users; it may be reserved for the system's use or users may be permitted to execute programs within it or read from it or write into it; it may persist, that is, remain allocated, for the lifetime of a job or only for a single step's duration; it may be reserved for programs that do not modify their own code or have no such restriction. The number of distinctions that may be useful cannot be stated positively, yet the number of distinct types of storage that may be necessitated by those distinctions is two raised to the power of that number!

4.3 MANAGEMENT OF ADDRESSED STORAGE (VIRTUAL)

Virtual storage is gaining fairly wide acceptance, because of the lack of real storage constraint. Both user and system programmers have had less of a storage constraint problem when using the virtual storage systems. Although a virtual storage system does not entirely solve the problem of main storage size, we find that since the entirety of a program does not have to be in main storage at once, but rather needs only those pages (subdivisions of main storage) which it is likely to access at a given time, the system and user programs can at the same time be bigger in the sense of absolute program length, but require less real main storage at a given time. This average amount of pages is sometimes called the working set size by Denning [Den68b] and others.

The first virtual storage system was the ICL-Ferranti ATLAS, in the 1960-1962 era, followed by the Burroughs B500 system. More recently, the MULTICS operating system has been implemented on the HIS/GE 645 system, and the OS/VS1, OS/VS2 (including MVS), and DOS/VSE on the IBM 370 series.

Virtual Storage

A virtual storage system may use the same type of strategy that we have been talking about, either multiple partition, fixed partition, or variable region. Most systems, for example, MVS (Release 2 of IBM's OS/VS2) system, actually allocate multiple address spaces. The difference is that through the addition of certain hardware and software functions, we can build a system using virtual storage that will have more of a range of storage addresses than the actual main storage limits will allow. Any program can run in a virtual storage environment. The basic mechanism of virtual storage is relocation, whether hardware or software. Many operating systems have virtual storage. The term *virtual storage* is used to describe many kinds of hardware-assisted or software-assisted program relocation. Each system has its own kind of virtual storage. One attribute of these is that program addresses do not require a fixed relationship to a real storage address. Main storage addresses (actually virtual storage addresses) are almost always permitted to exceed the limits of real storage. The latter point is sometimes used to define virtual storage. For our purposes, a virtual storage scheme is one in which a program address does not have a fixed relationship to a specific real storage address and, in fact, may exceed the boundary of available real storage.

Nondynamic Relocate Systems

The first category of virtual storage systems is those having no dynamic relocation hardware, that is, relocation is done by software. In these systems, address translation is either absolute or static. Absolute relocation occurs during compilation or linkage editing. To modify the starting location of a program, it is necessary to recompile. To alter the location of main storage data, one must use some sort of software adjustment technique. Many operating systems of the early 1960s and IBM DOS use this kind of technique. The program must always be brought into the same place in main storage.

With static relocation, flexibility of main storage utilization is improved by waiting until just prior to beginning execution of the program to assign a load address for the program. At load time, a base register, or its equivalent, is loaded with the address (which the operating system may provide), so that the program resides in the same real storage location as is contained in the base register. This approach is used in many recent operating systems. With this particular kind of system we find much fragmentation of storage. In Figure 4.5, three programs are resident and active in real storage; either because of partition sizes in excess of the programs' sizes or else because of small fragments being left over in the case of the variable region type of system, we find wasted main storage. This system does not permit the use of addresses larger than real main storage being utilized by programs. The following types of computers use this kind of address strategy: the HIS 200 and 2000 series; the HIS GE200 and GE400 series; the NCR Century series; the UNIVAC 9200, 9300, and 9400 series; the XDS Sigma 5 and Sigma 8; and the IBM System/360, excluding the Model 67.

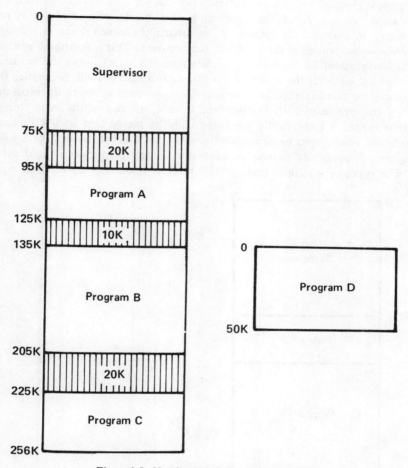

Figure 4.5. Nondynamic Relocate Hardware.

Dynamic Base Relocate Systems

Two types of systems use hardware in minimizing real storage fragmentation. First we discuss those that use dynamic base relocation (DBR). Upon termination of a program, and at periodic intervals, the DBR system can monitor the fragmentation of the programs and adjust the location of the active programs in main storage in order to compress out the wasted main storage space. This is accomplished by hardware circuitry within the computer. Basically, what happens is that the address in the base register for each (affected) executing user program is changed and the program is dynamically moved to a new address and execution resumes. Since the program is dynamically relocatable, it is not necessary to wait for the release of the originally assigned space in order to continue execution after the swap out has occurred. This makes these systems particularly useful for time-sharing applications. Also, this allows the inclusion of a critical job with the least amount of operator intervention, because as the programs are compacted this dynamic relocation tends to move the programs within the computer both together and toward one end of the main storage address range. A high-priority job can readily be placed first in a job queue, which will result in its being initiated sooner than if it had to wait for a given program of equal size to end its execution before this program could come in. The types of machines that use this kind of relocation are the Burroughs

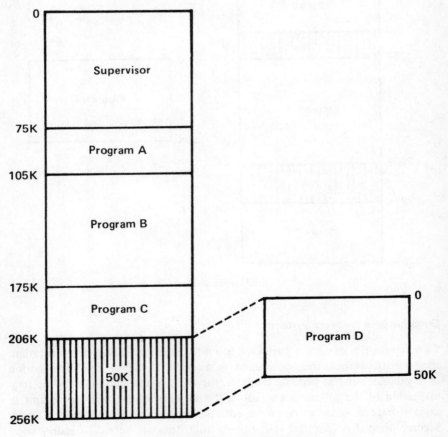

Figure 4.6. Dynamic Base Relocate.

2500, 2700, 3500, and 4700 series; CDC CYBER 70, 6000, and 7600 series; the DEC 1040, 1050, and PDP-10 series; the HIS 6000, 600, and 8200 series; and the UNIVAC 9700, 1106, 1108, and 490 series. This kind of virtual storage system, because relocation is occurring continually, does not necessarily tie a program to a specific real storage address, since the executing programs are constantly being moved toward one end of the real main storage; however, this type of system does not ordinarily allow use of an address greater than that of real storage.

Dynamic Segment Relocation

A third type of virtual storage system uses dynamic segment relocation. In this approach, each program is subdivided into several parts, generally of fixed length, that are called segments. Each segment has a relocation, or mapping, register associated with it during execution which allows the operating system to use fragments of available memory. (See Figure 4.7.) Addresses are still limited to real storage size. Systems which use hardware in this manner are: the CDC 3170, 3300, and 3500 systems; and the XDS Sigma 6, 7, and 9 systems. Rather than the perpetual compaction and migration of programs, the programs are subdivided into segments which can be placed into available free fragments of main storage. Other than the manner of avoiding fragmentation, the attributes of this approach are much the same as those of dynamic base location.

Note that fragmentation remains: the unused portion of each fixed-length unit of storage page or segment. In this case, the average amount of main storage unused at any instant of time may be greatest, but the flexibility of the mechanism mitigates the effect.

Paging Systems

The fourth kind of virtual storage system, and the only kind which allows the specification of program addresses larger than available real main storage, is the paging type of computing system. Very important issues not addressed by the above-mentioned relocating mechanisms are the following:

1. Programs larger than available main storage must be structured into overlays by a programmer or else modified until they fit into real main storage (see Section 6.1).
2. Programs cannot automatically make use of additional real storage when it becomes available.
3. Programs cannot be run on a back-up system with less available real storage than their size.
4. New applications being designed for a large system cannot be tested without tying up the entire system.

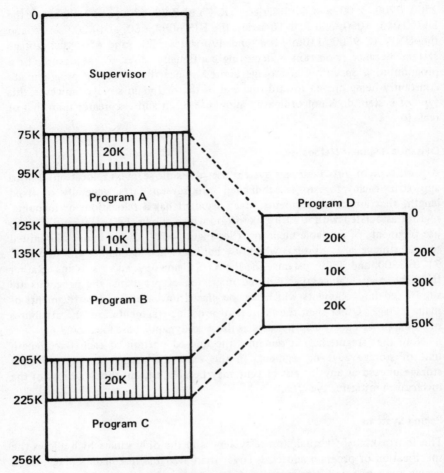

Figure 4.7. Dynamic Segment Relocate.

With a virtual storage system which allows program addresses larger than available real storage, a small system can be used for testing as well as for back-up. It runs, of course, significantly more slowly, but functionally it does all that the larger system does.

Systems using the paging method must include the necessary additional hardware to provide these capabilities. These systems carry the concept of dynamic segment relocation one step further by the incorporation of hardware that recognizes relocatable program subdivisions; there are actually three sub-categories of paging systems:

1. In segmented-only systems, programs are divided into logical segments, for example, an I/O area, or a subroutine of variable length.
2. In paged-only systems, programs are divided into fixed-length discrete units, pages, without regard to logical division.
3. In segmented and paged systems, programs are divided into pages which can be grouped into variable length *logical* subsets called segments.

For each process, there are tables called segment tables of segments addressable and their current residence. For each process or for each segment there are tables called page tables of addressable or contained pages and their current residence. Both types of tables are typically hardware-defined but software-accessible. Systems offering these capabilities are: *segmented only* — the Burroughs B5500, B5700, B6500, B6700 and B7700 systems and the UNIVAC 1110; *paged only* — the DEC 1070 and 1077, and the UNIVAC RCA 3, RCA 7, Spectra 70/46, and 70/61; *segmented* and *paged* — HIS GE645, the CDC STAR 100, and the IBM System/370s and System/360 Model 67.

Let us now briefly examine the general characteristics of each of the three approaches. In segmented systems, the smallest unit of allocatable space is the variable length segment. In Figure 4.7, it was assumed that program D could be divided to fit available spaces in storage. However, the definition of segmentation on systems such as the B6700 involves *logical* subdivision. Assume, then, that program D logically is divided into three segments of 25K, 15K, and 10K; further assume that segment 1 at 25K contains the initial code required to commence execution. If no available fragment of storage, although there may be many of them, is as big as 25K, we could not then commence execution of this program until a fragment of this size or larger was found. We have several choices then: swap or page out the first logical segment of program A or C if it is 5K or larger, or compact two of the available storage spaces by moving one of the active programs to create sufficient continuous space, or swap out one logical segment of A, B, or C if it is 25K or larger. We see that the operating system must perform a considerable amount of work just to find space for a new segment. With many programs operating concurrently, and limited available real storage, we can easily find ourselves in a real storage deficiency situation which necessitates much unproductive processing performed by routines of the operating system.

A page-formatted approach, on the other hand, eliminates the need for searching for sufficient space; since the system is always dealing with fixed-length units, whatever page is the best candidate for swap-out can be paged. However, the contiguous grouping of I/O areas or of code in a closed subroutine is lost. In other words, we do not have the advantages of the logical segment concept wherein we may have considerable variation in size from one segment to another depending on the structure of the program. In a page-only system, after the last instruction on one page is executed another page may have to be swapped back into main storage to complete the operation. If we could somehow cause the entire logical group to be brought in at the same time and *left* in main storage, we would not see so much overhead in terms of paging in and paging out. With the paging type of configuration, we lose the advantages of the logical segments. (See the discussion of paging strategies below for more on this topic.)

It would appear that the combination of the two techniques in *segmented* and *paged* systems — segmentation for flexibility of sharing and paging formats for efficient storage allocation — might give us the advantages of both without

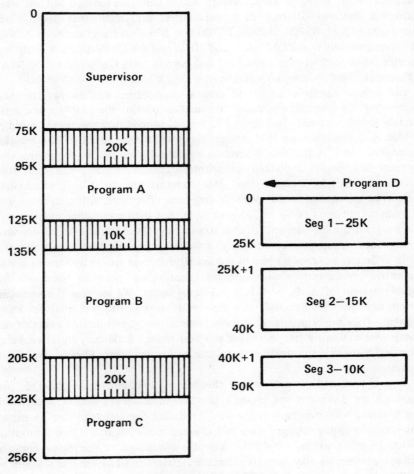

Figure 4.8. Demand Paging.

incurring the most severe penalities of either, and so it works out in practice. Let us examine the relationship of real storage to virtual storage. The virtual storage systems that have a larger address space than available real storage are actually physically limited only by the size of the computer's addressing structure. A typical limit is 24 bits in the case of IBM's System/370 series. This allows 16 megabytes (16 million bytes) of virtual storage. This 16 megabytes of virtual storage is mapped onto an area on an external paging device, also called the paging file or paging space. The process of assigning real storage to some address in the virtual storage address space is called dynamic address translation. The hardware takes an address reference somewhere within the 16 virtual megabytes and translates it automatically (through the use of hardware associative registers) into a real storage address. At this point, the program or data residing on the external paging device are brought into real main storage. Since this system is segmented and paged, we might see three or four pages of 4K, or some other finite constant size, apiece, actually loaded from the external paging device into real storage. We are assuming, for example, that four pages are sufficient to contain a logical segment of the program. The pages of constant size give the best control on available real storage because all real storage is also subdivided into correspondingly sized page frames. The data residing in some real storage page frame of 4K currently unused, are swapped out to the appropriate location on the external paging device, to remain there until they are needed again. The new material from another virtual storage location, which may contain a program executing at higher priority, is then brought into the freed page frame in real storage. For an excellent technical discussion on virtual storage and paging, see Parmalee [Parm72].

Virtual storage is subdivided in IBM virtual storage systems into either fixed partitions or variable regions, just as in the original discussion of fixed size real storage machines; the only difference is that the total amount of virtual storage may be larger than the partitions or regions of a nonvirtual machine. In addition, MVS has multiple address spaces. Previous IBM and some other operating systems operate as though they were in a real storage computer; that is, they allocate virtual storage as though it were real storage. With multiple address spaces there is a significant difference.

Multiple Address Space Systems

A multiple address space system is a hybrid system such as MULTICS or IBM's MVS combining the traditional storage system with the multiple virtual machine systems discussed in Section 2.6. Instead of having multiple virtual *machines,* however, the multiple address space system has only *one* complete machine. It does give each user a unique address space (16 megabytes in the IBM OS/VS2 Release 2 system). There can be numerous users, each with an address space, and each individual address space is pageable as indicated in the previous discussion. In addition, if a process is likely to be unready for a long time, waiting for a volume to be mounted on a device, for example, the entire address space is completely swapped out of the system until the wait condition is satisfied.

The difference between multiple address space and older systems is that the virtual storage space is not split up into partitions or regions, but rather each user has a very large unique address space of his own, and does not share virtual storage including "shared space" (see below), with anyone else except the system, leaving 10 to 12 megabytes to be used by a single user. Very few programs are as large as 10 megabytes in length, although working storage for some may exceed this amount.

Even 16 megabytes do not provide enough storage for some applications, for example, a subsystem serving many users. IBM systems introduced in the eighties permit 31 bits of addressability, two gigabytes, and the ability to address more than one address space from a single program.

Strategies for Virtual Storage Systems

In all page-based virtual storage systems, two algorithms are of paramount importance in determining the system's performance characteristics; those for bringing data into main storage and for displacing data from main storage. A separate algorithm may be used for moving data between the paging device and slower media in the storage hierarchy, but we choose not to say much about that here. The two principal algorithms, page-in and page-out, are our main concern.

We consider two basic types of algorithms, those which deal with individual pages and those which deal with groups of pages. A virtual storage system could have no algorithm of the latter type, but Denning has amply shown [Den70] the value of such an algorithm under a variety of circumstances.

Choosing a page to bring into storage is typically a trivial task. The system brings in pages as they are needed. This is called *demand paging.* Aho [Aho71] demonstrates that no other in-paging, or *placement,* policy is superior to demand paging. The absence from main storage of a needed page is called a page fault and causes a fault-handler or in-paging routine to be invoked by hardware. Finding the page may be more interesting. Little has been written specifically about the management of space on a paging device and optimal arrangement of the space. (See, however, [Sch73], which demonstrates that there may be merit in keeping on the paging device two copies of every page assigned to it.) The problem is little different from many others where a directory of some sort, such as page tables, must be used to access fixed-length records directly. (See Chapter 5.) Much, however, has been written about scheduling I/O operations on paging devices. See [Ful73], [Sch73], and [Cha73]. Section 3.2 is, of course, also relevant.

Choosing a page to replace is quite a different matter. Most algorithms or *replacement* policies in use today [Wil73] are based on the longest-unused-first-out (LUFO) principle. The page which has been unneeded for the longest time is the first to be overwritten. If it has been modified since it entered main storage, it must be written out; otherwise not. All out-paging algorithms are hardware-assisted, each page in main storage typically being associated with a resettable *changed bit* and a periodically reset *referenced bit*.

Working Set

Among the considerations for the user of a virtual system, particularly a demand paging system, is the concept of the working set. A given program of perhaps 96K bytes might only need at any one time to have 30K of itself residing in main real storage. It is probable that for execution of a particular instruction in the program, only locations within 4K of the instruction plus the data in the data-declarative portion of the program are needed. The total number of actual page frames needed to execute a program over a given time interval, taken on the average through the life of the execution of the program, is called the working set size. The working set size, then, is the amount of main storage required for efficient execution of the program in this kind of virtual storage system. On the average, it is considerably less than the total amount of main storage that a program might require in an environment with no virtual storage.

Many studies have been made on how the size and optimum contents of a process' working set may be determined by an operating system. Such studies examine the patterns of process references to storage addresses. If a program's behavior in this regard is not or cannot be properly anticipated, too small working sets and *thrashing* — excessive overhead due to frequent page faults — may result. (Some anonymous wag has referred to the minimum size of a working set as its "thrashhold.") It is important that the reader understand that an entire working set may be paged out when a process becomes unable (because it may be waiting for a resource) or ineligible (because it has insufficient priority) to use the central processor and paged in again when that circumstance no longer exists. (See Section 4.4 for discussion of priority.) This results in potentially great efficiencies in paging. The reader is referred to Denning [Den68b and Den70] for some valuable thoughts on the subject.

We find that we can execute more programs concurrently in a virtual storage system than we can otherwise; however, there is a very definite trade-off involved, because the paging mechanism is a source of considerable overhead. Additional use of the central processing unit of 25% is not uncommon in virtual storage systems; for example, an installation that has a CPU utilized an average of 23% of the time in a conventional operating system might find utilization averaging 50% or more after the installation of a virtual storage system. The *total through-put* of the system normally increases despite the increased overhead. An individual program may well take longer to execute in a virtual storage system than it did on another type of system; however, since more programs run concurrently, we find that the total throughput may increase dramatically in a virtual storage system. Virtual storage systems may also be self-tuning. The problem of deciding which components of the operating system should be resident and which should not be may no longer exist. Every performance-oriented module in a system may be made resident in a virtual storage system and merely paged along with the actual application programs. This can result in self-tuning, because main storage contains only the program modules required for high performance over a given interval of time. They are not resident at all times. There are no storage constraints, so that there is no necessity for overlaying or segmentation of programs. Application programmers have a much easier task and are much more productive because they therefore do not have to spend time planning overlay strategies for their programs. Operational ease is also greatly enhanced because of the decreased need for periodic redefinitions of the systems, particularly in fixed partition systems. Operator intervention is much less prevalent and the system tends, more or less, to run itself.

Comprehensive papers on virtual storage, recommended in the order of increasing depth, are [Wil73], [Parm72], and [Den73]. The latter two have exemplary bibliographies.

Shared Space

As obliquely implied above in this section and elsewhere, some programs resident in main storage are shared by multiple processes. This particular subject is discussed further in Section 5.6, but it is symptomatic of a broader topic, the sharing of addressed storage across processes. This is represented in a segmented store such as that of MULTICS by shared page tables; in a paged store by duplicate entries in multiple page tables; and in a system, such as OS/360 MVT, without virtual storage by a nucleus (the resident portion of the supervisor) and a separate area reserved for shared reentrable programs of the system.

Programs share addressed storage through such mechanisms as COMMON in FORTRAN, STATIC EXTERNAL in PL/1, and COMPOOL in JOVIAL. Implementations of these mechanisms differ from system to system, but are generally much more a concern of a compiler than of an operating system, although, of course, the system must not prevent the implementation of such concepts.

This section has dealt with the management of addressed storage. After a number of preliminary remarks, we treated principally the topics of fragmentation, relocation, virtual storage, and shared storage. We note now, incidentally, that such space as the system uses on secondary storage media for such tasks as spooling might be considered addressed space, but we choose to treat it in our discussion of named space, the subject of our next section.

4.4 MANAGEMENT OF NAMED STORAGE

We are concerned in this section with data collected together in named entities. To say that files are the only things which meet this description would be an oversimplification, but the attributes of files do provide the framework for our discussion. A file is identified by its name and its name must be used in the process of determining its location. The location of files is our first topic. We then look at other named entities which reside on the same media as files, secondary storage volumes. Some of these entities are the very objects used in locating files. For all of these, however, arise questions of optimum placement, our third and last topic.

Locating a File

As we have remarked above, a name is a convenience designed for human use. The system itself would naturally prefer to deal with more efficient identifiers, collections of bits with no redundancy. Files have names because people wish to communicate with the system about files. People communicate in programming languages and operating system control languages (OSCL). Every instance of use of a name is said to occur within a *context.* If context is insignificant in the interpretation of a verb, we say that its use is *context-free* or, more precisely, that the semantics of a verb may be context-free. Our concern here, however, is that apparently context-free uses of a verb may not be what they seem. Take the case of a DELETE command of an OSCL. This may mean something quite different (say, delete one line of text) when one is editing data from what it means (say, delete a file) in another context. The earlier use of an EDIT command might have established the former context. Further, "DELETE 35" may have the meaning of our former example, while "DELETE FILE = 35" may have the meaning of the latter. Here, context is established after use.

In some systems, qualified names are used to form context-free verbs. The entities to which DELETE may refer could be distinguished by verbs: DELETE LINE, DELETE FILE, PROGRAM DELETE, or PROCEDURE DELETE, for example. The qualifiers are merely alternative ways of expressing context. Where the naming scheme of a system uses qualifiers, however, these may participate in the process of locating objects. Actually, they may establish a *context* for search, a library of programs, for example, rather than a catalog of procedures.

The notion of context is vital in all programming languages. Suppose subroutine A defines an object X which can be referred to from anywhere in the program MAIN, X is of type integer, A invokes subroutine B of MAIN containing a definition of an object X of type label, and a statement of B is SET Y = X; then we would expect by the rule of locality of reference, which is in accord with the principle of least astonishment, Y is set to the value of the label X, unless that is forbidden by the semantics of the SET statement. The SET statement provides a static context for the interpretation of the name X. The invocation of B by A provides a dynamic context for that interpretation, one in which Y could conceivably take on the value of the integer X.

All this is preliminary to our exposition. The reader should note as we describe specific mechanisms what role the notion of context is playing.

In the remainder of this section, we focus on the mechanisms of large IBM operating systems for the management of named storage. These are adequate for illustrative purposes. It should be clear to our reader where our statements have broader applicability.

Location Mechanisms. In looking at the locating of objects in named storage, we consider in turn each of the mechanisms used by OS/VS in finding the files the names of which appear in its control language, the job control language (JCL). The objects involved are the passed data set (file) queue (PDQ), the catalog, the label and the volume table of contents (VTOC), and the directory.

If a user does not explicitly tell the system where a file is resident, the system first uses the PDQ in its effort to find the file. The PDQ is used to realize the context of a job for the interpretation of file names. The PDQ is maintained with the other tables that result from the interpretation of the JCL statements for a job. It is more closely associated with a particular job and, therefore, more efficient than a catalog, but has logically the same contents: an ordered list of symbol-location pairs, where a location is a list of identifiers of volumes on which the file resides. Other data, such as the medium on which the file is recorded, are also in each entry of the PDQ. No two entries in one PDQ may contain the same name. Names in the PDQ must include all qualifiers.

After searching the PDQ for a file, the system then searches the *catalog,* which contains, in addition to such pairs and other data as are in the PDQ, pairs which give the locations of other catalogs and the names used as qualifiers to make reference to them. The catalog represents the context of the entire system, although there is a way for a user to gain access to a catalog other than the primary catalog of the system. Entries in the catalog are ordered alphabetically, but, again, no two entries may have the same name, so ordering is academic.

If a file is named ANIMAL.CAT.TIGER, where ANIMAL and CAT are qualifiers, and the system must search the primary catalog for the file's location, an entry for ANIMAL is sought. This should lead to a catalog with an entry for CAT, leading in turn to a catalog with an entry for the file TIGER. If the system cannot find the named file in this way, it treats the situation as an error.

Once the system has learned on which volumes the file resides, it searches the label of the first volume (the label is called a VTOC for directly accessed volumes) to learn where on the volume the file is. This is the information which eventually finds its way into main storage for use during the execution of a program using the file. An exception of sorts concerns members of libraries, designated in JCL as FILENAME(MEMNAME). FILENAME is treated as a file name, but the first element of the file stored on a directly accessed volume is a *directory*. This gives the location of the named member. (See Section 5.6.)

These, then, are the objects involved in locating objects in named storage: PDQ, catalog, volume label and VTOC, and directory. We now look at other objects the system itself places in named storage.

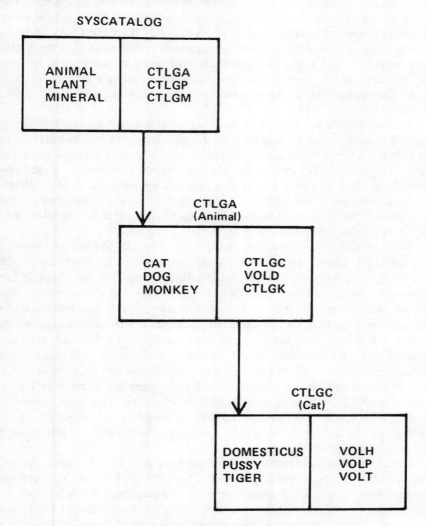

Figure 4.9. Catalogs.

System Use of Named Storage

The system uses directly accessed storage media to store much data it needs itself. The PDQ, catalog, VTOC, and directory are discussed above. We discuss below five other types of such data: paging space, spooling space, VSAM space, the system job queue (SYSJOBQE), and libraries of system programs.

Paging space, needed with virtual storage systems, is usually a dedicated block of tracks and cylinders on a particular drum or disk pack or entire volumes. The space must be contiguous for reasons clarified in Section 5.2. It contains a map of the virtual storage space discussed in Section 4.2. If an operating system has a closed virtual storage space stored contiguously on a volume, then the system may be able to read a large contiguous block of virtual storage from its location in the paging space into main storage, and start executing a program or using data. The management of paging space, as mentioned above, is critical to system performance.

Another system use of directly accessed space is spooling. Spooling can be defined as an intermediate step between the effective use of data and their input or output via a medium of direct value to people. Such data might be an output listing or punched card input; anything that must be processed by a relatively slow device such as a card reader or a printer is spooled, placed on a directly accessed volume and, for input, then read into the central processing unit at the appropriate time at a much higher rate of speed. Output is first spooled, then put out to such a device as a printer.

There are two types of spooling: individual and pooled. In individual spooling the operating system creates one or more temporary files that exist only for the life of the relevant job. The input and output of this job are placed in the temporary files as the job is processed. Then, when the job terminates, the output data are sent to the appropriate slow device, such as a printer, at the appropriate time. The data transfer is effected from the intermediate direct-access file to the printer after the job itself has actually been completed. It is not unusual to have a two-hour delay from the time the job is completed to the actual appearance of its output on the printer. During this time the output is held in the system's intermediate files until the system determines that it is the turn of that job to have its output printed. When the printer has completed writing all outputs from the job, the space occupied by the temporary files is relinquished by the system for use by another job, whether for an intermediate file or for some other file.

Pooled spooling involves single spool space reserved by the system. A good example of this type of spooling is seen in the IBM JES2 and OS/VS1 systems. In pooled spooling, a spool space is reserved on a given pack and is inviolate; no other user of the system may use this space. The space is subdivided into logical input and output units which are accessed by means of binary tables. It is a much faster way of handling the intermediate input and output data. It does, however, require more dedicated space and adds an additional layer of overhead to the operating system if done in addition to the already existing spooling facility of the operating system.

Virtual I/O is a method for handling system and user temporary files. In the past these files would have to be allocated like all other files. This was time consuming and undesirable, since most of these files would be the kind that are created and deleted within the same job. They served as temporary storage for the most part, and formal allocation should not have been necessary.

Virtual I/O simply works on temporary files by assigning them blocks or pages of virtual storage as required. When they are no longer needed they are of

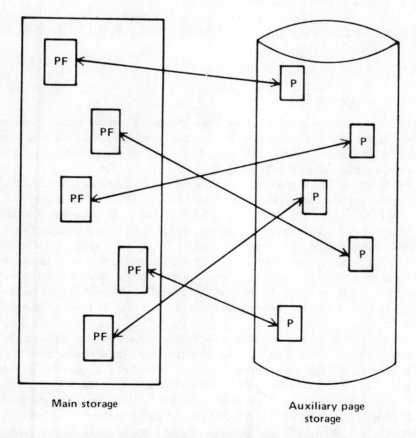

Main storage   Auxiliary page
                                storage

Figure 4.10. Relationship Between Main Storage and Page Storage, Including Main Storage Page Frames (PF) and Pages (P).

course eventually paged out of the system. By having files in virtual memory one can gain significant performance advantages, since the more cumbersome and generalized I/O supervisor is bypassed altogether.

The system job queue (SYSJOBQE) of IBM's System/360 and 370 operating systems without virtual storage is a reserved area on a directly accessed volume preformatted into blocks of fixed size (176 bytes). The system uses the area to contain tables built by its JCL processor and maintained throughout the life of the associated jobs, even until the completion of output spooling. The tables serve various purposes and are most frequently used between steps by the system's scheduler to accomplish interstep transition. (See Section 4.6.) The tables for a single job occupy potentially noncontiguous groups of contiguous blocks varying in number with medium.

OS/360 and successors use a large number of libraries to contain the system's programs. Nothing else really need be made of this here, but see Sections 5.6 and 6.1 for related information.

Placement of System Space

When an establishment installs a new large computing system, systems analysts devote much time and effort to arranging files on volumes in such a way as to optimize performance. How much more it behooves the designer of an operating system to concern himself with placement of the system's files!

For many such files, the criteria for placement may be meager or conflicting. For others, definite reasons for doing one thing rather than another may exist.

The PDQ is one of the tables on SYSJOBQE for a job. This is as it should be. Little can be said about the catalog except that frequent access thereof should be anticipated. The same can be said for spooling space, VAM space. SYSJOBQE, and system libraries. It follows, therefore, that care should be taken in separating these so that no one unit and no one channel is overloaded compared to others. Dispersal of these files is limited, however, by the number of distinct units and channels available for the purpose. It is, in all, a vexing problem.

For volumes frequently mounted, a decision to place VTOCs at the beginnings of volumes makes sense if, as happens, mounting leaves the accessing mechanism positioned there. This placement also permits the rest of the volume to be used contiguously. For fragmented, rarely dismounted disk volumes, a VTOC in the middle of accessible space might make more sense, to minimize the maximum and average distance between VTOC and files. A similar statement applies to the directory of a library of fixed size. As long as a spatial object is infrequently processed sequentially, but accessed by a moving mechanism, the placement of controlling data at the center of the object's extent must be considered.

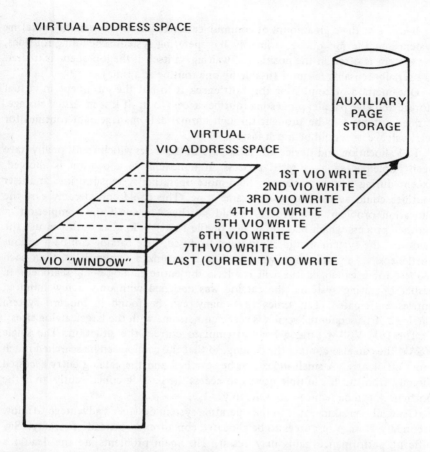

VIRTUAL ADDRESS SPACE

AUXILIARY
PAGE
STORAGE

VIRTUAL
VIO ADDRESS SPACE

1ST VIO WRITE
2ND VIO WRITE
3RD VIO WRITE
4TH VIO WRITE
5TH VIO WRITE
6TH VIO WRITE
7TH VIO WRITE
VIO "WINDOW"   LAST (CURRENT) VIO WRITE

Figure 4.11. VIO Operations, IBM VS2 Release 2. The VIO (virtual input/output) buffer, or "window," has been assigned to a permanent virtual address within a system or user address space. This buffer is moved to auxiliary page space when it has been filled, after which the VIO operation may be repeated, as shown.

Constraints on the placement of paging space have been stated above. Suffice it to say that when paging is done, no element of space utilization is more important than the placement and management of paging space.

Bottlenecks on Secondary Storage. The job (spool) queue can be a system bottleneck. It is ordinarily located on a direct access device, so that in the event of a system failure an audit trail is available for the jobs which have been entered into the system. In addition, there is less of a main storage requirement if the job records are on secondary storage.

Because of the high amount of communication required between the operating system and the job queue, primarily by operating system scheduling routines, the system is often in the position of waiting on itself if the job queue is treated as a serially reusable resource (usable by one routine at a time).

One method of combating this bottleneck is to put the job queue in virtual storage and give parallel processing routines access to it. If it is in virtual storage, it does not have to be brought through normal data management routines for retrieval; access should be much faster.

File allocation and device allocation are bottlenecks which traditionally have been implemented as a serial process. If nonexclusive allocation is allowed, except during update processes, then more operating system routines and user routines could access files at the same time. This could considerably ease the allocation problem; one process would not have to await the completion of another process which had the device or file first. As long as both can use the resource, the system should allow them to do so. The catalog can be a serious bottleneck in an operating system; if it is organized sequentially, then each request for a cataloged file will result in the entire catalog being searched. In earlier operating systems, the catalog was designed with only a few hundred entries anticipated. Ten times that many can be found in modern system catalogs. This sequential search is very cumbersome with the large catalog sizes.

The IBM VSAM catalog is an attempt to correct the situation. The single VSAM file can also contain the catalog, so that the catalog can be searched much more efficiently. A small index can be searched and the catalog entry accessed directly from it. If multiple users can access the catalog concurrently, then the bottleneck can be reduced considerably.

Generally speaking, it is to the operating system designer's advantage to allow secondary storage resources to be allocated concurrently instead of serially. Significant performance gains may result. The main problems are the deadlock problem, and the problem of one user updating while another inquires; locks have to be used more often.

In summary, the virtual I/O capability should markedly improve operating system performance when designers avail themselves of it.

This section has dealt with the management of named storage. The problem of allocating space on secondary storage, tied as it is to specific media and the use of files, is deferred to Chapter 5, the protection of data in named and unnamed storage.

4.5 SYSTEM INTEGRITY

If the protection afforded data by systems is to be effective, the system must have integrity. That is, it must prevent unauthorized access to resources and must resist penetration or modification by unauthorized individuals [McP74].

The problem can be addressed in terms of protecting data in primary and in secondary storage, but that protection involves other considerations. Processes that act on users' behalf must access protected data securely. The system does this by placing the data in primary storage accessible only to itself and to authorized users of the particular data it has fetched. The system maintains blocks of descriptive data it depends upon to accomplish this. Such descriptive data must themselves be protected. The regression from users' data to system data to even more intimate system-descriptive data is not infinite, but it is quite long and complex. Therefore, protection can be assured only if designers find and protect all data upon which the system relies to provide protection. Further, the system must ensure that unauthorized individuals cannot modify its behavior. This means that the system must ensure that code provided by unauthorized individuals never executes with any privilege, for example, running with system protection keys in effect or in supervisor or kernel state, that the system reserves for itself so that it can do what unauthorized individuals may not.

Even selection and protection of descriptive data is not enough. The system provides function requested by users. The system must analyze requests well enough to recognize and reject requests for unauthorized function. In the case of direct access to data or acquisition of privilege, the determination may be straightforward and mediated by the system's access control facility, but in the case of such subtler services as the signaling of completed activities, identifying a routine to be invoked for specialized processing, or the diagnosis or errors, the determination may be quite complicated and liable to error. The system is vulnerable to penetration when it:

1. Modifies storage as requested by a user's program; it must verify that the modification is authorized.
2. Transfers control; it must verify that it is branching to or invoking a program authorized to run with the privileges that it will receive.
3. Expands its own privilege; it must be sure that it will not do anything that its own lack of privilege should prevent.
4. Fetches system- or data-descriptive data; it must be sure that it is fetching protected data.

The points of vulnerability are listed above only for emphasis; any system bug might lead to a penetration of the system simply because the system behaves in a way designers did not anticipate. The penetration itself may occur at a point of vulnerability, but it may result from a flaw that was manifested long before.

The next section concerns task (or process) management and job management as such, subjects to which our first four sections of this chapter have been complementary.

4.6 MANAGEMENT OF TASKS

Tasks are logically independent units of work whose use of the computer's central processor(s) can be scheduled. The term derives from IBM usage. We treat it as wholly synonymous with *process,* the more common term in the literature, and use the terms here interchangeably.

In discussing task management, we consider the various states in which tasks can exist, types of strategies for scheduling their use of the system's central processor(s), the relevant effects of multiprocessing, and the matter of task synchronization and induced dependencies between tasks. Our discussion is most heavily influenced by the IBM Time-Sharing System/360, TSS/360. (See Hamlet [Ham73] for another view.)

States of Tasks

Once a task has been defined within an operating system, it can be either *active* or *inactive.* A task is inactive if it cannot proceed, pending some event other than the placement in main storage of a needed page. A task may be inactive because it is awaiting the completion of a nonpaging I/O operation or the availability of a needed resource. An active task is *dispatchable* if the system has placed the data it is known to need, such as its working set, in main storage. Otherwise, an active task is *eligible.* The transfer of control of a central processor to a task by the system is called dispatching. A page fault suffered by a dispatched, that is, running, task renders it unready until such time as the required page has been brought into main storage by the system, when the task becomes *ready.* The dispatcher dispatches only ready tasks.

Note that the distinction between dispatchable and eligible task applies to virtual storage systems. In these, the pages of an eligible task reside on a paging device. In other systems, the notion of *swapping* or *rolling out* a task, making it eligible rather than dispatchable, may maintain that distinction. In still more primitive systems, created tasks may always use main storage space, eliminating the notion of an eligible task completely.

Strategies for Scheduling and Dispatching

We have already defined dispatching. Scheduling is a strongly related function and the two are sometimes confused. A *scheduler* sets up the tables used by a dispatcher. To put it another way, a dispatcher is a rather simple, mechanistic program which obtains control of a central processor whenever another program relinquishes it and merely decides in an algorithmic, unsophisticated way which task shall run next. And it must decide this quickly because it is exercised more frequently than any other piece of code in the system, so often, in fact, that its code, like the code of a page-fault handler, is among the few identifiable items which will remain resident in main storage in any operating system ever designed, as we know such systems. A scheduler performs whatever analysis on competing tasks that the system designer deems appropriate so that these tasks can be ordered for the dispatcher's convenience. The scheduler is executed whenever an event worthy of its consideration occurs, for example, whenever the state of a task changes.

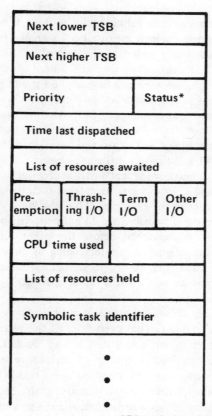

Of last 20 time slices, number ended due to:

Next lower TSB			
Next higher TSB			
Priority		Status*	
Time last dispatched			
List of resources awaited			
Pre-emption	Thrash-ing I/O	Term I/O	Other I/O
CPU time used			
List of resources held			
Symbolic task identifier			

*Bit switches denoting:

	bit
Waiting for Resources	0
Page wait	1
Terminal I/O wait	2
Other I/O wait	3
Foreground	4
Ready	5
Active	6
etc.	

Figure 4.12. Hypothetical Task Scheduling Book (TSB).

In looking at the strategies employed in scheduling and dispatching, we consider first the notion of priority, central to any scheme but the simplest. We then look at the goals of scheduling; the criteria by which tasks are accorded priority; the mechanisms, such as time-slicing, by which the apportionment of processing time is regulated; and some of the ways these criteria and mechanisms can be used to effect scheduling strategies.

Priority. Clearly, one way scheduling could be done is with a FIFO (first-in-first-out) queue. A single chained list of all tasks known to the system is maintained, each new task being added to the end of the list at birth and being deleted from the list at death. The dispatcher need always examine only the state of each task, beginning with the first in the list and proceeding down the list until a ready task is found, which is then dispatched.

This method is inadequate for many purposes. We can improve upon it by applying criteria of importance to tasks and reordering our list accordingly. We do exactly this, in principle if not in bits and bytes, in virtually every scheduling scheme, but, to avoid insisting on sufficient objective criteria to apply a strict ordering to all pairs of tasks, we accept a partial ordering, a finite categorization. Each task t_i is assigned a priority pr_i, an integer such that $0 \leqslant pr_i \leqslant n$ for all i and some convenient integer n, for example, $256 = 2^8$. We say that $pr_i = pr_j$ implies that tasks i and j have equal priority. We do not concern ourselves with which of tasks i and j would be dispatched before the other, all things being equal, because we know that, digital computers being as they are, nonrandom, all things can never be equal and we see to it that the inequalities are the ones which serve our purpose, usually a FIFO factor of sorts.

Criteria for Scheduling. When we establish a scheduling strategy, we must have specific goals clearly in mind. That every user of the system gets a fair shake is likely to be one of them in only a very limited way. Rather, we seek to maximize throughput, serve a maximum number of interactive users with acceptable response time, minimize worst-case response times within specified constraints, and/or something else. Whatever our primary goals, they suggest secondary goals, such as equalizing resource utilization and minimizing overhead, and these suggest algorithms or strategies.

As intermediate goals the reader can bear in mind as we proceed, let us take these:

1. Give preference to tasks likely to use underutilized resources.
2. Give preference to tasks that have not received that fair shake we mentioned.
3. Heed some notions of priority associated with important people, important processes, and the like.

4. Do not let noninteractive (batch) use interfere with interactive use.
5. If an important process is waiting for a resource held by a less important one, give preference to the latter so that the former can more quickly obtain the resource for which it is waiting.
6. Shun tasks with high overhead, such as high paging rates.

This is hardly an exhaustive list, but it should serve to place some of what follows in perspective.

With goals clearly in mind, we seek criteria by which we can prioritize tasks to meet those goals. These criteria must be applicable in a reasonably efficient manner; that is, we must see ways of collecting the data we need without unduly burdening the system. Some criteria we might choose on this basis are:

1. Number of I/O operations lately.
2. Page-fault rate.
3. Times preempted by a higher priority task becoming ready.
4. Priority of tasks waiting for held resources.
5. Urgency of task, such as the importance of opening a steam valve in response to signal of an impending explosion.
6. Importance of user for whom task runs.
7. Interval of elapsed time since last dispatch of task.
8. Total time in execution over some interval of real time.
9. Projected requirement of running time for completion of the task.

Whatever criteria are employed, the scheduler is responsible for maintaining the control blocks which contain the scheduling parameters and for performing whatever calculations and manipulations are necessary to provide the dispatcher with the data it needs.

Mechanisms. We have said that the dispatcher gains control of a CPU whenever another task relinquishes it. Let us now qualify that statement. A CPU processes a stream of instructions until some event interrupts that processing. We can classify such events as follows:

1. A task-related event which (a) can be processed forthwith as part of the process, that is, synchronously, or (b) requires processing beyond the continuous instruction execution by a CPU, for example, paging, other I/O or waiting for an unavailable resource; asynchronous processing.
2. An event associated with another task, typically the termination of asynchronous processing as described by 1(b).

Events of type 1(a), such as diagnostic interruptions for such exceptional conditions as underflow and division by zero, need not involve the dispatcher inasmuch as no *task switch,* the altering of the identity of the task to be processed by a CPU, is necessary. Type 1(*b*) is indicative of the reverse; a task can no longer make use of a CPU and must therefore relinquish it. Events of type 2 present the designer of a system with a variety of choices. The event can be cursorily noted and attendant processing can await the next dispatching of the related task; attendant processing, such as error-checking for a completed I/O operation, can be undertaken immediately followed by (1) resumption of the interrupted task, (as would be the case for cursory notation of the event), (2) dispatching of the task to which the event is related, especially if it is of higher priority, (3) normal entry to the dispatcher, or (4) some combination of the above, where the option chosen is dependent on some additional characterization of the event.

Understanding these options for implementation, the student is prepared to consider the mechanisms used in realizing a scheduling strategy. We discuss these next; priority queuing, time slicing, and preemptive dispatching.

The reader may already have inferred that a scheduler can produce at each of its executions an ordered list of tasks and nothing else, and have well fulfilled its purpose. When this is true, we have scheduling by *priority queuing.* In most virtual storage systems, because of our scheduling goals for interactive use, priority queuing is augmented by time-slicing. With each task is associated a maximum interval of time that the task can remain active. Expiration of a *time slice,* as the interval is called, is a task-related event always causing invocation of the dispatcher. The dispatcher may redispatch the same task, but only if it would have selected the task independent of the reasons the dispatcher was invoked. Typically, in implementation of our criterion 7 above, a task whose time slice has ended would be repositioned in the priority queue, logically or physically, by the dispatcher or the scheduler.

Bear in mind that a task may lose control of a CPU whenever an interrupting event occurs and time-slice expiration is just one such event, the one which occurs if no other event occurs before it.

Another mechanism involved in task scheduling is partitioning of active tasks into dispatchable and eligible tasks. The number of dispatchable tasks in a system is limited by the size of main storage. Let t_i be the list of active tasks in the system with priorities pr_i, such that $i<j$ implies $pr_i \geqslant pr_j$ ("greater than" is equivalent to "better than" with respect to priorities, for the sake of our discussion), and with working set sizes w_i and let K be the size of main storage excepting those areas reserved for the system's use. Then the number D of dispatchable tasks in the system is bounded by $D \leqslant$ the max n such that $\sum_{i=1}^{n} w_i \leqslant K$, assuming that we never wish to have a dispatchable task with a priority inferior to that of some eligible task.

Preemptive scheduling occurs when, in response to an event of type 2, asynchronous, the related task is dispatched, even though that would not have been true had the same type of event, related to some other task, occurred. We use

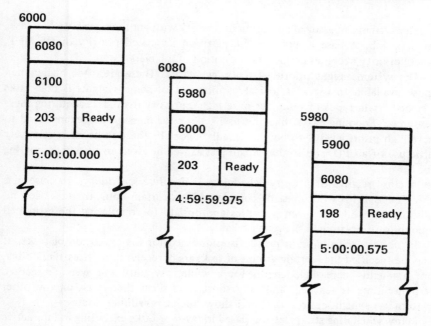

Figure 4.13. A Queue of Task Scheduling Blocks (TSBs).

preemption in response to criterion 5, for tasks of inherent urgency, such as defense against nuclear attack or destruction of an uncontrollable missile.

We now have the weapons of scheduling in hand. We next discuss some ways of using them.

Strategies for Scheduling. Scheduling strategies can be categorized according to whether they are oriented toward local optimization or toward global optimization. This is not to say, however, that a system must choose between the two. The total scheduling strategy of a system may consist of elements of all the separate strategies we discuss below.

Local optimization here implies focusing on the characteristics and behavior of individual scheduled entities. A prime ingredient of such activity is priority. We look now at the possible origins of priority specifications. We discount the case where another scheduling strategy generates a priority; that is merely a mechanism.

Users can specify a value for the priority of the work done on their behalf. The system or the installation may place bounds on this value, but the fact that it is specified by a user remains significant. A system may permit a user to associate a priority with each task or only with some collection of tasks, a step or job. See Chapter 6 for discussions of how such values as priority are specified by users.

The system can associate a notion of priority with another attribute of a task, step, or job. A case in point is the partition-associated priority of OS/MFT, where priority becomes implicit in the notion of job class.

The system assigns priorities to its own tasks. These are often higher than those available to users. A logical requirement of some systems is that tasks freeing certain types of resources have higher priority than tasks acquiring these resources. Spooling tasks, like the user's tasks for message processing, tend to have high priorities due to our intermediate goal 1: these tasks make relatively little use of a CPU, and so they might just as well be given an edge in competing for it.

A close relative of priority scheduling is *deadline scheduling*. If a user has specified that his work must be completed by a certain hour, the tasks accomplishing his work are given priorities appropriate to completing the estimated amount of processing in the time available.

In *pattern scheduling,* a profile is established for the execution of tasks. It may be specified that certain groups of tasks are to receive time-slices of middling, but gradually increasing, lengths for a while, say until the system's median response time is reached, and only short time slices thereafter, or any other pattern users might desire. Table 4.1 shows such a scheduling strategy.

Many scheduling strategies are biased in favor of tasks executing in interactive environments. This bias is justifiable in view of response-time requirements.

A more global type of scheduling strategy involves a *ring*, a cyclically ordered set of tasks. The ring merely serves to give each of n tasks every nth time slice; this is a strategy predicated on fairness, justice, and the like. Rings are often embedded in other strategies.

Another form of global optimization favors tasks which use little processing time compared with their need for resources, such as I/O processing capability. This is consistent with what we have said before: If a task needs little of a resource, we can pursue our goals of maximizing resource utilization and throughput by giving it that resource.

Finally, we can choose to try to please everyone. We can design a scheduler that collects all data that could conceivably influence scheduling, express a

Table 4.1. An Example of Pattern Scheduling (all times in seconds).

Elapsed Time	Maximum Time Used CPU	Time-Slice Duration
1	.01	.003
1	∞	.001
2	.02	.005
2	∞	.004
$\geqslant 3$	.06	.002
$\geqslant 3$	∞	.001

scheduling algorithm in terms of a parameterized combination of priority scheduling and pattern scheduling, and allow users to supply and periodically vary the parameters to be used by the system. Such schedulers are said to be *tunable*. If a system unilaterally modifies its own scheduling parameters, it is said to have a *heuristic scheduler*. It is not at all unusual to find that the designers of a general purpose operating system have, in defiance of Lincoln, tried in this way to please all the people all of the time. The cost of such a policy is measured in development expense, bugs engendered by complexity, overhead of processing inconsequential data, and, sometimes, bewilderment of the individuals intended to be helped. Yet, this cost may well be justified in particular cases.

This concludes our general discussion of scheduling strategies. Before passing on to the synchronization of processes, we consider briefly the implications of multiprocessing on scheduling.

Scheduling for Multiprocessing

At this point, the reader may wish to review Section 2.4 on multiprocessing systems. For our purposes here, we consider only systems having multiple central processors with identical capabilities and access to the same (common) resources, including main storage.

If tasks are assigned to specific processors, scheduling assumes the form of a general, well-researched problem. (See [Bru73].) With our assumptions, however, forcing a task to use but one processor is unjustified, and we therefore omit consideration of this problem.

In general, we can treat multiple CPUs in the environment we've described as indistinguishable resources to be allocated routinely as requested. The malfunction of a processor makes it distinguishable, certainly, but this poses system-dependent problems we choose not to discuss.

A problem that does confront us is *atomicity*, the uninterruptability of an operation. In a multiprocessing system, we must be cognizant of the fact that, insofar as hardware permits, two things can happen simultaneously. The dispatcher, therefore, must ensure that it does not allocate two central processors to the same task simultaneously. Locking — serializing operations on a common object — grows in importance in a multiprocessing system.

Process Synchronization

The serializing of operations with respect to some object or event of synchronization is a frequent requirement in all large, general-purpose operating systems. Dijkstra [Dij68a] has proposed that problems in synchronization be defined in terms of *semaphores*, variables with integral values and initial values S greater than or equal to zero. The initial value can be interpreted as a quantity of indistinguishable consumable resources. Two operations, P and V, and defined on semaphores. The P operation decrements S by 1 when S is or becomes nonnegative; that is, if S is negative, the issuing process is suspended until this is no longer true. The P operation corresponds to the consumption of one resource. The V operation always increments S by one and, if S becomes zero, causes some waiting process to resume execution, corresponding to the production of a resource. The resource in question may be viewed as a message from the process issuing the V operation to the process issuing the P operation.

Kosaraju [Kos73] has shown that some problems in synchronization cannot be realized using semaphores or, indeed, even Petri nets, as suggested by Patil

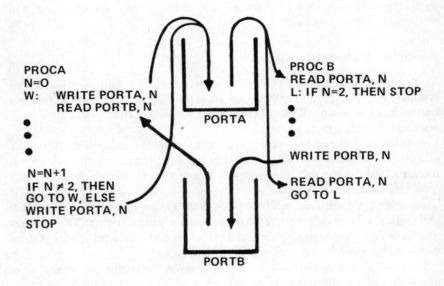

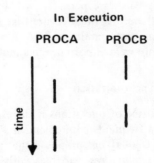

Figure 4.14. Synchronized Processes.

[Pat70]. Balzer [Bal71] has discussed communication with processes in a less theoretical context, using the notion of ports. A *port* is a medium for communication between cooperating processes, much like a semaphore.

In the practical case, designers of operating systems do succeed in providing mechanisms for communication between processes. These mechanisms differ from system to system, but most have these attributes in common:

1. All intercommunicating processes share knowledge — such as an address or a name — of some common object.
2. The object is a medium for the exchange of some information, at least an address of some other object, the contents of which are practically unconstrained.
3. Associated with the object of communication is some locking mechanism, preventing simultaneous access by more than one process.

This mechanism for communication is called a synchronizing device because, at the least, a message can tell a receiving process to resume execution. If two processes alternate sending messages to each other, using one such object for communication in each direction, and each attempts to receive a message immediately after it has sent one, the two processes never execute simultaneously but are synchronized with respect to each other.

To say that there is nothing more to task management than scheduling and synchronization would doubtless be unjustified. Yet these topics, certainly among the most important ones relating to the subject, have been the focus of our discussion. We proceed now to a discussion of collections of processes — jobs and steps — and the system's management of them.

4.7 MANAGEMENT OF JOBS AND STEPS

The user of an operating system communicates with it through a control language, an OSCL. The *job,* like the compilation in the case of a programming language, is the largest group of statements of the OSCL about which the individual can express himself in the language itself. Since a user may have something to say about a great many tasks, taken together as a unit, the term job defines an entity which may embrace many tasks. The same rationale leads us to define an entity intermediate in size, the *step.* A job comprises one or more steps and a step one or more tasks.

Because of the way the notions of job and step have been implemented in various operating systems, notably the large IBM operating systems for Systems/360 and 370, many attributes have come to be associated with the terms job and step. A job is:

1. A context for symbol definition (see Section 4.3).
2. A collection of interdependent steps.
3. A unit of accountability.
4. A sequence of JCL statements present in an input file beginning with one JOB statement and ending with the last statement preceding either another JOB statement or a null statement.

Analogous statements could be made about a step. These are not our concern here. We assume here that these groupings of tasks are useful and examine what functions might be and, in large IBM operating systems, are defined on and by them. We focus on the notions of job and step that permit us to give them scheduling attributes, including lists of required resources. Our principal topics are job scheduling and the housekeeping, especially with respect to the acquiring and releasing of resources, attendant on the management of jobs and steps.

Job Scheduling

In a uniprogramming operating system, jobs are executed one at a time. The job scheduling used for this kind of system is serial scheduling; in other words, a job is first presented to the computer, the computer starts the job, and, when that job has ended, the next job is allowed to come into the computer, and so on, until all the jobs have been executed. The goal of this particular type of operating system is to provide service for users. They do not have to maintain files entirely by their own programming, as they would if they did not have an operating system; the operating system handles the input-output operations and locates files, devices, or whatever other system resources are required. The user need not be concerned with the actual channel programming for input-output devices, since the operating system handles it. However, a serial system is a comparatively inefficient system. The time required for an input-output operation is appreciably more than the time required for a CPU operation, so that in a uniprogramming system, the central processor is often idle while input-output operations are going on.

In a multiprogramming system, we can still have serial scheduling; however, if we have the ability to run four jobs at a time, four jobs are read into the computer. Upon the completion of any one of these four jobs, a fifth job is allowed to come in its place, assuming there are sufficient resources for it, and so on. However, we still are scheduling jobs serially; that is, jobs are executed first-in-first-out (FIFO), in the order in which they are presented to the system. Job scheduling by priority is a different sort of scheme.

The priority job scheduler is a separate process of the operating system. The job scheduler in a priority scheduling system allows jobs to be presented to the rest of the operating system in the order of their priority. The user determines the job's priority and, in the system's control language, specifies what priority the job is to have; that is, the priority with which it goes into the system. There are various schemes of prioritizing in a fixed partition type of system such as System/370 OS/MFT or OS/VS1. Each partition accepts only members of certain job classes. If there are no members of a job class A available and a certain partition can accept only jobs of class A, that partition sits vacant even though there may be a waiting list of jobs to execute in other classes. Within a job class, the jobs are also arranged by a further priority, which is a numerical one. If a particular system recognizes priorities, the higher the priority a job is given, the faster it is passed from the priority scheduler to the operating system.

Scheduling is accomplish by the use of a directly accessed job queue. This job queue can be likened to a set of buckets. One of these buckets exists for each job class. The priority scheduler accepts all jobs which are available from the input reader and places the control language statements for these jobs in the appropriate class buckets. For example, let us assume the following situation: bucket A has ten jobs, bucket B has two jobs, bucket C has no jobs, and bucket D has two jobs. Taking the four-partition operating system we have mentioned, let us constrain each partition so that is accepts only one of the classes: partition 1 accepts class A jobs only, partition 2 accepts class B jobs only, partition 3 accepts class C jobs only, and partition 4 accepts class D jobs only. Assuming all jobs run the same length of time, we see that at no time is partition 3 used, because we have no class C jobs to begin with, and that after the two class D jobs run, that partition sits idle and we have the computer, in effect, running serial processing of the remaining class A jobs.

This problem is solved by assigning multiple classes to the partitions. The partitions accept jobs in the order in which the classes are assigned to them; for instance, if partition 2 has classes B, C, and D assigned to it, all B jobs are

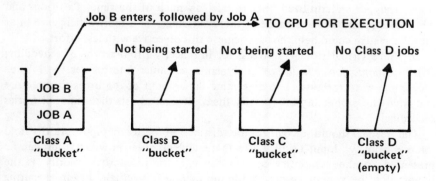

Figure 4.15. Detail of Priority Scheduler Input Queue.

executed, then all C jobs, and then all D jobs. We could hypothesize the following situation in a system with four partitions: that partition 1 would be assigned jobs of class A, B, C, and D, in that order; partition 2 would be assigned class B, C, D, and A jobs; partition 3 would be assigned class C, D, A, and B jobs; and partition 4 would be assigned D, A, B, and C jobs.

Note that classes cannot be assigned to partitions in a purely arbitrary manner. Jobs are assigned to a specific class because they have certain characteristics in common, such as resource requirements, that make them similar to one another for the system's purposes in scheduling. Were classes A and C to denote jobs requiring respectively, 50K bytes and 200K bytes, class C could not be assigned to a partition of only 50K bytes in size. The reverse assignment could be made, but would involve the disuse of 150K bytes every time a job of class A was assigned to a partition defined to process jobs of class C.

In our example, we see that partition 1 would execute only class A jobs, since there were ten of them; partition 2 would accept its two class B jobs, start accepting class C jobs, of which there were none anyway, and then accept the two class D jobs, if they were not already initiated. The B jobs probably would have been executed by the time partition 4 was done with its two class D jobs. Partitions 2 and 3 would be undoubtedly executing class A jobs, and the same argument applies to partition 4; in fact, parrion 4 would immediately start accepting class A jobs after the B and C jobs were completed.

We see that the user has a great amount of control over how he processes his jobs simply by the use of an appropriate arrangement of priorities and classes. However, in practice this becomes a little difficult, since there is often the problem of handling urgent jobs.

One objective a user of OS/370 MFT is expected to keep in mind is resource utilization. If partitions are defined in such a way as to permit the concurrent processing of a set of jobs such that either all or none of them use very few I/O operations, then either the computer's I/O equipment or its central processor, respectively, is underutilized, that is, idle for much of the time. Partitions and job classes permit the avoidance of these extremes. Still more intelligence built into the system could help the user achieve this objective with less effort.

In IBM's virtual storage systems, for instance, we find a type of scheduling called *dynamic job scheduling*. A dynamic scheduler interrogates the jobs as they come in to the system to determine the amount of resources they require and what the probability is of getting them. It then adjusts their input priorities accordingly.

The reader should recognize the distinction between input priority and internal priority. Input priority affects merely the order in which a job can be presented to the computing system for execution. Internal priority is the importance the system assigns to the job once it has actually begun executing within the system. The internal priority is what determines when a given process will receive control of the central processor for its turn with the system resources, as discussed in Section 4.4.

Another type of priority scheduling is called deadline scheduling. In this kind of scheduling, a job can be given a deadline by which time the job must have been completed. If it becomes evident that the job will not be completed by that time, the system raises the job's internal priority and, therefore, it uses more of the central processor's time until the job can be completed.

We have not really exhausted the topic of job scheduling. We have, however, given the student some idea of the relevant principles, of the problems involved and of some mechanisms designed to permit solution of those problems. We now turn our attention to the more mechanical aspects of job scheduling, the steps taken by an operating system before initiation and after termination of jobs and steps.

Housekeeping

At points in time, resources managed by operating systems are allocated to objects of one sort or another to be used for some set of purposes. Questions which confront the designer of an operating system are: What resources should be allocated to what objects? Upon the occurrence of what event? When should they be released? These questions are discussed in this section rather than in Section 4.1 because "to jobs and steps" is often part of the answer to the first of these questions.

That this is so should not be surprising. The process of resource allocation can be a very resource-consuming one itself, and a complex one. The less often the system undertakes it, the less overhead is endured as a result if resources are actually consumed or used by processes, and they are, why not consider allocating them to groups of processes, namely, steps and jobs?

Indeed, in the large IBM operating systems, while some resource allocation does take place dynamically, that is, in midtask, allocation is basically an interstep or interjob occurrence. Havender [Hav68] gives sound reasons for this in his discussion of deadlock avoidance for these systems. In this section, we consider the allocation of storage, I/O units, volumes, and files, directly or indirectly, to jobs and steps.

In virtual storage and fixed partition systems, the allocation of storage is clearly no problem. In OS/MVT, as [Hav68] points out, storage participates in the ordering of resources, which is crucial to the avoidance of deadlocks. This fact dictates at what point during interstep processing storage is allocated. How much storage is dictated by control language statements or default values for parameters of the control language. The determination of which storage is to be allocated is part of the allocation process.

The allocation of units to steps is in many systems a rather straightforward process. Complications arise when directly accessible (DA) volumes are considered together with the units on which they are to be mounted. This is the case in large IBM operating systems and these systems provide the basis for our discussion of the subject.

The volume is central to our discussion. A programmer states, via control language statements, which files are required for a step, but, insofar as interstep resource allocation is concerned, the identities of the DA volumes on which these files (will) reside are of prime interest. The system must ensure that the step runs in such an environment that it can always gain access to the volumes it needs. This is done by assigning units to contain the volumes.

Volumes are said to have attributes of two kinds: mount and use. A volume is said to be *permanently resident* if it can always be found mounted on the same unit. A drum has this attribute for physical reasons, the volume containing supervisory routines for logical reasons, and other volumes simply because someone so instructed the system. These distinctions are irrelevant to the basic fact of the volume's permanent residence. A volume is reserved if the system has been told not to order its removal from the unit on which it is mounted. Volumes neither permanently resident nor reserved have a mount attribute of *removable.*

If the system is told that a volume is *private,* the system cannot arbitrarily select that volume to contain a new file for which no residence is explicitly specified. A *public* volume may be so used by the system for files forbidden to persist beyond the life of a single job. Units containing removable private or public volumes become available for use by other volumes as soon as the mounted volumes cease to be needed by active jobs. *Storage* volumes, which are not permitted to have a mount attribute of removable, may be used by the system without restriction. These volumes may be considered a logical extension of the system's storage capacity.

The algorithms for allocating units and volumes are greatly complicated by such considerations as the sharing of volumes containing multivolume files and deferred mounting of volumes not immediately needed by a step being initiated. All the problems involved, however, yield to graph-theoretic approaches.

The allocation and freeing of units are basically interstep events, but they can also be accomplished dynamically, that is, within steps. Table 4.2 shows a complex allocation problem and its solution.

The only relevant allocation of files occurs on a interjob basis. A user may specify use of a file in such a way, for example, updating it, that concurrent use by another job must be prevented. Such a specification has in IBM systems a job-long effect.

The management of jobs and steps has been viewed in terms of job selection and the functions attendant on interstep and interjob transition. Note that the notion of step selection would apply to a system that permitted one to specify

Table 4.2.

Files

Name	Organization	Operations	Residence	Size (cyls.)
FILEA	Sequential	Read	333 (disk)	25
FILEB	Sequential	Wr., Rd., Delete	any medium	25
FILEC	Sequential	Wr., Rd., Delete	any dir. acc.	25
FILED	Indexed	Read	333,444 (disk)	100
FILEE	Sequential	Wr., Rd., Delete	any medium	15
FILEF	Sequential	Rd., Add rec'ds	222,555,333 other disk	100

Units

Address	Type	Space Left (cyls.)	Mount Attr.	Use Attr.	Vol. Assigned
1C1	drum	0	Perm. Res.	Public	AAA
191	disk	20	Perm. Res.	Public	111
192	disk	30	Reserved	Storage	222
193	disk	—	Removable	Public	333
291	disk	—	Removable	Public	444
292	disk	—	Removable	Private	555
181	tape	—	Removable	Private	Scratch

Solution

File Name	Units Used for Access
FILEA	193
FILEB	181
FILEC	192
FILED	193,291
FILEE	191
FILEF	192,292,193 (292 used for mounting of subsequent volumes)

asynchronous execution of steps, that is, steps not strictly ordered by sequence of execution. If such a system is designed, it nevertheless presents no noteworthy obstacles and we choose not to consider it.

This concludes our chapter on job and task management. This chapter has viewed the problems of job and task management largely in terms of the management of resources. It is altogether fitting and proper that we do this, for it is only by consuming and using resources that jobs and tasks can accomplish useful work.

Having looked at the objects defined to represent the work the system does, we next turn our attention to the objects upon which work is performed: data.

QUESTIONS

1. Name four queue management algorithms. Give existing operating systems as examples of the use of three of them.
2. Give examples of three linear dispatcher types of operating system.
3. Construct a main storage scheme for a multiprogramming system which does not use fixed partitions or variable regions.
4. State three virtual storage management schemes and give two examples of each.
5. List three positive effects and three negative effects caused by the implementation of virtual storage in an operating system.
6. In your own words, give an explanation of the working set concept.
7. Explain the term "virtual I/O" in your own words, and give four applications of its use.
8. What is a processor and why is it important to operating system designers?
9. Discuss the effects on addressed storage management of the relocation mechanism(s) in one computer with which you are familiar.
10. For the LUFO (longest-unused-first-out) out-paging algorithm, discuss (*a*) its rationale, and (*b*) the behavior of a program for which LUFO might be the least advantageous method.
11. Discuss the effect of storing a matrix in row order (first all of row 1, then all of row 2, and so on) and processing it in column order if the number of bytes needed to store one row is equal to the size of one page in a virtual storage system. If you cannot do so yourself, get up a group and thrash out the answer.
12. Describe diagrammatically the I/O configuration of a computing system and indicate where you would place system files and why.
13. Match the listed criteria for task scheduling (p. 178) to the subgoals listed in the preceding paragraph. Explain your answer.

PROBLEMS

1. The P and V operators defined to facilitate synchronization may be used to provide mutual exclusion of two or more processes in some critical region in which only one process should access a resource. Develop a flow chart using semaphores and two processes to provide mutual exclusion by ensuring that only one process at a time may be in its critical region. After completing its critical region, each process will be occupied for some arbitrary time doing noncritical activities. The flow chart must guarantee that mutual exclusion without deadlock is provided, regardless of the timing or frequency of operations in either process. The P and V operators may be assumed to be uninterruptible; for example, the changing of the value, testing the result, and queuing are all done without any interruption by another process. Since no real computers have the P and V operations implemented as machine instructions, how would you program to ensure that these operations could be carried out?

2. The two flow charts shown here are intended to provide mutual exclusion in the use of resource X by two processes. The Boolean variables P1 and P2 are supposed to be flags which control access to resource X to provide the mutual exclusion. Assume that the operations within any block in the flow chart are not interruptible, but otherwise that the operations by the two processes may be carried out in any arbitrary order. Does either flow chart provide mutual exclusion without any other difficulties? If so, show it. If not, show why not.

3. Deadlock situations may be displayed graphically if the resource needs of processes are known. The following data concern two processes needing resources A and B:

Process 1		Process 2	
% Done	Resource Needs	% Done	Resource Needs
0–10	none	0–20	none
10–20	A	20–30	A
20–30	none	30–40	B
30–40	B	40–50	none
40–50	A and B	50–60	A
50–60	B	60–70	A and B
60–70	A	70–80	B
70–80	A and B	80–90	A
80–90	B	90–100	none
90–100	none		

The values of percentage done cannot decrease for either process. Prepare a graph having percentage done for process 1 as one coordinate and percentage done for process 2 as the other. On this graph show regions which have the following states:

a. No resource contention exists.
b. Remove contention exists, but the requirements may be satisfied by making one process wait.
c. Deadlock.
d. Unfeasible.

4. One method for deadlock prevention is to make all users state their resource requirements in advance by declaring their maximum need for each resource before being allowed to start execution. The users must also request actual allocation of the resources one unit at a time. Deciding whether to grant such a request is done by determining if deadlock is possible after granting the request. If so, granting the request is delayed until some other change in the status of the resources makes allocation possible without the possibility of deadlock. To check the possibility of

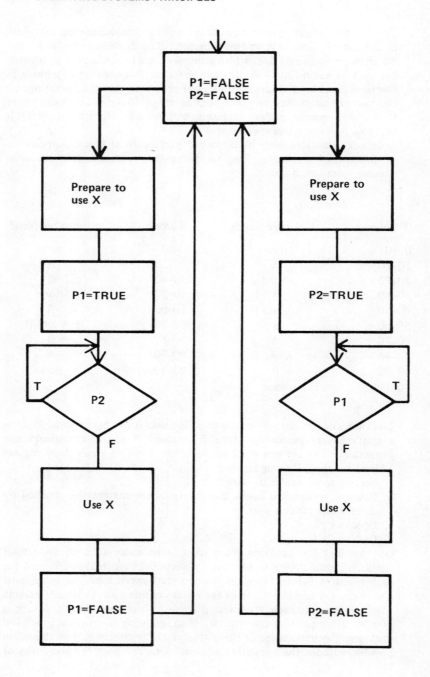

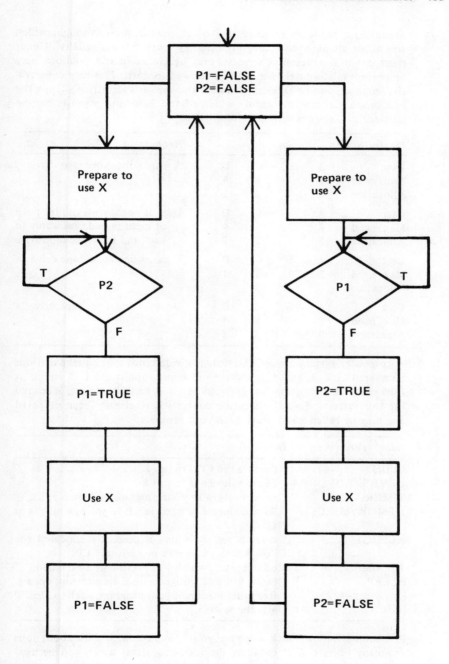

deadlock, a sequence of execution of all present users is sought which will allow all users to finish, even if they must execute serially. Under these conditions, resource requests may be evaluated and deadlock may be prevented absolutely for all users allowed to start. This very conservative method, due to Dijkstra, is called the banker's algorithm. Using the banker's algorithm, determine which of the following requests can be granted for a system with eight tape drives:

Present State					Request
User	A	B	C	D	A wants one more tape drive
Max. need	2	3	5	4	
Allocation	1	1	2	2	
User	A	B	C	D	User E with a maximum need
Max. need	2	3	5	4	of eight tape drives wants to
Allocation	1	1	2	2	start and have one tape drive
User	A	B	C	D	B wants one more tape drive
Max. need	2	3	5	4	
Allocation	0	2	3	2	
User	A	B	C	D	D wants one more tape drive
Max. need	2	3	5	4	
Allocation	0	2	3	2	

5. A computer system has a CPU; storage divided into four equal partitions numbered 1, 2, 3, and 4; and three I/O devices numbered 1, 2, and 3. A flow chart of a program for interrupt handling and dispatching is desired for this system. Several allocation routines have already been prepared and may be called as subroutines to your program:

Name (Parameter)	Description
CPU(J)	Allocates the CPU to job J.
DEVICE(J,D)	Allocates device D to job J.
TIMER(T)	Causes a return to your program in T time units.
MEMORY(J,P,C)	Allocates memory partition P to job J, which is of class C.
XCPU(J)	Suspends job J, which is presently allocated the CPU. Another job may be allocated CPU.
RESUME(J)	Restarts job J, which was previously suspended.
SLEEP	Deactivates your program until an interrupt occurs. After initialization of your program, a call to SLEEP starts the system.

A communication block supplies your program with data about jobs requiring resources. It contains the following data, which can be used without being defined by your program:

TIME — the current time in microseconds.

DEVNO — a device number for a device requiring a resource.

JOBID — a job identifier for the job currently requiring service.

CLASS — a job characteristic which is supplied with jobs entering the system. The values range from 1 to 4. All jobs with the same class have generally similar characteristics.

Requests for resources activate your program (after a call to SLEEP) at several different points by interrupts, as follows:

1. An active job requires the CPU. Unless DEVNO=-2, the device DEVNO has just completed an operation and can be reallocated.
2. An active job requires the device DEVNO. The CPU has just completed a period of operation and can be reallocated.
3. A job has just terminated. Both the CPU and a memory partition may be reallocated.
4. A timer interval has just expired.
5. A new job has just arrived in the system and must be assigned to memory or queued to start later.

Any attempt to allocate a busy resource will be identified as an error and the run will be aborted. When a job is allocated to storage by a call to MEMORY, it automatically starts requesting other resources. A job keeps its partition until it terminates. A job starts with a CPU request and alternates between CPU and I/O devices until it finishes with a CPU request. After the last CPU period has completed, the job requests termination. Two service routines may be used by your program to queue and dequeue resource requests which must be deferred until later:

Name (Parameter)	Description
ADD(J,Q,PR)	Adds job J to queue Q with priority PR. A job can be in only one queue at a time.
DELETE(J,Q)	Deletes job J from queue Q. If queue Q is empty, an error handler aborts the run.

A job must either be in a queue or allocated to a resource. Otherwise, the job will be lost in some undefined status. Your program must keep adequate information about each job to ensure that it can be run correctly.

6. Below are described eight classes of jobs. Construct a partitioning of a 192K area of storage and assign classes to partitions. Tell whether or not your scheme convinces you that a partitioned system is practical and why you feel that way.

Job Class	Size of Job	% I/O of Boundness	% of All Jobs
A	50	7	3
B	42	22	28
C	100	1	18
D	92	3	8
E	67	15	2
F	25	10	20
G	40	28	20
H	80	5	1

5
Data Management

Thus far, our discussions have concerned the incidental functions of an operating system and those functions which deal with the environment for the execution of programs. These programs, however, can accomplish little of value without data on which to operate. The management — input, output, storage, and control — of data is the subject of this chapter.

The first four sections of this chapter focus on data as they are stored in forms sensible only by the system. They deal respectively with where, what, how, and why data are stored, that is, with the media on which data can be stored, the formats which can be used for that storage, the operations involved in storage and retrieval, and a particular and important category of data: the data base. The last sections are devoted to data as they enter or leave the realm of human sensibility, that is, to I/O equipment having interfaces with people and its use, and to the management of programs as data.

5.1 SECONDARY STORAGE MANAGEMENT

In discussing the media used for the storage of data, we concern ourselves first with the physical characteristics of the media and the consequences of these characteristics. We then examine what the operating system must do to exploit them. These topics lay the foundation for the discussion of specific file organizations in the following section.

Hardware Considerations

The most basic distinction made among types of media for storing data intended for only the system's use is between those which require that all data on a given unit of storage be accessed serially or sequentially, and those which do not. A unit of storage is called a volume. A volume, a device containing that volume, or the data recorded on that volume, may be either sequentially accessed or directly accessed (DA). The term random access occurs synonymously in the literature for direct access. Below, we first consider magnetic tape, the only significant (if not the only) medium accessed sequentially. The remainder of this discussion deals with directly accessed media, of which there are many types.

A volume, called a reel, of magnetic tape is long (for example, 2400 feet) and narrow (1/2 inch). These attributes determine its characteristics as a recording medium. The width of the tape accommodates a single character or byte per unit length — six or eight bits of data plus check bits — and bytes are recorded at a density of up to a few thousand per inch. Physical records are separated by relatively long (say 1/4 inch) interrecord gaps. With some systems, reels of tape can be read either forward or backward.

The tolerances and error-recovery techniques involved in processing magnetic tape on some systems are such that one cannot overlay an existing record with another of the same or even of lesser length.

These physical characteristics of magnetic tape lead to certain logical restrictions and suggest certain techniques for its processing. For example, it is clearly impossible on some systems to update in place. Labels — records descriptive of files — are often placed before (leaders) and, optionally, after (trailers) files on the medium. Multiple files on a single reel must be delimited by unique, distinguishable recordings, called tape marks or end-of-file (EOF) markers, to separate them from one another. Data relevant to an entire reel must be placed at the beginning of the reel for expeditious retrieval.

Labels on the reels of magnetic tape are subject to standardization in the data processing industry and contain many types of data. Typical of these data are an identification of the reel (volume id), a date when the data on the reel are no longer needed (expiration date), data about the files on the reel, and, in a trailer label, a check sum, a sum of some field in all records of a file, modulo the word length of the system. The last item is indicative of the relative unreliability of magnetic tape as a recording medium. Yet, totally unlabeled tapes are very commonly used.

Labels, on tape and direct-access volumes, are used by the system to identify the volumes, and to learn what volumes have been mounted by the operator without the system's direction and whether the operator has mounted requested

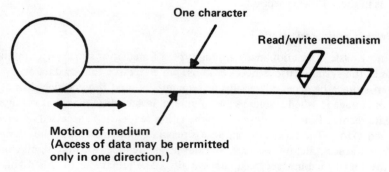

Figure 5.1. Logical View of a Reel of Magnetic Tape.

volumes as directed. Section 6.2 discusses the use made of file descriptions contained in labels. The access methods described in Section 5.3 are the routines of the system which make use of those data — record size and format, blocking factor, and so on.

Directly accessed volumes may be of many types. The most useful classifications of these distinguish between:

1. Volumes accessed by fixed read/write heads.
2. Volumes accessed by movable heads.

and among

a. Volumes accessed in place and wedded to a unit.
b. Volumes accessed in place, but movable from unit to unit.
c. Volumes which can be so moved and are even transported within a unit for accessing.

The following discussion is limited to drums (volumes of type 1*a*), disks (type 2*b*), and magnetic strips (type 2*c*). These are the only combinations of types extant, but other combinations are theoretically possible and our categorization helps to illuminate the effects these volumes' characteristics have on their use by operating systems.

A drum is a rotating cylinder whose recording surfaces are circles having their center at the drum's axis of rotation (center) and their radius equal to that of the drum. Each circle can be accessed by one or more heads fixed in position just beyond the drum's surface.

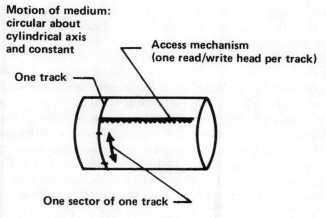

Motion of medium:
circular about
cylindrical axis
and constant

Access mechanism
(one read/write head per track)

One track

One sector of one track

Figure 5.2. Logical View of a Drum.

A disk volume, or pack, resembles a stack of phonograph records fastened at even intervals to their common spindle. The flat surfaces of the "records" have circular recording surfaces concentric with the disk pack and each other. They are accessed by heads which move between the "records" toward and away from the spindle in a radial direction. The heads move into position for data transfer, and the disk always rotates when mounted on a unit and ready for access. (A disk accessed by one fixed head per concentric recording surface [track] is logically indistinguishable from a drum.)

A magnetic card or strip is a thin rectangular solid. For access, it is transported from its storage location within a unit to a cylinder around which it is wrapped to form a shape like that of a wedding ring. Movable heads then assume positions such as those of the heads which service a drum, but not every recording surface (parallel to the card or strip's longer side and therefore circular when accessed) is accessed simultaneously.

The types 1 and 2 determine what data may appropriately be placed on a volume by an operating system. Volumes of type 1 contain data the system uses continually, such as the system's programs or pages of virtual storage. Other volumes are used for data of less constant use or a more transitory nature. (See Chapter 3.)

The types a, b, and c determine speed of access, respectively, from the fastest to the slowest, for reasons which should be clear. Time is required for heads to move into place; even more time is needed to transport recording media. The volumes most quickly accessible are used for paging; those most slowly accessible are used for less frequently needed and more voluminous data. The latter aspect is related to a facet of our discussion not yet mentioned: the more slowly a volume can be accessed, the less it is likely to cost per character. Volumes of type c tend to have far larger capacities than those of type b, without proportionally greater cost. Data transfer rate – the rate at which a record can be transferred to or from main storage – tends to be roughly proportional to access rate, for technological reasons.

The disk provides the prototype for addressing DA volumes. All recording surfaces equidistant from the center of a disk collectively form a cylinder. This unit is important because all the heads accessing a disk move in unison and, therefore, an entire cylinder can be accessed without moving a head. Each recording surface (two per "record") of a cylinder is a track. Drums, mass storage (cartridges of magnetic tape), and magnetic cards or strips are also said to have cylinders and tracks and these have similar accession characteristics. (A section, $1/n$th of a cylinder, of a drum is logically equivalent to a disk's track.)

On tracks, there are records, and between records there are gaps. Recording is precise enough that a record can always be overwritten with another of the same size.

A record on a DA volume may have a key, a record identifier, on which separate I/O operations are defined. Most usefully, if all the records in some

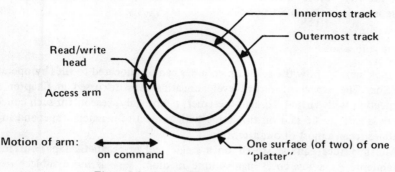

Figure 5.3. Logical View of a Disk Volume.

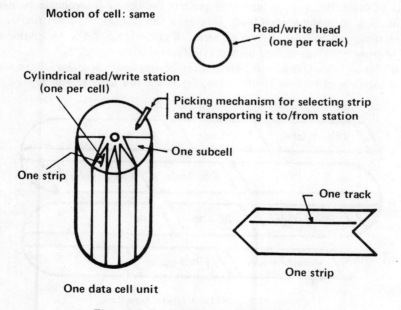

Figure 5.4. Logical View of a Magnetic Strip.

area of a volume are sorted by their keys, a single I/O operation can be used to find the first record with a key greater than or equal to a given key [Min72]. More is made of this in Section 5.3.

Space Allocation

We look next at how the space on volumes can be allocated to files by operating systems. The aspect of record-level allocation was discussed in Chapter 3 in connection with virtual storage, the chief, if not only, reason for such concern. There is little to be said on this topic with respect to magnetic tape, and so DA volumes receive most of our attention.

Multiple files can be stored on a single reel of magnetic tape, but this is infrequent. As a low-cost, high-volume medium, tape is more subject to the reverse treatment: multireel files. In either case, labels — reel header, file header, file trailer, and reel trailer — carry the necessary control data.

DA volumes lend themselves much better to the interleaving of files. For one thing, each record on a DA volume has a unique address (cylinder, track, record) which can easily be used for access. For another, separate segments of noncontiguously stored files can be accessed without great delay, that is, without passing all intervening data under a head.

That interleaving is convenient is fortunate because the cost of DA volumes argues strongly against leaving large portions of them unused (as happens with reels of magnetic tape). Interleaving permits the use of DA volumes by many small files of varying persistence (lifetimes from creation to destruction or expiration) and by files of varying sizes. A growing file on a DA volume can easily grow into areas vacated by small files recently destroyed.

If files on DA volumes were permitted to occupy space in undisciplined ways, gross inefficiencies could result. Thus, for much the same reason regions and

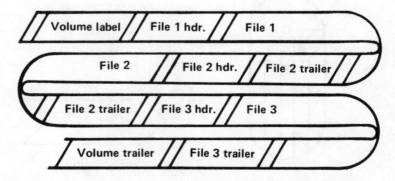

Figure 5.5. Multifile Magnetic Tape Reel.

partitions are employed in main storage (see Chapter 4), constraints are placed on the use by files of space on DA volumes. A file in the System/360 and 370 family of operating systems is permitted to occupy no more than 16 separate areas, called *extents*. Program libraries of those systems, partitioned data sets, are much more tightly constrained. These are really bound collections of sequential files sharing a common extent descriptor, called a directory.

In these IBM operating systems, a DA volume is said to have a label, but file labels are called data set control blocks (DSCBs) and form collectively a volume's table of contents (VTOC). One DSCB describes unused space on the volume and one the VTOC. The management of space on a DA volume is accomplished by manipulating DSCBs.

Users may describe requirements for space for a file on a DA volume in terms of units such as tracks, cylinders, or, more naturally, bytes. They may specify an initial size and an increment (size of a secondary extent) by which the allocation is to grow as the file grows. The system may impose a limit, say 15, on the number of times the allocation of a file can be extended.

One topic remains to be covered in this section: preformatting. The low-order component of an address on a DA volume is often record number. Each track thus resembles a sequential file insofar as addressing is concerned. In a file with direct organization, one may wish to store a record other than the first on a track before its predecessors on that track exist. This can happen because a record's address is a function of its key. This can be done only if dummy records are present to justify the calculated record number. Rather than create dummy records as needed, one can create all possible dummy records before storing the first record of a newly created file with direct organization. This function of secondary storage management is called preformatting.

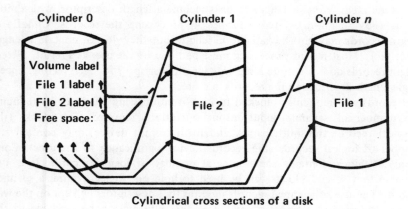

Cylindrical cross sections of a disk

Figure 5.6. Multifile Disk.

This section has discussed the media used for secondary storage, explained their critical characteristics and shown how these influence operating systems, and covered certain aspects of managing the space and data on the media. Having taken care of the media, we proceed to the message, the files themselves.

5.2 FILE ORGANIZATION

A file is a collection of logically related records treated as a unit. There is a connotation that a file is located physically on a secondary storage device, although some files used by an operating system may be partially resident in the computer's main storage. File sizes vary from a few records to any size desired. A file is usually thought of as providing a permanent repository for information, but some files are temporary and are called scratch, or scratchpad, files. The records constituting a file may consist of any data items a user may wish to have stored, but usually a file is thought of as containing records that have some characteristics in common and are stored in some consistent way. In some cases, descriptors are attached to files or records to identify them and provide information on their contents and characteristics. These descriptors may or may not be considered part of the file, depending on the nature of the use of the file. A typical descriptor would be a tape label, an end of file indicator, or an interrecord gap. Descriptors occupy space on the device and have to be considered when allocating space for a file.

The records which make up a file can have a variety of characteristics which are of concern to operating systems. Because not all kinds of records are permitted on all devices, the operating system must be able to determine the kind of records in a file. A file label kept with the file is one convenient way to do this. Three record-length formats are commonly recognized: fixed, variable, and undefined. Variable-length records include a length descriptor, which must be used by operating system routines in processing the records. Undefined-length records may also be variable in length, but they do not contain a length descriptor. Most record processing must be done by the user as a result. Fixed-length records do not require a separate length descriptor for each record, since a single length describes all the records in a file.

Records are frequently blocked to improve processing efficiency by reducing the number of separate input/output operations required. The blocks (the physical records transmitted back and forth from a device) may contain any number of logical records (the records having significance to the user). Commonly, a block contains some integral number of logical records. It is also possible that several blocks can be used to hold one logical record, a spanned record. The use of spanned records requires that descriptors be kept on the way logical records are segmented, and that this information be available to the operating system. The combination of blocking and spanned records allows the block size to be chosen to give the best device performance and the logical record size to be chosen for the convenience of the programmer.

The remainder of this section is divided into seven parts, one for each of the six file organizations listed below and one for further comments on the topic. This list includes, for each organization, a brief statement of why it might be used for a file:

1. Sequential — a file is always processed in its entirety and remains of constant size or grows only at its end.
2. Direct — additions to (or deletions from) a file are frequent and it is never processed sequentially.
3. Partitioned — a set of sequential files, for example, object modules, that have similar characteristics.
4. Indexed — rapid access to individual, randomly selected records of a file is essential, but the file may be processed sequentially in its entirety with some frequency.
5. Virtual — a file has practically the same attributes as one with indexed organization, but is processed by OS/VS [IBM9].
6. List — a file is processed sequentially, but suffers frequent insertions or deletions.

Inverted and hierarchical organizations are treated in the last part of this section.

Sequential Organization

The basic constraints on the organization of files are derived from the characteristics of the storage devices and media used to contain the files. Sequential devices, in which the next record to be accessed is physically adjacent to the present record, naturally lead to a sequential organization of the data on the recording medium by having each record have a distinct predecessor and successor. The most obvious examples are files on paper or magnetic tape, card files as processed by the usual card reader/punch device, and print files. Direct-access devices, in which the next record to be retrieved is specified by its location, naturally lead to a file organization in which the physical location of the next record relative to the location of the present record is irrelevant. The most obvious example of this kind of organization is data stored in the computer main storage.

In some files, such as a print file, the file organization is firmly locked to device characteristics. In other cases, the distinction is not so clear. For example, data present in a direct-access file may be accessed sequentially by specifying that the successive locations accessed are adjacent to each other. A magnetic tape file that can be processed by a tape drive capable of (1) rewinding or

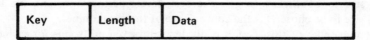

Key	Length	Data

Figure 5.7. Record on Disk with Key.

backspacing and (2) updating a previous record, could be programmed to act like a direct-access file in the sense that any record can be read or written next. Normally, this would not be done for a tape file because of the probable excessive amount of rewinding and nonproductive reading to be done to obtain the desired record. An IBM 2314 movable-head disk does a seek operation to find the correct head location. This is a direct-access operation in that the head location may be specified by an address. Once the head has been positioned correctly, the desired record is located by sequentially examining the descriptors or keys of each record until the correct record is found. The actual access is a combination of direct access and sequential access, so that the device can be used as either a direct-access or a sequential device.

Each logical record in a file may be thought of as having a key which identifies the record and serves as a basis for inserting it into the file or retrieving it from the file. For sequential files on a sequential device, the key is inherent in the physical structure of the file and is merely the location in the file established when the record was added to the file. In a sequential file maintained by pointers, the key may still be inherent in the file structure as the relative record number counted from the beginning of the file, but the key may change if an item is inserted in the file.

In some cases, the key of a record is all or part of the data of the record, an embedded key. As an example, in a personnel file maintained in alphabetical order, the names in the file constitute the keys, and the other data in the file are not considered part of the key. In this case, maintaining the file in alphabetical order makes it a sequential file based on this key.

Direct Organization

To establish a direct-access file, users must provide some means for transforming the key for their records to a location in the physical device. The location, or bucket, may hold more than one record. Occasionally, a key might serve directly to determine the location, if the number of unique keys equals the number of available locations, but this case is rare. More usually, some function is used to calculate the location of the data from the key. This technique is frequently referred to as randomizing. It is the same as the hash addressing technique described in Section 1.4. The division method was found to be one of the best in an experimental study [Lum71b]. In this method, the key is regarded as

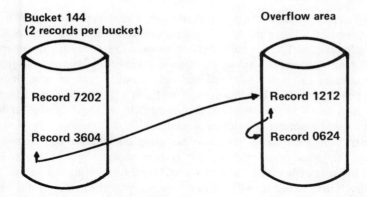

Hashing algorithm (very poor): first two digits multiplied by last two digits
Collision-handling routine: chain to overflow area

Figure 5.8. Direct-access Organization.

a binary number and is converted to a location by modulo division by a binary number equal to the number of available locations. The method works best if the divisor is prime or at least does not contain any small factors.

Webb [Web72] distinguishes between a hash coding function (HCF), the randomizing method we have just discussed, and a collision handling routine (CHR), which is used when the HCF yields an unacceptable result, that is, the address of a bucket filled with records other than the one which is sought or to be placed. His model has demonstrated that the choices of HCF and CHR are not independent and that the division method HCF is inferior to others for some choices of a CHR. The optimum CHR in this case is the quadratic quotient method due to Bell, wherein if k is the key, d the chosen divisor, and $k = q/d + H_1(k)$ for $0 \leqslant H_1(K) < d$, then the ith slot tried for $i \geqslant 2$ is

$$H_i(k = H_{i-1} + (q \cdot k^2)$$

Alternatively, a distinct area may be used for records which are the victims of collisions, but such an overflow area has been shown not to be of value.

In addition to the elemental sequential and direct-access organizations, several other file organizations represent combinations of characteristics of the elemental file organizations.

Partitioned Organization

The term *partitioned data set* is used by IBM to refer to a file consisting of any number of sequentially organized members. The records composing each member must have common physical and logical characteristics so that they can be described by a single set of defining parameters. Thus, once the file is open, this single set of defining parameters can be used to retrieve any member of the file. The most common uses of partitioned files are for libraries of commonly used programs and data. A partitioned file is usable only on disk. It may be stored on magnetic tape or other storage media by a process known as unloading, which is done by utility programs, but it must by restored to disk, or loaded, before it may be accessed by the usual methods.

A partitioned file has a directory indicating the location and name of each member. The location of each member relative to the origin of the file is used, so that the entire file may be moved without need for altering the directory. The directory is maintained in collating sequence order by the names of the members and is located at the beginning of the space allocated for the partitioned file. The directory consists of a number of blocks containing the entries. Each directory block also contains a key which is the highest name present in the block to facilitate searching the directory for a particular name. The last entry in the directory contains all 1's in the name field.

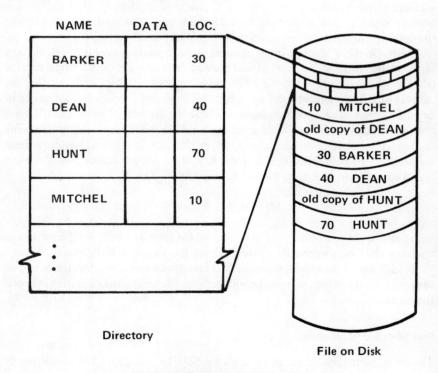

Figure 5.9. Partitioned Organization.

A partitioned file can be seen to be a variation of sequential organization. A saving of space is effected by not having to keep separate record characteristics with each member and by being able to use only one entry in the volume table of contents for the device. Balancing this are the time required to access the directory and to search it as well as the space required for the directory.

Indexed Organization

An indexed sequential file is basically a file in which keyed records are physically arranged in sequential fashion on a direct-access device. However, an index allows locating records anywhere in the file without reading or skipping through the entire file from the beginning. Since the file is physically a sequential file, it may be retrieved or added to at the end by sequential means. The use of the index allows retrieval, deleting, adding, and updating as for a direct-access file. Seen in this way, the indexed sequential file may be thought of as having both sequential and direct organizations.

Ghosh and Senko [Gho69] have shown that sparse indexes, those with entries for less than every record in a file, can be as efficient as more voluminous dense indexes. In this case, the same facility of a control unit to search for a particular key, used for fast searching of an index, is also used in searching for the desired record.

For some files, multiple levels of indexing might prove desirable. Each index serves to provide pointers to the next, until the desired record is located. This can be practical only where separate channels are used for each level of index, just as a separate channel may be desirable for index and records. Alternatively, a cylinder index may reside on one track of a cylinder and serve as the lowest level of index for all records on the cylinder, thus minimizing arm movement. An index to cylinder indexes may even fit in main storage, enhancing efficiency.

One of the complications involved in maintaining an indexed sequential file has to do with inserting a new record. Since insertion in a sequential file requires data movement, a considerable amount of data movement may be required to add new records. To minimize data movement, an overflow area can be used. As implemented by IBM in OS/VS, the data movement necessary to insert a record is restricted to one track and additions beyond that point force records into an overflow area in order of arrival.

Alternatively, records can be chained so that each points to the next. An insertion still requires the writing of two records and an extra record may have to be read to find a desired record, but this may be the most efficient organization for some files. If an overflow area, used as described above, is served by a separate channel, frequent insertions may not have a great adverse effect on performance. When such an effect becomes unbearable, it may be practical in some cases to recreate the file [Cha69a], for example, on Sunday, or a holiday, when it is not being used.

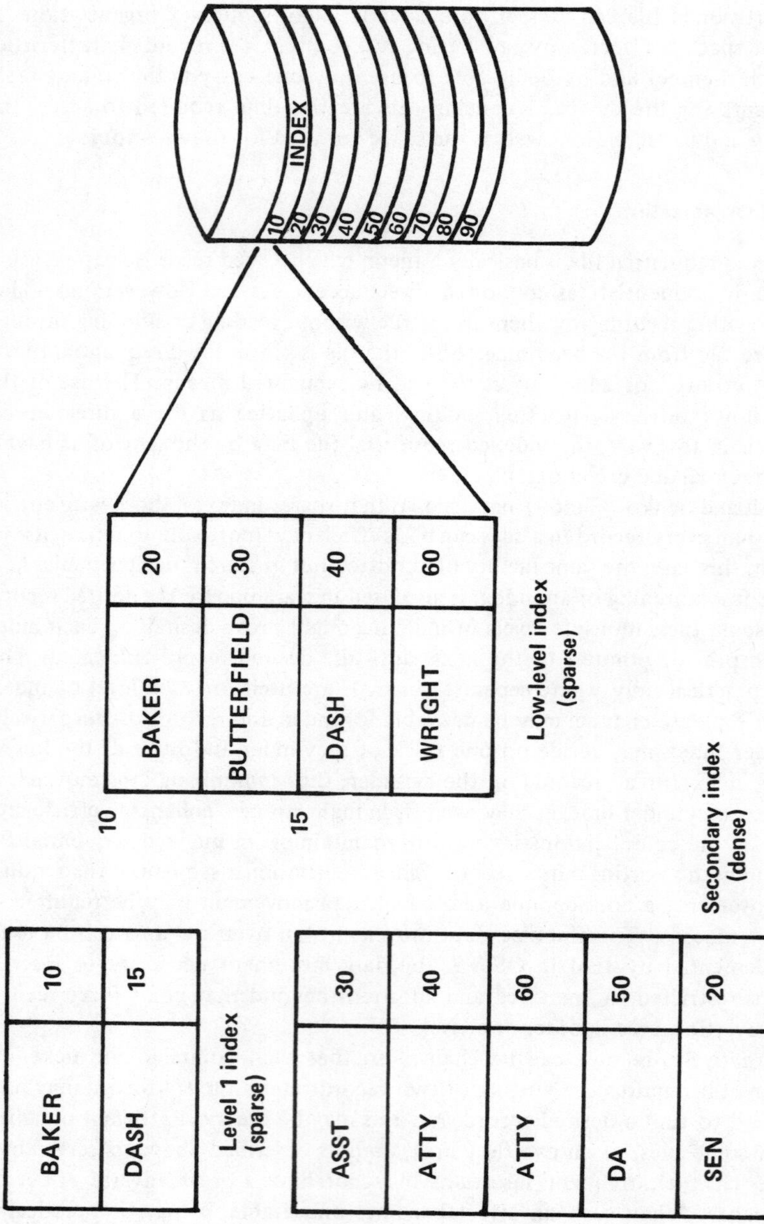

Figure 5.10. Indexed Organization.

Records of variable length can be inserted into indexed files with chaining into overflow areas more easily than into any other type of file. Even so, a system may not permit such an awkward use of data.

It is often desirable to be able to locate needed records by more than one key. No extant medium facilitates secondary indexing, but secondary indexes are nonetheless commonly employed, say, to locate a record for either John Doe or 267-58-4007 in a personnel file, depending on the information available to the application program. Lum and Ling [Lum71] have done considerable work in the area and have formulated objective criteria for determining whether or not a secondary index should be created. Secondary indexes which point directly to records must, of course, be dense, but a sparse secondary index could be used at a higher level. Of course, all secondary indexes on a file must be updated whenever a record is added to or deleted from the indexed file.

Virtual Organization

A virtual storage file organization is used by IBM in OS/VS [IBM9]. This is basically an indexed organization, but one uniquely adapted to the virtual storage environment of OS/VS. A direct-access device is used to hold the file in a virtual storage space. Records may be inserted in the file in the order of their addition (entry-sequence) or in collating sequence order by their keys (key sequence). The records may be retrieved by byte address relative to the beginning of the file, by relative record number or by key. The key-sequenced files include an index, which may contain one or more levels, as required by the size of the file. Data in a virtual storage file are stored in a fixed-length area called a control interval. The control interval must be larger than the largest data record. Information on the number, size, and organization of the contained data records is kept in each control interval. The index in the virtual storage file points to the control interval containing a data record. The data records in a control interval may be blocked or unblocked and of fixed or variable length.

The virtual storage file organization bears an obvious similarity to the indexed sequential file organization; for example, both allow sequential or direct access to the file. Conceptually, the virtual storage file exists in a storage space addressable by byte, so that the file organization is device-independent. An indexed sequential file exists on a direct-access device whose addresses are device-dependent. The entry-sequenced virtual storage file has no keys and is analogous to an ordinary sequentially organized file. The same access method (described in Section 5.3) is used for both entry-sequenced and key-sequenced virtual storage files.

Location		Next
10	ABLE	15
11	CHARLIE	14
12	FOX	16
13	EASY	12
14	DOG	13
15	BAKER	11
16	GLADYS	0

Figure 5.11. List Organization.

List Organization

The list-processing techniques described in Section 1.4 may be used to create files having any desired organization. By inclusion of pointer fields with each record, the immediate neighbors of a record may be specified. For example, a sequential file may be created by having each data item in the file contain pointers to its predecessors, successors, or both. A file may then be retrieved by starting with its first record and retrieving or accessing records in the order specified by the pointers. Techniques like this are best implemented on direct-access devices. The records for a file need not all be on the same device, or even the same kind of device, if the pointers are sufficiently indicative. Any technique like list-processing must be known to the operating system if the operating system is to move or process the files using it.

Other Organizations

The list-processing techniques also allow the establishment of inverted files [Dod69]. In these files, the records are kept on a secondary storage device in any desired order. A file consists of all the records plus an auxiliary list containing the locations of all the records having the attributes desired. For example, in personnel files, the records for one employee might all be stored in one place. Subsidiary files might then consist of the location of the employee records in numerical order by social security number, in alphabetical order by name, for

VALUE	RECORDS			
100,000	10			
75,000	20			
50,000	30	40		
45,000	50	60	70	80
30,000	90	100	110	

RECORD #	KEY
10	PRES
20	VPRES
30	STATE
40	DEFENSE
50	TREAS
60	JUST
70	LABOR
80	COM
90	INTER
100	HUD
110	HEW

Figure 5.12. Inverted Organization. The table at left may be used to find the records of personnel having given salaries.

those employees possessing certain skills, or any other arrangement desired. An operating system might be programmed to process files having this type of structure, and thus perform sophisticated information retrieval functions for the user.

List structures can be used to describe more complex relationships among the records of a file than a simple linear ordering. When the records of a file are as vertices joined by directed arcs in a connected graph and no more than one arc is directed to any one given record, a hierarchically organized file is described. The file has the form of a tree and any one record taken together with its outwardly directed arcs and the vertices connected to it thereby forms a subtree. The singular record of a subtree may be a header record, for example, those describing the departments' employees or the assembly's parts or subassemblies. Some

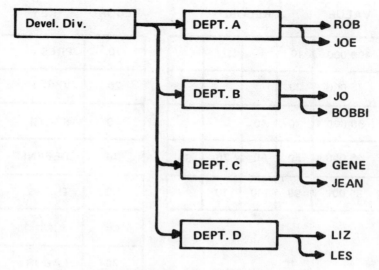

Figure 5.13. Hierarchical Organization.

treat the notion of connectedness as optional, so that any collection of subtrees may form a hierarchically organized file.

Associative, or content-addressable, memories represent a natural residence for files of inverted organization. Such memories really fall outside our stated scope and have not yet proven practical for files of respectable size, but much interesting work has been done on the subject [DeF72, Min72, Min71].

Some files are organized in ways which defy a unique categorization. These may employ directly accessed indexes, for example. They are said to have hybrid organizations.

Recommended treatments of the subject of file organization include [Cha71], [Cha69b], [Min68], [Dod69], [Sen69], and [Lef69]. In the next section, we treat access methods, the mechanisms through which data can be stored into and retrieved from files.

5.3 ACCESS METHODS

Since all programs must do some form of input or output to yield a result, the importance of an operating system's I/O facilities is clear. It should not be surprising that several levels of complexity are provided for use by programmers with varying needs and skills. The input/output supervisor (see Section 3.2) is the operating system component which actually schedules, initiates, and controls the input/output operations. The facilities for communicating with the input/output supervisor and for performing other services related to input and output are called access methods. Our discussion of the subject is based on IBM's OS/VS but is not meant to imply that there are no other ways of providing similar facilities.

Types of Access Methods

The amount and kind of information specified by a programmer to request input/output services depend on what access method, if any, is being used. The programmer may choose to use a basic access method or a queued access method. In a basic access method, an input or output request to the access method generates an actual operation on a device. The basic access methods also require that a programmer do any necessary blocking, buffering, or synchronizing. The basic access methods allow the programmer to control overlapping of computation and input/output operations.

With a queued access method, each input or output request made to the access method is for a logical record so that the access method does blocking or deblocking as appropriate. The queued access methods are limited to the processing of sequential or indexed sequential files. The queued access methods also perform other services, such as buffer management, synchronizing operations, error analysis, and error reporting. In addition, for an input operation, the physical records can be obtained before they are actually requested, assuming that a programmer will usually want to access all the records in a sequential file. Thus, an input buffer can be filled when the file is opened and whenever a buffer is released. A buffer will frequently be full when data are needed. This is the only overlapping of input/output operations with computation that can be done with a queued access method.

Finally, a programmer may choose to communicate directly with the input/output supervisor and not use an access method.

The language used by a programmer also influences the way input/output services are specified. In high-level languages, the programmer describes files and uses statements in the syntax of the language being used. The compiler may translate these statements into the data required by an access method, so that, in effect, the high-level language programmer is using the standard access methods. Alternatively, the compiler may generate the code to communicate directly with the input/output supervisor. The former method leads to easier maintenance and standardization, while the latter method may allow more efficient programming by not including coding for unused options of the access method. In assembly language, the same choices prevail. However, if the programmer chooses not to use an access method, the coding has to match that provided by the access method.

In the remainder of this section, we discuss techniques of buffer management, the mechanism which permits the overlapping of I/O and computation; a representative algorithm for buffer management; and an implementation of a set of access methods.

Buffer Management

Buffer management by the access method relieves a programmer of having to locate main storage for records and of having to keep track of their status. Knuth [Knu68] has described a number of buffering techniques and provided algorithms for implementing them. He distinguishes three states that a buffer may have:

State	For Input	For Output
Ready	Full of new input	Free area for new data
Assigned	Processed by user	Processed by user
Released	Free for more input	Full of new output data

A buffer passes successively through these states. The actual input or output operation may occur while a buffer is in the released state. Completion of a device operation causes a transition to the ready state. The transitions to assigned and released states occur as a result of user requests to assign and release buffers as required by the program.

Knuth also shows that a circular list structure or buffer pool can be constructed to utilize any number of buffers. The technique requires keeping pointers to the next ready buffer, the assigned buffer, and the first released buffer. The circular list structure can be implemented by keeping a pointer to the successor of each buffer.

Under some conditions, both input and output operations can be conducted from the same set of buffers having another state:

State	For Input or Output
Ready	Full of new input
Assigned	Processed by user
Released	Can be output
Empty	Can receive new input data

These states correspond to the sequence of events required for updating data. The transition from released to empty is caused by the completion of an output operation, and the transition from empty to ready is caused by the completion of an input operation.

Synchronous algorithms for buffering are given by Knuth. In these algorithms, when an input/output operation has been started, a program can continue to

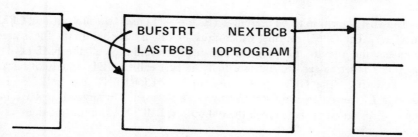

Figure 5.14. Buffer and Buffer Control Block. The header of each buffer control block contains pointers to the block's buffer, successor, and predecessor and to an associated input/output program.

compute, but the device status must be interrogated periodically by the program. This may be accomplished as Knuth suggests by incorporating the necessary testing into the user program approximately every 50 instructions. Alternatively, timed interrupts can initiate device polling to see if any device has completed an operation. Unless extremely fast polling is possible, such a procedure is likely to generate intolerable overhead and may cause errors when fast devices subject to overrun are used. Such algorithms are not extensively used.

Asynchronous algorithms allow computation to continue without repeated testing for completion by depending on interruptions to indicate the end of device operations. To illustrate asynchronous buffering, the use of an input/output supervisor is assumed. The following supervisor calls are used to request services:

Supervisor Call (SVC)	Meaning
1. FILL A	Fill a buffer associated with A. On completion, POST event A. Queue a request for a busy device.
2. WAIT B	Put this process in a wait state until event B is posted.
3. POST C	Mark event C as having happened.

The algorithms assume an array of buffers, which are identified by subscripts. The following variables are used to describe the buffering:

1. L — the number of assigned buffers.
2. M — the number of released buffers.
3. N — the number of ready buffers.
4. CURRENT — the subscript of the assigned buffer.
5. FULL — the subscript of the next ready buffer.
6. EMPTY — the subscript of the first released buffer.
7. NEXT (I) — the successor to buffer I.
8. STATE (I) — the state of buffer, that is, READY, ASSIGNED, or RELEASED.

The first algorithm to be presented (Figure 5.15) uses two subroutines, OPEN and GET. The OPEN routine, which must be called once before the file is used, connects the file to the program and requests filling of all the buffers. The variable J is set to zero to indicate that the first call to GET should not release an old buffer. The GET routine first updates CURRENT and EMPTY. The variable J is tested to see if a buffer is to be released. On any call to GET but the first, a request is made to fill the old buffer, EMPTY. The routine then waits

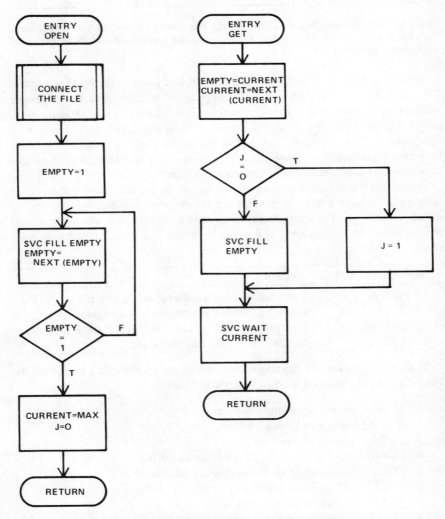

Figure 5.15. Buffer Management Using OPEN and GET.

for the current buffer to be filled, if necessary, and then returns the location of the current buffer to the user program. This algorithm is relatively simple because the releasing of a buffer and the request for assigning a new one always occur together. Thus, after the first call to GET, one buffer is always assigned to the program. A request to fill this buffer cannot be generated until a new buffer is desired by the program. These conditions mean that is is not necessary to keep track separately of empty and full buffers.

If the assigning and releasing are to be separated, a more complex algorithm is needed (Figure 5.16). This algorithm uses three routines, INITIALIZE, ASSIGN, and RELEASE. The INITIALIZE routine connects the file to the program and initializes the variables such that all buffers are in the released state. An independent

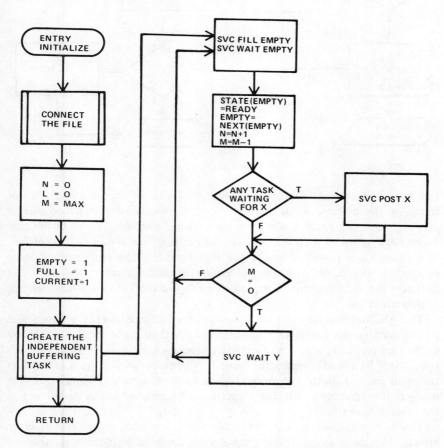

Figure 5.16. Buffer Management Using INITIALIZE, ASSIGN, and RELEASE.

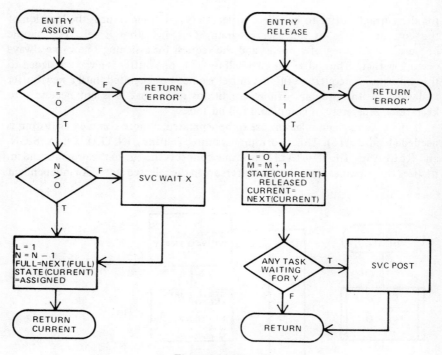

Figure 5.16. (Cont.)

task is then created to fill all requests for filling and waiting for completion of filling of the buffers. When a buffer is filled, the variables are modified to indicate one more ready buffer (increased N) and one less released buffer (decreased M). A test is then made to see if any other task is waiting for a buffer. If so, event X is posted to notify the supervisor that the other task can now proceed. If the number of released buffers M has been reduced to zero, the buffering routine must wait. A request to wait for event Y notifies the supervisor of that condition.

The ASSIGN routine tests to make sure no buffer is already assigned and returns with an error message if one is. A test is then made on N to see if any buffers are ready. If none are, the ASSIGN routine must wait for a buffer to fill as indicated by a WAIT request for event X. When a buffer is ready, the variables are modified to indicate one more assigned buffer (increased L) and one fewer ready buffer (decreased N). The location of the assigned buffer is returned as the value of CURRENT.

The release routine tests to see if a buffer is assigned, and returns an error message if none is assigned. The variables are modified to indicate no assigned buffer ($L = 0$) and one more released buffer (increased M). If the independent buffer task is waiting on event Y, event Y is posted before returning. The recording of the status of each buffer in the array STATE is not necessary to the operation of the algorithm. It would be useful for debugging purposes, but would probably be deleted from a working program. The equivalent information is inherent in the variables L, M, and N plus the states of the events X and Y.

The ASSIGN and RELEASE routines are called by the user program and are effectively an extension of it. The independent buffering task is effectively an extension of the input/output supervisor. The fact that two independent tasks may modify the status variables creates additional problems. If one of the routines were to be interrupted while modifying L, M, and N, an incorrect result might be obtained. One solution to these problems is to let all the routines run with interruptions masked off, at least while modifying and testing these critical variables. Alternatively, locks could be placed on the critical sections by the use of uninterruptible instructions. To analyze what locks are necessary, one must assume that any of the routines could be halted at any arbitrary point and another one started. The problems of buffer management are a special case of task synchronization problems considered in the discussion of multiprogramming and multiprocessing. The problems involved are practical ones, as demonstrated by Wood [Woo73], who described a synchronization problem involving the CDC 6600 system, which uses a considerable number of independent peripheral processors. The complication arises there because the peripheral processors are too valuable resources to remain idle. The conventional synchronizing mechanisms did not work well because they could not be implemented as uninterruptible operations. The solution involved double checking of some of the critical variables to verify that an improper sequence did not occur.

The techniques described may be applied to both queued and basic access methods. For queued input, a buffer in the released state can be filled just as soon as a device is available to fill it. For basic input, a buffer in the released state is filled only when the program requests it. The basic access methods can thus be used with buffering for sequential or direct-access files. The latter is possible if processing of one record does not influence the location of subsequent records.

The number of buffers to use depends on the kind of demands the programs make on the input and output units. Given a fixed amount of main storage to devote to buffers, there is a trade-off between the number and size of buffers. Hellerman [Hel67] and Hellerman and Smith [Hel70] have analyzed this trade-off for several possible modes of overlapped operation involving constant cycles of input, computing, and output. They compared the results obtained to those obtained for sequential, or nonoverlapped, operation. Because overlapping of input/output operations with computation requires more buffers, the buffers must necessarily be smaller. The results of the analysis showed that some form of overlapped operation was usually better. However, for I/O-bound systems with a single channel, nonoverlapped operation with a larger buffer was better when access times were large compared to computation times. For a computation-bound problem, two buffers were all that were effective, because all input or output operations were completed before required by the problem.

The management of buffers in a multiprogramming system should be done on the basis of the overall system mix of computation and input/output, if the overall system utilization is to be maximized. When multiple users are present, the overlapping of computation and input/output operations for any particular user is not as important for efficient performance as when only one user is present. Thus, if one user in a multiprogramming system is waiting for an input/output operation to be completed, another may wish to compute. Cohen [Coh70] points out that an unbuffered system may provide improved throughput, especially if the space released by not buffering can allow more programs to be in the system. A buffered system may provide better turnaround for individual users. The choice depends on the design objectives of the system.

Implementation

In OS/VS, the programmer who chooses not to use an access method still has some coding aids provided in the form of macroinstructions, or macros. Recall from Section 3.2 that the requestor of an input/output operation must supply four data inputs to the input/output supervisor: input/output block, event control block, data control block, and channel program. The EXCP (execute channel program) macroinstruction requires that the programmer code these four items directly, but supplies the supervisor call and a pointer to the input/output block. The data control block may be constructed by using the DCB macro. The XDAP (execute direct-access program) macro for direct-access volumes allows reading or updating a file. The macro constructs all the data inputs to the input/output supervisor except the data control block, which is formed by using the DCB macro. The incentive for using EXCP or XDAP comes from the reduced program size, compared to that required for the access methods. The services provided are reduced accordingly; for example, any blocking, buffering, record-length checking, or error analysis must be programmed.

The OS/VS access methods are invoked by using assembly language macroin-structions. Different sets of macroinstructions are used for each file organization and for queued and basic access methods. The combinations available are summarized in Table 5.1. A particular file need not always be processed by the access method used to create it. For example, a file might be created by BSAM and processed later by BDAM. In addition, an ISAM interface is provided to allow processing of ISAM files by VSAM. The distinction between basic and queued access methods is not so clear in VSAM, because a program may either do simultaneous computing and input/output, as in a basic access method, or

Table 5.1. OS/VS Access Methods.

File Organization	Basic Access Method	Queued Access Method
Sequential	BSAM	QSAM
Partitioned	BPAM	—
Direct	BDAM	—
Indexed sequential	BISAM	QISAM
Virtual	VSAM[1]	VSAM[1]

[1] VSAM allows both synchronous and asynchronous processing.

automatically wait until input/output operations are complete, as in a queued access method. The level of auxiliary services provided by VSAM is similar to those of the queued access methods.

The functions provided by the OS/VS access methods are summarized in Table 5.2. Not all these functions need to be used in every program. A minimal set of the functions needed for simple applications is:

1. DCB or ACB — to specify file attributes.
2. OPEN and CLOSE — to connect and disconnect files and programs.
3. GET and PUT, or READ and WRITE — to cause records to be input or output.

The rest of the functions are provided so a programmer can control specialized elements of the input/output system or specify things that would be done automatically or by default by the operating system.

The buffer management techniques provided by OS/VS allow both simple buffering, in which a buffer stays in a fixed location, and exchange buffering, in which buffer areas may be exchanged with work areas provided by the program. Four modes of record movement are

1. Move mode — The physical record is located outside the program area, and the system moves logical records into a work area in the program area.
2. Data mode — Same as move mode for variable-length spanned records.
3. Locate mode — The physical record is located outside the program area, and the system returns the address of the logical records to the program.
4. Substitute mode — The system returns the address of the logical records to the program. The program supplies the system with an address of an area that is no longer needed as a logical record.

The GET macroinstruction causes retrieval of a logical record by one of the modes. The PUT macroinstruction causes writing of a logical record by one of the modes. With simple buffering, only move, data, and locate modes can be used.

Table 5.2. OS/VS Data Management Macro Summary [IBM9, IBM12].

Macro	Function	BSAM	QSAM	VSAM	BPAM	BDAM	BISAM	QISAM
GENERAL DATA MANAGEMENT								
OPEN	Link file to program, merge file attributes, specify disposition.	X	X	X	X	X	X	X
CLOSE	Detach file from program, specify positioning and disposition.	X	X	X	X	X	X	X
DCB	Construct data control block, specify file attributes.	X	X		X	X	X	X
ACB	Construct access-method control block, specify file attributes.			X				
GET	Obtain a logical record.		X	X				X
READ	Obtain a physical record.	X			X	X	X	
PUT	Output a logical record.		X	X				X
WRITE	Output a physical record.	X			X	X	X	
ERASE	Delete a record.			X				
CHECK	Test I/O for completion, errors, and exceptional conditions.	X			X	X	X	
RELEX	Release exclusive control.					X		
ENDREQ	Terminate a request			X				
PUTX	Output an updated logical record.		X					X
SYNADAF	Analyze I/O errors and return error message.	X	X		X	X	X	X
SYNADRLS	Release data areas used by SYNADAF.	X	X		X	X	X	X
XLATE	Translate ASCII to/from EBCDIC.	X	X		X	X	X	
ESETL	End sequential retrieval.							X
SETL	Begin sequential retrieval.							X
RPL	Define a parameter list.			X				
EXLST	Specify location of exit routine.			X				
GENCB	Combine ACB, RPL, and EXLST.			X				
MODCB	Change fields of ACB, RPL, and EXLST.			X				
SHOWCB	Display fields of ACB, RPL, or EXLST.			X				
TESTCB	Test fields of ACB, RPL, or EXLST.			X				

Table 5.2. (Cont.)

Macro	Function	BSAM	QSAM	VSAM	BPAM	BDAM	BISAM	QISAM
BUFFER MANAGEMENT								
BUILD	Construct buffer pool in data area supplied by program.	X				X	X	X
BUILDRCD	Construct buffer for spanned records.		X			X	X	
GETPOOL	Construct a buffer pool in data area supplied by the system.	X	X			X	X	X
FREEPOOL	Release a buffer pool.	X	X			X	X	
GETBUF	Obtain address of buffer from pool.	X				X	X	
FREEBUF	Return a buffer to pool.	X				X	X	
FREEDBUF	Return a buffer obtained automatically.					X	X	
RELSE	Release current buffer.		X					X
TRUNC	Force current to be marked full.		X					
DIRECTORY MANAGEMENT – PARTITIONED FILE								
FILE	Get address of specified member.				X			
STOW	Update directory.				X			
BLDL	Construct main storage address list.				X			
DEVICE MANAGEMENT								
CNTRL	Specify device control for online device.	X	X					
PRTOV	Test printer carriage overflow.	X	X					
BSP	Backspace.	X						
FEOV	Force end of volume.	X	X					
NOTE	Get address of last record output.	X			X			
POINT	Position device at specified record.	X			X			

A special PUTX macro can be used for updating or copying a file without adding new records or changing the record size or blocking.

Several aids are provided to programmers for buffer management with the basic or queued access methods. Buffer pools can be created or destroyed in three ways.

	To Create	To Destroy
1. Statically	BUILD macro with storage area in program	Close file
2. Explicitly	GETPOOL macro with storage area provided by system	FREEPOOL macro
3. Automatically	Open file	FREEPOOL macro or close file

GETBUF and FREEBUF macros are used for obtaining buffers from a pool and returning them. These correspond to the assigning and releasing functions discussed previously. The system uses control blocks contiguous with the buffers to maintain pools.

An assembly language, as is used to code the OS/VS access methods, is not necessary for communication with input/output supervisor routines. The Burroughs [BUR4, BUR6, BUR9] Master Control Program (MCP) does not provide the programmer with an assembly language. All programming is done with high-level languages. Consequently, the compilers for these languages must construct directly the tables needed to convey information from the user program to MCP. A file information block containing about 120 file attributes serves as the primary vehicle for these data.

5.4 DATA BASES

Every job performed by an operating system involves the use of some data, but unique problems arise when a set of data is shared by many jobs of diverse types. In this section, we define such a collection of data, a data base, and show why data bases are employed. We then examine the views of the data base seen by various persons who interact with it. The mechanisms by which the system manages the data base are explored next, and, finally, we investigate some specific problems engendered by the use of data bases.

A data base is a collection of data viewed as separate, but overlapping, files by programs executing under an operating system. An inventory data base may be viewed as a file of assemblies and subassemblies by an engineering division, a file of items and warehouses by a manufacturing division, and a file of assemblies and warehouses by a distribution and marketing division of the same enterprise. If each division kept its own separate independent files, reconciling these files, keeping them consistent with one another, would pose a huge, essentially hopeless problem. A data base eliminates that problem or, rather, trades it for other, more manageable problems. It is these, in fact, which are our central topic in this section.

Roles

With the advent of data bases, a new individual, or group of individuals, was identified in the data processing environment, the data base administrator [COD71b]. The data base administrator does everything necessary to permit those writing application programs which use the data base to concentrate on their own jobs, programming, not data management. Among the functions of the data base administrator are:

1. Defining (*a*) the residence of the data base, (*b*) the physical structure of the data base, (*c*) the logical organization of the data base, and (*d*) the contents of the data base.
2. Creating the data base.
3. Creating subschemata (descriptions of parts of the data base) for use by application programs.
4. Redefining the data base as necessary.
5. Accomplishing the recovery of the data base's integrity following a mishap.
6. Working with users of the data base to help them use the data base efficiently and to understand himself what is required of him.

The data base administrator must decide, among other things, through indexes on which fields the data base should be accessible; how much space should be allotted for the data base and its indexes; what data should be included in the data base; when and how procedures for recovery of the data base should be exercised; and what mechanisms are needed to protect the data base from error.

The application programmer writes programs which use the data base and are in turn used by individuals whose knowledge of data processing is more superficial. An application programmer communicates needs for data from the data base to the data base administrator, who creates an appropriate subschema for the programmer's use.

The application user simply uses the programs provided by the application programmer. While these programs may include the traditional applications of payroll preparation, billing, and so on, they also increasingly include programs which permit querying of a data base. Today, many managers can sit at terminals in their own offices and ask how much money Lee Doe is paid each week. (How much Lee earns might be a separate question.) One can easily see that structuring a

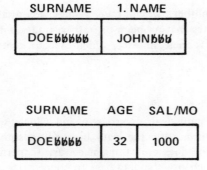

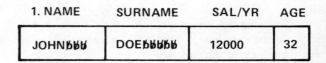

Figure 5.17. Two subschemata and a schema.

data base to serve many diverse applications efficiently is a task of considerable complexity.

These, then, are the individuals who work with data bases: the data base administrator, the application programmer, and the application user. An appreciation of their roles should serve to place the following discussion of data base mechanisms in clear perspective.

Mechanisms

Our terminology and organization for what follows are due in part to [COD71b] and [Schu72]. The details of our exposition follow more closely [Eng71], a position paper on [COD71b], and [Eng70].

We begin by distinguishing four tasks and four corresponding languages used to accomplish those tasks:

1. Allocation of space for the data base — device media control language (DMCL).
2. Definition of the schema (structure) for the data base — schema data definition language (schema DDL).
3. Definition of subschemas for the data base — subschema DDL.
4. Specification of operations to be performed on the data base — data manipulation language (DML).

Having so said, however, we note that the schema DDL can be a superset of the subschema DDL and we therefore often fail to distinguish between the two in referring simply to DDL.

The languages of which we speak, DMCL, DDL, and DML, are conceptual and generic. We do not mean to imply that any language of any of the three types exists or ever will. The designations are mere conveniences, acceptable because the tasks they address have unquestionable significance.

In most cases, a DMCL can simply be a control language (OSCL). An OSCL has, typically, the ability to express what a DMCL must express: what space with what format must be allocated on what volumes for the data base or named parts of the data base. The DMCL is the first mechanism used by a data base administrator in creating a data base.

The DDL is the second. The data base administrator uses the DDL to create a schema, that is, to define the data base with respect to, among other things:

1. Its file organization.
2. The names of its fields.
3. How its fields are represented.
4. How its fields are grouped into records.
5. Relationships among records.
6. What fields are to serve for primary and secondary indexes over the data base.
7. How the integrity of the data base is to be maintained.

The data base administrator uses the DDL to create subschemata to meet the needs of application programs. The first four characteristics listed above apply as well to subschemata. One may summarize the purpose of subschemata as keeping the application programmer happily and harmlessly ignorant of:

1. The volumes and media used to store the data.
2. The physical or logical organization of the data.
3. The method employed for access to the data.
4. The relationships of fields to records and, perhaps, records to subfiles within the data base.
5. The length, bit representation, and encoding of a field.
6. How the integrity of a field is maintained.
7. What units, such as British pounds, West German marks, or American dollars, the stored field represents.
8. Whether or not the field is physically stored (as opposed to being calculated from other fields as necessary).

These items are aspects of data independence. Data independence is at least theoretically possible whenever a subschema describes precisely what a program expects to see and a schema describes precisely what is stored and algorithmic mappings between the two are known and are within the system's capability.

A unique subschema DDL may exist for each programming language being used to write application programs for a given operating system. The same can be said of DMLs. A DML is used for accessing and operating on the data of a data base through a programming language. It is not unlike the sum of a system's data management macroinstructions (see Section 5.3) taken together, or all the I/O statements of a higher-level language.

The operations of a DML are purely incidental processing (OPEN and CLOSE), positional (descriptive of a particular record, as defined by the subschema, to be processed next), or functional (GET, PUT, or MODIFY). Positional operations are particularly interesting in their variety. A record may be identified by:

1. Its key.
2. The value(s) of some one or more of its fields. (This is valuable for responding to queries and suggests an inverted organization.)
3. Its relationship to another record directly above, below, or next to it in a hierarchical structure.
4. Scanning within a defined subset of the data base.

Functional operations include notions of reading, writing, and updating. The latter is critical to the maintenance of the data base's integrity, as we show below.

DMCL, DDL, and DML are the external mechanisms of data base management. Beneath them may lie routines of great complexity and sophistication. This is illustrated as we proceed to discuss a few of the problems posed by data bases.

Implementation Problems

The mapping of subschemata to schemata is a difficult task and one whose complexities are just now being investigated. The problem is so large, the effects of hardware so significant, and the theoretical feasibility so obvious, that we choose not to pursue this matter in the present text. We leave it as a multitude of exercises for the reader.

Problems we do wish to discuss are (1) maintaining the integrity of the data base, (2) coping with the scheduling problems engendered by this maintenance, and (3) recovering the integrity of the data base. It is no accident that these problems seem to spring from the same root cause, sharing of data. Only this and the topics of privacy and data independence (which we largely avoid here) distinguish data bases from more tractable files.

The data in a data base are shared. This is the very essence of its *raison d'être*. But it is also the source of its greatest problems. Consider the case of two processes, A and B, which update field X. A and B may handle airline reservations and X may be the number of reserved seats on the 5:10 P.M. flight from Boston to Pittsburgh. A issues a request for X, obtaining the value 25. B does the same. A, handling a request for 4 seats on that flight, adds 4 to 25 and stores the value 29 in X. B, for similar reasons, may store 32 in X, being unaware of A's action. Clearly, someone may have to take a later flight. What we have here is uncontrolled access to shared data, and this cannot be tolerated. Let us try to find a solution to this problem.

Let A, requesting X, say "GET X for UPDATE." Now we can recognize X as a resource and set a corresponding lock on behalf of A. B behaves similarly, but cannot obtain X while A has it, and so our problem is solved. (Let us ignore deadlock for the moment, since it is covered in Chapter 2.) But what if the request A is handling is canceled? Must A store X anyway? This would seem inefficient, and so we invent a RELEASE operator for A to use instead. As long as A does not fail to release X, all is as it should be.

But suppose we wish to conceal the ugly UPDATE and RELEASE operands from users. Can we do this? We can if we keep careful track of what A is doing, interpret a STORE operation as a "GET and verify what I got before, then STORE if OK" operation and, in the event that the verification fails, can go back in A to the original GET. This would minimize contention, our next subject, as well as provide a simpler interface to the user. Yet, what must be done cannot be done simply and we know of no such implementation.

The point of our discussion is that shared data are resources and the system and its users share the burden of managing them.

When you have shared resources, you have contention. Contention can lead to bottlenecks, and thus to unacceptable degradation of performance. To avoid these consequences one must minimize contention. Three strategies exist for this task:

1. Plan ahead as much as possible, in a word — schedule. Schedule processes with cognizance of their requirements for sources. (See Chapter 4.)
2. Delimit as finely as possible the resources for which there may be contention. Treating the entire data base as a single resource clearly engenders far more contention than treating records as resources.
3. Reduce to a minimum the length of time that a resource is retained. Do not allocate a resource earlier than absolutely necessary and retain it no longer than necessary.

All three strategies should be employed whenever they apply to given problems, but not without consideration of compensating disadvantages: too much processing power expended on scheduling, too much time spent locking many things that are always used simultaneously, and too much time spent gaining the flexibility needed to delay acquisition of resources. In these as in all things, moderation.

When an inconsistency or inaccuracy has been introduced into the data base, corrective measures are needed. Little more than human ingenuity can be brought to bear unless the possibility of error has been anticipated. Such anticipation takes three general forms:

1. Checkpointing — recording the status of the data base at some point in time so that the data base can be restored to that status if an error is subsequently detected.
2. Journaling — keeping track of successive modifications to the data base and their sequence in time so that the modifications can be undone one by one until an acceptable state is reached.
3. Backtracking — constructing for each process an inverse process capable of undoing what has been done despite any independent modifications that the data base may have undergone.

Associated with each technique are costs and shortcomings. Checkpointing requires much storage space, a significant period of time when the data base is frozen, considerable delay in accomplishing recovery, and preparation to reexecute all processes whose effects are lost by restoration. Journaling places a severe strain on the system's resources, also requires reexecution of processes, and requires that one know how far back in time to go. Backtracking requires intimate understanding of the interactions of processes, prodigious preparation in the form of the needed routines, and precise knowledge of just what has gone wrong.

We have shown only that the problem of recovery is a great one. Easy solutions cannot be offered.

Preserving Privacy

One of the most common uses for data bases is the storage of information about people, for example, all the employees of a business, all the patients of a hospital, or all the residents of an area. Countries and various smaller governmental entities have (justifiably) passed laws [Tur76] that require those who store information about people to preserve those individuals' privacy. Laws vary considerably, but the same techniques apply to assuring adherence to all of them.

A first step is preservation of the security of the data and the integrity of the system used to process them. This is not a concern unique to data bases. Unique concerns arise from the fact that an important use of many a data base is the extraction of summary data about the individuals described. No one person's privacy is compromised if an auditor at a hospital learns how many patients were in the hospital on some particular day, but if that same auditor learns that Ronnie Smith is from Podunk, a seemingly useless datum in itself, and that no patient not from Podunk is the gonorrhea victim that the auditor knows was admitted yesterday, Ronnie's privacy is compromised.

Some preliminary conclusions can be drawn from the example above. People seeking summary data should not be told anything about a very small set of people or a very large set of people, almost everybody. Further study of the problem [Den80] leads to much stronger and rather discouraging conclusions. It is, in fact, not possible today to specify constraints on queries to which correct responses can be given from the information in data bases without possibly revealing data seemingly concealed by summarization. One leading worker in the field has told us that she could discover no privacy-preserving technique obviously better than the very restrictive one the United States Census Bureau has been using for many years. Consider this: Does the above description of our informant itself constitute an invasion of her privacy?

To protect people's privacy or for any of a number of other reasons, people control users' access to individual records and individual fields of data bases. Conventional access control programs can be used for these purposes, but an alternative way of controlling individuals' access to fields is attractive. One defines a subschema for each unique set of fields to which one wishes to restrict users' access. Then one need only ensure that users are given only the fields in their subschemata each time they obtain a record from the data base. They never see any other fields.

A related point is worth mentioning here. Some have suggested that cryptography be used to enhance the protection of data in data bases. Suggestions of this nature are subject to misinterpretation. If data bases are copied onto portable media with some frequency so that their contents can be stored securely, to be used if files online are damaged, then one may want the data on the portable media to be encrypted for protection, since control over physical access to the media may well be impracticable. A data base may be so large and data from it may be accessed so rarely or in such small quantities that keeping the data base encrypted online, to obviate encryption each time its contents are copied, may be desirable for efficiency's sake. If this is not the case, however, encryption of a data base is of questionable value.

Look at the matter this way [McP78]. If online data are encrypted, decryption must involve the use of a secret key. If it is resident in the system, it is just as vulnerable as the encrypted data being protected. If the key is provided by a user, just as a password is provided, the key is nothing but a resource-oriented password, a poor instrument of security.

With this discussion of problems, we conclude this section on data bases and our view, in general, of data in secondary storage. We next look at the equipment which communicates data between people and the system.

5.5 DATA FOR PEOPLE

Thus far in this chapter, we have dealt with secondary storage, the residence for data both read and written by the system. In this section we concern ourselves with the data portion of the man-machine interface and what lies behind it, that is, on the machine's side of it. We first discuss unit record equipment: printers, card readers and punches, paper tape readers, and optical/magnetic ink character readers (OCR/MICR). We then consider terminals, their characteristics and uses. Our last topic is display-producing equipment and the consequences of line-drawing capability.

Unit Record Equipment

In general, unit record equipment appears to the system no different from other media for sequential files. In fact, data destined for or received from unit record equipment are most often spooled into sequential files in secondary storage. Characteristics of particular devices show through only in output files in the form of embedded data interpreted by the receiving equipment.

Our questions, then, are what can a printer/reader/punch do and how can it be told to do it?

We start with a printer. A printer can move paper varying distances between lines of printing. This may mean double spacing, overprinting, skipping to the top of a new page (ejecting), skipping to the bottom line of this page, and so on. All these things may be controlled by the first character of a line of output. This character may be supplied by a user or by the operating system.

Some printers have far more function than is described above. This function is exploited [IBM39] by what can be regarded as application programs, not parts of the system itself.

The mapping from characters in main storage to printed characters is controlled by two factors: hardware or microcode within the printer and a physical printing mechanism, such as a print chain or train or a matrix of wires. A system may be capable of altering microcode, responding to changes in the physical mechanism (by performing a translation on data), or communicating with the operator about physical characteristics of the printer. The latter capability is also relevant to printing forms, absence of paper, ply of forms (number of copies), and a carriage tape (which controls spacing or ejecting in some printers).

Forms are also relevant to card punches and are treated similarly. Punches can also accept commands which alter their behavior. Relevant characteristics are stacking of cards or documents and mode of reading (binary or character for a card reader). These are among the functions which may require close synchronization between processing and I/O operations. A preliminary reading of an OCR document may have an effect on the next operation one might want performed on the same document. This requirement forces a system to provide capabilities, otherwise unneeded, for synchronous I/O operations on unit record equipment (as opposed to spooling, which is asynchronous).

Much communication with the operator concerns unit record equipment. This is discussed in Section 6.3.

Terminals

With the aside that we have nothing special to say about equipment for processing paper tape, we move on to terminals. Terminals present unique problems to the designer of an operating system (1) because they provide an interactive interface, (2) because they are character-oriented rather than record-oriented, and (3) because they can be attached to the system via common-carrier lines. A line is seen by the system as a port or socket to which calls can be made.

The prime distinguishing characteristic of terminals is that they are a medium of synchronous interaction. Data are passed between the system and a terminal in both directions, often alternately.

Another unique attribute of a terminal is that input from it is entered a character at a time rather than an entire record. For this reason, a single trans-mission may be self-correcting. A user may key in a character and then decide that this was an error. This is an event which must be anticipated; provision must be made for the user to correct such an error immediately, easily, by keying in characters which are part of the same transmission which contains the error.

Finally, the attachment of terminals via lines supplied by public utilities raises concerns we choose to discuss in the context of terminals, acknowledging at the same time that terminals are not the only things that can be attached to a system in this way.

Before proceeding to discuss particular consequences of the three character-istics we have listed, some words are in order about how terminals are used. We can distinguish basically between remote job entry (RJE), or batchlike, use, and true interactive use. In the former, the terminal resembles nothing so much as a combination of a printer and a card reader. The system may provide facilities for correcting errors without having to reenter correct data and for routing jobs, output, and messages to specific units, but even these are offered in the limited context of job entry.

True interactive use is something quite different. The user at an interactive terminal issues commands of an operating system's control language (OSCL). (See Section 6.2.) Each command is separately interpreted and results in some well-defined action taken before the next command is interpreted. In some cases — the collect or input mode of an editor or language processor — the action may simply be the concatenation of the entered statement with existing data in a named file or work space for later use. But this is nonetheless an action and the line of input an implicit command to collect the entered data.

The facilities made available through commands are typically a superset of those provided in batch, and additionally include remote job entry, text editing, interactive debugging, message routing (among users), a desk calculator facility, and an interpretive programming facility (such as APL). Systems with display terminals may support their use for product design, game playing, and any number of other somewhat specialized functions.

The reader may at this point wish to review Chapters 2 and 4 for more information about systems designed for interactive use.

In the context of what we have said, we can now discuss those portions of an operating system which deal most directly with terminals. We treat first those aspects of the subject which arise from the interactive nature of terminals' use. Their manner of attachment and character-entry nature are then treated in turn. We do not, however, explore here the problems of message queuing, a subject worthy of a book of its own.

The interactive nature of a terminal's use affords the users of a system the opportunity to protect their data, the system, and themselves in ways unavailable otherwise. The user who submits a deck of punched cards to a computing center and receives printed output in return has no way of knowing who has handled or read either. A user alone at a terminal in a locked room need only trust the system itself to feel secure.

If a system's access control is individual-oriented, users verify their identities when they begin a series of interactions, a session, with the system. The users first log on (or in) to a system and supply the identifiers by which they are known to the system. The verification mechanism, a password or magnetically encoded card or something like a fingerprint, is provided next. [Mei76] That is, users' identities are verified by something they:

1. Are or can do (a fingerprint, signature, or the like);
2. Have (a card or badge); or
3. Know (a password or the answers to personal questions).

Each mechanism listed above provides less security, but lower cost, than the one(s) above it, if any [Mei76].

A characteristic such as a signature may be most distinctive, but a system may have to store vast quantities of data for each user to avoid error, either false acceptance, a security exposure, or false rejection, a nuisance at best. Designers may trade storage for error as management directs.

A possession has the advantage that a loss should be readily apparent to the user suffering the loss, something not true of a password. On the other hand, anyone who acquires the identifying mechanism can masquerade as its owner with impunity until the loss is known to the system, no questions asked, as it were, unless a password is used in addition to the possession for verification.

A password, as noted above, can be unknowingly lost if it is known to another, without being lost in the sense of being unavailable to its owner. So it is with secret knowledge.

There are many important considerations in the design of a password-processing mechanism. While most of these concern the passwords themselves, perhaps the most important do not. We consider these first [Orc78].

Password processing must be designed to provide maximum security. Security is compromised if an opponent can learn or guess a password. The former threat is countered if a system exposes passwords to view as little as possible. Therefore, the display of passwords on screens or paper should be avoided. If display cannot be inhibited, a small measure of protection appropriate to a relatively benign environment can be obtained from a mask of over struck characters laid down to obscure the password after entry. Further passwords should be held in primary storage as briefly as possible and should be maximally protected in primary and secondary storage. As to guesswork, the system should discourage repeated entry of incorrect passwords, as would be necessary if one were merely guessing. It does this by introducing a delay, for example, by disconnecting the input device, after a fixed number of errors. In this case, a designated security administrator is simultaneously notified of the presumed attack on the system.

The first line of defense against an opponent who would guess a password is, however, a scheme that discourages users from selecting passwords that might be guessed [Woo77]. Users should be required to use any one password for no longer than some specified number of consecutive days out of some longer interval, say, for example, for up to four weeks once a year. Vowels might be excluded from passwords or integers required to prevent the selection of some obvious word or name. A minimum length might be imposed to enlarge the set of possible passwords within which an opponent must find the one chosen. Passwords might be chosen randomly by the system and assigned to prevent the selection of vulnerable passwords, but such passwords may be more difficult for users to remember without a written, and therefore vulnerable, reminder. System-selected passwords might be seeded with vowels to increase memorability [MIT75], a ploy that studies indicate is futile [Win75], or left vowel-free to prevent the generation of some word that a user might find offensive.

Fail-safe procedures must be made available to give management acceptable alternatives for recovery should users or administrators forget their own passwords. Also, it should be possible for users to prevent even administrators, managers, and auditors from successfully masquerading as someone else. For example, the system should let users know when they last used the system and when their passwords were last changed.

In some systems, the system prevents the user from getting ahead of it by locking the user's keyboard, rendering it inoperable for a time. There are few things in a terminal user's life so frustrating as a locked keyboard, and this ploy should be avoided as much as possible.

Because terminals are used interactively and data must be carried both to and from them, we can distinguish among the ways a terminal can be connected to a system as follows: a transmission line is duplex if it can carry data in both directions simultaneously, half duplex if it can carry data in both directions but not at the same time, and simplex if it can carry data in only one direction. The critical distinction from the system's point of view is that the system will send back to a terminal attached with a full duplex line the same data it receives. This mechanism, impractical with a half duplex line, permits the user to see whether or not his input is being received correctly.

A related subject is terminal identification. If a terminal is used by dialing up the computer and sending audio signals over a common telephone line, the system may not know at the time a connection is made what type of terminal is on the other end of the line. There are many ways the system can find out whether the terminal sends data unsolicited or must be polled (that is, asked for data), and what character code the terminal employs. The terminal may immediately send an identifier to the system. The system may wait some period of time and then poll. The system may send in some number of character codes a message requesting data.

When many terminals are attached via a single line called a multidrop line, the system must distinguish among them by attaching a terminal address to each polling or output message. The same address must be stripped from every incoming message.

It is a characteristic of lines supplied by public utilities or common carriers and of the equipment that is attached to them that they do not always function properly. One phenomenon for which every system must always be prepared is called line drop, the unintended severance of a connection between a system and a terminal. When line drop occurs, the system must preserve the status of the user's job, usually called a session in the interactive case, and perform whatever processing is associated with the termination of a session. If the workspace were not preserved, all the work reflected in it since the user last saved or checkpointed it would be lost. This preservation might not be so easy as one would first think, because the user must have the ability to refer and gain access to the preserved workspace from any terminal. Lines he entered but which were not processed when the line dropped must be either processed or saved for processing when the user restores the preserved workspace, or else the user must somehow be able to learn what lines were lost so that he can reenter them. In the latter case, the system must make some sort of disposition of the lost lines so that the space they occupy is not forever lost to the system. A similar concern applies to preserved workspaces which are never restored by the users whose work was interrupted.

Another possible consequence of line drop is that the system, unaware of the event, wastes a great quantity of resources waiting for input which will never come. Systems often take some exceptional action, such as terminating a session, if no input is received from a terminal over a certain preestablished period of time. From a user's viewpoint, the incident is called time out.

There is often on a terminal one key which has a system-defined significance quite different from that of every other key. This is the attention key. Depending on the system, the key may be used as an identifier to distinguish commands from textual input; as an escape character to leave some mode of operation; as a mechanism to interrupt ongoing processing, such as continuous printing at the terminal; as a signal to begin or recommence such activity; or any combination of the above.

The tabulating (tab) and carriage or carrier return (CR) keys pose problems because, when the system is sending data to terminals, it must avoid sending another character before the action of a tab or CR has been completed. If this is not done, assuming the terminal has no interlock, printing may be done on the fly, that is, before the printing mechanism and the paper are properly aligned with respect to each other.

The tab key presents an additional problem in that the actual tabulating positions set at a terminal can in no way be sensed by the system. It must rely on the user to supply this information if it is to use the tab key on output, as it should for efficiency's sake. Several design decisions appear here: Should assumed tabulating positions be held constant or allowed to vary across different users at the same terminal, across different printings of the same document, or across different terminals being employed by the same user? How should the user describe tabulating positions to the system?

The backspace key is another source of problems for system designers. Should the key be assumed on input to signal deletion of previous characters? If so, how can a user underscore anything? If not (the more common case), how are misstruck characters to be deleted? How is the system to accommodate lines of extraordinarily many characters due to the presence of backspace characters between CRs, the normal line delimiters?

As mentioned above, if access to data cannot be controlled physically, one can control access to the meaning of data by transforming the data through the use of some mechanism whose effects a potential opponent cannot reverse. Data traveling across lines not physically inaccessible to unauthorized parties fall into this category. The mechanism used for hiding the data's meaning is called encryption [IBM32].

The United States' National Bureau of Standards has promulgated a standard, called the Data Encryption Standard (DES) [NBS77a], that contains an algorithm for encryption. The algorithm, developed by scientists at IBM's T. J. Watson Laboratory, is used with a secret quantity called a key. The key is known by both the sender and the receiver of each encrypted communication and used by them for encryption and decryption. In the case of line encryption, necessary devices are placed at the termini of lines and the system is not involved in any way (save perhaps the selection of lines so protected for communications designated sensitive). End-to-end encryption involves processes at both ends of a logical line, in either systems or terminals. Some process must select keys for use in encrypting each set of communications; for example, all those of a session. The key must not be sent over the vulnerable line unencrypted, so a protocol involving a key known to both system and terminal must be used to insure that both know the key to be used for a session.

The DES' algorithm acts on 8 bytes, 64 bits at a time, but a process called chaining can be used to achieve the effect of encipherment of an entire message. This increases security because, for example, it provides unique encipherments for the same data replicated at different points in the message, yet it preserves integrity in that a single error will show itself, through gibberish, and data beyond the 8 byte block in error will not be affected.

An elegant scheme for encryption using dual keys, one secret and the other not, has been devised for certain applications of cryptography for which particular properties, other than efficiency, are of greatest importance. The importance of the scheme, called public-key cryptography [Sim79], in the context of operating systems, has not yet been demonstrated well enough to justify detailed treatment here.

By far the most thorough and useful material on encryption in the context of data processing is in [Mey82].

We have really just scratched the surface of our topics. It has been the subject of many books and we leave the details to them [Mar65, Mar67, Mar69, Mar72, Wat70].

Graphic Display and Other Equipment

We next consider graphic display equipment and more specialized equipment at the person-machine interface. All of the equipment we discuss here is almost always connected to the system by communication lines, so that our earlier comments on that subject remain relevant.

Graphic display equipment is distinguished principally by two characteristics: the temporary nature of its output, a characteristic that is exaggerated in audio (voice) response equipment; and the continuous nature (vs. discrete characters) of some data it is capable of producing, a characteristic it shares with plotters, tablets, and video (television) output. Note that not all display equipment exhibits this latter characteristic. Those which do not may be termed character-display equipment.

Two consequences of impermanent output are: (1) the system may be asked to duplicate output on other media, such a duplicate being known as a log; and (2) the system must be prepared to make incremental changes in output records. Thus graphic display equipment can be used as an aid to product design. An engineer causes a product, assembly, or part to be displayed and then instructs the system to rotate it, take something away from it, add to it, or display hidden lines. These functions, of course, do not apply to the more impermanent medium of audio response.

Continuous output is in some cases an illusion. In these cases, where curved or diagonal lines are constructed from short straight line segments that are all in reality either horizontal or vertical, the system may be required to store vast quantities of data to represent a single record. This does not apply to plotters, but does apply to planar and holographic tablets and most strongly to video output. One could say that one picture may be worth more than ten thousand words!

Where diagonal lines can be drawn directly, each line need only be represented as two pairs of coordinates on the grid of the medium.

A light pen can be used in conjunction with display equipment. A light pen is actually a light-sensing device housed in a stylus and flexibly attached to display equipment. What appears to be a steady image on a display screen is actually a series of rapidly recreated images formed by sequentially produced points of light. By noting the precise instant when the light pen detects light and calibrating with the known rate at which the image is produced, a unit can determine exactly which point of light on the screen the pen is detecting, that is, at what the user is pointing the pen. This provides a uniquely convenient way for a user to choose among options. He is shown a list of options (menu) with a large dot next to each. He points the pen at a dot to select the associated option. (See Section 6.3 for one application of this technique.) Regardless of the application, it is clear that the system must provide facilities whereby the function of a light pen can be exploited.

Some specialized equipment presents a quite ordinary interface to the system. For that reason, we shall only mention in passing magnetic strips used for recording typed data and point-of-sale (POS) devices which automate check-out at self-service establishments.

Audio (spoken) output can be produced in two ways: selection of prerecorded segments, or electronic reproduction of sounds in units of words and phrases (most often) or phonemes. The former method presents no unobvious problem to the system, but the latter may require a sizable quantity of data.

This concludes our discussion of equipment that permits a system to communicate directly with people. As we have noted, much more could be said on the subject, so much that we must leave that task for other texts. We proceed to a discussion of data which are unique in the requirements that they place on the system's data management facilities: programs.

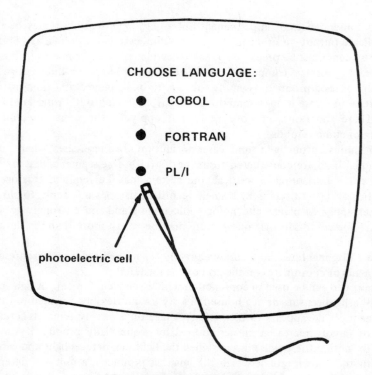

Figure 5.18. Menu and Light Pen.

5.6 PROGRAMS AS DATA

All of the information contained within the main and secondary storage of a computing system is data and all of it must be the concern of the operating system. This is no less true of programs than it is of more mundane data like sequential files and trailer labels.

In this section, we concern ourselves with programs seen as data. We examine those properties that make programs unique as data items and the requirements placed upon the system's handling of programs as data. In the context of the IBM System/360 and 370 family of operating systems, we look at the libraries that contain programs and the constraints placed on the residence of programs in main storage. We conclude with a view of analogous subjects in MULTICS.

The outstanding characteristics of programs as data are their homogeneity — every program is like every other program in certain ways — and their status as resources of the system. Other data may, of course, be viewed as resources, but programs must always be handled with concern for the notion of resource control.

These properties and the unique role of programs in the functioning of an operating system contribute to these requirements on their management:

1. Attention must be paid to the speed with which programs can be found and transferred to main storage.
2. The system's own programs must be protected to preserve the system's integrity.
3. Care must be taken for the programs' own integrity lest an accidentally modified program yield destructive bugs of almost undetectable origin.

Libraries

For the storage of programs, the IBM System/360 and 370 family of operating systems provides partitioned data sets (files), which we call libraries. A library comprises a directory and zero or more members. (See Section 5.2.) Libraries address primarily the accessibility requirement of program management.

A directory may be viewed as an extended label for the file. It comprises, for each member, a list of characteristics of the member, including its name and the location of its first record. The name is used as a key, permitting searches for specific members to be performed outside the central processor.

A member is a sequential file occupying contiguous space within the library. Any sequential file may be a member of a partitioned data set, but source modules, object modules, and load modules most often are, and we limit ourselves for the present to the case where load modules populate libraries. Contiguity, of course, contributes to the speed with which programs can be transferred to main storage by the loader, but it presents the problem of space management mentioned in Section 5.2.

Collections of programs are grouped into libraries for simplicity, efficiency, and the preservation of integrity. Private libraries are illustrative of the former point, libraries for programming languages contribute to efficiency, and the system's own libraries illustrate our last point. We discuss these libraries below from the inside of the system outward.

Three libraries that contain the system's programs are:

1. SYS1.NUCLEUS — contains the nucleus and must be on the system residence volume.
2. SYS1.SVCLIB — contains supervisor programs designed to run only in the system's transient areas and must be on the system residence volume.
3. SYS1.LINKLIB — the link library, which contains other programs and may be on the system residence volume.

Programs residing in these libraries are accessible to any user, although, of the libraries listed above, only SYS1.LINKLIB contains routines, such as utilities,

Program name	
Program location	Program attributes*
Stor. needed for program	Overlay description
Offset to entry point	List of authorized users

*Bit switches:

Attribute	Bit
Reentrable	0
Reusable	1
In overlay	2
Has symbol table (for debugging)	3
Protected	4
.	.
.	.
.	.

Figure 5.19. Contents of a Hypothetical Program Directory Entry.

which would normally be executed as user programs. System programs operating in supervisor mode use only specially marked libraries, to which write-access is tightly controlled, when invoking other programs without changing modes. An installation, with the aid of mechanisms provided by the system, is responsible for preventing its programmers from adding to or modifying these libraries. This protection of the system's libraries is necessary to preserve the system's integrity.

Compilers typically have separate libraries which provide run-time subroutines for the executing programs. The assemblers have macro libraries which provide the source coding for accessing most system functions. The SORT/MERGE program has a supporting library. The purpose of providing these libraries is to allow user programs to include only those features which they actually need in their programs, thus securing a measure of efficiency.

Private libraries are established in OS/VS for either a step or a job by data definition statements in the job control language for a particular job. These libraries consist of executable programs in load module format and reside as members in a partitioned file. A program in a private library may be executed as the primary program in a job step if its name is specified in the EXEC statement of the job control language.

Temporary libraries containing the load modules for a program to be executed immediately can be established for use only once.

The various permanent libraries are searched in fixed order to allow a user to control which programs are loaded when duplicate names are present in different libraries. To locate the program to be executed for a step, a search is made in the following order: (1) the step library, (2) the job library, and (3) the link library. This permits the user to use a single program name in multiple jobs, but fetch a different program depending on his use of data definition statements, for example, for testing multiple versions of the same routine.

Programs in Main Storage

One characteristic of a program is the discipline with which is was written. If a program stores a value into itself and never reinitializes the affected location but is dependent on that location's initial value, the program is neither serially reusable nor reentrant. Reinitialization is one requirement for serial reusability — the property of a program that can be used many times after being loaded into main storage only once, but cannot be used by two independent invoking programs simultaneously. A reentrable program, one free of that qualification, can never store data into itself.

More can be said on the subject, but our point is made. Reentrable programs can be loaded into areas of main storage into which they cannot write. This preserves their integrity. Serially reusable programs and others cannot. Control blocks must be associated with reentrable and serially reusable programs so that the system can always know when they are unused. In that case, the reentrable program can be deleted from main storage and the serially reusable program can be either used or deleted from main storage.

Libraries, then, are not the only places the system can search for requested programs. When a program is to be loaded dynamically by the supervisor, it searches for a usable copy of the desired program in the following order:

1. The job pack area, containing previously loaded modules in the user's storage area.
2. The task library, established for a task by the ATTACH facility (OS/VS2 only).
3. The step library.
4. The job library, if no step library is used in the current job step.
5. The linkpack area or resident reentrable module area, which contains link library routines resident in main storage.
6. The link library.

The system uses the first available program it finds of the desired name to satisfy the request.

Multics

The management of libraries in MULTICS [Ben69] reflects the segment concept of that system. Any user can refer to a named segment and cause it to be placed in his logical address space. In MULTICS, both program and data files exist as segments. Access to segments is controlled by a tree-structured directory, which is searched by starting at its root subdirectory and searching along allowed paths. The allowable paths for a user are kept in the directory to control access to segments at a lower level. Any node of the tree may be another subdirectory or a nondirectory file, the latter terminating a particular branch of the tree. Additional paths, called links, allow users to access directories on alternate paths. Each subdirectory entry has an attribute list, which consists of a name, a segment length, a segment map, and an access list. The operations on the directory are all performed by the supervisor according to directions given by the creator of a segment. The directory also contains entries for library routines accessible to anyone and for the supervisor. Segment protection is provided by the access attributes of a file, which include free access or restricted access [Wat70]. The various kinds of access restrictions include execute only, read only, write only, read and write, add, delete, and modify. References to a segment which is not already present invoke a dynamic linking facility in the MULTICS supervisor, which verifies access rights and then makes the segment available. Different users can reference a segment at the same time because all MULTICS programs are reentrant.

In this section, we have explored the unique properties of programs as data. This concludes our discussion of data management. Having discussed the way operating systems work, how they manage the system's resources, units of work, and data, we now proceed to the mechanisms for tying the system's facilities together and making use of them, the system's symbolic (external) interface.

QUESTIONS

1. What medium should be employed for each of the following files:
   a. Assembly listing.
   b. File on graves at a large cemetery.
   c. The circulation file for the Library of Congress.
   d. The library of system (object) programs.
   e. Inventory of parts.
   Explain your answers.
2. How should the files described above be organized? Why?

3. Given the records described below in terms of their fields, on which fields of each might primary and secondary indexes be maintained and why:
   a. Part Number, Part Name, Supplier, Component Parts (by number), Quantity on Hand.
   b. Employee Name, Employee Number, Social Security Number, Department, Salary, Skills, Position, Telephone Number.
   c. Customer Name, Charge Number, Address, Balance, Credit.
   d. Flight Number, Origin, Destination, Capacity, Departure Time, Duration, Frequency, Ticket Prices, Movie, Stops, Airplane.
4. Draw a flow chart for a buffering scheme of your own devising, for instance, for two cooperating programs performing different operations on the same file.
5. Give ten examples of uses for data bases with two or more uses of each.
6. Discuss causes of error uniquely likely to arise in the use of data bases.
7. Devise five means for man-machine communication not mentioned in this chapter (such as odoriferous-response), and speculate as to their effects on operating systems.

PROBLEMS

1. Modify the buffering algorithms in Figures 5.15 and 5.16 so that they may be used for output. Use SVC EMPTY X to write out records.
2. Modify the buffering algorithm in Figure 5.16 by using TEST and SET instructions to prevent interruption of critical sections of the algorithm.
3. Modify the buffering algorithm in Figure 5.15 to include unblocking the records. Each call to the GET routine is supposed to return the location of a logical record. The blocking factor, the number of logical records per block, is to be called F and is set by the user program.
4. Develop the flow charts for asynchronous buffering for an updating operation in which a record is read, modified, and written out immediately before the buffer is released. Assume a supervisor call EMPTY X, which may be used to write out a record.

6
Symbol Binding

When we speak of the functions of an operating system, we do not use the word "function" lightly. Our meaning is close indeed to that of the mathematician who speaks of the function $f(x)$ which is defined on some set $x \mid x\epsilon I, x \geqslant 0$, that is, the domain of f is the nonnegative integers. The domains for system functions — such as create, destroy, and execute, as well as add, subtract, and multiply — are sets of objects. We may define a function "execute" on the set of all objects of the type "program." If x_i is the set of all objects defined within the operating system X, and t_i is the type of object x_i, we can speak of the function "execute $(x_i \mid t_i = \text{program})$." Other types might be integer, file, semaphore, and procedure.

To identify objects uniquely and unambiguously, we name them. We use names which comprise familiar graphics, alphabetic and numeric characters, for our own convenience. Such names are easy for us to remember and to use in our communication with the system. We place certain limitations on the formation of names for the system's convenience. We may limit the length of a name or symbol, to some small multiple of the number of characters which can be encoded in one of the words of the computer's storage. We forbid the use of certain characters or combinations of characters to avoid confusion between symbols and other lexical objects, such as function names and syntactic delimiters. We may even encode information as to the object's type in its name; for example, symbols denoting floating-point numbers in FORTRAN may not begin with the letters I through N.

Associated with every named object in the system are three things: a type, a value, and a location where that value can be found. The last is logically superfluous. If a system is merely the sum of its objects, we could define a system simply by keeping a list of all its objects, their types, and their values. Searching this list for an object of a given type with a given name, however, would be most difficult and time consuming. It is much simpler for us to keep a well-structured list of named objects at hand which points to each object's value. This also facilitates giving one object several names — aliases — and naming parts of objects. Employing separate lists for different types of objects, such as a directory for programs in a library or a catalog for files, further simplifies our task.

Symbol *binding* has two meanings. These can always be distinguished in context. In some contexts, a symbol is said to be bound when the location of the value associated with it is fixed. In other contexts, binding is the fixing of the value itself. (This is sometimes called *evaluation*.) A *linker*, or *linkage editor*, for example, is primarily concerned with binding of the first type. The passing of parameters by value is an instance of the second type of binding. Binding of the former type tends to be automatic in some sense, while binding of the latter type tends to involve people.

Symbol binding always occurs within some *context*. That is, the scope within which a search for a definition of a symbol occurs is always specified or assumed. If this were not so, every named object in a system would require a unique name. Limiting scope by type of object would provide little relief. Symbol binding may be confined to a library of programs or a list of libraries, a catalog, a program or list of programs, and so on. A scope may be specified by name qualification — for example, "A.DD1" means the statement named DD1 in the group of statements named A — by preexisting specifications of scope limitation — such as "find my programs only in these libraries: . . ." — or implicitly by context and/or default — for example, "EXEC X" means "find program (context) X in the system's library (default)."

In this chapter, we first discuss the mechanisms involved in symbol binding. These are discussed in a natural chronological order, with emphasis on the linking of separately translated programs. The remainder of the chapter deals with two most important mechanisms for binding: the operating system's control language (OSCL) and the system's interface with the system operator(s).

The reader should bear in mind that binding for objects of certain types can occur only at certain times, that is, by certain mechanisms, and for objects of other types at other times. The designer of a system strives to permit binding to occur whenever a user might reasonably desire it, and not otherwise. A range of binding times or mechanisms is required, because early (tight) binding improves efficiency by permitting the tailoring of operators, while late (loose) binding offers greater flexibility by permitting decisions as to operands to be deferred. Users must be permitted to exchange efficiency for flexibility as they see fit, within the bounds of reason. Readers may wish to decide for themselves whether certain systems they encounter or those mentioned herein exceed those bounds in certain cases, excessively limiting the function of binding, or offering too many gradations of flexibility beyond reasonable bounds.

6.1 MECHANISMS

An operating system comprises a very large number of named objects. Some of these determine the system's characteristics, its appearance to all of its users. Others are relevant only to an individual user or to sets of users. With respect to the system itself, the environment within which jobs are executed, symbol binding may occur when the system's components are coded when a system is individualized (that is, custom-tailored for an installation), when the system is initialized or reinitialized after having been inoperative, and when individuals with appropriate authority alter the system's physical (hardware) or logical (software) characteristics. With respect to a particular job being run on the system, symbol binding may occur when the associated programs are coded, when these programs are combined or linked, when the job is described via the OSCL, and dynamically as execution proceeds. This section deals with the processes which accomplish symbol binding at these times.

Sysgen

The system as coded by its developers may be incomplete in many respects. This is true because a single unmodifiable system cannot satisfy enough people to be a viable commercial product. Just as Ford had to offer colors other than black and, eventually, so many options that millions of Ford automobiles could be produced without any two being identical, so too each operating system must be tailored to meet the needs of individual installations. The process by which the raw system is modified to meet an installation's requirements we call, following IBM, *System generation,* or Sysgen.

There are a number of techniques by which variability can be introduced into a system during its development. The most obvious is incomplete assembly: assembly-time parameters govern whether this code or that code or no code is inserted at a particular point in the program. Alternatively, an entire module containing data rather than code could be built in this way and interrogated by various routines to affect their behavior. This is a second technique: table-driven programming. Various modules with the same name could be shipped with a system from the factory and one of these chosen via some selection process at Sysgen time. A given set of modules could be combined in any of various ways specifiable when the system is generated. Whole components could be included or excluded when the system is generated. All of these techniques involve symbol binding of some sort (exclusion of a component may be viewed as binding to a null value) and all permit the tailoring of a generated system.

Many diverse decisions may be embodied in the generation of a system. A specific or maximal configuration of hardware may be established fixing such variables as: what devices with what features are at what addresses, what is the capacity of main storage, and what features are installed on the central processor. Software configuration may also be established: which compilers are included, which utilities, which devices the system's operators are assumed to be using, and so forth. The functional characteristics of a system may be determined at Sysgen time, such as level of multiprogramming, sizes of partitions for jobs of given types, and the contents of scheduling tables. Less significant decisions embodied in the specifications of Sysgen may establish default options or prevent the bypassing of security/integrity procedures, for example.

System generation for OS/VS systems is a two-stage process. The first is an assembly, the input for which is supplied by the installation that will use the resulting system. The input is in the form of a deck of assembly language macroinstructions. These instructions permit specification of all the data needed to generate an individualized system. The output of the first stage is the job control language (JCL) and data for one job, a sequence of steps. This is then fed back into the starter system which was used for the assembly. The execution of this job constitutes the second stage. It consists mainly of executions of the linkage editor and the move/copy utility. A minimal deck for system generation of OS/VS2 is shown in Figure 6.1. Note that much of the deck consists not of assembly language statements but of JCL statements needed for generation of a new system.

Even system generation does not yield a system ready for use. Many aspects of tailoring a system to a particular establishment's needs may involve software such as vendor-provided subsystems or applications.

IPL

After a system has been generated, the next opportunity for binding of system-related symbols comes when the system is loaded. We again follow IBM in referring to this process as *initial program load,* or IPL. IPL occurs not only immediately following Sysgen, but also after each interruption of service, such as power-down or system crash, whether caused by hardware or software. Like Sysgen, IPL primarily involves binding to values rather than locations. The values entered by the system operator at IPL deal almost exclusively with software configuration: where the job queue is to reside, the current date, modules to be permanently resident in main storage, and the like. Some of these data are provided directly, while others are provided via named files. Some of the values are used immediately, while others are stored away for reference.

OCL

There are some pieces of information the system is always prepared to accept. These may be classified as operator commands, but they are so varied in nature that one can hardly imagine such a single individual as an operator competent to furnish all of them. Commands may alter the software configuration, initiate recovery procedures, and request data from the system. The operator's interface with the system is the subject of Section 6.3.

```
//         JOB    MSGLEVEL=1
//         EXEC   PGM=ASMBLR
//SYSLIB   DD     DSNAME=SYS1.AGENLIB,DISP=SHR
//SYSUT1   DD     UNIT=SYSDA,SPACE=(CYL,(15,2))
//SYSUT2   DD     UNIT=SYSDA,SPACE=(CYL,(10,2))
//SYSUT3   DD     UNIT=SYSDA,SPACE=(CYL,(16,2))
//SYSPUNCH DD     UNIT=180,LABEL=(,NL)
//SYSPRINT DD     SYSOUT=A
//SYSIN    DD     *
         DATASET   name,SPACE=allocation,VOL=volno
20 of ·  CENPROCS  MODEL=145R
         CHANNEL   ADDRESS=0,TYPE=MULTIPLEXOR
         CHANNEL   ADDRESS=1,TYPE=SELECTOR
         IODEVICE  UNIT=3210,ADDRESS=009
         IODEVICE  UNIT=2520,MODEL=B1,ADDRESS=00C
         IODEVICE  UNIT=3211,ADDRESS=00E
         IODEVICE  UNIT=2420,ADDRESS=180
         IODEVICE  UNIT=2314,ADDRESS=130,IOREQUE=PRIORITY
         PAGE
         SCHEDULR  IOC=009
         UNITNAME  NAME=SYSDA,UNIT=(130,131,132,133,134,135,136,137)
         UNITNAME  NAME=SYSSQ,UNIT=180
         GENERATE
         END
/*
//       EXEC  PGM=IEFBR14
//X       DD   DSN=SYS1.OBJPDS,SPACE=(CYL,(7,1,12)),UNIT=130      X
//             VOL=(,RETAIN,SER=SYSLIB),DISP=(CATLG)
```

Figure 6.1. A Minimal Sysgen Deck for OS/VS2.

One function of the *operator's command language* (OCL) gives rise to what may be considered an additional time for binding — subsystem initiation. The initiation of a subsystem involves the invocation of a program which may establish default values for attributes of jobs running under the subsystem. Loosely, we may include a job reader or input spooling program as such a subsystem. Even an initiator of OS/VS is started in this way and provides some binding. This mechanism, while useful, seems too contrived and ad hoc to merit separate consideration. We choose to categorize such binding with the interface through which it is effected, OSCL, and say no more about it.

This concludes our discussion of mechanisms specially designed to bind the system's symbols, that is, to provide values for system-related objects. Note that the symbols involved are hidden. Their only external manifestations are the keywords of statements in various languages. Somewhere inside the system's code, however, those objects are named, and their binding to values is no less real for the covert nature of their names.

Linking

We deal next with the binding of job-related, program-related, or user-related objects. One of the types of binding we encounter here is not easily to be subsumed by the two types we have defined above. It is common to write a program which makes reference to a logical file named, for example, DAILYXAC. Some statement of an OSCL is used to equate DAILYXAC with an existing (physical) file, say MONDEC18. We could call this binding by equation of symbols, or supplying an alias. Alternatively, we can assign the object named DAILYXAC the value MONDEC18 and say that using the former object involves making a search with its value as an argument, and then using the result of that search, that is, the location of the file named MONDEC18, as the value of interest. Utilizing the latter interpretation permits us to retain only our original two types of binding. In the terms of OS/VS, we say that the DDname DAILYXAC has the value of the symbol MONDEC18 and the binding of the latter symbol to a data set permits use of a given data control block (DCB).

The mechanisms we consider in the remainder of this section are program translation, program linking, control language (OSCL) processing, and dynamic binding. Linking receives by far the greatest part of our attention here, but OSCLs are the subject of Section 6.2.

The binding of symbols to locations is the very core of program translation. The operative notion of location differs from system to system and among types of objects within programs. A symbol may be associated with an offset from the beginning of the program or from the value assumed to be in a given register, rather than with an absolute location. When the register in question is always to be loaded with an address within the program, the symbol, as in the first case, can be called an *internal label*. Otherwise, the symbol is an *external label* and may address different storage for each invocation of the program. External labels permit recursive use of programs. Some symbols, called *external references,* cannot be bound during the translation process at all, but must be bound when programs are linked together. Some symbols defined within a program may be those to which references are made by other programs. Such symbols are called *external symbols* or *external names*. A dictionary of external references and external symbols must be one output of a program translator if the programs it produces are to be linked with others.

Within a single program, the same symbol may be validly used more than once. For that reason, the concept of scope for symbol binding is involved in the translation of a procedural language. The reader may wish to review the discussion of this point in Chapter 3.

One type of object for which many times of binding by value are provided is the file description, the data control block (DCB) of OS/VS. Certain characteristics may be ascribed to a file when a program to process it is written, others when OSCL statements are coded, others when a file label is read, and still others when the executing program examines the results of the other resolutions and inserts additional values. (See Tables 6.1 and 6.2.) We say more about this below.

Once a program has been translated, further symbol binding awaits a *linking* routine or linker, called by IBM a linkage editor.[1] The function we call linking is also known as *building, collecting,* and *binding.*[2] Linking here is treated as distinct from loading. The functions of a nonlinking loader are treated separately after the discussion of linkers.

A linker combines separately translated programs into a single entity we call, again after IBM, a load module [IBM2]. It does this by resolving (binding) external references to identically named external symbols (external names), and concatenating the *text* of the programs being combined. Typically, however, linkers do far more than this. They accept not only translated programs, but also load modules, control statements, and libraries of modules. They not only perform symbol resolution, but also equate, define, alter, and delete symbols as specified by control statements; build complex overlay structures; and produce valuable printed descriptions of the resulting load modules.

The linker's *raison d'etre* is the combining of separately translated programs into single executable load modules. To perform this function, the linker accepts as input the output of program translators. These are called here *object programs,* as distinguished from *source programs,* the input to translators. The terms *block* [Weg62] and *object module*[3] have also been used for this notion. An

---

[1] Although we may not always say so, most of our terminology (e.g., RLD, ESD) follows [IBM2].
[2] [Pre72], 151.
[3] [Pre72], et al., after IBM usage.

object program is composed principally of program text in machine-interpretable form and a dictionary of symbols. An entry of the dictionary describes a named object in terms of its name, type, location of definition or reference within the associated text, and certain other data, such as length, as appropriate. An object program may include delimiting records and other data descriptive of the program as a whole. A *relocation dictionary* (RLD) is included in an object program to permit a loader to initialize address constants in program text. An RLD entry indicates via a pointer the *external symbol dictionary* (ESD) entry for the containing program and an offset where the constant appears in text. A second pointer to an ESD entry designates the symbol whose value is to be added to the indicated word of text to bind the address constant in main storage.

The linker may accept inputs other than object programs. It may combine object programs with load modules to form new load modules. It may accept control statements which invoke functions other than simple combination. It may permit the specification of libraries to be used in searching for object programs or load modules to be included because their names match unresolved external references appearing in inputs already processed.

The basic functions of a linker are relatively simple. The textual portions of inputs must be concatenated to form the text of the resulting load module. The entries gleaned from dictionaries in the input to the execution of the linker must be collected to form the load module's composite external symbol dictionary (CESD). These entries must reflect offsets relative to the text of the load module unless, in some entries, offsets are carried relative to specified associated symbols. Where an external reference and an external name associated with the same symbol appear in different inputs, the reference must be resolved to the name. Resolution may involve placing at the textual location of the reference a value indicative of the location defined by the external name. This value may be absolute, in the case of nonrelocatable text, or relative to some other location,

Table 6.1. DCB Binding Mechanisms in Order of Precedence.

1. Values coded in the DCB macroinstruction of the Assembly Language.
2. Values inserted into the DCB subsequent to program loading, but prior to the OPENing of the file (a process which logically encompasses the mechanisms 3 through 5).
3. Values coded in the DCB parameter of the DD statement having a DDname matching the DDname coded in the DCB macroinstruction.
4. Values inserted into the DCB by a routine identified in a list associated with the DCB via the DCB macroinstruction.
5. Values present in the standard label of the file identified by the DD statement of 3.
6. Values inserted into the DCB subsequent to the OPENing of the file, but prior to first use. (This mechanism is effective only for some types of files and some characteristics.)

Table 6.2. List of File Characteristics [IBM4].

DCB Keyword	Meaning
BFALN	Buffer alignment; full- or double-word boundary
BFTEK	Buffering technique: simple, exchange, record, or dynamic buffering
BLKSIZE	Block size
BUFIN	Number of input buffers for a terminal
BUFL	Buffer length
BUFMAX	Maximum number of buffers allocated concurrently for a terminal
BUFNO	Number of buffers in a pool of buffers.
BUFOFF	Length of block prefix for ASCII file on magnetic tape
BUFOUT	Number of output buffers for a terminal
BUFRQ	Similar to BUFIN
BUFSIZE	Similar to BLKSIZE; for terminals
CODE	Encoding technique for paper tape
CPRI	Relative priority of sending vs. receiving; for terminals
CLYOFL	Number of tracks to be used for overflow per cylinder of ISAM file
DEN	Recording density on reel of magnetic tape
DDNAME	Symbol used for pairing DD statement with DCB
DSORG	File organization
ERROPT	Action to be taken when an uncorrectable I/O error occurs
GNCP	Number of I/O operations which may be in progress simultaneously for a graphic terminal
HIARCHY	Level of the storage hierarchy to be used for file
INTVL	Polling interval for terminals
KEYLEN	Length of record key
LIMCT	Limits searching characteristics for directly accessed file
LRECL	Length of a logical record (a physical record is a block)
MODE	Mode of operation for file of punched cards: binary or character
NCP	Similar to GNCP for a nongraphic file
NTM	Similar to CLYOFL for index rather than overflow
OPTCD	Catchall for miscellaneous options
PCI	Similar to BUFTEK with emphasis on utilization of main storage; for terminals
PRTSP	Spacing on a printer
RECFM	Record format; blocking, embedded descriptors, anomalies permitted or prohibited, etc.
REPOS	Program using primitive method of access (EXCP) will simulate SAM's record counting
RESERVE	Descriptive data to be included in records for terminal
RKP	Offset in record to position of key

Table 6.2. (Cont.)

Verb	Function of Statement
SOWA	Size of work area; for terminal
STACK	Stacker for cards; for card reader or punch
THRESH	Relates to integrity mechanism associated with telecommunications
TRTCH	Parity and 6-to-8 bit conversion data for file on magnetic tape

for example, the first character of text. Alternatively, an index to the directory entry for the external name may be associated with the entry for the external reference. In the latter two cases, further resolution must be performed by a loader. A reference to an external name within a block is treated as a reference to a fixed offset beyond the start of the block containing it.

A linker may perform a number of other functions involving symbol resolution. A symbol may be modified or deleted altogether by the linker as directed by control statements. When a symbol identifying a block of code is deleted, the then inaccessible block is deleted as well. The user may specify that an external reference may remain unresolved for this (no-call) or for this and all subsequent (never-call) operations by the linker on this module, without invalidation of the resulting load module. Such a specification implies that resolution is not to be effected through implicit searches of libraries. Conversely, it may be specified

Table 6.3. OS/360 Linkage Editor Functions: Rough Semantics of Control Statements [IBM2].

Verb	Function of Statement
ALIAS	To provide more than one entry point to a load module
CHANGE	To alter the symbol associated with an entry, CSECT, or external reference
ENTRY	To specify the primary entry point (first instruction) of a load module
HIARCHY	To assign a CSECT to a level of the storage hierarchy
INCLUDE	To include all or specified modules from a library
INSERT	To order CSECTs within a load module
LIBRARY	To control the searching of libraries to resolve external references
NAME	To name a load module
OVERLAY	Used with INSERT to specify an overlay structure
REPLACE	To delete a CSECT entry name or external reference from a load module or replace one CSECT with another
SETSSI	To associate hexadecimal data with a load module

that a particular library is to be searched to effect a resolution of all unresolved symbols or one or more designated symbols. A library may contain either object programs or load modules. The no-call and never-call facilities are employed when a front-end object module is to be included in load modules with only some of its back-ends. For example, TRIGFNS may have no-call or never-call references to SIN, HSIN, COSIN, and so on, the latter routines being included only via INCLUDE statements as needed.

The linker should respond in a completely predictable way to multiple definitions of the same symbol (via external names). The OS/VS Linkage Editor rejects all but the first definition it encounters of the same symbol. It could just as logically have been defined to prefer the last definition or to permit specification by the invoker of an algorithm for choosing the preferred definition.

Folding. The linker is one of a number of possible agents for accomplishing the *folding* of a program, that is, permitting a program to execute in less storage space than would be needed to hold all of its code and data areas at one time. When a linker is used to fold a program, the operation involved is referred to as the building of an overlay structure. Since this was once the most widely used method of program folding, we choose this point to insert a general discussion of folding. What we call semiautomatic folding, the building of an overlay structure, is discussed next. Automatic folding is effected by mechanisms involving virtual storage, which is covered in Chapter 4. Totally manual folding is not discussed in detail.

It is sometimes convenient or necessary to write programs larger in size than the main storage available to contain them. These programs can be executed in intrinsically inadequate storage space if they are folded, that is, divided into chunks which fit into the available space as they are required. Folding may be done automatically by the system, employing either static or dynamic analysis of program behavior; semiautomatically with the aid of a linker; or manually [Pan68].

All folding techniques yield the same result: more than one part of the same program may occupy the same location in primary storage at different times.

Automatic folding with static analysis is said to occur when a source program is analyzed by some component of the operating system and segmented for folded execution [Say69]. It may involve either semiautomatic folding or the simulation of manual folding, depending on what facilities are available. It is interesting, but its value has not been demonstrated.

Virtual storage may be seen as a mechanism for providing automatic folding with dynamic analysis. This clearly provides a solution to the same problems addressed by other folding mechanisms. In this case, symbols are bound to locations by hardware mechanisms. We say no more about this technique here, but refer the reader to Chapter 4.

S/370 Assembly Language			Assembled Text (Object Module)	ESD Entries				Text in Storage (Load Module loaded at 48000)
				Symbol	Type[a]	Offset	Length or Reference	
	CSECT				PC	000000	00001A	
	BALR	12,0	05 C0					05 C0
	USING	*,12						
	L	15,WBASE	58 F0 C0 0C					58 F0 C0 0C
	L	11,WBASE(3)	58 B3 C0 0C					58 B3 C0 0C
	BALR	14,11	05 EB					05 EB
	BR	4	07 F4					07 F4
	EXTRN	NTREE		NTREE	ER	000000	000000[b]	
	EXTRN	WATRGATE		WATRGATE	ER	000000	000000[b]	
WBASE	DC	A(WATRGATE)	00 00 00 00[c]					00 04 80 20
	DC	A(NTREE)	00 00 00 00[c]					00 04 80 22
	DC	A(NTREE+2)	00 00 00 02[c]					00 04 80 24
	END							
WATRGATE	CSECT			WATRGATE	SD	000000[d]	00000E	{6 bytes of any data}
	USING	*,15						
	LCR	1,1	13 11					13 11
	ENTRY	NTREE		NTREE	LD	000002	000001[e]	
NTREE	AR	2,1	1A 21					1A 21
	A	2,CON8	5A 20 F0 0A					5A 20 F0 0A
	BR	14	07 FE					07 FE
CON8	DC	A(CON8-NTREE)	00 00 00 0A					00 00 00 0A
	END							

[a] PC=Private Code, SD=Section Definition, LD=Label Definition, ER=External Reference.
[b] Entries absent from CESD of load module due to resolution.
[c] Constant represented by RLD entry in both object and load modules.
[d] Becomes 20 in CESD of load module.
[e] Becomes 2 in CESD of load module.

If A is in Register 1, B in Register 2, and either 0, 4, or 8 in Register 3, B-A, B+A+8, or B+8 is returned in Register 2 by WATRGATE (assuming it has no bugs).

Figure 6.2. Various representations of a program after successive binding mechanisms are applied.

Semiautomatic folding occurs when the programmer breaks his program into segments and maps their occupation of some known quantity of main storage. This mapping is expressed by statements presented to a linker. The necessary binding of symbols to locations is accomplished by the linker and loader, as with nonfolded programs.

Manual folding occurs when semiautomatic folding is simulated by explicit user-written code. Specialized operators or standard I/O operations are employed.

Overlay. Figure 6.3 depicts some overlay structures a linker might construct. P1, . . ., P15 are routines (the text of independently translated programs); S1, . . ., S11 are segments; E1, . . ., E6 are entry points (external names); and R1, R2, and R3 are regions. A region serves to partition the storage occupied by a program. Its contents are determined without regard for the contents of other regions. Within each region, a tree of segments may be defined, the tree being a map of the region. Branches descending from the same node — for example, S2 and S3 — may not reside in main storage simultaneously. In fact, each segment is associated with some fixed range of addresses relative to the beginning

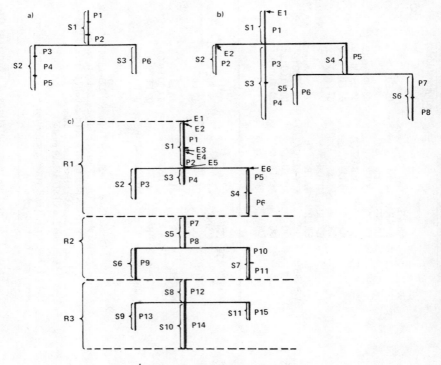

Figure 6.3. Some Overlay Structures.

of a region, and two segments associated with overlapping ranges cannot coreside in main storage. The single segment at the top of a tree, the root segment (S1), occupies the lowest range of addresses in a region. Each segment is associated with a range which begins where the range associated with the segment above it ends, and each region represents a separate area of main storage, that is, the regions of a load module do not overlap.

Individual linkers place particular restrictions on overlay structures beyond those implicit or explicit in the preceding paragraph.[4] The number of levels of overlay permitted, that is, the maximum number of segments in storage at one time, may be limited to as few as four. Intersegment calls may only be allowed up the tree, toward the root, with all downward linkage funneled through a single entry point permitted in each segment. The loading of a segment might imply the loading of all its lineal descendants — the segments which connect it in the tree to the root — even if the code causing the loading is overlaid as a result. Resolution of external references may be required within a segment and its lineal descendants, making communication down a tree tricky, though not impossible. A call from one segment to another with which the first cannot coreside may require preplanning or be prohibited altogether. Returning from subroutines to invokers in other segments may be restricted or prohibited. And there may be other restrictions.

Two functions associated with overlay structures are of particular interest: promotion of common areas and calls between segments which cannot coreside. The name of the former function is a reference to the COMMON facility of FORTRAN. The static external storage of PL/1 is but another of many examples of similar facilities. A linker may place all common areas in the root segment. Alternatively, a common area may be placed in the root of the subtree containing all references to it if and only if that root remains resident or is preserved and reloaded together with the common area as long as the area remains in use. Since a length is associated with each reference, the length of the common area is the greatest of all the lengths associated with the references to it. A common area may be named or blank (unnamed). All references to blank common are treated as references to the same unnamed common area.

A call between segments which cannot coreside. termed by IBM[5] an exclusive call, may appear to be impossible. In a way, it is; that is, although the exclusive call appears to the programmer to be a simple branch instruction with an entire segment magically loaded between the time the branch instruction is fetched from main storage and the time control is actually transferred, this is not really the case. A supervisory function is, as one might imagine, invoked, albeit by covert means. The key to the puzzle is an object called a virtual constant, a V-con.

---

[4] [Lan69] is a principal source for what follows. [Pan68] is also relevant.
[5] [IBM2], from which much other information on this topic is derived.

The linker, in resolving a V-con used for an exclusive call, does not use the address of the named entry point but the address of a table, called the entry table or ENTAB, inserted by the linker into the root segment. An entry in the ENTAB contains an instruction to invoke the supervisor and an identifier of the related entry point. Because of this indirection, a V-con used for an exclusive call cannot be used to reference data, but only for a call, exclusive or not. Also, a routine called via an exclusive call cannot simply return to the instruction following the one which caused its invocation. To effect a return to the calling segment, it must perform another exclusive call. A V-con not used for an exclusive call is at execution time indistinguishable from any other address constant which makes reference to an externally defined symbol.

Specifications for an overlay structure govern the relative locations of segments of input text in the resulting load module. The OS/VS Linkage Editor does not otherwise specify the order in which segments of text will appear in its output. If order is important to the user for some reason, INSERT statements must be employed.

Linkers' Output. The OS/VS Linkage Editor produces three types of printed output beyond the mere listing of input parameters, control statements, and identifiers of diagnostic messages. The first is a map showing the relative locations of all named objects in the load module produced. The second is a cross-reference listing showing where references are made to external symbols. These two can be of great aid when a large program is being debugged, especially in the early stages of development. The third is an English description of errors or anomalies for which diagnostics were generated. The value of such output from any processor should not be underestimated, yet it can always be produced simply and inexpensively.

Loaders

The linking functions we have described are most often performed by a program which is also responsible for loading programs into main storage and executing them. A significant exception, but not the first nor by any means the only one, is the OS/VS Linkage Editor, a program which demonstrates what we consider to be a very important point: that these functions are logically separable. The incurring of the overhead of linking only once per load module, as opposed to once per execution, is crucial in production-oriented environments, that is those where a program is produced over a period of days, weeks, or months, but used every day or week for years.

Loaders, as distinct from linkers, load text into main or virtual storage and perform that relocation which is the last form of binding to precede program execution. (In the light of this chronology, we might well have inserted here our discussion of control languages, but the close relationship between linking and loading functions dictated the ordering we have used.) Loading is also a function of an overlay supervisor, a specialized loader used to load segments of a load module having an overlay structure. The overlay supervisor is simply a loader sensitive to the description of an overlay structure provided by the linker.

The functions of a loader are few and simple: determine what is to be loaded where; read records of text into the proper locations in main or virtual storage; use the RLD records (in the case of OS/VS) to find address constants to which a value must be added; and perform that addition.

Loading need not refer to an operation performed by the system once per step. Routines may be loaded explicitly under program control while steps are being executed. LOAD and DELETE operations permit what we have called manual folding. Some operating systems define these operations to be comparable in function to linking, providing thereby facilities for manual folding as powerful as those provided for semiautomatic folding.

The most comprehensive work on linkers and loaders is [Pre72]. Other works of interest are [Weg62] and [McC63].

OSCL

The next binding mechanism we consider is the operating system's control language (OSCL). The OSCL binds by value rather than by address. We can think of a step as being represented within the system by a set of tables. One table contains entries for attributes which apply to the step as a whole. One or more entries in that table serve to point to the other tables via lists or chains. In the latter case, each table points to the next until the chain is ended by some sort of last-table indicator. Those tables beyond the first describe the files to be associated with the step. The entries of the tables correspond to file characteristics. We can think of each table as bearing the symbolic name of the object it describes, step or file, and each entry in a table as bearing the symbolic name of the keyword used in OSCL, or some other language used for binding, to assign a value to that entry. The full symbolic name of an entry might thus have several components: job name (for we assume that each step must exist within a job and each job must be uniquely named); step name; file name, and file characteristic name. Our conceptualization gains credence from the fact that such tables as we have described are actually used by operating systems, but that need not have been the case. The items of data in question might have been kept in a single table or in widely scattered storage locations. Their logical purposes and identifiers would remain.

Most of the values supplied by the user through an OSCL are merely descriptive. They describe a step in terms of what programs are to be executed and where they can be found; what facilities it will use; under what conditions it should be aborted by the system, for example, if too much time is consumed or too much output generated; and so on. They describe files in terms of where they can be found; how space on a direct-access device is to be partitioned (for main, overflow, or index records); when the file should be considered obsolete; and the like.

Some values, however, specifically request services, usually the allocation of resources from the system. For a step, the allocation of space in main storage is requested. For a file, requests are made for the allocation of auxiliary storage devices, volumes, and space; specific forms or print chains; and so on.

Two functions of OSCLs are rather unlike all the others. An OSCL permits the passing of data not in any file to the first program of a step. The parameters so passed are bound to the variables established as parameters when the program was coded. Such data could be read from a file, but are of insufficient volume to justify the overhead associated with the processing of a file.

The other unique function of an OSCL is the binding of logical and physical files. This occurs when a symbol used within a program to denote a file (DDname) — its logical name — is equated, or bound, to the symbolic name of an actual file (data set name, or dsname). The ability to perform binding of this type, sometimes called file independence, adds significantly to the generality which can be incorporated into a program. The same flexibility could be provided by changing the physical names of files to match logical names which are unique and remain constant, but this technique is clearly more awkward than the first described, particularly for files that are accessed by more than one program.

The ability to omit the specification of a value is crucial to the usability of a control language. If users must specify every detail of a function each time they invoke it, the function must be either a very simple one or very difficult to use. Defaults, assumed values, if chosen so as to be widely applicable, permit most users to invoke a complex function with a simple statement.

It is sometimes necessary to specify a value which is to take effect even in the face of contradictory values specified for the same symbol by mechanisms which normally have precedence. Such a specification is said to *override* all others. Orders of precedence are necessary whenever several mechanisms exist for the binding of the same symbol. This order of precedence is most often temporal, a later specification overriding an earlier one. There are, however, often reasons for reversing this order or altering it in some other well-defined way. In some cases, the relative time at which specifications were made may not even be clear. An order of precedence may be specified with respect to mechanisms, with little or no regard for the temporal order in which the mechanisms are usually employed.

The OSCL of OS/VS, Job Control Language (JCL), exhibits an extraordinary range of orders of precedence with respect to individual parameters of the language. These are described by Table 6.4. Omitted from the table is the DCB

Table 6.4. JCL Defaults and Overrides.

Statement and Parameter	System[1] build	Sysgen	IPL	S RDR[2]	S INIT[3]	JOB	PROC[4]	EXEC PGM	DD
JOB									
name[5]	d			(s)		s			
CLASS	d					s			
MSGCLASS	d	d		d		s			
MSGLEVEL	d			d		s			
PRTY				d	s				
JOB and EXEC									
ACCT[5]				(s)		o	o	s	
COND						s[11]	s[11]	s[11]	
DPRTY	d			d		o[12]	s	s	
RD	d					o	s	s	
REGION			d[10]	d		o	s	s	
ROLL				d		o	s	s	
TIME				d		o[13]	o[13]	s	
EXEC									
PARM						o[14]	s		
DD									
ddname[6]					d[6]				s
DISP	d								s
Label=BLP[7]	(o)	(o)		(o)					s
SPACE[8]				d					s
UNIT[8]				d					s
DCB=BLKSIZE[9]				d					
DCB=BUFNO[9]				d					s

d = default; effective if no later specification occurs.
o = override; effective if no earlier overriding specification occurs.
s = specifiable; effective in absence of overrides.

[1] Where no default is indicated, a later specification is required to invoke a function. No means of negating the effect of an invocation (e.g., via a value of NO) is provided. Some defaults are no longer applicable due to the obsolescence of the uniprogramming version of OS/360.
[2] The PARM field in the procedure used to start a reader of jobs is meant. Default for all indicated parameters except MSGLEVEL *must* be specified.
[3] DD statements in the procedure used to start an initiator are meant.
[4] Parameters to whose keywords "procstepname" (designating an override of a single EXEC PGM statement) is not appended are meant.
[5] The parenthesized value refers to a specification of whether or not the parameter is mandatory on JOB statements.
[6] The specification of statements to provide defaults and overrides of similarly named DD statements in initiated jobs is meant. Some parameters of the DD statement are given default values, others are given overriding values, and still others obtain merged values.
[7] Any specification that the value of BLP is to be treated as though it were NL overrides contrary specification. The parenthesized values refer only to this fact.
[8] Reference is made only to parameters for SYStem OUTput files of jobs read by the relevant reader.
[9] Reference is made only to SYStem INput files (those specified with the * or DATA parameter) of jobs read by the relevant reader.
[10] Via the definition of fixed partitions. OCL is also a source for this information.
[11] All specifications are valid in the presence of others and refer to the entities job, procedure, or step defined by the statements of which they are part.
[12] The earliest specification is the only one which retains validity. It refers to the entity, job, or procedure, defined by the statement of which it is part.
[13] A specification takes effect for the first step of the procedure and later specifications are nullified.
[14] Specification is accomplished via the PRTY parameter of the JOB statement and overrides only the first subparameter of the DPRTY parameter of the EXEC statement.

(data control block) parameter, which is treated separately in Table 6.1. The DCB parameter is used to specify the characteristics of a file. The data control block is the control block specified at the time of program translation to hold this information. Some parameters of the DCB provide programs with what is called device independence, the ability to process, without being modified, files resident on diverse media.

Dynamic Binding

Binding of both addresses and values may occur even after a program has begun execution. While all systems with virtual storage have some form of dynamic address binding, the segmentation mechanism of the Honeywell (formerly GE) 645 MULTICS system merits our particular attention. We also discuss in the following paragraphs the role of catalogs, file labels, and prompting.

Segmentation[6] involves the retention of symbols through the loading process and the resolution of these symbols as they are encountered during execution. Unnecessary binding is thus avoided; the named objects, residing in separate segments, can grow to the maximum size of a segment and the sharing of named objects is easily managed. All the benefits one would expect from this latest of all possible binding accrue: the ultimate in flexibility.

While the involvement of a *catalog* can be inferred from the description of segmentation, we treat the subject of catalogs separately. A catalog is basically a set of ordered pairs, each pair comprising a symbol as a first element and an address as a second element. Among the objects which can be cataloged are programs, segments of programs in overlay structures, and files. Searches of catalogs to effect the binding of symbols may be constrained in various ways. Constraint is strictest when a segment of a load module is sought within the load module. An ordered list of libraries to be searched for a program may be supplied by a user. This is an explicit, but fairly loose, constraint. Between these is the constraint which may be placed on files: that part of their names — called qualifiers — name the catalog through which the search must be made. For example, the file ANIMAL.MAMMAL.PRIMATE.LEMUR would be found in the catalog named LEMUR, located via the catalog named PRIMATE, which is located in turn via the catalogs named MAMMAL and ANIMAL. The types of constraint described above may be designated implicit, explicit over a set of symbols, and explicit by symbol, respectively. Other means and scopes of constraint can easily be devised. A constraint defines a context for the binding of symbols and each symbol defined within a context is usually required to have only one definition.

---

[6] Our present discussion of segmentation (see also Chapter 4) follows [Pre72], although many more detailed treatments exist.

We have mentioned above the role played by file labels in the binding of file characteristics. We add here only that the directory of what is called in OS/VS a partitioned data set, that is, a library, is for all intents and purposes a label for the file which is a single program — load module or object program. The directory entry describes the member of a partitioned data set in much the same way a file's label describes a file.

[COD71b] describes another type of dynamic binding, that of data formats. In a data base system, one where huge amounts of data are stored in highly structured ways for efficiency of random access, an executing program may access and interrogate a record template, called a schema, to bind dynamically a view of data. Since the program is insensitive to changes in the schema, it is said to be *data independent*.

In an interactive environment, dynamic binding of values can sometimes be the result of human intervention. If a program finds that a required value has not been supplied, the program can send a message to a user at a terminal to ask the user for the value. When such a message follows the entry by the user of a deficient command language statement, the function is known as prompting. In this case or otherwise, such a mechanism is properly considered post-OSCL binding.

This concludes our discussion of mechanisms for binding symbols to addresses and values. The remaining sections of this chapter deal with the two languages specifically designed to accomplish binding, OSCL and the operator's command language (OCL). The latter is treated in the context of the total interface between the operating system and the operator. Our treatment of binding is novel and no general references can be cited. The reader may pursue the subject in the works mentioned in the discussion of individual mechanisms.

6.2 CONTROL LANGUAGE

Control languages for operating systems have existed as long as operating systems themselves. Yet, they have been the subject of far less concern, proliferating wildly at the whim of the systems' designers without so much as a nod toward consistency. This is a matter of considerable importance, and an effort directed at standardization[7] has been undertaken, but what constitutes a good operating system control language (OSCL) is still poorly understood.

Let us define our terms. OSCLs are the languages used to request services of generalized operating systems. An OSCL may be used from any input device, including a terminal, Excluded are query languages, information systems such as IMS, MIS, or GIS, and dedicated systems such as APL and QUIKTRAN.

---

[7] ANSI X3.4.2f. (later called the Ad Hoc Committee on Operating System Control Languages), and successors. A *CO*BOL *Da*ta and *Sy*stems *L*anguage (CODASYL) task group was formed to the same end.

OSCLs should make available the full power of the systems they serve and they should be "easy to use." It is easy to speak of "usability," "good human factors," and so forth, but hard to define these terms. While one qualification of experts on human factors is that they be human, it is not the only qualification. That all designers of OSCLs think that they know better than any previous designer how to make a language "easy to use" can be inferred from the fact that no two OSCLs are alike. Yet, the usability of no OSCL has been widely acclaimed and these designers have made little of their thinking publicly available. (An exception is [Bar72] on the GEORGE 3 system.) See, however, [Sch80].

We set forth here a large number of considerations which must be taken into account in the design of an OSCL. In so doing, we illuminate the process of designing an OSCL and suggest how existing OSCLs may be evaluated.

This task is by no means simple. An OSCL does not exist in isolation. An OSCL can only be evaluated in terms of:

1. Its environment — the system described by the OSCL, its power and complexity, users and their characteristics, its very nature, for example, data-oriented, interactive, or multipurpose.
2. Its processor — the program which translates the OSCL into the requests for system functions.
3. Its functions — the things which it enables its users to do and say.
4. Its syntax — the rules for composing valid statements in the language.
5. Its documentation — the description of the language.

An OSCL can be characterized only when all of these aspects of its nature have been considered.

Environment

An OSCL is strongly influenced by its environment. We define the environment of an OSCL by how jobs are entered into the system, by what kind of work is performed by the system, and by the homogeneity and level of sophistication of the system's users.

Many distinctions among OSCLs can be made on the basis of the manner in which jobs are entered into the system. Two main categories are recognized: batch and interactive. The latter is distinguished by the fact that a user reacts synchronously to the system's processing of the job. For this reason, OSCLs for interactive systems tend to be interpretive, while OSCLs for batch systems are "compilable," if not actually compiled.

The distinctions between OSCLs for batch and interactive systems have been great enough to merit a distinction in terminology. We acknowledge this distinction by referring to OSCLs for batch systems as *control languages,* while OSCLs for interactive systems are here called *command languages,* a distinction consistent with [Bar72]. An OSCL may, of course, be either.

Command languages take some of their characteristics from terminals, the devices through which they are entered into the system. Thus, command languages make use of backspace keys and attention keys. These keys, quite naturally, facilitate the editing of OSCL text, normally possible in command languages. The ready availability of upper and lower case has led to enlarged character sets in some command languages.

A command language need not be so invulnerable to errors as a control language. A user of the former can easily see his input and can easily correct it in "real time." An error in control language is far more likely to escape undetected and is likely to cause a delay of one turnaround or more.

All this is not to say that a single OSCL cannot serve a system to which jobs may be submitted either interactively or in batch mode. The IBM System/360 Time-Sharing System's Command System [IBM3] and SDC's Advanced Development Prototype (ADEPT-50) Time-Sharing System's Command Language [Ken69] are two of many such OSCLs. In each case, a command language became a control language as a batch capability augmented an interactive capability.[8] In fact, most command languages have a facility for defining procedures which simulate batch processing; that is, they contain a control language as a (not necessarily proper) subset. The use of a control language as a command language is also known [Cla70].

Further differences among OSCLs result from the different orientations of the systems they describe. A system oriented toward computation is likely to have an OSCL with very limited facilities for data description and data handling. Such an OSCL is often designed for rapid processing so as not to incur overwhelming overhead in a system where most jobs last less than a minute. A data-oriented system is likely to bring many more facilities, even some considered utilities or applications in other systems, out to the user via OSCL.

A system aspiring to generality must serve data-oriented and computation-oriented requirements. To do this, significant procedural, or "macro," capabilities must be present to facilitate the OSCL's use. OS/VS is an example of such a system. The extent to which its Job Control Language [IBM4], or any other OSCL, achieves the objective of generality is debatable.

Highly specialized systems offer control functions concisely and inflexibly. Such systems, as is noted above, are excluded from the present discussion.

An OSCL is heavily influenced by the power and complexity of the system it describes. A complex system can have a complex OSCL or an inadequate one.

---

[8] This statement is supported by the use of LOGON and LOGIN, respectively, in the two languages, where OSCLs designed for batch systems more typically use JOB or RUN (UNIVAC 1108 EXEC 8). LOGOFF and LOGOUT, used by these systems, are also typical of command languages and unknown in OSCLs restricted to batch systems.

Those are the only alternatives. The value of the OSCL may be measured by its success in using the homogeneity of segments of the system's user population to conceal the system's complexity wherever possible, without sacrificing flexibility. If, for example, 80% of a complex system's users use 80% of the OSCL's parameters less than 20% of the time, the OSCL has achieved some degree of success (an application of the oft-used 80-20 rule). Yet, it must also be said that users who do not require a function should be able to remain ignorant of its existence. This is largely a problem of documentation and is addressed below.

A system far more sophisticated than its users is unlikely to have a well-liked OSCL, and conversely. A system used by only "the faithful," at a university, for example, can hardly have a poor OSCL. This is all the more true when the users and designers of the system are the same or similar individuals. While OSCLs may be tailored to input media and the purposes of operating systems, their acceptance is apt to depend on the relative simplicity of the systems they describe and the users they serve. This point can hardly be overemphasized and it is one to which we return below. The powers of an OSCL designer are heavily constrained by such factors.

Processor

The appearance of an OSCL to its users depends to a great extent on its processor. The processor gives the OSCL its character as an interpreted or a compiled language. It may permit or deny the user functions because of the way it is integrated with an operating system. And its efficiency determines to what extent the OSCL is seen as imposing overhead on the system. While the function of an OSCL may be to describe an operating system, the OSCL often includes a large number of statements addressed solely to its processor. These statements specify how other statements are to be interpreted, altered, excluded, or included.

The most basic thing which can be said of an OSCL processor is that it is an *interpreter* or a *compiler*. Yet, this distinction is sometimes blurred. All command languages are processed interpretively. This is implicit in the interactive nature of the host operating system. Most control languages go through some sort of compilation which permits a degree of interpretation. That OS/VS JCL is in some sense compiled seems clear from the way procedures, data set integrity functions, and operator commands are implemented. Yet the testing of condition codes is synchronous with the execution of steps, a faint hint of interpretation.

Note that in the absence of forward references, a compiled OSCL could always be interpreted, but the reverse is not necessarily true. The functions gained by interpretation, statement modifications triggered by prior processing, are valuable in some contexts, and definitely visible to a user.

An OSCL processor may offer any number of functions which facilitate communication with the operating system. A useful, but probably not exhaustive, list of these follows:

1. Default mechanism — facility whereby the failure of a user to make a choice among options is interpreted as an implicit expression of choice for one of the options. The most primitive implementation would have all defaults prebound, that is, defined as part of the language, assembled or compiled into the OSCL processor, and not subject to change by any means. More sophisticated implementations permit default values to be bound:
   a. at Sysgen,
   b. at IPL,
   c. when an OSCL processor is activated, that is, START READER time,
   d. when a new statement is defined to be added to the OSCL,
   e. via a *profile* when a user or group of users is described to the system, or
   f. dynamically, across the system or per user, by specific request.
2. Control of sequencing — facility for executing OSCL statements other than in strict sequence, such as by branching or looping. This facility includes statements similar to the IF, GO TO, and DO of FORTRAN and the ON of PL/1. (See [Barr71].) A specification that all branching must be forward would not be surprising nor unduly restrictive. An OSCL might permit one to specify that two units of work may be performed concurrently [Bar72].
3. Expression evaluation — facility for expressing values of OSCL parameters as sums, products, or other combinations of elemental values. In the extreme, most of the power of, say, APL could be incorporated into an OSCL without altering the language's basic purpose. Parnas [Par69a] has mentioned a trend toward such ideas. (One might, conversely, propose the extension of APL to an OSCL [Bar72], but that is not a topic to be discussed here.) The notion of variables [Bar72] is meant to be subsumed under this item.
4. Data types — acceptance of data in forms other than simple integers, for example, exponential representation, character strings, octal, or hexadecimal.
5. Data conversion — facility to include in an expression data of more than one type. Thus 1.5E2+5+X'FF' might be a permissible expression of 410 in some OSCL. (It is not today.)
6. Language extension — facility for adding statements to the OSCL. The OSCL processor might be capable of invoking programs or sequences of OSCL statements in response to statements defined by the user. The invocation of programs might be considered a purer implementation and is certainly a more flexible one, but the other alternative, a "procedural," or "macro," [Bar72] capability, is more common and also valuable. Often included in a facility of this kind is a mechanism for defining synonyms to be used in addition to or instead of keywords (including

verbs or command names) of the language. This permits among other things, reorientation of an OSCL to a natural language other than the one originally employed as a model for keywords.

7. Recursion — extension of the facility for language extension to permit a statement to invoke a sequence of statements including itself; that is, the statement identified by the character string (verb) "ABC" might conditionally cause the invocation of a sequence of statements, one of which is also identified by the string ABC. Conditionality, that is, an IF-like statement, permits the avoidance of infinite looping.

8. Editing — facility for emending OSCL statements as they are entered. A command language interpreter may permit character, line, and, by extension, command deletion or emendation.

9. Statement modification — facility for specifying that some or all instances of some (type of) text are to be replaced by some specified text. This covers the overriding of parts of statements within procedures as well as the evaluation of symbols appearing in previous or subsequent text. The "override" and "symbolic parameter" facilities of JCL [IBM4] are examples of this facility. Modification or parameterization may be linguistic, that is, constrained by the OSCL's syntax and semantics, as in the former case, or purely textual, as in the latter.

10. Invocation of functions — facility for obtaining a value by passing one or more parameters to a specified program. Such a function might be "built-in" or defined by a user. This facility may be used in conjunction with expression evaluation or data conversion in obvious ways.

11. Prompting and instructional facilities — facilities for reminding the user of a command language that he has omitted a syntactically or semantically required parameter. Also, the provision to the user of a command language, upon request, of brief descriptions of commands or parameters which may be of interest to him (the HELP function).

The functions listed above are described in the context of an OSCL, but our comment to item 3, that all features now found in any interpreted language might find their counterparts in a command language, is valid for all of them.

The OSCL processor, like many other components of the operating system, must sometimes communicate with the user. Such communications may be, for example, error or warning messages or indications of default values which the processor has assumed. These communications should be precise and couched in terms familiar to the intended recipient. Complete, meaningful, helpful messages can do much to enhance the usability of an OSCL.

The user's view of an OSCL is affected by the quality of the OSCL processor. No evaluation of the OSCL is complete without a statement as to the usability, reliability, availability, and efficiency of its processor. Inefficiency may be masked by a well-designed operating system and availability may be only a function of the system's accommodation of the processor itself, but reliability of the processor should be totally under the control of those responsible for the OSCL. No OSCL can be well thought of if its processor is unreliable.

Functions

Once the language-oriented facilities described in the previous section have been stripped away, one can see the functions an OSCL was meant to make available to the users of the operating system it describes. Woon [Woo72] has formulated a categorization of these, which we paraphrase here:

1. Those functions which the user genuinely requires of the system to accomplish useful work.
2. Those functions which permit optimization of the system's performance through familiarity with the user's expectations or requirements.
3. Those functions which are required only because of deficiencies in the system's design or realization.

Genuine functions are not so numerous as one might think. They fit into three categories — structure of work, context for work, and definition of work. The first category includes specification of parameters, such as account number, user identification, priorities, sequencing of work, which apply to a job. We define the word *job* with the loosest possible constraint: a job is the largest collection of work about which a user is able to make generalizations. This seems to embrace most other definitions and approach some of them quite closely.

Within the second category, context for work, are three subcategories: mechanisms for the indirect binding of symbols, requests for resources, and descriptions of objects. Symbols, particularly file names as expressed in programs, may be bound with reference to a hierarchy of catalogs, lists of named objects and their locations (consider the step library, job library, and link library of OS/VS, for example). Resources may be: primary or secondary storage space, secondary storage devices of specific types, or processing time or features (such as floating-point hardware or one of many CPUs in a network). One can conceive of a system wherein all resources are requested dynamically and implicitly. Therefore, the characterization of this subcategory as necessary is open to some question. Descriptions of objects, such as characteristics of files, are necessary in the sense that a system which required this information from sources other than OSCL would seem to be of limited usefulness. But this, too, is open to question.

Definition of work includes: the specification of programs, including utilities, to do useful work; the specification of parameters, including account numbers, priorities, and so on, to be associated with units of work; and the stipulation of conditions under which work is to be initiated, suspended, or halted. Some conditions might be: failure of some other work, excessive use of resources, unavailability of resources, and the attainment by a variable of some value. Statements for control of sequencing (for example, IF statements) provide one medium for the specification of such conditions, but others may be required.

Functions which contribute to the optimization of a system are usually estimates of resources which will be required. A primitive example is the request of a first-generation assembler to know how many input statements it could expect. Yet, more contemporary examples may be even further removed from the typical user's concern and control, as witness the SPLIT, SEP, AFF, and SUBALLOC parameters of JCL [IBM4]. These functions are evidence of the inadequacies of some operating systems.

Functions of the third type are abundant in most systems. The IN, OUT, and BLP parameters of JCL [IBM4] are examples. One measure of the adequacy of an OSCL is certainly the absence of such functions.

Syntax

OSCLs are characterized by their syntax. Everyone who uses an OSCL leans its syntax — what its keywords and delimiters are, where blanks are permitted, and so on. Yet, these things usually have little bearing on what one can do with the OSCL. Because this is true, the designers of an OSCL feel strongly about its syntax. It is their creation, their contribution, virtually unconstrained by product requirements (except to be unambiguous), and almost always totally unlike any previously developed syntax. Each OSCL has to its designers' minds the ultimate, easiest-to-use syntax. It is to the syntax that Keyser refers when he specifies the following design criteria [Key65]:

1. Empirical adequacy.
2. Ease of translation into computer control.
3. Ease of use for the human operator.

These are goals which must be met by a good syntax for an OSCL, and any given syntax may be judged by the extent to which it meets them.

There is no optimum syntax. Each one is the product of tastes and trade-offs. This section seeks to cast light on these trade-offs and how they should be made.

Model. The first decision a designer usually makes about the syntax of an OSCLs are characterized by their syntax. Everyone who uses an OSCL learns its with respect to systems (an earlier language developed by the same manufacturer) or higher-level languages (APL, QUIKTRAN) may make this decision trivial.

Many designers think of natural language, usually English, as a model. This possibility is recommended by Parsons [Par70] and analyzed by Keyser [Key65]. It is interesting to note that an English-based (nonnatural, unambiguous) language is likely to be susceptible to mechanical translation to any Romance or Germanic language, somewhat justifying what might appear to be a parochial view. Even Germanic and Indic languages preserve the verb-object-list form. But the imitation of natural language has proven of limited practicality and most designers have passed on to other models.

COBOL, the most widely used higher-level language, is another candidate for a model. Although the usefulness of its syntax, like that of any other higher-level language, has been demonstrated, we nevertheless find that generalized operating systems tend not to favor users of particular languages by this device.

Rather, we find that fixed formats, with identifiers to distinguish OSCL statements from data, predominate. This seems to be a carry-over from earlier generations, in violation of the second law of product design: Don't continue to do things as they have been done just because someone "must have had a good reason for doing it that way."[9] The good reason in this case probably related to how few characters the user had to punch to do a simple thing. (Skipping unused fields is easy on a keypunch, but not always so easy on a terminal where tabulator stops replace a program drum card.) Things may no longer be simple, but some justification for this approach remains and is discussed below.

Some OSCLs, most notably JCL, are modeled on assembly languages. This may be because someone thought the same individuals would be coding in JCL and the assembly language. The validity of that hypothesis is open to question.

Still another basis for OSCL syntax might be a sort of stilted English adapted to a certain context. This is meant to describe the approach generally taken for command languages. These tend to have no identifiers and, because they are processed interpretively, no labels. A very useful discussion of the syntax of command languages is to be found in Heine's paper [Hei71].

Whatever the model for the syntax of an OSCL, the goals remain fairly constant. These goals are constrained by the need for expressing unambiguously all those things which the user of the operating system should be able to express. Within this constraint, the syntax should be easy to use and extensible. Ease of use comes from simplicity and consistency, a few rules and no exceptions; familiarity, similarity to something in the user's experience, such as natural language or a programming language; and ease of entry, paucity of keystrokes required, limited use of special characters. Extensibility refers not only to the mere ability to add statements and parameters to the language, but also to the absence of restrictions on these additions. An oversimplification of the latter

---

[9] First Law is: Don't innovate just to be innovating (or because the other guys, whatever their motives, couldn't have been as smart as you are).

point is: "Thou shalt have no reserved words," that is, keywords which cannot be coined or arguments forbidden due to their identity with or similarity to existing keywords.

Statement Parts. The statements of OSCLs characteristically consist of at least *verbs* and *operands.* Statements of OSCLs processed noninterpretively typically include also identifiers, labels, and comments. Provision may also be made for a statement-end delimiter and a sequence number. The first syntactic decision facing the designer of an OSCL is which of these components to include in the syntactic definition of an OSCL statement.

An identifier serves to distinguish OSCL statements from data. The identifier is ipso facto precluded from use in data when the system might expect OSCL statements. Yet, if OSCL statements might usefully appear as data, say, to be transcribed to some storage medium for periodic retrieval and use, an escape convention must be defined to permit this. In this way, the identifier may become totally redundant. This is the case with JCL. The identifier could be justified in systems where OSCL statements can never be useful data and useful data can never contain identifiers. In this case, the identifier may obviate mode-switch (OSCL to data and vice-versa) statements entirely and thus be justified.

A label may be used to distinguish an OSCL statement so that a modification to it, a reference to data in it, or a transfer of control to it may be defined. The second function is clearly a nicety rather than a necessity[10] and the last has been shown similarly unnecessary by Böhm and Jacopini [Böh66]. Planned modification of a statement in a procedure can be accomplished via a parameter of the procedure. Unplanned modifications require either a label or a sequence number, which can serve as a conceptual label. The utility of this function may vary from system to system and so, therefore, may the usefulness of a label.

The value of comments in an OSCL is a matter of some disagreement: The better (that is, more usable) an OSCL, the less the need for comments, and so, it may be said of a poor OSCL that the inclusion of a facility for comments is one of its few virtues.

A statement-end delimiter permits the specification of multiple OSCL statements within a single logical or physical record, assuming that an end-of-record condition is treated as an implicit statement-end. (If end-of-record is not an implicit statement-end, no continuation convention is required, but the statement-end character must then be coded for each statement.) The definition of a statement-end delimiter costs only the use for other purposes of the character used. The value of the function obtained seems almost equally small.

---

[10] Consider, for example, the DSNAME = *.DDNAME of JCL: if the named DD statement contained no DSNAME parameter, a function *seems* to have been provided. But this function is simply the avoidance of devising a name (such as &&ANYNAME). This is, at most, a convenience, not a function.

A sequence number, besides serving as a conceptual label, may facilitate editing of a procedure. For the latter purpose, it suffices to define an area not processed by the OSCL interpreter. Even a field defined to contain comments could contain sequence numbers instead.

Delimiters. Once the content of an OSCL statement has been fixed, some manner of distinguishing among the various fields must be devised. Conventionally, one characterizes OSCLs as fixed-form or free-form depending on whether specific record positions or defined delimiting characters are used for this purpose. Many OSCLs are hybrids wherein certain record positions (such as 1 for the identifier) are significant, but delimiters for certain fields are also defined. Record positions other than the first three should not be significant in OSCLs where statements of the language are likely to be entered from devices, such as terminals, which do not make a record position easily visible to the user. Positions near the end of a record should not be significant, as users may have to space rather than tab (use the tabulation key) to them.

When delimiters are used, the blank is an obvious choice. If a blank is a field delimiter, however, it cannot also be used unambiguously as a delimiter of subfields (in a field other than one known to be the last of a statement), unless "all blanks are not created equal"; that is, blanks delimiting subfields might appear within parenthesized strings to distinguish them from field delimiters. Parentheses, quotation marks, and equal signs may be used as delimiters when use of the blank creates more problems than it solves. The function of blanks in an OSCL is a matter of some seriousness and should not be casually determined.

A statement of an OSCL typically has the format of a function, that is, it has a verb and an operand field separated from each other by some sort of a delimiter, more often a blank than the parentheses most commonly used in the specification of mathematical functions. A conditional (IF) statement is not easily adapted to this format and various alternative formats may be used. These may represent anomalies in the general syntax of the OSCL. The treatment of the words THEN and ELSE in a syntactical description is a nettlesome problem. The best solution may be the definition of a statement different from all other statements and containing statements as components.

Groups of Statements. Once the general form of an OSCL statement has been determined, the combination of statements can be addressed. Jobs, steps, and so on can be dismissed for the present as system-dependent notions. A linguistic entity, however, is the *procedure.*

An OSCL procedure is any representation of OSCL text which is retained within the system, and which may therefore be interpreted more than once. A procedure may be *included* or *invoked.* In the former case, there is no semantic distinction between the inclusion of the procedure in the stream of input statements at some point and the actual occurrence of the same statements at the same point. This is textual parameterization (see item 9 on p. 274) at a level greater than a single statement. No new level of a naming hierarchy is created; that is, no scope for symbol binding is defined to be coterminal with the procedure. This is wholly analogous to the COPY function which is found in some assembly languages. An invoked procedure, however, which is the more common case, has all the characteristics of a called subroutine; that is, local named objects, if an OSCL permits any, must be passed if they are to be accessible, and distinct objects with previously used names may be introduced without effect on the preexisting objects. This form lends itself to the passing of parameter values and variables by name, but is constrained to have some sort of logical beginning and end, a first statement and a last of some definable process. Thus, JCL procedures must consist only of complete steps. An included procedure may be subject to textual overrides, either statement-oriented or parametric — for example, the "overrides" and symbolic parameters of JCL, respectively — but its lack of structure makes the passing of values difficult to define, since they are not passed to a cohesive unit of work, such as a program or procedure.

A textual parameter is analogous to an included procedure. It is unstructured and it interpreted just as though it occurred where it is invoked. A parameter value acts as a variable at the point of invocation. It may be maintained that textual parameters provide all the functions of evaluated parameters and then some, but this entails, of course, some expense in terms of complexity for the user and difficulty of implementation. Textual parameterization also raises the question of recursion: if a textual substitution yields a nested invocation — that is, text suggesting that a further substitution should be made — should that invocation be honored? If so, an unintentional loop can easily be defined, for example, wherever a string of text is replaced by itself. If not, some valuable function may be lost. The former concern seems easily the greater.

The functions involved in defining procedures are, with the exception of defaulting, relatively straightforward. Yet, defining what parameters can be specified in invoking a procedure and what value they can be given can be quite complex. In some cases, one may wish to distinguish between the keyword used to invoke a parameter and the values used to make a statement about the parameter (for example, that the parameter to be called COLOR can be represented by one of the three keywords RED, WHITE, and BLUE). One may also have to associate with a parameter a range and/or a type of permissible values, such as a number between 0 and 15 or a file name. All this can lead to undesirable complexity if the definition of a procedure is to permit defaulting and/or validity checking.

The specification of dependent default values adds to the complexity described above. Certain defaults may only be effective in the presence or absence of others. This sort of complexity — for example, "if STATUS=NEW, WHITE is the default for COLOR; otherwise BLUE is" — can and should be buried in the procedure itself.

Parameters. The parameters which can be specified at the time a procedure is invoked are analogous to the operands which are specified at the time a system function is invoked via the coding of an OSCL statement. Thus, designers of an OSCL would do well to study the ways users specify parameters for the procedures they have defined and define statements similarly. They would probably find that few procedures had more than five or six parameters which were used with any frequency. This and some obvious human-factor considerations suggest the following rules for defining OSCL statements:

1. In most cases, the user should have to specify no more than five parameters on any one statement.
2. It should be possible to specify the most commonly used parameters most briefly.
3. Default values should be those most frequently used, but all the default values for a single statement should be consistent with one another. (That is, their appearance together on one statement should not make that statement invalid.)
4. While it may be necessary to permit the specification of each atomic function of the operating system independently, useful groups of functions should be identified and made available through single parameter values. (This might be accomplished via a built-in procedure internal to the OSCL processor.) Little-used atomic functions should be segregated so that they may easily be documented in places typical users can and will ignore.

One mechanism designed in response to the third rule is the positional parameter. A statement containing positional and no other type of parameters may be easiest to code and even English-like. The definition of more than one positional parameter for a statement from which a positional parameter other than the last may be omitted, leads to the requirement for a syntactic mark meaning "this positional parameter has been omitted." Alternatively, following positional parameters may be distinguishable by value (for example, only the last positional parameter can be numeric and it must be), but any such convention induces coding errors. Any time an error of a single keystroke can result in a valid, but unintended form, the usability of the OSCL has been diminished.[11] Since the proliferation of syntactic marks is also undesirable, one can say that no positional parameter other than the last of a statement should be optional. A useful discussion of forms for the mixing of positional and keyword parameters is given by Heine [Hei71].

---

[11] An outstanding example is the trailing comma in the operand field of a JCL statement to be continued. The omission of the comma causes the intended continuation to be treated as a comment, so that parameters which are syntactically optional may be ignored, with disastrous results.

Keyword parameters, with or without associated values, present several problems to the designer of an OSCL. The choice of keywords themselves, and the choice of verbs as well, should be based on the user's view of the system. This is a very controversial area, as the following examples [ANS71] should serve to indicate. (The verbs in the examples were chosen for their cross-system applicability.)

1. Does a user CALL any routine which executes at the same level (processed by the same mechanism) as the CALL statement itself (for example, OSCL procedures), or are only programs the object of CALL statements? What is the distinction in the user's mind between CALLing and EXECuting (or EXEQting or EXQting)? Is it related to the distinction between programs and procedures?
2. Would a user rather LOG ONto a system or LOG INto it? Or would he rather just define a JOB or RUN his programs? Or is it enough that he supplies his USERID or IDENT?
3. Should a user ALLOCate or ALLOCATE or ASsiGn space or Define his Data or give a Data DEFinition?

The choice of a keyword should be based on criteria such as the following:

1. The word should be meaningful to the user. It should be one of the first to come to mind to describe the corresponding function.
2. The word should be short or lend itself to a short, easy-to-remember abbreviation. A pronounceable abbreviation may not be easier to remember than one that is not [Win75].
3. The same keyword should be used consistently to invoke the same (that is, appearing identical to the user) function, regardless of the object upon which the function is defined. (DELETE all types of objects; don't EXCISE some and ERASE others.)

An OSCL may permit multiple abbreviations of keywords according to some fixed rule. The first n characters of a keyword, where n is large enough to assure uniqueness of an abbreviation in a context, may be all that is required, as in the Time-Sharing Option of OS/VS2. This, of course, limits extensibility by discouraging the addition to a statement of a new keyword, in such a way that a formerly valid abbreviation of an existing keyword would no longer suffice for uniqueness. Fixed abbreviations avoid this problem, but are more restrictive.

Automatic error correction [Mor70, Jam73] may be offered to decrease the number of times jobs are aborted due to errors of a single keystroke. Such a policy is not without its attendant risk of "correcting" incorrectly with disastrous results, or insignificant results expensively obtained.

A *keyword parameter* is typically followed by an argument list, most often delimited by parentheses, sometimes preceded by an equal sign. An argument list may degenerate to a single item, in which case the parentheses may be omitted if an equal sign is used.

It is sometimes necessary to provide in an OSCL a means of negating the specification of a keyword parameter. This is done to permit the user invoking a procedure to nullify the effect of a keyword parameter appearing on a statement of the procedure or of a default parameter value. There are two basic ways of providing this facility:

1. By defining distinct keywords mutually exclusive with and opposite in meaning to existing keywords. These may all begin with NO, for example, but they are valid keywords of the OSCL.
2. By defining a convention for the negation of keywords, such as preceding the keyword to be negated with a minus sign or the letters "NO."

The former method facilitates precise definition of the OSCL, but the latter facilitates the extension of the OSCL in that new keywords need not be defined in pairs.

A *hybrid parameter* is one which may receive a value from either a positional or a keyword parameter [IBM3]. Hybrid parameters can significantly complicate the implementation of an OSCL, are easily overused once they are admitted to an OSCL, and tend to cause problems of reserved words (keywords associated with hybrids cannot be used as positional parameters with argument lists, in some cases). Judicious use of hybrids, however, can enhance the usability of an OSCL to some extent by minimizing the adept user's keystrokes.

Values. Parameters serve to associate values with variables. The designer of an OSCL has considerable latitude in defining the ways in which these values can be expressed. A value can be expressed as the name of a variable, in which case the value is, by extension, the value of the named variable. A value can be a constant or "self-defining" value. Or a value can be an expression, that is, a well-formed arithmetic or Boolean expression comprising elemental values and relational operators.

Any value may be said to be of one of several types. A type may be character string, floating-point, or integer base n, where n may be 2 (Boolean), 8 (octal), 10 (decimal), or 16 (hexadecimal). While syntactic mechanisms used to distinguish among these types are in all cases controversial, no type presents more problems than the character string. It requires both starting and ending delimiters, which may be identical, to set the string apart from contiguous text. The problem of permitting inclusion of the ending delimiter within a character string may be solved by specifying that such an embedded delimiter must be doubled (coded twice in succession) or preceded by an *escape character.* (An escape character is one which indicates that the following character is not to be interpreted as a syntactic marker, but rather only as another ordinary character of text.) The latter method can be extended to permit the embedding of editing marks such as line-delete and character-delete characters in strings.

Operations are defined on values to permit the specification of expressions. An operator is defined to operate on values of a given type. A hierarchy is defined among operators to provide rules for the omission of parentheses, assuming infix notation. (This assumption is safe, since any human user of an OSCL would prefer it overwhelmingly.) Operations which might be defined are addition, subtraction, multiplication, division, concatenation, conjunction, disjunction, negation, and, in the extreme, all the operations of APL.

A user might well wish to embed blanks in expressions. This can always be permitted except preceding operators which may be either unary (prefix) or binary. In this case, if a blank delimits fields, the blank may seem to delimit operands. If this restriction on the embedding of blanks is intolerable, and it should be, a unique unary operator can be devised, or each unary operator and its operand may have to be enclosed in parentheses.

Much more could be said about syntax for OSCLs, and much of it, as with what has been said, could apply as well to other languages designed for use by people and for interpretation by computer. Yet the present exposition should suffice for illuminating the relevant issues. With it, one should be able to take an OSCL and evaluate how well its designers coped with the problems that confronted them. And with it, designers should be able to see clearly the problems that lie ahead. They should be able to design an OSCL aware of identifiable objectives and not have to justify unconscious decisions with "it seemed desirable at the time."

Documentation

A discussion of all the technical aspects of OSCLs and their processors does not suffice for an understanding of OSCLs, because not even the best OSCL can be of any value if it is poorly or inadequately documented. The documentation of a good OSCL is not usually a difficult task. But for one large class of OSCLs, it is not only difficult, but also critical to the acceptance of the OSCL by its users. This class comprises OSCLs for complex, generalized systems whose users are relatively unsophisticated.

That this class has many members should not be surprising. Large systems are built for large numbers of users and large numbers of users tend to have diverse problems. The system which aids in the solution of all those problems is likely to be complex. And the diversity of its users ensures that at least some are naive.

To cope with this situation, the set of all users must be broken down into subsets of users with some useful set of characteristics in common. Then, the tasks these users perform must be isolated and each task must be described *as it appears to the user.* These descriptions should lead to uncomplicated examples of OSCL statements the user might wish to employ. Only after these examples have been provided, can exotic functions be described without intimidating the naive user.[12] In this way, the most troublesome of OSCLs can be helpfully documented.

The syntax of an OSCL must be described by some sort of metalanguage. Backus-Naur Form, also called Backus Normal Form, (BNF) is preferred by academicians for its precision and relationship to ALGOL. Easier for typical users of OSCLs to understand may be what Boettner [Boe69] calls IBM notation. This notation does not allow the precise expression of necessary concepts, such as (for JCL) the interchangeability of keyword parameters and the inclusion or exclusion of delimiters for positional parameters not coded. These deficiencies can be remedied by *ad hoc* extensions to the notation, for example, a ∘ operator within brackets for interchangeability and a　　operator to indicate that a delimiter need only be coded to denote the absence of a positional parameter other than the last of a statement.

In summary, any discussion of OSCLs must not be limited to the languages themselves. The environment of the OSCL, its operating system and users, its processor, and its documentation must also be taken into account. With respect to the language itself, one must consider: the functions it provides (are some missing? extraneous? poorly grouped?); the syntax it employs (is it extensible? easy to use?); and its keywords (are they meaningful? consistent?). All these things are relevant to the quality of the OSCL.

Works covering much the same area as this section are [Bar72] and [Boe69]. Both of these and [Barr71] contain ideas which happened to be developed concurrently by others, but only the published works are cited.

Many people have contributed ideas expressed in this section. Many of the points made herein arose from discussions involving one of the authors (K) and K. Bandat, and G. Seegmuller, the late M. J. Harrison, and others, in 1969. More recently, collaboration with J. B. McKeehan, T. F. McBride, and P. Y. Woon on relevant projects has contributed to our insights. Relevant references not cited above include [Cut70], [Lic65], [Ste73] and McKeehan's [McK68], as well as manufacturers' publications [DEC1], [DEC2], [GEN1], [HIS1], [NCR5], and [UNI1].

6.3 THE OPERATOR'S INTERFACE

As is noted briefly in Section 6.1, the nominal interface between an operating system and its operator(s) may support much more than any individual earning

---

[12] Another view of this problem can be found in [Nic68].

an operator's salary could be expected to comprehend. We might be better advised to speak of the operator-administrator-librarian-security manager-etc. interface, or the system's interface for nonprogrammers. We hew to tradition, however, and use the simpler, more familiar term.

We speak of more than one operator not only because we are likely to be referring to many individuals of varied skills, but also because many systems are served by multiple operators even in the narrowest sense of that designation. Yet, there are smaller operating systems served by only one operator who is supposed to know a little about everything. Henceforth, we tend to use the singular form exclusively, but our meaning does not change and should not be forgotten.

We first enumerate the classes of functions associated with the operator's interface. We then discuss the various ways in which the system and the operator interact. There follows a discussion of the language the operator must use to communicate with the system. The system's communications with the operator next come under scrutiny. A discussion of the general usability of the operator's interface concludes this section.

Operator's Functions

The functions which involve the operator can be placed into three categories: those involving some positive action on the operator's part (physical functions); those nonphysical functions where the operator responds to a stimulus from the system (responsive functions); and those nonphysical functions where the operator exercises his initiative (initiative functions). We fail to distinguish physical functions by the agent, system or operator, exercising initiative, because that agent is almost always the system.

Physical functions involve principally the care and feeding of I/O devices attached to a system. The operator is expected to mount and demount disks and reels of magnetic tape, to load paper into printers and cards into readers and punches, to feed OCR/MICR devices and paper-tape devices, and so forth. For input devices which process self-identifying volumes — reels of labeled tape, labeled disks — the operator may mount media spontaneously and inform the system of the actions or trust it to become aware of the actions by itself. Otherwise, the operator generally does what the system says to do. The operator is expected to remove paper tape and cards which have been punched, cards, paper tape, and magnetically imprinted documents which have been read, and so on, as they accumulate, without the system's guidance. The operator is also expected to clear card jams, stop runaway printers, and otherwise respond to visible malfunctions, with a minimum of aid from the system.

Also at the operator's disposal may be dials, sense switches and lights, and other mechanisms for determining and altering the status of the system. These should be employed only for diagnostic purposes and are normally of no real concern to the individual known as the operator.

In connection with physical functions, mechanisms must be available for the operator to tell the system what has been done at its request, for example, loaded the proper form in the printer, or that it cannot be done.

Responsive functions are those which result from the system's requests for human guidance. Most often, the system is aware of several alternative courses of action it may take in response to a given situation and wishes the operator to choose among them. There are few justifiable instances of this type of function. Whatever algorithm the operator may use to select an option can usually be exercised more easily by the system, that is, preprogrammed. Only when the algorithm involves human nature — is Jan's work important enough to deserve special treatment today — or prediction of things to come — anticipated workload — is it unsuitable for mechanical implementation. In other cases, responsive functions are symptomatic of incomplete system design; the means has not been provided for making the appropriate algorithms part of the system's behavior.

Initiative functions are those which result from the operator's knowing something that the system should be informed of, from the operator's desire to influence the system's behavior directly, or from the operator's requirement of function from the system. Examples of the first type are: that a specified device is about to be made unavailable due to preventive maintenance; that the system's workload will soon increase significantly; or that a specified printer is malfunctioning. Examples of the second type are: That the level of multiprogramming should be altered; that the partitions of main storage should be redefined. Most, if not all, functions of the second type either reflect the system's inability to do as much for itself as it theoretically could, or are designed for use by someone of greater competence than the typical system operator, or both. Functions of the last type, requests for service from the system, include the specifications of messages to be placed on the system's log or broadcast to all users of the system; and requests for the display by the system of information needed by the operator.

The foregoing discussion of the system operator's functions is intended to serve as a basis for categorizing the functions present in a particular system. Such categorization might well lead to the addition or omission of functions as the categories for that system are seen to be inadequately filled or unnecessarily large, respectively.

Consoles

The operator converses with the system through an operator's console — one or more I/O devices — which may be a terminal, a graphic display device, or a card reader and a printer. If a system has multiple operators, each operator may have a separate console. The following paragraphs describe how consoles of the various types are used for communication between the system and the operator and what the functions of multiple operators might be.

Most consoles today are simply terminals. They are used for two-way conversation in the usual way, with some few exceptions. Special keys or combinations of keystrokes might have specialized meanings, such as "Listen, I'm about to say something," "end of multiline input," or "ignore this message" (also called line-kill). If the terminal has upper- and lower-case alphabetic characters, as most do, the system may choose for the sake of efficiency of input not to distinguish between the cases as entered by the operator.

A graphic display console permits and requires much more control than a terminal. The fundamental distinction is that the content of a display screen is limited, while the paper feeding through a terminal is theoretically infinite in length. An operator at a terminal who wishes to review a conversation with the computer need only pick up some paper and look at it. The operator may have difficulty finding some particular unfulfilled request the system has made, but it can be found eventually. This is not true for the operator at a display console.

A display screen may be divided into two or more areas.[13] One area serves to display the most recent communications not yet deleted and another is used for new communications. Other areas might be set aside for messages requiring particular attention, for *menus* (lists of options), or for informational displays. The operator may be given the ability to delete specific communications or all communications which meet specific criteria; to "roll" the list of communications forward or backward; to select with a light pen a communication or an option from a menu; to indicate similarly compliance with a request; or to alter the bounds of the screen's areas.

The graphic console has the advantage of being visible from a much greater distance than a terminal and of facilitating selection from a menu, a list of options presented to the operator by the system. It can also serve to keep messages requiring operator action in sight and, therefore, in mind. It has the disadvantages of limited content, impermanence (for which reason it is customarily supplemented by a hard-copy log), and increased cost in terms of equipment, programming, and management by the operator. A graphic console tends to be favored over a terminal at large installations where equipment covers a greater area and fixed incremental cost is less significant.

Consoles made up of a printer and a card reader are cumbersome and most often a mere stopgap in the temporary absence of a more suitable console. They are used in the obvious way and require no further attention here.

As we have noted, each operator typically has a separate console. More precisely, the system perceives as many operators as it distinguishes active consoles, regardless of the number of persons actually attending those consoles. Multiple operators are a consequence of a large or physically decentralized, sprawling installation. The operators at particular consoles may be restricted as

---

[13] This discussion of display consoles is based on [IBM26].

to their use of operator commands. Some designations suggested by IBM [IBM5] for operators are: master, tape pool, direct-access pool, tape library, disk library, unit record pool, teleprocessing control, security, maintenance, and programmer liaison.

OCL

The commands available to system operators constitute a language the operators use to communicate with the system. We call this the operators' command language, or OCL.

The first virtue of an OCL is consistency, that it is, in fact, a language and not just a collection of input forms designed individually by diverse programmers. The operator is just as entitled to a syntax, a consistent set of rules on which he can rely when framing a statement, as anyone else. In fact, if we hold that an operator is less skilled than a programmer, we can only conclude that there is a greater requirement for the simplicity born of consistency.

An OCL must bear evidence of an understanding of an operator's unique requirements. The operator works in real time and needs a language which permits brevity and, at the same time, does not lead to mistakes. The commands used most often must be the briefest and easiest to remember. All of the language's keywords must be meaningful. One must not be forced to speak of a "processor" if one thinks about a "CPU." The OCL's syntax should be tailored to the device(s) to be used most often for expressing it. Attention should be paid to avoiding case shifts and other multikey characters, and words which cannot be entered quickly because of their spelling (those with consecutive characters typed with the same finger or with many "pinky" characters). Multiline commands are certainly to be avoided.

The OCL is only part of the operator's interface, the portion which deals with initiative functions. Responsive functions arise from messages sent by the system to the operator.

Messages

Messages typically consist of two parts: an *identifier* and natural-language text. The identifier permits rapid recognition of a message by anyone familiar with it. The identifier may also contain a code of some sort which serves to categorize the message as to whether, for example, it requires the operator to make a decision, it requests some action, or it is provided solely for edification. This code permits the operator to scan a list or log of messages and select those to which a response is still needed.

As a message is seen by the system, it may have a third element: a *routing code* to specify those consoles to which it is to be sent. Messages requesting the mounting of disk volumes clearly need not be sent to the unit record pool. Routing codes permit such discrimination.

As operators become more proficient and better acquainted with the messages the system sends, they may wish to suppress the text of many messages because they recognize these messages by their identifiers alone. The operators should be able to control the system's verbosity in addressing them, just as the users of some time-sharing systems can today.

The operator's responses to the system's messages must meet many of the same criteria applied to the OCL. They are, after all, entered by the same individual via the same input device. Responses should be brief, meaningful, and directly responsive to the messages which instigate them. A response of "U" (for unchanged) to a request for the specification of parameters is at least nonintuitive, if not irrational; "none" or "defaults" would be preferable.

One appealing mechanism for operators' responses is the menu, mentioned above. A menu clearly lists the options available and allows the operator to select one, instead of trying to guess what responses might be acceptable. Of course, the provision of a menu does not relieve the system of the responsibility for specifying meaningful responses. A choice among "wait," "nosep," and "abend," is more meaningful than a choice between "1," "2," and "3," where the numbers have the same effect as the words.

If a message requiring a response is always to receive the same response, then the message probably should never have been included in the system at all. If it is too late to delete the message or if a few installations really require the variability

```
1.  a.  M 191 X3587

    b.  MOUNT DISK X3587 ON DRIVE 191, PLEASE.


2.  a.  2R 1-3

    b.  2 REPLY 1=NEW PTR 2=NEW FM 3=NONE

    c.  SPECIFY RECOVERY ACTION; USE id=2 IN REPLY

        1 MEANS USE ANOTHER PRINTER.

        2 MEANS USE ANOTHER FORM -- GIVE ITS NUMBER.

        3 MEANS NO RECOVERY IS POSSIBLE. THANK YOU.


3.  a.  3JB283 JB375 DDLKD

    b.  JOBS JB283,JB375 DEADLOCKED; CANCEL 1; USE id=3 IN REPLY.
```

Figure 6.4. Messages with Varying Levels of Verbosity.

provided by the message, an installation should at least have the option of suppressing the message and having the system assume some prespecified response.

Each component of the operator's interface has now been discussed. We conclude this section with some more general observations concerning the usability of the interface.

Other Aspects of the Interface

Individuals should not be presented with information which cannot conceivably affect their behavior. This general verity applies most pointedly to the system operator. A flood of informational messages about situations the operator cannot prevent, encourage, or even understand is guaranteed to reduce the operator's efficiency, and consequently the system's, and yield no compensating benefit. Routing codes are one mechanism designed to eliminate noise − useless information − but they are not in themselves a preventative. Designers and implementers must use the codes and must eliminate messages of interest to no one, if noise is to be avoided.

We have already noted the common attributes of OCL and responses. We now assert further that these mechanisms should be homogeneous. They should appear to the operator to be parts of the same language. And why not? They are used in the same environment to accomplish similar ends. That the operator is stimulated by extrasystem events or initiative in one case, and by messages from the system in the other, seems irrelevent, as it should be. The system should not compel cognizance of such a useless distinction.

A clear conception of the operator as an individual or as a group of individuals should be borne in mind as the operator's interface is designed. To require of a single individual that he do things of widely varying complexity is to define a job that cannot be filled. [Kur83] If an operator is someone who performs dull, essentially manual tasks 90% of the time and exercises initiative, skill, and superior judgment 10% of the time, then there is no such person as an operator. Persons satisfied with dull tasks are generally incapable of superior judgment and persons of skill are discontent with dull tasks. Similarly, if an operator is an expert at scheduling the system, administering an installation's security procedures, maintaining the system, and exercising discretionary judgment with respect to other people's work, that person is far too valuable to keep in an operator's job. In fact, that person is also unlikely to exist at all. "The operator" is more likely to be a group of individuals with distinct well-defined responsibilities.

All these things must be considered in the design of a system so that the people who make the system work can be found. These persons must have enough work of consistent complexity to do to justify their existence, although, of course, a small number of jobs can be combined at smaller installations.

s=system

o=operator

	Message	Meaning
s	FM138 CD INP1 TO RDR OOC	Place deck INP1 in reader
s	FM281 RL 35678 TO LIB	Return reel 35678 to library
s0	IO126 ERR PCH OOC	Check punch for problem, e.g., jam, no cards
s1	FM316 FM N2856-3 TO PTR OOD	Load form N2856-3 in printer
o	1 n	Unable to load form
s2	FM 1=ANOTHER PTR,2=SUBST FORM,3=NONE	State recovery possibilities
o	2 0 n2856-4	Have substitute form
s3	FM316 FM N2856-4 TO PTR OOD	
o	3 y	OK, use it
o	0 y	Done
s	FM138 DK 58762 TO 191	Problem repaired
o	sd	Mount disk 58762 on 191
s	SC105 20MINS LEFT	Shut down system / Jobs in execution will need 20 minutes
s	JOBS NOT STARTED:JB387,JB128,JB276, INVENT, SAMSJOB, PRESJB,QUIK1,XYZ	Jobs in system which won't run
o	d presjb,user quik1,pgm jobs,gt,10m	Display data
s	USER PRESJB=BIGMAN,PGM QUIK1=FORTRAN,	
s	JOBS$\geq$10MINS=(PAYROLL,TEST1,BILLSJOB)	
o	r presjb,quik1. c test1,billsjob	Run PRESJB and QUIK1, Cancel TEST1 and BILLSJOB

Figure 6.5. A Hypothetical OCL Scenario.

As mentioned in the previous section and discussed with greater generality and at greater length in the next chapter, documentation is critical to the usability of any component of the system. The less gifted and less well-trained the user of a component is, the more important the quality of the component's documentation. So it is that the documentation of the operator's interface merits special attention.

The operator requires documentation of at least the following types: an introduction to the system as it appears; a procedural manual telling step by step, how to accomplish certain vital or frequently required tasks; a user's guide (see Chapter 7) for the system's OCL; a reference guide for the OCL, detailed and intended for use only as a reference and only after some competence in the use of the OCL has been attained; a reference guide for the system's messages and possible responses to them; and, optionally, a document explaining the customs, procedures, and idiosyncracies of the particular installation. The latter document is, of course, not supplied with the system. Documentation of each type may account for a separate publication, or some of them — such as the reference guides — may be bound together for convenience and efficiency. Some large set of operators' functions may require separate documentation where they obviously represent the responsibilities of some distinct individual or set of individuals. [Wal69] contains a useful outline for what is called "an operations guide for an operating system."

A well-designed operator's interface can contribute significantly to the efficiency of the system and to the ease with which it can be used. The importance of human factors, aspects of the system which reflect its adaptation to people as opposed to the reverse, must not be overlooked in the development of any product. An operating system is no exception.

Some of the material presented in this section derives from conversations between one of the authors (K) and R. M. Patterson, and reflects the work of a number of persons who have worked with Patterson, notably H. C. Dearborn.

This chapter has dealt with the assignment of values and addresses to named objects, symbol binding. We have treated the various mechanism involved — Sysgen, IPL, OCL, program translation, linking, OSCL, and dynamic binding — in summary and some in greater depth. This chapter concludes our discussion of the mechanics of operating systems. Our final chapter is devoted to the production of the system, the development process.

QUESTIONS

1. Tell whether each mechanism is concerned primarily with binding to value or to location:
   a. Sysgen.
   b. IPL.
   c. OCL.

294 OPERATING SYSTEMS PRINCIPLES

d. Program Translation.
e. Linking.
f. OSCL.
g. Dynamic Binding.
2. Give examples in some programming language known to you and your instructor of statements which define a symbol X of each of the following types:
  a. An internal label.
  b. An external label.
  c. An external reference.
  d. An external symbol.
  e. None, although symbols X and Y appear in the statement.
3. Draw a diagram of an overlay structure, list control statements which might be used to create it with some linker, and use the diagram to illustrate the execution of an exclusive (indirect) call.
4. From the list in Question 1, suggest appropriate binding times for the following values:
  a. Physical organization of a user's file.
  b. Address of a subroutine called by a user.
  c. Identifier of a volume containing a user's file.
  d. Amount of primary storage needed for jobs of a given class.
  e. Addresses of magnetic tape drives.
5. Categorize as necessary, optimizing, or superfluous the following OSCL functions:
  a. Estimated running time.
  b. File name.
  c. Amount of primary storage required.
  d. File is not to be read after writing.
  e. Name of checkpoint from which restart is to be done.
  f. Recording density for input file on magnetic tape.
  g. Recording density for output file on magnetic tape.
  h. Volume identifier.
  i. Record with split cylinder technique.
  j. Expiration date of file.
6. Comment on the aptness of the following OSCL keywords and permitted abbreviations:
  a. DSNAME or DSN
  b. IN
  c. DEN
  d. DCB
  e. SYSOUT
  f. VOLUME or VOL
  g. START or S
  (*Hint:* If you cannot deduce the function invoked by a keyword, it is not apt.)

7. Discuss the virtues and vices of (*a*) blank, (*b*) comma, and (*c*) semicolon as delimiters for the separation of parameters on OSCL statements where OSCL input comes from (i) punched cards, or (ii) terminals.

8. Consult an operators' manual and categorize the listed commands according to the likely job title of the person(s) qualified to issue them: operator system administrator, security chief, maintenance personnel, or other positions.

9. Answer Question 6 for an OCL instead of an OSCL.

10. Comment on the usefulness (how much and to whom) of the following informational messages sent by the system to the operator. Indicate what function must be available to the operator if he is to take effective action in response to each message.
    a. JOB X ABENDED
    b. DISK DRIVE AT 192 FAILING
    c. CARD READ ERROR ON O1C
    d. JOB X RESTARTING
    e. SYSTEM OVERHEAD BEYOND THRESHHOLD

11. Reword the following messages for brevity and meaningfulness:
    a. FILE X ON VOLUME 528 NEEDED ON DISK DRIVE AT 293.
    b. INSERT FORM 4876X INTO PRINTER AT OOE.
    c. EXCESSIVE PARITY CHECKS ON TAPE DRIVE AT 183.
    d. LOCATIONS 58800-60000 NEEDED FOR JOB X TO RESTART.

12. Indicate to which operators listed below the following messages should be routed (unabbreviated for clarity):
    a. MOUNT TAPE XYZ ON 183
    b. PASSWORD FOR FILE X?
    c. JOB X THRASHING
    d. DISK 528 ON 191: 6 COR'D ERRORS
    e. PARITY ERROR: PAPER TAPE RDR AT 013
    f. SEND TAPE SYZ TO DUBUQUE
    Operators: (i) master, (ii) tape pool, (iii) direct-access pool, (iv) unit record pool, (v) tape library, (vi) disk library, (vii) security, (viii) teleprocessing, (ix) system administrator, (x) maintenance, (xi) programmer liaison.

13. Prepare a critique of an OCL of which you can obtain a description.

PROBLEMS

1. Two programmers write identical FORTRAN programs and submit them to the computer operator for execution at the same time with the same job name. Discuss various methods by which the symbol conflicts might be resolved or made unambiguous. The following kinds of symbols should be considered:
   a. Variable names in the FORTRAN source.
   b. Statement numbers in the FORTRAN source.

    c. SUBROUTINE definitions in the FORTRAN source.

    d. References to FORTRAN run-time routines for I/O or mathematical functions.

    e. The scratch-file names used in various parts of the jobs.

    f. The names of the compiler and linker programs used to prepare the FORTRAN programs for execution.

    g. The permanent file names of files updated by the two programs.

    h. The names of supervisory modules used to do I/O and provide other supervisor services.

    i. The identical job names.

Under what conditions could these two programs be run concurrently by a computer system? Explain why this could or could not be done at an installation with which you are familiar or at a hypothetical one. Can you do this at your installation with the operating system in use?

2. Use the outline of operating system functions in Appendix B to compare two systems from documentation provided. In making the comparisons, also include your evaluation of the operating system control language according to the criteria presented in Chapter 6. Is the outline adequate for the purpose? How would you change it to make it better? What is missing? Do any of the systems obviously not fit the outline because they are organized by unique concepts?

7

The Development Process

Thus far, we have considered the properties of operating systems themselves. We now look at the process whereby operating systems are produced. This process begins long before the first instruction of the system is coded. Preliminary documents describe requirements, objectives, the system's design, and the plan for its development. A new organization is created or an existing one is used to accomplish the production of the system. Certain tools are employed, not the least of which is the language to be used for implementation. In the coding of an operating system, certain techniques are used, some of which have little or no application to other types of programming. And after all is said and done, the product remains to be measured, modified, and maintained.

7.1 PRELIMINARIES

The development of an operating system begins with a need. Someone or some group of people must decide that they need an operating system and they are both willing and able to pay for it. Most often, this need is that of the manufacturer of a new computer, who wants to sell the computer and he concludes that the people most likely to buy it will want an operating system. If the existence of an operating system will increase probable profit by more than the cost of developing an operating system, one will be developed. Of course, the manufacturer could ask others to produce the system under some sort of contract, but this is not relevant to the process itself.

The unique fact about a manufacturer in search of an operating system is that the users of the system are unknown. Some sort of a survey of the marketplace could be taken to categorize potential customers in some useful way. But the system will eventually do more to determine its users than vice versa. Nevertheless, the manufacturer must draw up some sort of list of prospective customers' requirements that the system will be designed to fulfill.

Such a list is composed with greater confidence by an actual user, that is, the person or organization which, unlike that amorphous entity, "the marketplace," has a specific set of jobs to do. Organizations which can afford to have operating systems developed to meet their own detailed specifications usually fall into one of three categories:

1. Corporations of such great size as to make sufficient use of the system to justify the cost of its development. (This category accounts for very few operating systems.)
2. Organizations which use taxpayers' funds to pay for the operating systems.
3. Universities, which derive substantial benefits (research, theses, dissertations) from the mere development of a system, before it is even used for productive work.

The last two categories overlap when, as happens, a governmental agency provides a grant to a university for the development of a system.

Whatever the tasks it is decided that an operating system will have to perform, the descriptions of the tasks are only a beginning. "Lots of computation," "terminals for students at three universities," and "business applications" are not phrases which instantly prescribe a particular design for an operating system. Quantitative specifications are required. One must talk about response times with given loads, failure rates, visible and invisible components, flexibility, and simplicity. (What we are calling quantitative requirements are sometimes called system objectives. In that case, our "objectives" above become component objectives.)

The responsiveness required of an operating system is expressed by curves. The parameters for each curve are pairs from the following set: response time, number of users, and cost of hardware. The assumptions which must be made to derive the necessary curves involve among other things: effective capacities of various levels of the storage hierarchy after overhead has been subtracted, data transfer rates, transaction sizes, and whichever of the aforementioned parameters is to be held constant for a given computation. A study of such curves will suggest a certain configuration of hardware. The hardware will, in turn, become an assumption for the design of the operating system.

Failure rates may be expressed in quantities of data, the loss of which is acceptable if it occurs only once, on the average, over every time interval of some specified length. For an example, the loss of 10 records of 800 characters each twice per year might be acceptable. If the unaided hardware of a system does not offer an acceptable rate of failure, the operating system must be designed to augment the hardware in this regard. The same is true for other types of failure — software errors necessitating some sort of reinitialization, possibly with attendant loss of data; operator errors; device errors leading to degradation of the system's capabilities; and so on. The operating system must be designed to cope with each type of failure to the extent that the normal result of such a failure would be unacceptable.

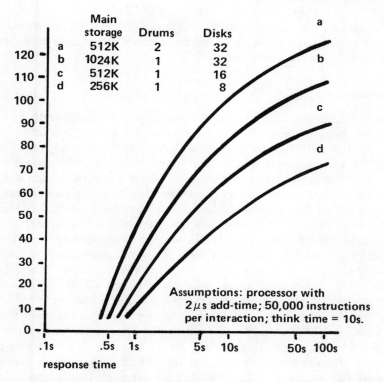

	Main storage	Drums	Disks
a	512K	2	32
b	1024K	1	32
c	512K	1	16
d	256K	1	8

Assumptions: processor with 2 μs add-time; 50,000 instructions per interaction; think time = 10s.

response time

Figure 7.1. Graph Relating Response Time, Number of Interactive Users, and Configurations of Equipment.

It may be required that the users of a system be unaffected by the invention of new I/O devices, the physical storing of data in media of diverse types, or even the substitution of an entirely different computing system for the original one. These requirements for the hiding from the system's users of certain characteristics of the system are known, respectively, as device-independence, data-independence, and machine-independence. The first of these is provided by modern data management routines, the second by data description routines, and the last by standardized higher-level languages.

Flexibility is used here to denote the degree to which an operating system is parameterized. The later the user is able to assign values to more parameters, the more flexible an operating system may be said to be. Flexibility, more than any other attribute, must result from the design of an operating system. It cannot be added later.

The simplicity required of an operating system may be expressed in terms of the education certain users of the system might be expected to have had, and the use that the users must be able to make of the system. While no operating system should be made unnecessarily complex, a system to be used by graduate students in computer sciences need not be so simple as one destined for use by homemakers or business executives.

Objectives

Product requirements lead inevitably to product objectives. The path, however, is neither short nor easy. First, to the functional and performance-oriented requirements must be added statements which relate the operating system being developed to others with which it might be compared. With respect to an existing operating system or one being developed concurrently, the new one might have to be: compatible, more reliable, easier to repair, more secure, and so on. When all the requirements and desires have been noted, they must be broken down into measurable objectives. The rate at which data can be transferred from an indexed file on a direct-access device to main storage may be an objective derived from requirements stated in terms of response times or the performance of object programs produced by given compilers. The mean-time-between-failure (MTBF) and duration of unscheduled interruptions (DUI) are measurable objectives derived from requirements for reliability and availability.

In the best of all possible worlds, a list of objectives would be unordered. In this world, such a list must be prioritized, so that when it becomes apparent that all objectives cannot be satisfied, designers can know which are the first to be sacrificed. The operative term is "trade-offs": "Performance must be traded off to assure full function."; "Trade off_____, but don't slip the schedules." – these are statements which might be made during the development of almost any operating system. The ordering of objectives at the outset facilitates and provides rationalization for the decisions these statements support. More importantly, the list helps reveal and thus prevent undesirable trade-offs.

Objectives should do more, however, than provide criteria for design decisions. They should be used to measure the extent to which the system is succeeding or has succeeded. In the former case, a model of a developing system can be used to determine that a component or the entire system must be revised, or that the project is totally unfeasible. In the latter case, measurement of the system may determine whether or not the system is accepted and paid for by a purchasing agency.

Design

With a prioritized list of quantified objectives, design can begin. [COS71] distinguishes six types of system design: the levels approach, the top-down approach, the nucleus-extension approach, the modules-interface approach, data base or transaction-oriented system, and ad hoc techniques such as the iteration method and the deadline method. As we shall see, these approaches are not mutually exclusive, but rather overlapping and complementary. Before this can be explained, each method must be described separately. This is done well in [COS71], from which the following descriptions are adapted. Quoted material is taken directly therefrom, except as noted.

The *level approach* involves the definition of a series of systems or machines, M_i, each one realized on its predecessor, M_{i-1}, by means of a program P_i. M_0 is hardware and M_k, where $k \geq i$ for all i, is the operating system. In the case of the only system designed by this approach to date, M_k is the THE system [Dij68b] and the technique is due to Dijkstra. Advantages of this approach are "clarity of description and elegance of design," and the feasibility of proving "by induction that the correctness of M_{i-1} and P_i implies that of M_i." Of course, selecting suitable M_i is not a trivial task.

The *top-down approach* involves functional analysis, a high-level description of the system as the sum of some number of nonoverlapping parts. Each of these parts is similarly divided, and so on, iteratively until a convenient level for implementation is reached. Not every system lends itself to this approach and, when one does, it is likely that the lowest level of description will not match well with the hardware available. This approach has, however, definite merit, as is discussed below.

The *nucleus-extension approach* involves a prototype of minimal system which is extended to the final product. The value of a "throw-away" prototype as a tool in the development of operating systems is discussed in Section 7.2. Such prototypes, contrary to original intentions, sometimes evolve into products, but this is not the issue here. Prototypes can provide a legitimate path to product development [Bri70].

The *modules-interface approach* involves a division of the operating system at some early stage of development into components the size of a single module of code. This is understandably difficult to do well, and its exclusion from the list of ad hoc methods might not be justified. It is often tantamount to nondesign or "design by junior-level coder."

Data base or *transaction-oriented systems* are constrained by the specialized tasks they must perform. These are not so much designed as they are specified. So little generality exists that the term "operating system" is only marginally applicable to such systems.

The *iteration method* is similar to the nucleus-extension method except that what turns out to be the nucleus of the system was originally believed to be the operating system itself. This could also be called the "growed-like-Topsy" approach [Sto92].

The *deadline method* is a form of nondesign wherein specific demonstrations are scheduled and given (or faked), but are rarely relevant to the development of the system, which proceeds lamely in parallel.

From the foregoing, one could easily conclude that there is no good way to design an operating system. The conclusion is overstated. A better case could be made for the assertion that no single approach is adequate for the design of a large, general-purpose operating system. Small operating systems can be designed well with any of several approaches [Lis72, Gai72]. Specialized systems, such as the aforementioned transaction-oriented systems, also lend themselves to several techniques of design [Kei64]. Large general systems normally require some combination of the approaches listed above.

The level approach is almost always implicit in the design of an operating system. The underlying computer is one level of the system. The services invoked by assembly language macroinstructions define another level. A control language processor and the programs implicitly invoked through the control language, such as scheduler and loader, form a third and possibly the highest level. Or, a higher level might be part of the operating system, a level at which a higher-level language such as ALGOL is implemented. If the levels are not defined with precision, proofs of correctness cannot be produced. But the value of levels in subdividing the totality of what must be done remains.

The top-down approach is also nearly inevitable. The fact that the objectives of a system are specified before design is begun is, in a sense, top-down. Before the details of a system can be hammered out, some gross specifications of the system's components and interfaces must be established. This is also top-down. What distinguishes a pure top-down approach is that the derivation of lower-level requirements from the functions above is carried down to the level of code. More commonly, at some higher level a collection of functions is treated as a single machine and implementation below that level is free to optimize globally; that is, there is no requirement for identifying code at one level with one specific function visible at the next higher level.

We have already pointed out that the nucleus-extension approach plays a part in the development of most operating systems. The prototype which is used to produce some kind of running code as soon as possible is a manifestation of this approach.

The modules-interface approach is seen at the lowest level of each operating system design. When no other design is visible between the operating system control language and the computer, the approach can be said to have been used in its pure form. More often, this approach, like the others mentioned, is one of a number used in a single design. Parnas has provided [Parn72] a useful discussion of criteria for modularization.

Elements of the iteration and deadline methods are also present in every design. Nothing worth doing is done perfectly the first time. Iteration is the natural consequent of this truism. No one will finance a project as large as the development of an operating system without setting a deadline for its completion. And no deadline, no matter how unrealistic — too close *or* too distant — is either met by developers or totally ignored.

Operating systems have typically been designed, as has been indicated, with a combination of approaches. The definition of levels for the implementation of an operating system seems to have definite value. That these levels could be sufficiently numerous and defined with sufficient precision to permit proofs of correctness and error-free implementation seems highly unlikely. Rather, levels should be defined to reduce the tasks of design and implementation to manageable proportions. Between levels, top-down implementation seems quite appropriate. Functions at each level are likely to be sufficiently isolated that generalizing across functions is unnecessary. At the level of code modules, some version of the modules-interface approach is required; that is, for each module, its inputs and outputs must be defined. These, taken together with the transformations performed by the module, define it. The incidental roles of iteration and deadlines cannot be avoided and need no further explication.

Specifications

The products of design are external and internal specifications. An *external specification* describes the product as it appears to its users. Precision is to be desired in an external specification, but for a product as large and complex as an operating system, it is not always a practical objective. A precise description of an operating system would most likely be written in a language such as APL [Fal70]. The description would treat the system as a machine having an internal state defined by a number of parameters, and, for each possible input, the effects on those parameters (state transitions) would be described. Regardless of the precision of the external specification, however, it is the statement of what the product must do when it is completed. Once the external specification has been written, the designing of test cases can begin, for the matter of what the product must be proven to do has been decided. In practice, the external specification of an operating system remains in a state of flux long after a product has been delivered and even unto the day of its total obsolescence.

It should not be surprising that external specifications vary with time. They are produced by people and people make mistakes. The specifications may fail to meet the objectives or contain contradictions and inconsistencies or describe a product which cannot be developed within the constraints imposed by the availability of resources (for example, it may cost too much). The external specification permits all these errors to be found. That is one of its prime values. Another is to serve as a base for the next steps, the internal specification and the plan.

External specifications often change for reasons less laudable than those listed above. Operating systems being developed under contract, whether government or private, are often subject to the whims of the party for whom the work is being done. The failure to control changes in specifications has doomed more than one operating system and it might be said that the extent to which external specifications undergo change is inversely proportional to the quality of the resulting system and the degree to which it meets its cost and scheduling objectives.

External specifications describe not only what the system and each of its components will do, but also how fast, how reliably, and so on. In short, the external specifications of the system's components illustrate what the components will do to permit the system to meet its objectives.

The *internal specification* describes how the external specification is to be realized. An internal specification should include:[1]

1. Semantic description of all external interfaces of the system.
2. Detailed specifications for all interfaces in the system, including the format and usage of all data areas used for communication through the interfaces.
3. Overall flow diagrams for the system, subsystem, and components.
4. Specifications for each module in the system, including: (a) narrative description, (b) estimates as to resource requirements (such as space in main and auxiliary storage, time), and (c) definitions of interfaces, entry points, exits, exceptional conditions, error messages, and the like.

An internal specification gives evidence as to the feasibility of development and embodies the lowest level of development which can be called design. Below an internal specification, all is implementation.

The specifications described above may be of any of a wide variety of levels of formality. Simple natural language has been the medium most used. Recently, however, improvement has been sought. If one could specify operating system components in some formal, at least quasi-mathematical language, one might be able to use formal techniques both to implement the specification and to derive formalisms that give evidence about the adherence of the specification to well-defined criteria. Such formalism has been the object of a number of efforts [Ame79] stimulated by the United States' Department of Defense's Advanced Research Projects Agency.

In particular, if one could use formal techniques to develop the kernel of an operating system and that kernel included all functions that related to the mediation of access, one might be able to certify with an expressible, if not mathematically derived, level of confidence that unauthorized access cannot occur. The structure needed to achieve such a goal may place great burdens upon the system in terms of development costs and ultimate efficiency of the resulting system, but such burdens may be acceptable to those who most value security.

---

[1] Adapted from [Mea69], p. 5. Also of interest is [Las70].

Plans

To say that the development plan for an operating system is built on an internal specification is to oversimplify. Of course, plans must have been made for the resources expended in doing market surveys, establishing requirements, deriving objectives, and designing the system. Yet, implementation is the greatest part of development and requires the most planning.

A plan must provide for many of the items treated in the sections which follow on tools and techniques. These items are simply listed here:

Bootstrapping base (for example, simulator or emulator of a yet-to-be-built computer)
Model
Prototype
Programming Development System (PDS)
Documentation Systems
Standards Development and Enforcement
Testing
Maintenance
Follow-on efforts
Procedures for controlling change

The aspect of the plan on which we dwell here is that of staged implementation.

In every development project there is pressure to "get something on the air." This is true not only because managers like to display functioning products to justify expenditures, but also because running systems facilitate further development. As additional components of the system are produced, they can be appended to the part that works to form a precursory system. This allows components to be tested more easily, more efficiently, and more thoroughly, than they ever could be tested in isolation. For all this to be done, some order of precedence must be established among the various pieces of the system. It must be established what components make up a minimal running system. The plan will state that these are to be implemented first. For each component, a list is prepared of components which must preexist for integrated execution. An order of implementation can then be determined. Where cycles appear, such as A needs B and B needs A, all components in the cycle must be treated as one.

The order of implementation can be represented by a form of PERT[2] chart, which permits scheduling of development on the basis of projected costs in

---

[2] PERT (*project evaluation review technique*) employs graphic representations of subproject dependencies to answer questions such as "What should/must be done before what?", "What happens if X isn't done on time;", and "What can be allowed to slip its schedule without affecting the final delivery date;" See [Fla67].

resources and elapsed time for each component. Such costing is still a primitive science wherein the most thorough effort to date[3] has yielded a costing polynomial of 11 variables and a standard error of 42.3 against a mean of 39.5 man-months for the 169 programs involved. In other words, even if you could quantify a dozen or so imponderables such as "innovation," "stability of design," and continuity of personnel," the scientifically derived expression for cost of development in programmer-years would be of little practical value.

Trapnell has observed [Tra69] that modularity is critical to effective planning. If estimates of the resources required for each component of a large product are reasonably accurate, the cost estimate for the entire product may be accurate (unless all errors are of the same type, either high or low, in which case their cumulative effect may be disastrous). The smaller the components, the better the chances for accurate estimates.

Estimates must be based on some assumptions of productivity, but these assumptions are very dangerous. Ercoli and Endres have noted[4] that the cost per instruction for a program may vary by a factor as large as 20 or even 50, depending on techniques, projects, and personnel. The importance of the last variable can be seen from the following list, which gives the ratio of worst to best performances by experienced programmers in a test [Dav68] :

Debug time used	26/1
Computer time used	11/1
Coding time	25/1
Code size	5/1
Running time	13/1

Organization

However suspect estimates may be, however, they will be made. The job of organizing for the production of an operating system then follows. The modularity which played such an important part in estimating is even more vital here. A great deal has been written about the number of workers one manager can supervise, and when the workers are programmers the number seems to vary between five and ten.[5] This number of people must have an identifiable, isolable, precisely defined task to perform. That task is to code one or more modules with inputs, outputs, and functions that were defined before the development group existed and which can be altered only due to design bugs or contract modification, and then only by procedures which guarantee that all affected parties will learn of the change.

---

[3] See [Nel66], p. 76. A large number of small programs exaggerates the error of the method. Excellent discussions of the topic are [Pie70] and [Aro70].
[4] [NATO68], p. 82.
[5] The estimate of A.J. Perlis, in [NATO68], p. 85.

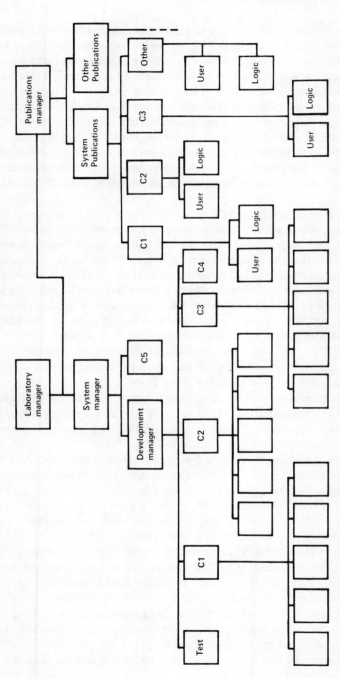

Figure 7.2. Hypothetical System Development Organization Chart. This chart foreshadows an operating system with three major components of five subcomponents each. One minor component (C4) will be well integrated, but another (C5) will have few or poor interfaces with the rest of the system. The system will be of poor quality, and its documentation will be as poor as it will be voluminous. Any similarity between this organization and any real organization, past or present, is coincidental

Mealy [Mea69] paraphrases Conway [Con68] in saying that "systems resemble the organizations that produce them." Since this is true, and since the system should be, and often is, designed without regard for existing organizations, the organization must change to conform to the design of the system. If this is not done, there is no chance of the system matching its design.

The organization we have been discussing is just a skeleton. To produce a system, one must have not only organization charts and managers, but also implementers. Implementers are by no means all alike. To take advantage of the fact that different individuals in an organization have different skills, Mills [IBM22] has developed a concept of *programmer teams*. The following material on programmer teams is adapted from the works of Baker [Bak72] and Aron [Aro68].

A programmer team is a group of individuals led by a chief programmer, who does the most important work, the design work which remains to be done within the context of the assigned task, and the most intricate coding. A team is assembled around the chief programmer to free that individual from more arduous and less productive tasks. A technician keeps track of latest versions of modules, notes what has and what has not been done, and handles other clerical chores. Less skilled programmers code less complicated routines, generate documentation, and provide control statements. A manager handles administrative matters and a secretary performs secretarial functions. An analyst might be concerned with flaws in design and relationships between the modules being developed and the rest of the system. A back-up programmer can and does do what the chief programmer does, only not quite so well.

The concentration of work in the hands of a single individual greatly mitigates the problems of communication which typically plague a large programming project. The team represents a tribute to specialization with, Baker estimates, a doubling of productivity.

A weakness of programmer teams is that the members of the team take their technical direction from the chief programmer, but they are managed by someone else. "One cannot serve two masters," yet the duality of direction is a natural consequence of the fact that few people can do a good job of managing both ideas and people. Most organizations ignore this fact. Programmer teams acknowledge it and accept the challenge it represents.

Not all projects lend themselves to development by teams. For example, the right skill mix must be present, as well as tasks defined with sufficient precision. These requirements are always present in system development but become more critical when teams are involved. The unique prerequisite for effective use of programmer teams is a number of chief programmers, individuals of the necessary competence and motivation to perform the tasks described. Too many of those Aron might call "superprogrammers" are not interested in coding. Such people cannot be chief programmers. But where bothersome semiclerical

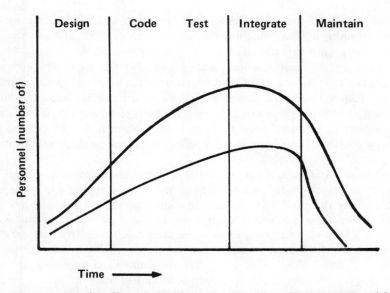

Figure 7.3. Variation of Staffing Level with Development Time. The chart, adapted from one prepared by A.M. Pietrasanta, shows staffing levels as a function of elapsed time on a program development project.

tasks have not been eliminated by a programming development system (PDS) and the appropriate personnel exist, and, particularly, where erstwhile designers can serve as chief programmers for components they have designed, providing continuity and faithfulness of implementation to design, programmer teams can be of immense value.

The contributions of Weinberg to our understanding of how programmers behave and how programming projects can be managed can hardly be overstated. His books, [Wei71 and Wei73], and article [Wei72] are recommended without qualification for further study on this and related topics.

Pietrasanta has estimated[6] that developers represent only half of the people necessary to produce an operating system. The designers, coders, testers, and so forth, are no more numerous than managers, project control personnel, test developers, developers of standards, writers, developers of models and other tools, educational personnel, and so on. The jobs of most of these people are easily understood. Less obvious is the role of project control personnel. These people do more than simply keep track of what has happened and what should happen next. They must establish procedures to be followed. They are the guardians of the PERT chart, mentioned above, which says what must be done

─────────────────

[6] See [Pie70]. The entire volume [Wei70] is relevant to the present discussion.

before what. They report to responsible parties when schedules have not been satisfactorily met. But, most importantly, they are the first and often last line of defense against that mortal enemy of orderly development: change. Changes in design are, of course, often justified and even necessary. The procedures established by project control personnel must ensure that only justified changes occur. Failure to control change guarantees chaos,[7] while overcontrol ensures strangulation of the project by red tape. The balance between these is not easily struck, but that is what must be done if the system is to be produced in an orderly manner. The project control personnel are the ones entrusted with this critical task.

Another little-appreciated aspect of system development is review. The market for key verifiers[8] is ample testimony to the fact that two heads are as much better than one when applied to computer-related tasks as at any other time. Every document, every design, every line of code, should be studied and understood by at least one person other than its author. It is too easy for a person to make the same mistake twice, for desk-checking to take the place of review in the verification of code. The procedures and personnel for review should appear in every operating system development plan.

Those responsible for the development of an operating system cannot always choose who will do the developing. Since choice *is* sometimes available, however, a word about the selection of good programmers is in order. Mayer and Stalnaker [May68] report that six years of research revealed no test "capable of consistently predicting job performance." While therefore unable to recommend an infallible method of hiring programmers, they did find something wrong with present procedures. Studies by Bairdain and Dickman had shown that the criteria most commonly used in *hiring* programmers — professional activity, age, appearance — are those least esteemed in *evaluating* programmers!

The preliminary steps of operating system development — surveys, statements of objectives, design, planning, and organization — have been discussed in the natural order indicated above. This is somewhat misleading, however. Each step is, in fact, an iterative process. Requirements, objectives, design, plans, and organizations change over time, each perturbed by its predecessor, by a changing environment, and by the discovery of flaws — such as surveyed customers who cannot afford the product, designs which cannot be implemented, or plans containing checkpoints which cannot be met. The only stable object is a dead object, be it a plan, an organization, or a system. At every step, change must be anticipated, controlled, and absorbed. That is how progress is made.

---

[7] That "chaos" ends in OS may be significant.
[8] Key verifiers resemble key punches, but are fed with already-punched cards. The operator reads the original source material and keys as if punching new cards. If two operators do not punch identically, that is, if the operator of the verifier does not key in a way which might have created the card originally, an indication of error is given. Two operators must make the same error for a punching error to go undetected.

With the formation of an organization to develop the operating system, the preliminaries are over. Ahead lies the implementation. We thus proceed to discuss the tools and techniques which facilitate implementation and that most critical tool of all, the language of implementation.

7.2 TOOLS

No job can be done well without the proper tools. The development of an operating system is no exception. One of the most valuable tools one can employ on such a project is a programming development system (PDS), which can be of use in almost every facet of system development. A computer simulator or emulator is needed when an operating system is being developed for a computer not yet available in sufficient quantity for use by all developers. Simulative models are used to gain insight into the system's performance characteristics. Prototypes are developed for several reasons: as part of a nucleus-extension approach to design; to provide a vehicle for testing early versions of programs which must use the operating system; to demonstrate feasibility of the system; or to have a usable product, albeit of limited capability, even if the system as originally planned is never built.

The PDS

A PDS is intended to aid the development of an operating system in several ways. Much of what the PDS does could be done by clerical personnel, but neither as quickly nor as well. Such clerical functions include keeping track of various versions of a single module; updating source decks; providing reports of the usage of system macros; associating source modules with object modules, flow charts, historical data, documentation, and so on; and keeping track of which modules have and have not been coded.

The tasks described above are performed by programs which execute as part of the PDS. Some of these may be standard utilities, such as the update program. Others are specially written for the PDS. The PDS includes many other programs which would be used in the development of the system in any event: language processors, linkers, test case generators, text editors, flow-chart-preparation programs, and other programs. What distinguishes the PDS from bare control language procedures is that the PDS presents a single interface to the developer, one which permits the expression of all requirements for programming support in a single convenient language. These are some of the possible components of a PDS:

Module libraries (source/object, current/under test/next)
Catalog of modules
Source module editor

312 OPERATING SYSTEMS PRINCIPLES

Processor for implementation language
Conversational symbolic debugging monitor
Flow-charting program
Text processor
Procedure library
Test case library
Management reporting system
Standards enforcement program
Code-charts-documentation correlation program
"Where used" analysis program
Security/authorization routines
Development network
Remote job entry facilities
System build/modify routines
Job stream generator
Loader

A PDS may also include an interactive system for program preparation and testing. Controls may be included to prevent unintentional or unauthorized updating of programs. The PDS may play a major role in the distribution procedures for the system by providing for the placement of all the system's modules on some appropriate storage medium. Direct control of program production may be exercised through a validation of code against flow charts. Alternatively, flow charts may be produced directly from code. Verification of compliance with standards, such as use of standardized names [Mer72], is yet another possible PDS function. All sorts of useful data may be collected incidentally by the PDS, yielding statistics on system usage, debugging time, and other information of great interest and value to management [Denv66].

The CLEAR-CASTER[9] (Controlled Library Environment And Resources - Computer Assisted System for Total Effort Reduction) system developed by IBM has proven of particular value in coordination of the efforts of programmers at many widely separated locations. This is to be expected, inasmuch as the PDS is not sensitive to the physical location of its users and influences all of their productive activities. It is as though all the developers existed, in some sense, *within* the PDS. One could imagine no better example of centralized development.

---

[9] See H.M. Brown's remarks in [NATO70], pp. 53-59. Other PDSs are described by R. Bemer in [NATO68], pp. 94-95 and by Section 6.26. "Real Time Program Management Supervisor," of [IBM20]. The RTOS (Real-Time Operating System) was produced in connection with the activities at the NASA Houston Space Flight Center. Corbato et el, in [Cor72], note that MULTICS served as its own PDS ("Maintenance tool"). AUTOFLOW/ LIBRARIAN® is a PDS running on IBM's System/360 and was developed and is marketed by Applied Data Research, Inc.

Simulator

Another possible component of a PDS is a *computer simulator.* Such a tool, or its hardware-assisted counterpart, the *emulator,* is needed when the computing system for which an operating system is being developed is well defined, but nonexistent.

The term *simulator* is used here in a narrow sense. Simulators of existing computing systems or systems of other types are not our concern. The simulators of interest here are those which precisely imitate the behavior of a computer, except for the dimension of time. They are built because a computer manufacturer would like to realize revenue from new computers just as soon as the first production models have been built and tested. But customers will not pay for computers if they are not accompanied by operating systems with facilitate — indeed, make feasible — their use of the computer. The operating system must have a computer as a base on which to be developed. And the first models of a new computer, those produced in advance of the ones which will actually be sold, are apt to be too few, too late, and too unreliable to permit the efficient development of an operating system on them. What the manufacturer needs, then, is something that acts just like the new computer, but can be available and reliable sooner. This is the simulator. It must simulate the following elements of a computer:

Main storage space
Instruction set
Registers
Auxiliary storage devices and volumes
Interruption mechanisms
Protection mechanisms
Relocation mechanisms
Notions of privilege
Timers

The development of a simulator is made difficult by nearly unique problems of time, pressure, and requirements for innovation. First, the product is likely to be scheduled for use some time before the specifications it is to meet have been completely determined. Programmers can easily code, and clamor to test, modules long before engineers have proceeded from basic instruction set to detailed interruption mechanisms. Second, the secondary storage devices of a new computer may be totally unlike any that are available. Simulating a directly accessed storage medium with one that is accessed sequentially is not a trivial task. Third, mechanisms devised for a new computer may also be completely new. It may not be easy to break down mechanisms such as relocation and storage protection to primitive operations that can be simulated without the assistance of hardware components.

Simulators include routines for the mapping of the host system's storage to the storage of the simulated system and for the execution of the simulated computer's instructions, and, perhaps, a small supervisory system which is itself a prototype of the operating system being developed.

The mapping of storage is relatively simple when the simulated system and the host system, the system used to implement the simulator, utilize the same internal representations for data. Complexities arise when the systems have different word lengths, different character and data representations (floating-point, decimal), and different collating (sorting) sequences. These differences all applied to "SUPPAK," the IBM 7090/7094 Support Package for IBM System/360 [IBM21]. Only variable-length words such as are found on the IBM 1401, could have made mapping much more difficult, although the fact that the host computer had a longer word was probably an advantage.

SUPPAK simulated up to 65,536 8-bit bytes in 32,768 36-bit words of 7090 storage, a 1:2.25 ratio in bits; that is, the simulator could run programs about half as large as the largest programs the host could accommodate. This is a satisfactory and typical capability.

Few useful generalizations can be made about the simulation of instructions. About the only aid to brute force is the actual hardware implementation of the simulated instruction set. Particularly if that implementation, which is being attempted simultaneously, is in microcode, but even if it is not, those working on the simulator are likely to find that the engineers' tricks have their analogs in code of the host machine.

The simulation of devices by using similar devices of greater or equivalent capacity is relatively simple. Where complications arise, no better solution may be available than to simulate a device by mapping its contents into a virtual address space. This is possible, of course, only when the simulator is to run under a virtual storage operating system. In the absence of such a system, devices of new design or great capacity may sorely test the programmers' ingenuity.

Interruptions usually pose less of a problem than one might first think. Since the functions of the simulated machine are being performed "in slow motion," as it were, it is not difficult to suspend them entirely at some well-defined point and mimic the behavior of a real computer signalling an interruption. Here again, those coding the simulator are likely to benefit from an analysis of concurrent development of the real computer and its microcode, if any.

Like any bare computer, the simulated machine needs some sort of supervisory program to be of practical value. The simulator could be programmed to an interface somewhat above that of the expected hardware to include a primitive supervisor, but it seems more practical to code such a program concurrently with the simulator. This serves two purposes: it yields code which may be carried forward to the real machine, perhaps even to the actual operating system, and it provides a first test case for the simulator itself.

An *emulator*[10] is just a computer simulator, part or all of which is microcoded. All or parts of the instruction set of the emulated machine may be implemented in the control storage of the host. Access to the emulative code is likely to be provided via an external switch, in the case of total microcoding, or a single instruction of the host machine. Any supervisory routines provided and programs for the simulation of I/O devices may be coded directly in the instruction set of the host machine, on the premise that the advantages of efficiency outweigh the disadvantages of rewriting routines for the emulated machines. Emulators are now most commonly used to allow those obtaining a new computer, the host, to run, without modification, programs that ran on previously used computers. This discussion of emulators is included because the technique is clearly applicable to the problem usually solved by computer simulation, the anticipation of a new machine.

IBM's Virtual Machine Facility/370 (VM/370) [IBM18], a successor to Control Program-67/Conversational Monitor System (CP-67/CMS), permits the simulation of various operating systems within a single System/370 computer. Techniques employing virtual storage permit the simulation of up to 16 million bytes of storage on a virtual machine and a number of virtual machines in one physical system. VM/370 illustrates the feasibility of running one operating system under another. This is important because the facilities of the "master" operating system are then available for debugging of the "slave." While no new operating system has yet been developed in this way, McGrath describes [McG72] how this technique has been used with CP-67 to test modifications to OS/360.

Model

As Zurcher and Randell have shown,[11] a *simulative model*[12] can be of great value in the design of an operating system. The simulative model represents activities and events, in contrast to the equations (involving averages of time for complex processing over some mix of transactions) of an analytical model. This concentration on *what* happens, as opposed to *how* it does, encourages a similarly

---

[10] The term is used here in the natural sense employed by IBM and some others. See [Tuc65], [Ben65], and Schoen and Belsole [Sch71]. Instruction speeds comparable to the 220, but four times slower than the System 360/25, are reported in the latter. Various IBM and RCA publications describe other emulators.

[11] [Zur69]. See also Randell's "Towards a methodology of computing system design," in [NATO68], pp. 204–208, and the related discussion on pp. 53–55. Much of the following paragraphs is adapted from these sources.

[12] The term is used (in preference to *simulation model*) after [Pom72]. The definition is also due to Pomeroy.

activity-oriented "outside-in" design. The activities can be broken down more finely as design progresses, yielding a model of increasing detail and accuracy.

The reasons for modeling an operating system under development are:

1. To compare the performance of alternative designs.
2. To evaluate the adequacy of a given design.
3. To predict the performance of the resulting system.

The performance aspect of modeling will be considered further in the section on measurement. During the design stage, only relative measures of performance are likely to be reliable. Yet these suffice for reason 1 and, in the case of a grossly inadequate design, for reason 3 as well. Also, if the system is not destined to work, neither will the model. The model reveals this much sooner. If the model keeps pace with the system under development, the value of its performance data becomes greater as the system approaches completion.

Many languages can be used for the implementation of a simulative model of an operating system. The System and Software Simulator [L.Coh68] was written in FORTRAN, the same language Zurcher and Randell [Zur69] used for IMMM. Stanley and Hertel [Sta66] used GPSS [IBM19], one of a number of languages — including SIMSCRIPT [Mar64], SOL [Knu64], and SIMTRAN [Bra65] — developed particularly for simulation. Teichroew and Lubin list [Tei66] 22 such languages. These are characterized as discrete-change simulation languages (as opposed to continuous-change languages) which are suited to the study of transactions, such as jobs passing through successive states and served by distinct components.

Prototype

Regardless of the detailed plan for the development of an operating system, some portion of the system will of necessity be developed first. That portion is likely to consist of the components on which most others depend on which themselves, of course, depend only on one another. Almost by definition, these components form the nucleus of the operating system. If it is intended that this nucleus, which may be developed with undue haste ("quick and dirty") to "get the ball rolling," be recorded later, it can be called a prototype. This type of prototype is consonant with the nucleus-extension approach to design. The nucleus is both designed and implemented first, providing a basis for further work.

The greatest value of any such prototype is as a vehicle for three types of testing. First, the hardware or computer simulator on which the prototype is built is tested by the prototype's use of it. Second, the prototype itself and its design are tested by its successful implementation. Third, the prototype provides a vehicle by means of which other components of the operating system can be tested.

Prototypes need not be limited to the nucleus of an operating system. They may be more elaborate, growing in response to pressure for demonstrations of capability to justify additional expenditure. The more pressure under which a prototype is developed, the more likely that it will be, or, at least, should have been a true prototype: a model not destined for actual use. However, "The best laid schemes o' mice and men/ Gang aft a-gley." The "quick and dirty" code that was to be rewritten may become part of the final product because, for one reason or another, the rewriting never happens. Indeed, this possibility may occur to those who suggest the production of a prototype. They know the vicissitudes of life and a prototype is one form of insurance that a development manager can buy.

Programming development systems, computer simulators, models, and prototypes are the primary tools of operating system development. Below in this chapter, in the section on system measurement, tools employed in later stages of a system's life are discussed. Included there is a different view of models, one more concerned with performance than design. Barely mentioned in the discussion of PDSs were tools of a more general nature, applicable to large and small systems and application programs: conversational symbolic debugging monitor, a flow-chart processor, and a text editor. Sammet has described [Sam70] the roles these and other tools play in program development. Pomeroy has summarized [Pom72] IBM's inventory of generally available aids. Evans and Darly provide [Eva66] a useful discussion of facilities for conversational debugging, while Chapin discusses[13] [Cha72] programs for production of flow-charts.

7.3 TECHNIQUES

Our discussion of the development process has covered the steps leading up to implementation and the tools which facilitate it. Before going on to discuss the language in which the coding is done, we shall discuss the techniques which are employed in the development of operating systems. In particular, we shall be concerned with the establishment of standards and conventions for coding; graphic and tabular aids to the development of the system, such as flow charts; methods of coding, such as structured programming and top-down programming; the testing of the system and its components; the integration of components into precursory systems; and the documentation of the system.

Standards

Standards and conventions are established:

---

[13] See also [Abr68] and [Pom72].

1. To categorize certain undesirable coding practices as "nonstandard" as well as, say, inefficient, bug-inducing, or unduly restrictive.
2. To facilitate development by obviating trivial decisions which might result in bugs and would, at least, be time-consuming to make.
3. To facilitate maintenance by endowing the virtues of uniformity, meaningfulness, and "modifiability" on code.
4. To provide flexibility in naming where, due to restrictions in the language of implementation, it might not otherwise exist.

Standards must not, however, stifle creativity, a point which must be borne in mind and made clear if coders are to accept and respect standards.

The first rationale for standards is partially psychological. Poor coding practices could be described in some document and coders left on their own to read and understand the document and avoid the poor practices. One advantage of establishing good practice as "standard" is that that label carries more moral suasion. Another advantage is that in establishing a standard, one tries to be precise as to its definition. This precision has the obvious virtue of providing clear criteria for adherence to the standard. It may also enable the mechanized, that is, programmed, checking for violations of standards.

An example of a standard dealing with efficiency of code is one stating that the less common result of a test should cause a transfer of control to another location while the more common result "falls through." Greater efficiency results from for mainline code, but does not do this for other branches of code. This standard also contributes to readability of code, illustrating the valid thesis that many standards are motivated by more than one of the four basic rationales listed above.

An example of a standard designed to reduce the number of bugs in programs is a standard requiring the saving and restoring across a call to a subroutine of the contents of all registers, except those participating in that call. The saving of the contents of fewer registers may be more efficient, but as programs grow, the list of unused registers tends to shrink. Programmers modifying someone else's or even their own code may not notice a subroutine call which occurs between two uses of a previously unused register. Not only might this result in a bug, but the bug might not appear until the innocent subroutine is modified to use the exposed register. At that time, the bug may be very difficult to find.

Other standards designed to reduce bugs, or aid in their detection, are those sometimes categorized as *defensive programming* [Con72]. One such standard might require that all parameters passed to a routine be checked for validity (for example, that they be integers between 2 and 5) before use. Another might require that even a variable already known to have integral values between 2 and 5, inclusive, be tested for equality to 5 after having been found unequal to 2, 3, or 4.

A standard intended to avoid undue restriction of function might require that a field containing the length of a control block be large enough to contain an integer, say, 20% greater than the maximum size of the control block as constrained by initial design. This permits orderly growth.

Standards which obviate arbitrary decisions might involve register usage, record formats, or the increment to be used in numbering successive source language statements. Standards dealing with terminology are also in this category. The magnitude of the problem of getting everyone in an organization to use the same words to mean the same things is directly proportional to some power of the size of the organization. What is needed are standards to assure the meaningfulness of coined terms and a glossary to assure the wide distribution of accurate and precise definitions and to combat the proliferation of new meanings for old terms and new terms for old concepts.

Program maintenance is facilitated if those who will maintain the system can be assured that certain things are done the same way throughout the system. If each field in a control block has only one name by which reference is made to it in every module, cross-reference listings can be used to find every reference to a given field. To this end, a standard might require the use of control block definitions, provided by macroinstructions, for all references to control blocks.

Flow-charting conventions may be established so that those maintaining the system can infer certain sequences of code from notations or specifications of flow charts. This should reduce the number of times actual source code must be consulted. Notational conventions may be the subject of similarly motivated standards. Boettner has provided [Boe69] a useful discussion of notations, for example, Backus-Naur Form (BNF), for descriptions of syntax.

It is impossible to place too much emphasis on standards relating to the meaningfulness of source code. Many "self-documenting" programming languages have been developed, but none of them are in fact self-documenting. Comments will always be necessary and standards should compel their use. [Flo72] amplifies this subject at length. The standards should make it perfectly clear that comments are not merely to echo the accompanying statement, such as

ADD POINTER, 4   ADD 4 TO POINTER

but should add to the reader's knowledge, as

ADD TABLPTR,L'ENTRY   POINT TO NEXT ENTRY IN TABLE

The latter example illustrates adherence to other useful standards. Names should convey a maximum of meaning ("TABLPTR" is more specific than "POINTER"); and the most meaningful of all possible equivalent expressions should be used ("L'ENTRY" suggests the code's meaning more than "4" does).

Indentation of lines of codes can be the subject of a standard with the objective of meaningfulness. The equal indentation of two lines of code may mean that they delimit the same loop or block. Such a convention has already spawned a program to accomplish meaningful indentation, NEATER2 [Con70].

There are certain coding practices which make program modification difficult, perilous, or virtually impossible. Standards should be established prohibiting code that:

1. Branches to "myself plus ten," or the like. (Such an instruction may acquire a meaning radically different from the one intended when a new instruction is carelessly inserted immediately after it.)
2. Specifies an operation on two or more of a table's currently contiguous fields. (The fields might be separated by a redesign of the table.)
3. Approaches in size the maximum for a unit of code (such that no room is left for modification without the splitting of the unit into two units).

In an operating system, there is likely to be some context, some universe of discourse, wherein symbols created by many different coders must coexist. To ensure that two coders do not define identical symbols to be associated with different objects, such as messages, programs, or entry points, it may be necessary to establish a standard which a coder can apply algorithmically to derive unique symbols that no one else will use. Such a standard might involve coders' initials, for example, but a breakdown of symbols' initial characters by component and subcomponent is usually more useful.

The reader may have noted that some of the examples given relate to assembly language code and not to code written in higher-level languages. This is a reflection of the fact that assembly language code is inherently less disciplined. In fact, compilers often enforce what would be standards in their absence.

Our discussion of coding standards has not touched upon the standards to which the end product, the operating system, may have to conform. Statements regarding adherence to the standards for magnetic tape labels, COBOL, and so on, are part of an operating system's external specifications and are not really relevant to the subject of this chapter.

Graphic Aids

Standards dictate how code is to be written. Flow charts tell what the code is to accomplish. Actually, a flow chart is but one of a number of possible graphical or tabular representations of a program. Others are *HIPO* (Hierarchy-Input-Process-Output [IBM30]) diagrams, logic flow tables, and decision tables. The flow chart is, however, far and away the most popular of these and deserves most of our attention.

Flow charts serve two quite different purposes. Before coding has been done, flow charts help programmers to gather and express their thoughts.

After the system has been implemented, flow charts form part of the system's documentation.

Prior to coding, flow charts representing gross detail might be prepared by the system's designers to communicate their design. Individual programmers will certainly prepare flow charts at the most detailed level of the system. It should be possible to code directly from the lowest level of charts.

The foregoing is well known and generally accepted in the programming community, but some questions do arise: Do flow charts help? Do some languages of implementation obviate flow charts? If coding from charts is so easy, why not compile a set of low charts?

The answers to the first two questions differ from programmer to programmer. Some people find the two-dimensionality of flow charts practically indispensable to their thought processes.[14] Others do not. The value of flow charts varies with individual and with programming language. Some programmers will always use charts, some never. For a given individual, the use of charts will vary with the language of implementation. As to the compilation of a set of flow charts, there is no obvious reason this cannot be done.[15] Certainly a nontrivial amount of processing, depending on the suitability of the flow-charting language, might be involved if efficient code is to be generated, but a valid, though unsophisticated, algorithm (BRANCH to every box on every chart) is obviously available. Implicit, of course, is that the textual material of the flow charts is code of some sort. One intuitively feels that if chart and code have merged, two different representations have become one and something must have been lost. This intuition is not easily substantiated.

Flow charts must not simply be created and forgotten. They must be continually updated to reflect the state of the corresponding programs. Updating the charts incrementally helps in the preparation and evaluation of design and code changes and is more efficient than producing new charts to document the finished product.

Flow charts can be used in a rather limited way to validate coding. Transfers of control may be matched against flow lines and inconsistencies flagged. This operation is very nearly the converse of the compilation of charts, discussed above. The precise converse, producing charts from code, has been done,[16] but this technique seems more susceptible to the "two representations merged into one" objection raised in the other case.

---

[14] Yet this seems strange, in that our lives are in some sense one-dimensional; that is, things happen to us one after another and we rarely think about the simultaneity of events that affect us. But psychology is not the subject of this book.

[15] Such programs are described in [Ell68] and [Sut66]. See also [Kar55] for a description of a "block diagram compiler" used in system simulation. The phrase "set of flow charts" acknowledges the values of cross references among charts, as made possible by AUTODOC, which is described in [Cha72].

[16] For surveys of relevant programs, see [Abr68] and [Cha72].

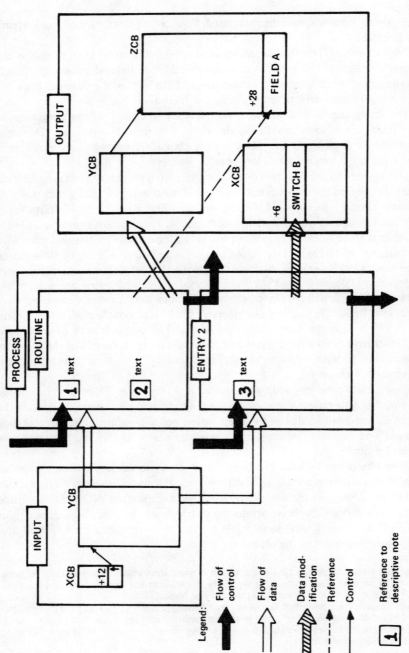

Figure 7.4. A HIPO Diagram.

Charting techniques have been the subject of a number of works[17] and is not discussed here. Gruenberger's review [Gru70] is of greater relevance to our topic than any of the books cited, and is recommended for its insight.

The HIPO (Hierarchy plus Input-Process-Output) technique, credited[18] to Wolfe, is illustrated in the accompanying figure. It capitalizes on the fundamental fact that any program can be characterized by its inputs, the functions or transformations it performs on those inputs, and the resulting outputs. The "hierarchy" is suggestive of the technique's particular suitability for describing top-down programs. HIPO diagrams, also called method-of-operation diagrams, may be used in conjunction with or instead of flow charts, before coding is done or after coding, to document a program. Their use is largely a matter of personal preference, although, of course, management may elect to make their use mandatory. HIPODRAW is the name of a program used to draw HIPO diagrams mechanically.

Logic Flow Tables [Sel67] are completely analogous to flow charts, preferable to the latter only in that the forms from which they can be prepared encourage by their detail the rigor that should be, but often is not, applied to flow-charting. Decision tables also provide an alternative method for describing the flow of a program. While mechanized processing of decision tables is possible [Cha67],[19] they seem ill-suited to systems programming and inadequate by themselves to document a system. Both tabular methods lack the helpful visual cues of flow charts.

Coding Techniques

One might think that a great deal had been written about the science or art of coding and, indeed, much has. However, most works on the subject have dealt with specific languages. Few instances of generality across all programming languages have been brought to light. One subject for generalization is modularity. This is discussed above in connection with the design of operating systems. Another generally structured program is also defined to have only one entry and one exit. A third, related topic is *top-down programming,* which is related to the notions of modularity and top-down design, as explained below. Most writers ([Mil72], [McG74], Dijkstra, Hoare, and others) specify that a structured program must by definition be a top-down program. We do not contest this view, but omit the constraint for the purposes of our exposition.

---

[17] Recommended is [Cha70]. See also [Far70], [Gle70] and Schriber [Sch69].
[18] An in-house nonconfidential newsletter of IBM links HIPO to Wolfe. See also [Van73]. The HIPO technique is described and exploited, among other places, in [IBM23].
[19] Extensive bibliographies appear in the comprehensive works [Pol71] and [Lon72], [Ver72] shows well the value of decision tables in optimizing decision-dominated code, but also the indispensability of flow charts.

Line	Label	Operation	Op	1	2	3	4	5	6	7	Exit P	L	C	Cond
1		Read Card	IO	10							2	1	1	EOF
2		Header	Q	20 N	Y									
3		Error Msg	IO	30										
4		Halt	H	40										
5	HDR	Process Header	A		10									
6	READ	Read Card	IO		20						2	1	1	EOF
7		Detail	Q		30 Y	N								
8		Process Detail	A		40									
9		In Sequence	Q				10 Y	N						
10		Error Msg	IO				10							
11		Halt	H				20							

Exit: Page : 1 1
            Line : 6 5
            Column: 2 2

Figure 7.5. A Logic Flow Table.

Manager/Worker	M	W	W
Salaried/Hourly		S	H
Compute Hours			1
Compute Pay	1	1	2
Add to Dept. Total	2	2	3

Figure 7.6. A Decision Table.

Böhm and Jacopini [Böh66] have proven that any program with one entry and one exit can be converted into a structured program, that is, that GO TO statements can be eliminated in favor of conditional and iterative statements. Dijkstra, Mills [Mil72], and Baker[21] have argued that this is desirable on the following grounds:

1. The order imposed on the sequence in which statements are executed makes the program conform more closely to the way programmers, and all people, think, and therefore facilitates coding.
2. Since the program does not "jump" around, it can be read from entry to exit, and is thus easier to understand in the absence of supporting documentation.
3. The prominence of criteria for transfers of control (all in IF statements) makes the various functions of the program easier to see, thus facilitating the writing of test cases.

The validity of the latter two arguments is difficult to challenge, but not so the first. Perhaps the fact that programmers have been coding GO TO statements for years biases them, but many programmers who have been asked to code without DO TO statements have been most uncomfortable with the restriction.[22] Hopkins cites [Hop72] instances, such as handling of asynchronous events or escapes from blocks, where GO TO statements seem desirable and all but unavoidable.

The simplification of programs afforded by structured programming is a potential aid not only for conventional testing, but also for proofs of correctness. While such proofs have been attempted and recommended only for relatively small programs, advanced coding techniques — modular, top-down, and structured programming — may break operating systems down into components the correctness of which can be proven.[23] This topic is not pursued here, but London has compiled a bibliography [Lon69] on proofs of program correctness.

Top-down programming is analogous to top-down design. The first code written for a component reflects the highest level of design. The code may contain nothing but conditional statements and calls to subroutines. For a control language processor, for example, the uppermost level might include only a

---

[21] Dijkstra, E.W., (letter to the editor), *CACM* 11 No. 8 (1968), 538, 541. [Bak72] is the source of the arguments dealing with legibility and testing. Dijkstra acknowledges the influences of P. Landin, C. Strachey, H. Zemenek, and C.A.R. Hoare on his thinking on this subject. See also [Lea72] and [Mil72].

[22] [Bak72] supports this view, which is primarily based on personal conversations. He and we concur, however, with Dijkstra on the appeal of the method to those familiar with it.

[23] [NATO70] contains a discussion of this subject. [Kah71] asserts unconvincingly the applicability of the method described to operating systems.

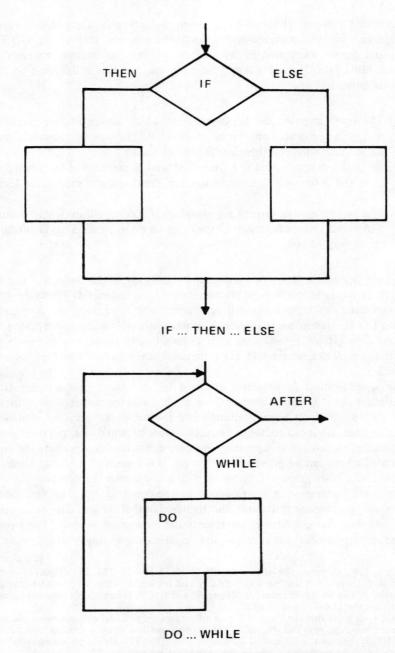

IF ... THEN ... ELSE

DO ... WHILE

Figure 7.7. Flow Chart Representations of Program Structures.

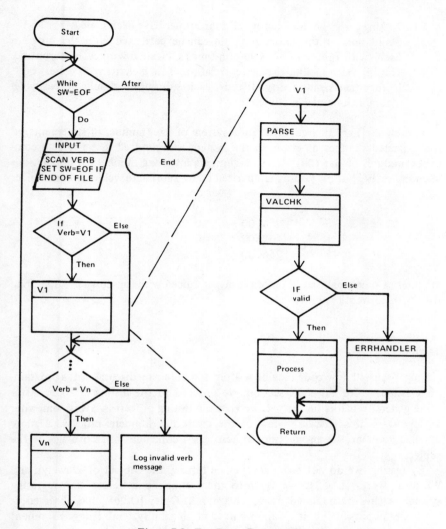

Figure 7.8. Top-Down Programming.

comprehensive DO statement, a call to an input subroutine, tests and subroutine calls for every valid verb, and an "invalid verb" routine. All the rest of the processor's code is buried in the subroutines, and their subroutines, and so on. Each subroutine has one entry and one exit, or return. A simple RETURN statement can take the place of a subroutine not yet coded. Some advantages of top-down programming are the following:

1. Testing can begin long before all subroutines have been coded.
2. Simulation of the entire program can be patterned after the program itself, with functions of execution times associated with each subroutine.
3. The approach facilitates close correlation of flow charts with code.
4. It encourages modularity; that is, each subroutine should be easily replaceable by a new module.

Ferdinand [Fer72] argues that for a system of size (number of statements) n, the expected number of errors in the system is minimized if the system comprises modules of size $(2n)^{1/3}$. His arguments involving numbers of interactions seem imprecise, but his results, tabularized below, correlate well with experience:

n	$(2n)^{1/3}$
4000	20
62500	50
256000	80

Modules of such small size are more easily produced with top-down programming than with conventional methods.

Testing

Having discussed how code may be written and deferring discussion of a programming language for the next section, we proceed to the testing of code. After some general remarks on testing, we view the testing process in a way somewhat analogous to this chapter's view of the entire development process. A more detailed look at the production of test cases concludes our coverage of the subject.

By testing, we do not mean acceptance testing, the subject of Llewelyn and Wickens' work [Lle68]. We refer to the testing done before the operating system reaches its intended users. This job, as Opler [Opl68] has observed, is "virtually impossible" in itself and we need not let the system's true environment complicate matters. It is this virtual impossibility about which a special remark is due. Formularization and quantification are worthy goals in the effort to make inherently imprecise work manageable; that is, if a job can be done more or less well, but not perfectly, rules which can be followed to ensure that the job is done reasonably well are worth seeking. So too are measurements, although they may be subjectively derived (such as performance ratings from 1 to 100 on personnel factors such as conscientiousness, initiative, and so on), when they are used in measuring how well the job is done. The danger these worthy objectives engender is objectification — the *illusion* that a subjective matter has become objective [Kur83]. One must not lose sight of the fact that subjective measures are just that and no more reliable taken together than they are separately, indeed, less so. In the present instance, let no one think that any procedures for the testing of programs are any better than the persons who apply them, assuming that rigorous proofs of correctness are unfeasible. A program which runs 100% of all scientifically selected test cases can only be said to have no *known* bugs. (As Dijkstra has said [Dah72], "Program testing can be used to show the presence of bugs, but never to show their absence!") A program can be called bug-free only when no one will ever use it again. In testing programs, evaluating employees, and many other areas where subjective biases cloud every quantification, objectification is a snare and a delusion, a myth.

So saying, we prepare to discuss formularization of testing procedures secure in the knowledge that the reader has been forewarned of its fallibility.

Testing begins with an organization. As with documentation, discussed next, testing can be subsumed by development groups or delegated to a separate group. Delegation has the disadvantage of separating testers from developers, thus lengthening line of communication. Since objectivity is a tester's virtue, lack of intimacy with details of implementation may be a blessing in disguise. A clear advantage is the concentration of testing expertise in a group of individuals who can apply that expertise to a variety of projects. That group may, however, be difficult to gather and hold, because testing programs is an unenvied job. The absence of a product to be admired is crucial to this fact. One can hardly expect to do a spectacularly outstanding job of testing a program. Yet, all things considered, a separate group seems desirable.

Testing objectives must be established. It is not enough, as Knopp points out [Kno72],[24] to specify that all test cases must run successfully before the system is considered tested; quantitative criteria relative to functions, modules, instructions, and combinations of inputs must be stated. Testing may also include documentation — not only that it describes the product accurately, but also that it serves well its intended purpose, such as tutorial or reference. Objectives may apply not only to the system as a whole but also to each component. The objectives serve as a guide to what must be done and as a yardstick against which what has been done must be measured.

The test plan describes what units of code are to be the subject of testing, relevant schedules, criteria for passing from one stage of testing to the next, and the resources to be allocated to testing.

Modules are typically the smallest units to be tested. They are tested by their developers. This has the advantage of permitting the developer to test functions which may seem trivial from an external point of view, but about whose implementation he himself is unsure. Yet, little faith must be placed in this sort of testing due to the implementer's natural bias ("Of course that function is implemented correctly; I coded it, didn't I?").

---

[24] See also [Elm69]. Much of the material on this subject is adapted from these two works.

If modules are combined into subcomponents, testing of the subcomponent is properly the responsibility of the group implementing the subcomponent. It is at the level of system components that testing may be entrusted to specialists, for it is at this level that external characteristics are specified and details of implementation lose significance. Testing of the entire system is most difficult, since the possible combinations of input are almost infinite in number. The most useful testing of the entire system is actual use. The more diverse the environments in which the operating system is expected to function, the more difficult and costly this testing is and the less confidence one can have in its thoroughness.

For a version other than the first of an operating system, additional problems arise. The test cases devised for previous versions of the system are likely to be too numerous for rerunning of all of them to be feasible. For this reason, some subset of previously written test cases, "regression test," must be chosen to be used in the testing of the new version. The test plan specifies this subset.

Schedules for testing are established for each unit to be tested as well as for the precursory systems created along the way to serve as bases for further development. These schedules must, of course, be consistent with the development schedules and be updated (slipped or, rarely, advanced) when developed schedule changes. Criteria, usually specified in terms of what percentage of all test cases execute without error, must be established for such events as when a component may be integrated into a precursory system, when the system may be announced (if it is a commercial product), and when the system may be released to its ultimate users. These criteria are not all identically equal to 100%, since it may be far preferable, for example, to construct a precursory system known to fail in certain well-defined, avoidable circumstances than to delay the construction of the precursor for days, weeks, or months.

The resources required for testing are not inconsiderable. Trapnell attributes [Tra69] 15 to 20% of all development cost to testing by independent groups. Knopp reports [Kno72] that 1750 machine-hours were consumed in the testing of Release 17 of IBM's System/360 Operating System, that is, ten months of 22 eight-hour workdays. An effort of that magnitude cannot be taken lightly.

Analysis of the results of testing is, as Pietrasanta points out [Pie66], critical to effective management of operating system development. While testing is proceeding, records should be kept of how many test cases have been coded, how many run, and how many run successfully. A plot of these figures against time is likely to yield a curve of the type shown in Figure 7.9, which depicts what Pietrasanta calls [Pie66] a Test Trend Graph. Projections of current figures provide management with the best objective estimates of when testing criteria will be met.

Analysis of the thoroughness of testing is also advisable. Quantitative measures of test cases coded, run, or successful may be misleading if their complexity and

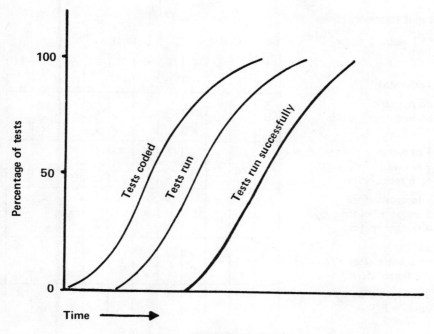

Figure 7.9. Chart of Testing Procedure.

usefulness are ignored. Figures on percentage of instructions or branches executed
are more indicative of how much code has been tested. To this end, a program
such as MEMMAP [Elm69], which traces the execution of branch instructions,
is valuable.

In deciding what test cases should be written for a component, one begins
with its external specifications. There is a "language" one uses to tell the
component what to do and all valid statements or "sentences" of that language
specify all possible functions of the component. For many programs, such as a
sorting program or a utility, the functioning of the tested program is affected by
input data over and above its ostensible control language. These effects must
also be taken into account in specifying all the things the component can do.

It will not, of course, be possible to test any component with all valid combinations of input. It is therefore necessary to categorize possible inputs intuitively
in some useful way. These categories are then listed and decisions are made as to
what combinations of inputs should be used for testing. The result is a test matrix,
as shown in Figure 7.10. Inputs are listed at the left and test cases across the top.
A cross indicates that a test case includes an input of the specified type. A column
is indicative of a combination of inputs included in a single test case.

Input statement:

SET name [,name]^{max7} $<$EQ$>$ { integer }^{max3} [.[integer]^{max2}]

Variations \ Tests	1	2	3	4	5	6	7	8	9	10	11
no operand	x										
no name		x									
1 name				x				x	x	x	
8 names					x	x	x				x
9 names			x								
no integer before .	x										
1 integer before .			x		x		x	x		x	
3 integers before .		x				x			x		x
4 integers before .				x							
no .			x								x
no integer after .							x			x	
2 integers after .		x		x		x		x	x		
3 integers after .					x						
name = EQ							x		x		

Test case 9 consists of the statement:

SET EQ $<$EQ$>$ 123.45

Figure 7.10. A Test Matrix.

Where many combinations of a few inputs are possible — say five parameters having six possible values each, where all combinations of values are to be tested — the generating of test cases can be mechanized. One program written for this purpose is the Test Matrix Generating Program (TMGP) [Gol72]. It is coded in APL and generates JCL statements as described by a simple input language. The technique involved is clearly applicable to many other problems. A much more elaborate program (predating TMGP) for generating test cases for compilers has been described by Hanford [Han70].

In selecting categories of inputs, limiting conditions play a major role. If up to nine file names may be supplied, test cases supplying nine and ten file names are mandatory. The latter case suggests another principle of testing: all error messages must be elicited. To do so may require the simulation of hardware errors. This is rarely impossible and should not be omitted on any grounds short of total impossibility.

As to the writing of test cases, two points are most important. First, the coder must remember that failure of the test case is a very likely result and, in that case, the blame must be fairly and quickly ascribable to the component being tested *and not to the test case itself;* that is, it is just as important for test cases to be free of bugs as it is for system components. What is more, test cases should more easily be rid of bugs because they are much smaller programs. When a test case grows in complexity because of the tester's desire to test a great deal and not because a great many functions must be tested in combination, the test case should be divided into several smaller test cases so as to improve the likelihood of avoiding test case errors.

Second, tests are likely to be run many times and in great batches of test cases. It is therefore important that results of test cases be quickly and easily discernible. A test case should not only exercise some combination of functions, it should also determine whether or not the functions were performed correctly. If and only if an error is detected, the test case should report this fact, with as much diagnostic data as possible, in a way which the person running the test case cannot possibly overlook.

We have thus far limited our discussion to test cases. Sometimes, testing can only be done well through the use of a program which simulates actual use of a system without the expense of such use. The Multi-User Environment Simulator (MUSE), described by Pullen and Shuttee [Ful68], is such a program. It simulates the use of the CDC RESPOND system by 64 users at terminals. Such a simulator can serve many of the purposes of an analytic model, while being at the same time an economical source of testing not otherwise feasible.

The concept of testing need not be confined to the notion of using the system to see what it will do. One can examine the system itself and analyze it to establish with some level of confidence the extent to which it has certain properties, for example, integrity and reliability. To do this, one can use analytical tools [Bel75] that apply quasimathematical procedures to yield proofs of the system's secure or correct behavior. These proofs must be understood and interpreted in the light of their acceptance by the community of competent practitioners and their limitations due to the state of the art at the time they are applied [DeM79], but their value in some contexts is undeniable. Another evaluative tool one can use is the penetration study [Att76, For75]. A team of particularly competent individuals is assembled and given the task of penetrating the system. One may draw conclusions about the system's integrity from their results [Car78].

Integration

As was stated above, the most useful testing of the entire system is actual use. For that reason, the system which is actually shipped may see few specially designed test cases not previously run on precursory systems. The testing of these precursory systems is crucial to the quality of the end-product. The testing occurs as part of the most delicate phase of the system's development cycle, integration of a precursory system.

At intervals during the period of development, precursory systems are, in accordance with the product and test plans, created. These systems permit the consolidation of development and the debugging of integrated components of the operating system in stages rather than all at once just prior to delivery. The steps of this process are:

1. Submission by the departments responsible for developing parts of the system of their theoretically thoroughly tested system components to the department responsible for integration.
2. The assembling by the latter department of all submitted components into a single integrated precursory operating system.
3. The testing of that system.
4. The application, tightly controlled by the integration department, of fixes supplied by the submitting departments for all bugs found by the testing.
5. The release by the integration department of the tested precursory operating system to be used as a basis for further development by all developers.

The process seems straightforward, but is fraught with pitfalls.

The submitted components have bugs. That is axiomatic. What is more, they do not do all they must to support the other components of the precursory system; interfaces between separately developed components are often misdesigned, misunderstood, misimplemented, or missing altogether; test cases are written to test functions not yet implemented; and so forth. But these misfortunes are only the *cause* of the biggest problem: the process of integration consumes so much time, and development proceeds concurrently to such an extent that developers may lose track of what it was exactly that they submitted for integration. They cannot fix what they cannot find, and they cannot apply whatever fixes they *do* make to the evolved component that has come into being by the time the precursory system is delivered. Zimmerman has produced [Zim69] a thorough and insightful paper on the system integration process. It is highly recommended for its faithful account of the grim realities of integration.

The problems of integration greatly complicate the question of how frequently precursory systems should be produced. Developers responsible for a system component can tell you that they would like such a system monthly, but they can contribute to such a system only once a year. Clearly, compromise is called for. The usefulness of precursory systems must be balanced against the havoc they wreak.

It is worth noting here that precursory systems are but one of a number of causes of an insidious schedule-wrecking phenomenon which might be called the deadline effect. Human nature dictates that some developers work hardest under pressure of deadlines that are difficult to meet. On the one hand, deadlines are needed to stimulate these individuals. On the other hand, most system programmers, like other mortals, make more mistakes, that is, inject more bugs, when under pressure. The more deadlines there are, the more bugs there are in the system. What can be done? Ideally, there should be only a single deadline for the development of the system. It should be sufficiently challenging to be stimulating, but sufficiently credible as not to be disheartening. And, since it will not be met, it should *not* be the basis of planning. This ideal is, of course, unattainable. Coders have access to the planners' schedules. Programmers other than the type described must be considered. Multiple deadlines are a practical necessity and a comfort to management. The only moral we can draw is that frequent deadlines are far from an unmixed blessing and a minimization of deadlines has its justifications.

Trapnell describes [Tra69] some ways that a PDS can be used to control the integration process. A PDS provides tools to be used in segregating and correlating different versions of the same module. It also permits restrictions to be placed on which persons can effect changes to individual modules. The precise procedures implemented to control integration vary with the PDS employed. The themes — apply fixes quickly, control access to the systems, keep careful account of what happens — remain invariant.

Documentation

A well-designed, thoroughly tested operating system is nonetheless worthless in the absence of documentation. Documentation is of two types, internal and external. The former describes how the system accomplishes what it does, while the latter describes what the system is in fact capable of doing. Taking these topics in chronological order, we first treat internal documentation, its objectives and components. External documentation is treated in greater detail to conclude our section on the techniques of operating system development.

Let us first note, with Chapin [Cha68] [25] that the production of internal documentation is an unpopular but vital task. Programmers, the sole source of internal documentation, produce it so reluctantly for a combination of reasons:

1. The value of internal documentation is not readily apparent. Internal documentation is not seen as a product which serves a vital and well-defined purpose.

---

[25] Much of our discussion of internal documentation is adapted from [Cha68], with liberal interjection of our own views. See also [Cha71].

2. Documenting is seen as a waste of valuable time that could otherwise be spent on the only job programmers think they are getting paid to do — programming.

3. If programmers wanted to write, they would call themselves writers. The jobs of programming and writing are quite different and require different skills rarely coresident in the same individual.

The obvious, albeit incomplete, remedy to the first two of these conditions is for management to clarify and to stress the importance of documentation. For the third item, only the employment of documentation specialists can provide relief. The practicality of such a step has been demonstrated, and even bright but inexperienced programmer trainees (or undergraduates, in the academic environment) can serve.

Documentation serves first of all as an aid to the programmer in designing his product. In this connection, graphic aids were discussed above. More importantly, however, documentation communicates with others. It permits a new or newly transferred employee to familiarize himself with code for which he is assuming responsibility. It serves the same purpose for those who must add function to system components or fix bugs in them. Also, it helps those working on related modules to understand how their modules and others interact to provide a system component's externally visible functions. Internal documentation is also useful in determining the accuracy of the system's external documentation. When internal and external documentation fail to match, one or the other must be changed. That change may also imply a change in code, the need for which might not have come to light for some time without the correlation of documentation.

The circumstances which make internal documentation most valuable — high personnel turnover, separate responsibility for maintenance, high degree of component interaction, importance of accuracy in external documentation — are uniquely characteristic of operating system development.

Some of the components of an operating system's internal documentation are:

1. Graphic aids, such as flow charts and HIPO diagrams.
2. Table and data record formats.
3. Prose descriptions of modules.
4. Module-descriptive information, such as entry points and exists, errors detected, messages, tables, and bytes used.
5. Program listing.
6. The associated comments.

An alternative list can be found in [Cha68]. Trapnell points out [Tra69] that the data of item 4 above lend themselves to mechanical processing, from which such useful results as where-used listings for bytes and tables can be obtained. Again, the PDS comes into play by providing the vehicle for such processing. The other items listed above require no amplification here.

Possible schemes for organizing internal documentation are suggested by Trapnell [Tra69] and Laschenski [Las70] in the contexts of an internal "specification" and a "product design book," respectively. These contexts reflect the view of internal documentation as an aid to design, but the organizations suggested, which are similar to that implied by the listing above, are no less relevant to the same documentation as seen from the perspective of the system's delivery date.

Some people contend that internal documentation can be obviated. In this connection, it has been said[26] of many programming languages that they are "self-documenting." The strongest claim is probably that of Mills [Mil70]. PL360 is so structured that he was able to write a program that interrogates coders as to the motivation for each line of their code. The answers form the documentation. Certainly, the results are impressive. But Mills' program documents the way computers play chess: with great attention to detail but no grand design. The coder cannot be interrogated about blocks which are logically cohesive, but not delimited as such (by "BEGIN" and "END"). Also, the useful content of the documentation can be obscured by an avalanche of obvious minutiae. The absence of graphic documentation is another cause for complaint, but this lack could be remedied by an automatic flow-charter. The work of Mills is valuable and may well lead to a "self-documenting" language, if that term is construed to include the coders' answers to mechanical interrogation, but to say that one exists would undoubtedly be premature.

Internal documentation begins as internal specifications. As time goes by, more and more details are added. Changes are made to reflect fixes for flaws of design or implementation. This process of constant modification suggests the desirability of mechanizing the documentation of the system. A text processing program may well be included in a PDS for this purpose. Flow-charting programs provide facilities for updating old charts as well as creating new ones. The updating of comments is each programmer's responsibility. In summary, all procedures needed to keep documentation in step with development exist. Yet, because the factors which made documenting distasteful to programmers in the first place are magnified by the environment of continuing development and testing, documentation often falls behind. The fact that changes to documentation are as important as changes to code must be made clear to all who are responsible for either task.

External documentation is at least as important as internal documentation. Potential users of the system must be made aware of its capabilities, be told how to invoke desired facilities, and be advised how best to exploit the system's power. Without a description of the system, no one can use it.

---

[26] [Cha68] cites COBOL, FORTRAN, PL/1, and ALGOL. See also [Cha71].

From the point of view of the firm marketing an operating system, external documentation must do more than merely describe the system. It must also contribute significantly to the ease with which customers use the system and get the most out of it. External documentation is therefore an integral part of the product — and an expensive one. Schöneborn estimates [Sch72] that 20 to 25% of a system's cost is expended for documentation.[27] Such an expenditure justifies the detailed planning which is our next topic.

The basis of a plan for external documentation is the gross design of the system. From the gross design it should be possible to derive some concept of the totality of the system's function. This concept must be broken down into logical components, in terms of users' views of the system, which do not always correspond with the system's physical components. With respect to these logical components — such as APL interpreter, operator interface, data organization, symbol resolution — it is then necessary to describe the body of descriptive literature to be produced. Up to three publications might describe each component:

1. A tutorial text — designed to be used with or without a human instructor, for persons totally unfamiliar with the function of the component.
2. A general information manual — for persons already acquainted with the component's purpose, who must make efficient use of the component.
3. A reference guide — a detailed specification of the component's characteristics, to be used by those working most closely with the component or those who require knowledge of some obscure function or error condition. This publication must be a completely accurate reflection of the component and can be used as a criterion for the correctness of other publications and the component itself.

In addition to books specific to each component, supplemental publications should describe the intended audience with respect to specific and general competence (that is, what the readers already know and how capable they are of learning), and objectives in reading the book (what the reader wants to know and why). The plan must also contain, of course, schedules and estimates of resources required for the production of each book.

To implement the plan requires an organization. This organization is likely to be a separate one, having the following virtues:

1. All parts of the organization have things in common, such as talent (writing), product (books), resources, and so on.

---

[27] It is left to the reader as an exercise to show that all the empirical cost estimates of this chapter lead to a contradiction.

2. Lines of communication for the coordination of subject coverage, terminology, and consistency of approach are short.
3. The organization is detached from physical components of the system, which might obscure logical components.

There is, however, one strong argument for associating writers with corresponding development groups: the writers are then closer to the sources of the information they need. In practice, this concern is not an overriding one.

The individuals who do the work of the organization are technical writers and editors. They must have competence in their chosen professions, of course, but they must also be familiar with two other disciplines: systems programming and data processing. That these fields are distinct should be clear from the very existence of the technical writers' job. They must understand the products of systems programming well enough to translate their specifications into terms the systems' users can understand. While the users process data in many different ways, most share an ignorance of the mathematical nature of the computer itself. The operating system hides the computer, and the technical writer must hide, or at least disguise in familiar garb, the system. Thus, the technical writers and editors must understand the system programmers and communicate with the data processors. The diversity of uses to which operating systems are applied makes effective communication with all of the system's users a uniquely challenging task.

The production of external documentation can be mechanized to a large extent. What is required is a text processing system, such as IBM's Document Composition Facility (DCF). This is not just a simple text editor of the type found in many time-sharing systems, but a versatile system capable of producing print-ready copy. Salient features of DCF and its predecessor, TEXT360[28], are automatic hyphenation, single or double column formatting, right and left justification, and even a spelling check. TEXT360 printed ten pages per minute on a System/360 Model 65 [Sch72].

As far as figures for external publications are concerned, DCF can incorporate simple tables without any hand-drawing. The program can be ordered to leave room for more complex graphics. Pages with flow charts can be prepared separately with flow-chart-producing programs. A program known as HIPODRAW can be used to mechanize the production of HIPO diagrams.

The writing of tutorial texts and reference guides for operating systems presents few, if any, unique problems. The general information manual, or "user's guide," as it is called by Selig [Sel68], is characterized by several attributes which make it difficult to write well. For one thing, it describes but one part of a very complex system. In many cases, frequent references to to other manuals

---

[28] As cited by [Pom72]. See also [IBM24].

are unavoidable. For another thing, most users will be desirous and capable of learning about only a small subset of the component's functions. Needless complexity must be avoided without such obvious omission of detail as might arouse a reader's curiosity without satisfying it.

The following is a list of suggested contents for such a manual:

1. References to related publications.
2. Overview of the logical component (that is, the component as viewed by the user, not necessarily a separately developed component) being described and the environment in which it is used.
3. Descriptions of the component's most frequently used functions.
4. Realistic examples of the use of these functions.
5. Descriptions of more exotic functions and examples of their use.
6. Reference material.

References to related publications should include a list of books with which the reader is assumed to be familiar and a list of those which should not be read before the one at hand. Books which give more information on subjects mentioned in the present book should also be listed. Such lists must *not,* however, serve as an excuse for omitting from a book information which every reader of the book should have.

The overview should so familiarize the readers with the component that they can subsequently use the book's table of contents and index to read only those portions of the book which are likely to be of interest, that is, the overview must divide the component into named and briefly described parts, whose functions the reader is able to comprehend.

The component's most frequently used functions are those that satisfy 100% of the requirements of 80% of the component's users. Typically, these are less than half of the total number of the component's functions. By presenting material in this way, the writers permit most of their readers to read only half of the book. This may be a blow to a writer's ego, but the discriminating reader will be very grateful.

Examples included in user's guides should be numerous, realistic (typical of large classes of users), optimized (not merely adequate for the task, but superior to some obvious alternative), complete (showing both input and output), and tested (and therefore accurate).

After a note admonishing the typical user that what follows is probably not necessary for his understanding and use of the component, the rest of the component's functions can be described.

Reference material should include a list of all options of the component, a list of diagnostic messages produced by the component and their meanings, specifications as to the component's resource requirements in terms of time and storage space, a glossary, and an index.

A book written in accordance with the points made above may be totally redundant with a reference guide with respect to content, but its value is not likely to be questioned.

[Wal69] provides useful models, or templates, which can be of immeasurable value in the preparation of outlines for documents.

An external publication, like any other product, must be tested. Burkenshaw recommends [Bur70] an "intelligent ignoramus" for this purpose. This is someone of better than average reasoning ability who knows nothing whatsoever about the component being described. This person is best suited to discover what has been omitted from a book and what section of it is misplaced or cannot truly be omitted in reading as recommended. Other errors which can occur in manuals are lack of aptness for the intended audience and simple inaccuracy.

A well-planned, well-executed set of external publications can greatly enhance the value of an operating system. Their absence can make the system virtually worthless.

This section has dealt with those things which can or must be done to facilitate the development of an operating system. We next consider one indispensable tool the selection of which has a profound effect on the finished product – the language of implementation.

7.4 IMPLEMENTATION LANGUAGE

When one chooses a programming language for the implementation of an operating system, one cannot avoid thinking about efficiency – the efficiency with which the system is developed and the efficiency of the resulting system. The choice, however, has other implications which may be less obvious. The quality – reliability, serviceability, and so on – of the system is also at stake, as is portability, an attribute of importance for some systems. In this section, we discuss the criteria by which an implementation language can be chosen, with emphasis on quality, efficiency, and portability. Additional factors, such as compatibility of object code and the availability of debugging aids, are then considered. Some possible implementation languages are then discussed with respect to their past use, their distinguishing characteristics, their advantages and disadvantages, and their suitability for future use. Finally, ways in which more than one implementation language may be employed during the development of a single system are considered.

Criteria

An implementation language makes its greatest contribution to quality when it permits – or, even better, forces – the coder to say what he means. Corbató points out [Cor69] that an assembly language instruction may have more than one result; for example, it may load a register with a quantity *and* clear the high-order portion of the register. There is no way that one can tell from looking at such an instruction whether the coder required both results or only one of them. This imprecision is felt when it becomes necessary to modify the original code to fix a bug or add a facility. Such actions often, therefore, result in bugs which could have been avoided if only the intention of the code had been clear.

The precision of higher-level languages contributes to quality in two other related ways. It discourages the type of tricky coding which is so difficult to understand and leads to so many bugs, and it contributes to the documentation of the system. While, as is noted above, no programming language is truly self-documenting, the higher the level of the language, the less supporting internal documentation is needed.

Our discussion of standards, above, touched on the enforcement of standards through compilers. This, too, is a contribution toward quality. A coder can hardly forget to save a register if his compiler saves all of them. Nor can one write nonreentrable code if the compiler does not permit it.

Higher-level languages tend to foster more universally desirable coding practices. Modularity is innate in many of them. If a language, BLISS [Wal71], for example, contains only statements of types that encourage structure and lacks a GO TO statement, its use can lead to better-structured programs.

With respect to the efficiency of system development, the theme of higher-level languages' superiority is repeated. Corbató estimates [Cor69] that one line of PL/1 code can be written and debugged as fast as one line of assembly language code, yet ten times as many instructions result. Mitigating this result is the fact that about twice as many instructions may be generated as are needed, that is, as would result from assembly language coding.

Against this 5:1 ratio in efficiency of development must be balanced the cost of developing a compiler if none exists. This cost varies widely across languages and computers and no good rule for estimating its value can be given here.

An additional contribution of a higher-level language to efficiency of development is the ease with which the language may be learned. Indeed, a pool of programmers already familiar with the language may exist. One cautionary note: familiarity with a language is no assurance of ability to write efficient code in the language. Total ignorance of machine characteristics coupled with ignorance of code-generation mechanisms and sheer inexperience has been observed [Cor69] to boost ratios of inefficiency to five or even ten to one.

Developmental efficiency applies not only to initial development, but also to the cost of modifying the system. The superior efficiency of higher-level languages is magnified as a system matures because the attributes of precision, readability, simplicity, and so on, come into play.

There is, however, another kind of efficiency, that of the resulting system. No code can be more efficient in this regard than assembly language code. A higher-level language may totally bar access to certain valuable instructions (such as editing) of the target machine. Yet Wulf et al. [Wul71] express the opinion that "efficiency, except possibly for a very small number of very small code segments, is determined by overall program design and not by locally tricky, 'bit-picking' coding practices." This contention is substantiated by the MULTICS experience [Cor72], where only a few of 1500 modules are coded in assembly language (rather than PL/1) for efficiency's sake, and about as many have been coded in PL/1 preference to the original assembly language!

To understand how an inefficiency ratio of two or more to one may be tolerable, we must appreciate the effect of inefficient code on system performance. Corbató estimates [Cor72] that 10 to 50% of the system's time is spent executing supervisor code. If the CPU were never to be idle, inefficient code might cut performance by 50%, although 20% is a more realistic figure. One should realize, however, that there is such a thing as CPU idle time, and code running when the CPU would otherwise be idle has no effect on throughput, except as serialized events are delayed, as when progress through a system bottleneck is impeded. Taking this into account, and considering that some parts of the supervisor must be exercised far more frequently than others, we can fairly conclude that much of the system can be coded inefficiently with little impact on the total system's performance. Program design, maximizing the utilization of processing and I/O facilities, is much more significant.

Among the most sensitive portions of any operating system is that dealing most directly with I/O. Coincidentally, this is the area in which a higher-level language is most often inefficient, inflexible, and inadequate to the task of exercising specific hardware features. I/O programming is therefore most likely to be done in an assembly language.

Efficiency of code can be gained by exploitation of the computer's characteristics. This possibility exists not only for code in machine-dependent languages, however, but also for code in such higher-level languages as PL/1. The storing of binary and character data in arrays geared to the word size of the target machine is one relevant practice. This is more easily forgotten by someone writing in a machine-independent language, but should not be.

Such machine-dependent coding is, however, a bar to portability. Portability is the ability to take an operating system developed for one computer and transfer it to another, with as little recoding as possible. If an operating system is coded in a machine-dependent language, the system is not portable. To the extent that an operating system is tailored to a particular computer, it is not portable, despite a machine-independent language of implementation. If portability is one's goal, one virtue of a machine-independent language may be called "poverty" (as contrasted with "richness" — the ability to express in a language directly any useful concept). Lang applauds [Lan70] [29] the Basic Combined Programming Language (BCPL) in this regard. He argues that it should be possible to construct any desirable mechanism, such as a push-pop stack, from a basic set of fundamental facilities. The mechanisms needed for a particular task can be constructed in a machine-independent way without burdening the writers of the BCPL compilers for various machines with needless complexities. Strachey notes [Str70] that a BCPL compiler written in BCPL was transferred to a new computer in "about a week."

The relative values of quality, efficiency (both of development and of the resulting system), and portability must be established if one is to make a rational choice of an implementation language. Criteria less clearly related to the language, as opposed to some particular implementation of it, are compatibility of output, availability of debugging aids, and inclusion of run-time packages.

As Lang notes [Lan70], it is unlikely that any single programming language will be ideal for the implementation of all portions of an operating system. It will therefore be necessary that the programs written in various languages communicate with one another. Where languages have different notions of data, this may be very difficult, if not impossible. ALGOL, for example, makes such communication unfeasible in some systems.

Little need be said here about debugging aids. Clearly, they are needed for operating system development, and the existence of aids tailored to a particular language argue in favor of the use of that language.

The absence of run-time packages is cited by Lang [Lan70] as a virtue because the coder has more complete control of the programming environment. Yet, he also states that "input operations are most easily provided by subroutines," and, we would have to add, "loaded behind the user's back." Run-time packages that run on the same machine as a boot-strapping compiler — one producing code for a different machine, the target — are, of course, intolerable. But the substitution of a suitable package should be easily accomplished. The issue of run-time packages seems moot.

Languages

With the stated criteria in mind, we can proceed to the evaluation of languages whose use for programming of operating systems has been seriously proposed. These are assembly languages (AL), PL360, Systems Assembly Language (SAL), BLISS, BCPL, PL/1, and ALGOL. PL/S, MOL940 and FORTRAN are given less attention. Discussion of more recently developed languages, including ADA, the language developed for use in programs of the United States Department of Defense, of whose AJPO it is a registered trade mark, is omitted for lack of proper time for evaluation.

---

[29] This paper covers much the same ground as this section.

An assembly language has been the principal language used for coding almost every operating system produced to date. That an assembly language has the greatest potential for coding efficiency is clear. An assembly language may provide the only way of invoking essential machine-dependent functions, for example, addressing specific locations, exploiting unique I/O characteristics, or manipulating protection or relocation mechanisms such as keys, registers, and page tables. An assembly language is also translated quickly into machine-processible text.

But against these unchallengable advantages are arrayed some very significant disadvantages: (1) Assembly language programs do not "mean what they say"; that is, tricky code is almost inevitable *and* indecipherable. (2) Assembly languages are geared to the expression of what the engineer has made the machine capable of doing, not what the programmer would like it to do; that is, the language is not even intended to lend itself to the expression of the coder's thoughts. (3) More steps are necessary, more statements, and consequently, more opportunities for error are involved in the coding of each routine. (4) Portability of a system written in an assembly language is beyond even consideration. Every disadvantage save the last contributes to the conclusion that routines coded in an assembly language take longer to write, longer to debug, and longer to modify.

An assembly language should be used, therefore, when: (1) machine-dependent functions can be invoked in no other way, or (2) optimum efficiency is mandatory. An assembly language should be avoided; otherwise, especially when development time is critical, many modifications to original code are expected, or portability is a consideration.

PL360 [Wir68] was developed in 1965 and 1966 at Stanford University for use in implementing a compiler for a derivitive of ALGOL. It is only slightly removed from an assembly language, having the following distinguishing characteristics:

1. ALGOL-like statements are used for declarations and common constructs such as IF . . . THEN . . . ELSE.
2. Access is provided to all machine operations and objects.
3. Self-modifying programs are forbidden.

PL360 facilitates program coding and analysis without restricting the functions available to the coder. Yet the language lacks some of the virtues associated with higher-level languages, such as prevention of the errors caused by a coder's having to be concerned with detail, and, of course, portability.

Where portability is not a concern and access to the machine-dependent features of an IBM System/360 computer is, one can hardly imagine an implementation language significantly superior to PL360. The requirement for intimacy with the computer must be present, however, for the efficiency of PL360 to outweigh the increased risk of bugs (as opposed to, say, PL/1) in the typical systems programming case. PL/S, a proprietary language of IBM, seems to have much in common with PL360, but has not been publicly documented.

SAL [Lan69] was developed at Cambridge, England, in 1966, for the writing of systems programs for the Titan (Atlas II) computer. SAL has much in common with PL360, differing in target machine, paucity of data types (floating-point calculations require assembly code), the lack of an ALGOL-like block structure, and the presence of complex facilities for address manipulation. SAL thus shares PL360's virtues and vices, translated to the Titan computer. MOL940, developed at Stanford Research Institute for the SDS940, has similar characteristics.

BLISS [Wul71] was developed in 1969-1970 at Carnegie-Mellon University for the writing of large systems programs for the PDP-10 computer. An implementation, BLISS-10 is designed for efficient use specifically on the PDP-10, although it contains no intrinsically machine-dependent structures. The language appears ALGOL-like, but is an "expression language," that is, one in which every character string connotes an arithmetic value. The data structures of BLISS are especially complex and PDP-10-oriented. BLISS encourages structured programming by lacking a GO TO statement, but suffers eight escape mechanisms as a result.

Success is claimed for BLISS by all reasonable criteria. One cannot say how much the success of this or any other innovation is due to the fervor of its first adherents, but in any event the applicability of BLISS-10 is limited. One must need to develop systems programs for a PDP-10 computer, be willing to forego the efficiency of machine-dependence, but virtually forsake portability. BLISS-360, for IBM System/360 computers, is described by Bahler [Bah72]. It remains to be evaluated.

BCPL [Ric69] was conceived at MIT and developed at Cambridge and London Universities for the KDF9 computer. BCPL is machine-independent and BCPL compilers run on eight different computers. All data items are treated simply as bit patterns, although the usual arithmetic operators are defined on them. BCPL has mainly its simplicity and the mobility of its cleverly constructed compiler to recommend it. It falls between PL/1 and languages such as PL360 in ease of use, tendency to error, facility of program comprehension, and so on.

PL/1 is, of course, one of the general-purpose higher-level languages discussed in Chapter 3. The outstanding example of its use for systems programming is MULTICS [Cor69], the system developed for the GE (HIS) 645 by the Bell Laboratories, the General Electric Company, and Project MAC of MIT. The characteristics which distinguish PL/1 from other higher-level languages are:

1. The richness of its data structures and syntax, such as long names and ASCII Character set.
2. The modularity of its object code (as opposed to ALGOL's).

3. Its "subsettability," that is, the ease with which one can omit implementing unwanted features of the language.
4. The higher cost of compiler development, difficulty of optimization, and innate inefficiency of object code due to 1 and 2 above.

Otherwise, PL/1 shares the attributes of higher-level languages in general: debuggability, ease of use, machine independence, and so forth.

MULTICS' experience with PL/1 and dialects thereof was generally favorable. For those environments wherein PL/1's shortcomings are tolerable, it or some subset of it must be considered preferable to any other higher-level language for systems programming.

ALGOL, developed in the late 1950s for the programming of algorithmic computational processes [Sam69], has been extended and used by Burroughs for systems programming [Sam71]. This was a natural consequence of the fact that Burroughs computers had been designed to be uniquely suited to the processing of ALGOL programs and lacked an assembly language. ALGOL and its derivatives are characterized by their procedural nature, their nonsupport of modularity, and the poverty of ALGOL's data definition facilities (derivatives address this aspect). The latter characteristics give evidence of its clear inferiority to PL/1 for most systems programming. Only computers such as Burroughs' and the specter of PL/1's complexity could argue for the use of ALGOL. FORTRAN and its derivatives, while once widely used, suffer similarly by comparison to PL/1.

Multilanguage Strategies

We have now seen the languages used or suggested for systems programming. It should be noted, however, that a system need not be written in only a single language. A machine-dependent language might be used only when absolutely necessary. A modified version of some chosen language may be used, in preference to the standard version, for an entire project or just to get started. Thus, EPL (for Early PL/1) was used to code MULTICS before a full PL/1 compiler could be implemented. Modules can be recoded in the same or a different language for efficiency as performance bottlenecks are detected. David reports [Dav68] an improvement of three to ten times in making EPL code more efficient. Hand-translation of all code down to assembly language is another option.

We have discussed the criteria by which a language of implementation may be chosen, several candidate languages, and possible strategies involving more than one language. Much the same topics are covered more extensively with a somewhat different approach by Sammet [Sam71]. Other papers in the same edition of SIGPLAN Notices bear on the subject. Our discussion of the development process, up to the first use of the system, is complete. We go on now to the post-production phases of development, the period from delivery to disuse.

7.5 MEASUREMENT, MODIFICATION, AND MAINTENANCE

Once a product has been developed, it can be measured or evaluated, modified or made better in some way, and maintained or repaired. We proceed now to discuss these three activities as they apply to operating systems.

Measurement

Operating system measurement has been the subject of many papers over the past several years. A bibliography restricted to the measurement of time-sharing systems [And72] contains 259 citations. Indeed, whole books could be devoted to this topic. We seek here only to provide a context wherein these sources can be understood and appreciated. Our approach most closely approximates those taken by Lucas [Luc71] and by Calingaert in his early, frequently cited paper [Cal67].

We begin by exploring the parameters of performance, seeing what measures are of value to developers, users, and potential users. We next discuss the steps which might be taken in response to measurement. With goals firmly established, we look at the various techniques that have been developed for measurement and assess their strengths and weaknesses. Finally, we consider the mechanics of actually performing an evaluation: preparation, execution, interpretation (data reduction), analysis, and action.

Measures. Calingaert cites [Cal67] throughput, turnaround time, and availability as the three basic measures of system performance. *Throughput* is a measure of the work accomplished by a system over some interval of time. The unit of work must be standardized or held constant across a number of measurements if a meaningful notion of throughput is to be obtained. Typically, work is defined anew for each instance of measurement and no one's definition is acceptable to anyone else. (In this regard, see the discussion of benchmarks below.) The same difficulty is encountered in measuring *turnaround time:* the interval between presentation of work to the system and receipt of the system's resulting full and accurate output. Again, the definition of work is critical. *Availability,* the likelihood that the system is functioning properly at any given instant of time, may be seen as a multiplier of throughput: If 100 work units can be processed per hour and the system is available 98 of every 100 hours on the average, the figure of $(98/100) \times 100 = 98$ may be called the effective throughput of the system in work units per hour, or

$$\% \text{ availability} \times \text{throughput} = \text{effective throughput}$$

This reduces our parameters of interest to two: effective throughput and turnaround time.[30]

---

[30] For this discussion, we rely most heavily on [Luc71], [Got70], and [Ano70].

It should be noted here that these parameters are only basic measures. If they were the only figures of interest, system measurement would be a virtually vacuous science. In practice, for reasons explored below, systems are measured by many other units.

Before proceeding to these, however, we touch upon some measures seen as basic by others, but omitted from our list above. Of response time, the time required for a single simple transaction of interaction processing, we can say that it is an alternative expression for turnaround time in a primarily interactive environment. Notions of productive time and idle time express the single concept of utilization, a measure applicable to each component of a system. This is treated below as a notion of direct measurement, not a result. Overhead is a measure of efficiency lost with respect to a single piece of work because the computer is not slavishly devoted to that work alone. While the reduction of overhead without loss of function is certainly desirable, a single figure for overhead tells us little about an operating system. In particular, it fails to tell us what the system can do, and does not permit us to compare systems except, possibly, as two systems of equal function are implemented on the same computer. While it seems unlikely that any system which spent, say, 50% of its resources (time over component) doing work of no value to any single user could be called good, such might be the case if that expenditure purchased invaluable function or extreme efficiency during periods of productive use.

Actions. The actions taken in response to the results of measurement may be characterized as asserting or affecting performance of accounting. Assertive actions include establishing an assumed level of performance in planning the use of a system, and comparing levels of performance in purchasing a system. Actions which affect performance include the purchase, lease, or discontinuance of hardware components (that is, hardware reconfiguration); the modification of parameters used by the operating system (tuning or software reconfiguration); the reworking of critical programming components which are discovered to be frequently used and needlessly inefficient; and the rescheduling of work presented to the system at regular intervals or at prescribed times (load-balancing). Our reference to accounting is due to the fact that the measurement techniques under discussion can be used to gather the data needed for accounting, that is, for charging the system's users in proportion to the amounts of the system's resources they consume. In this light the reader may wish to review Section 3.6.

The reader should now have a good idea of what one hopes to gain by measuring operating systems. One hopes to be guided in the actions described above to achieve the best possible match of operating system to the workload with which it is to be presented and, having found that system, to optimize its performance.

Tools. To measure systems, the following tools are used: hardware and software monitors, analytic and simulative models, and benchmarks. The *hardware* *monitor* typically measures utilization of hardware components — devices, control units, channels, central processing units, storage locations — alone and in combinations. It has the advantage of having no effect on the system being measured, but lacks, however, the ability to distinguish between useful and useless activity (such as wait loops). The action hardware monitors are mostly likely to motivate is hardware reconfiguration, such as the movement of a device from a channel for which there is much contention to an underutilized one.

A *software monitor* permits discrimination among executing instructions. It depicts utilization of programs rather that of physical components. It does, however, inevitably degrade system performance to some, usually minuscule, extent. It also requires integration into the system being measured. Software monitoring is most likely to result in the reworking of critical programs. The monitor may also be used for accounting.

An *analytic model* is a system simulator based on mathematical equations. The effects on performance of continuous changes in workload can be predicted by such a model, but the complexity of the model is limited by the difficulty of mathematical analysis. Analytic models are most commonly used to predict system performance. McKinney's survey of analytic models for time-sharing systems [McK69] is a primary source for further data on that important topic.

Simulative models, mentioned briefly in Section 7.2, permit the effects of changes to system components to be predicted. The model is necessarily far simpler than the system and may ignore critical interrelationships among components. A simulative model may aid system tuning and load-balancing and also serves frequently as a predictive tool.

Benchmarks are standard units of work used in comparing the performance of a number of systems. They are generally sequences of several jobs but may be single jobs, single programs, kernels of code, or add instructions, as one chooses. Particularly large numbers of jobs may be needed to evaluate multiprogramming systems effectively. Benchmarks are most often used in comparing the performance of multiple operating systems. The designing of a benchmark sequence to be truly representative of a potential user's workload is a most difficult task and crucial to the value of the benchmark. Benchmarks have the advantage of being useful in the absence of costly monitors and models. Timing can simply be done with a stopwatch.

Table 7.1 lists performance measurement tools in current use. Each tool is described in terms of its type and developer. A source for further information is also listed, as well as a note on the availability of each tool.

Steps. The measurement of a system begins with a need for data and ends with an action based on the data obtained. In between are preparation, execution, interpretation, and analysis. Let us examine each of these stages.

Table 7.1. Performance Measurement Tools.

	DEVELOPER	TYPE OF TOOL	REFERENCE(S)[1]	AVAILABILITY[2]
AMAP (Advanced Multiprogramming Analysis Procedure)	IBM	Software monitor	2	b
BTM	XDS	Software monitor	6	a
CASE	Tesdata	Simulation model	1, 2	c
CIMS	Boothe	Software model	1	c
Compumeter	Computer Efficiency	Software model	1	c
CPA7700	Computer Programming & Analysis	Hardware monitor	2	c
CPM II	Allied Computer Technology	Hardware monitor	1, 2, 3	c
CSS (Computer System Simulator)	IBM	Simulation model	4 (GH20-0874), 5, [Pom72]	c
CUE	Boole & Babbage	Software monitor	1, 2, 3	c
Dynaprobe/Dynapar	COMRESS	Hardware monitor	2	c
GTF (Generalized Trace Facility)	IBM	Software monitor	4(GC28-6719)	a
Job Accounting	Diversified Data	Software monitor	1	c
JSM (Job Stream Manager)	IBM	Software monitor	4 (360-D-03.6.010)	c
LEAP	Lambda	Software monitor	5	c
LOMUSS II	Lockheed	Simulation model	5	d
M-test/AFAS	Computer Management Sciences	Simulation model	2	c
MUST	Webster	Software monitor	1	c
MVTANAL	IBM	Software monitor	3	b
OS TRACE (OS/360 Trace Table Option)	IBM	Software monitor	4 (GC28-6554)	a
PPE	Boole & Babbage	Software monitor	1, 2, 3	c
PROGLOOK	Sanford University	Software monitor	2	a
SAM	Applied Data Research	Simulation model	2	c

Table 7.1. (continued)

	DEVELOPER	TYPE OF TOOL	REFERENCE(S)[1]	AVAILABILITY[2]
SCERT	COMRESS	Simulation model	1, 2, 5	c
SIPE (System Internal Performance Evaluation)	IBM	Software monitor	2, 4 (TR53.0013)	c
SMF (System Management Facilities)	IBM	Software monitor	4 (GC28-6712)	a
SMS/360	Boole & Babbage	Software monitor	1, 2	c
SUMPER	UCLA	Hardware monitor	2	d
SPY	Western Electric	Software monitor	7	d
SUM	Computer Synetics	Hardware monitor	1, 2, 3	d
X RAY	Tesdata	Hardware monitor	2	c

[1] References
1. Anon., "How to find bottlenecks in computer traffic," *Computer Decisions* 2, No. 4 (1970), pp. 44–48. ([Ano70])
2. Hart, L.E., "The user's guide to evaluation products," *Datamation* 16, No. 17 (1970), pp. 32–35.
3. [Got70]
4. IBM Form (Number)
5. Huesmann, L.T., and Goldberg, R.P., "Evaluating systems through simulation," *Computer Journal* 10, No. 2 (1967), pp. 150–155.
6. Shemer, J.E., and Heying, D.W., "Performance modeling and empirical measurements in a system designed for batch and time-sharing users," *Proceedings AFIPS 1969 Fall Joint Computer Conference*, AFIPS Press, Montvale, New Jersey, 1969, pp. 17–26.
7. Sedgewick, R., Stone, R., and McDonald, J.W., "SPY — A program to monitor OS/360," *Proceedings AFIPS 1970 Fall Joint Computer Conference*, AFIPS Press, Montvale, New Jersey, 1970, pp. 119–128.
Works 1, 2, 3, 5 are surveys of sorts which include references to other sources.

[2] a. available at no cost
b. proprietary but publicly described
c. commercial
d. unknown

A need for data arises when a system must be selected for use, when the precise configuration of the chosen system must be established, when performance must be predicted, and when the system is to be optimized. Corresponding with these needs, benchmarks, hardware monitors, models, and software monitors are likely to be employed. The appropriate tool must be selected and obtained or constructed. Preparation continues with decisions as to the details of measurement. One must decide precisely what is to be measured, how often measurements should be taken, what work should be executed while measurements take place, what exceptional results might be anticipated, who (user, vendor, or consultant) should design and perform the measurements, and so on.

When all is in readiness, the measurement is performed. Tools, whether hardware or software, must be connected to the system. Parameters of the tools must be set. Work to be run must be assembled and presented to the system. Facilities for receiving the results of measurement must be made available. Measurement is done, and, eventually, someone decides that enough measurement has been done.

The raw results of measurement are likely to be strings of apparently random integers. These must be associated with meanings if some value is to be derived from the measurement. This association is one component of interpretation. Another is data reduction, the compression of what might be a huge volume of data into a collection of manageable proportions, without loss of significant results. This step is often accomplished by a program of little less complexity than the tool itself.

One convenient mechanism for expressing the result of measurement by a hardware monitor is the Kiviat Graph [Mor73]. This is a circle with eight equally spaced radii, numbered 1 to 8 consecutively clockwise from noon and marked off to indicate the percentage of time:

1. The CPU is active.
2. Only the CPU is active.
3. The CPU and at least one channel are active.
4. Only one or more channels are active.
5. At least one channel is active.
6. The CPU is waiting.
7. The CPU is in problem (productive) state.
8. The CPU is in supervisor (overhead) state.

Zero is at the center and 100% at the circumference. Results are plotted on the eight radii and the resultant data points on adjacent radii are connected by straight lines. The more nearly the eight-sided figure formed about the center by these straight lines resembles a plus (+) sign, the better the utilization of the system.

AXIS	ACTIVITY	%
1	CPU in use	75
2	CPU, but no chan.	25
3	CPU/chan. overlap	50
4	Chan., but not CPU	5
5	Any chan. busy	55
6	CPU not in use	25
7	Problem State	25
8	Supervisor State	50

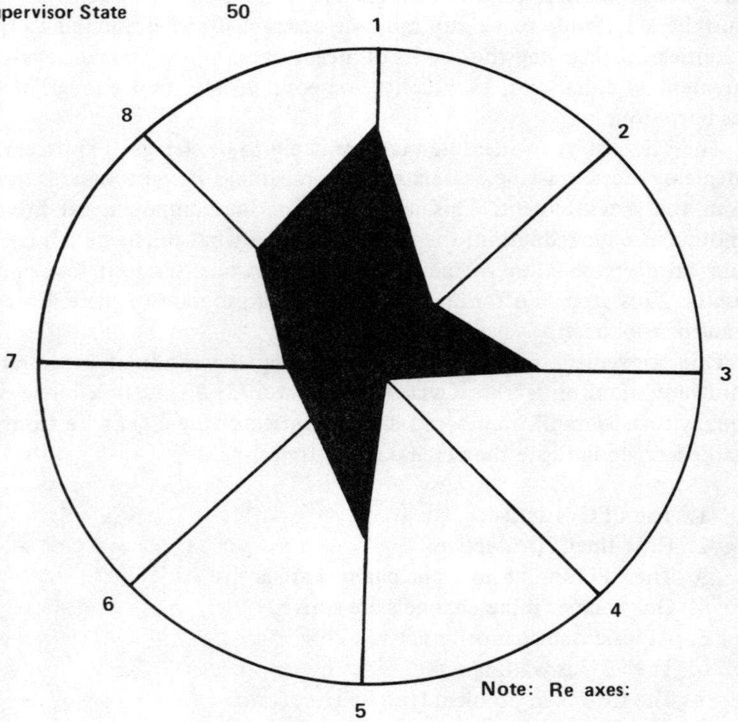

Note: Re axes:

$$2 + 3 = 1$$
$$3 + 4 = 5$$
$$1 + 6 = 100\%$$
$$7 + 8 = 1$$

Figure 7.11. A Kiviat Graph.

The last analysis must be human. What system is best, what component is underutilized, how system utilization can be improved, what module could profitably be made more efficient — all these are somewhat subjective issues. When people have resolved them, action can be taken and the cycle can begin anew. The result of such a cycle is never demonstrably ideal, but a point can always be reached where decisionmakers are convinced that the gains to be realized from further measurement are unlikely to outweigh the costs of measurement. That point is an end to measurement.

We have seen that measurement has its causes and effects, its techniques and its tools, and its chronology. The contents of many papers are relevant to this discussion, but only those already cited can be recommended unqualifiedly. They, especially [Luc71], should be consulted by the student for references on particular topics. Some more recent references are [Ant72], [Bard71], [Kim72], [Kob72], [Lyn72], [Mor'n72].

Modification

While much has been written about measuring systems, little has been written about modifying them. This despite the fact that at least as many (all) operating systems are modified as are measured. One probable reason for so little attention having been paid to system modification is that modification appears very similar to development. But appearances can be deceiving and it is our contention that this is so here. Modifying an existing system poses unique problems. These are our next subject.

We first discuss the reasons for modifications. We then look at how frequently modifications may be made available to users and, in so doing consider two quite different environments and their implications for modification. Alternative methods of program modification and their consequences are considered next. We then address briefly the activities principally associated with developing modified systems: integration, regression testing, and distribution.

Reasons. The modifications of which we speak are those made because function is to be added to the system or the interfaces of existing functions are to be altered. The elimination of bugs from the system is termed maintenance, the third and last topic of this section. Modification may result in the addition to the system of new components or the reprogramming of existing components. Activity of the former sort involves the following problem: Although the function is almost impossible to add; that is, you can design a system to provide, for example, restarting from checkpoints, but you may not be able to add that function later if the designers gave it no consideration originally.

Reprogramming, on the other hand, presents the problem of compatibility. New functions, must be offered in such a way that those individuals who have been using a system and wish to ignore the new function can safely do so. The addition of new functions must not affect the execution of existing programs and job descriptions, if possible.

Frequency. One of the critical questions that arise when systems are modified is how much code can be changed in a single modification or equivalently, how much time elapses between the releases of consecutive modifications. This depends largely on the effects of small and large modifications on users and developers, which in turn depends on a question of environment. In the academic environment, there may be few copies, often only one, of a system and correspondingly few users. Making a modified system available means modifying one or few systems and telling all interested parties about the modification. In a commercial environment, hundreds of systems and thousands of users may be involved. The cost of distributing one modification may be very large. It is therefore desirable that modifications be made infrequently, although not so infrequently that the system fails to respond to changing users' requirements or modifications are so large that they cannot be managed. This balance is difficult to maintain and objective criteria impossible to find. Hopkins has facetiously suggested [Hop70] that releases of OS/360 might be so spaced as to keep the number of bugs in the system at a constant. We know this to be false, but the real criteria are not readily apparent.

Where frequent small modifications are feasible, and especially where only a single system exists, other problems arise. Modifications must often be tested while the system is being used productively; the sequence in which modifications are made must be remembered; interdependent modifications must be made simultaneously; and so on. Landy and Needham have discussed [Lan71] techniques for coping with these problems. They are briefly addressed in the appendix to [Cor72]. VM/370, as has been mentioned, provides virtual machines, a great aid to solving these problems.

Methods and Activities. As to the mechanics of making modifications, these are quite clear in the case of adding a new component. The task is little different from that of developing any system program. When an existing component is to be modified, however, one must consider replacing the component instead of modifying it. A much-modified component or module rarely has a low error-rate and is never efficient. As bugs are found more frequently and redundant code proliferates, recoding must become a more viable alternative.

When modifications are infrequently released and voluminous, problems of integration and regression testing loom large. These subjects are discussed in Section 7.3. We confine ourselves here to emphasizing that these problems, which arise in the development of precursory systems, are also relevant to system modification, but with greater magnitude due to the size of the system and the fact that an external commitment to make function available to users is involved.

Modified systems may be distributed in the same way original systems are. In this case, the discussion of system generation in Chapter 6 is relevant. Alternatively, replacement components may be supplied separately. This is fairly natural in the case of a totally new component, such as a compiler. When, however, modified code includes values bound by the process of system generation, some form of such a procedure is unavoidable.

Maintenance

The last activity associated with an operating system is maintenance. This may continue, under contractual obligation, long after modification has ceased. Gillette has observed that the "cost of maintenance frequently exceeds that of the original development." [Gil68] He includes not only the removal of bugs, but also the optimization of code for critical routines, and the adding of code to extend the system in support of new hardware, such as faster and/or more capacious I/O devices. We accept this definition, but concentrate in the remainder of this section on the first aspect, debugging.

Maintenance begins with development; that is, many things which occur during development have profound effects on the system's maintainability, or serviceability. We have already mentioned, in our section on techniques, standards relating to such topics as defensive programming. This constant checking, to see if anything has gone wrong *yet*, permits bugs to be detected soon after they occur, before the evidence which may lead to their eradication has been destroyed. Diagnostic routines, such as traces and formatted dumps, are also keys to effective maintenance.

The bugs which are the subject of maintenance, those caught after the system is released, are, of course, the most recalcitrant. They often lie in the most rarely exercised routines and are exposed by abuses of the system no developer could have anticipated. But such bugs hardly account for all maintenance. Indeed, experience has shown that even the most obvious combinations of circumstances encounter bugs presumably undiscovered at the factory.

Bugs may be categorized as resulting from either poor design or poor implementation. The use of a higher-level language, as we have noted, may do much toward eliminating bugs of the latter type. Simulative models seem to offer the greatest hope for early discovery of bugs in design.

One of the greatest problems of maintenance is reproducing the manifestation of a bug. If all possible diagnostic data could be gathered as soon as a bug is manifested, reproducing the circumstances of the bug would not be a concern. But, as we have said, post-release bugs are the most recalcitrant, and they are therefore often detected far too late for the recovery of useful diagnostic data. To reproduce the bug, however, may require that the covert relationships of many seemingly unrelated events be recognized, a challenging task.

Because on-the-spot debugging is often unfeasible in the commercial environment, a manufacturer might keep a file of symptoms and fixes of bugs. This file would be made available to service personnel so that fixes can be applied promptly with a minimum of redundant diagnostic work. Fixes are not applied indiscriminately, that is, before symptoms appear, because they are not tested so rigorously as manufacturer-supplied modifications, and may engender undesirable side effects. The analogy with the prescription of medication is striking. The RETAIN [Ste71] system of IBM fits the description above.

When a fix is to be applied, two basic alternatives are available. A patch may be applied to the affected module or, where simple patches are insufficient, entirely new copies of affected modules may be linked together. Recompilation or reassembly is a less attractive alternative.

Systems and their customized configurations may become so complex that separate programs are needed just to keep track of what fixes apply to a system and in what order they may or must be applied. IBM's System Modification Program (SMP) [IBM40] is such a program.

In the academic environment, fixes may be applied in much the same way modifications are made available. In any environment, the fix must not be lost; that is, a PDS or some other mechanism must be employed to ensure that subsequent versions of fixed modules do not exhibit old bugs. It is, of course, to the source code that the fix must be applied if this problem is to be avoided.

Effective maintenance of a system is made more difficult by being unattractive as an occupation [Gun73]. The programmer responsible for maintaining an operating system sees no product of his own design, no creativity in his endeavors, no end result in which he can take pride. He can only have eliminated a small number of the many annoyances the system's users have encountered. To recruit and retain programmers of appreciable talent in maintenance positions is a nearly impossible task.

This, then, is the development process, or what [COS71] calls the pragmatics of operating systems. We have offered a mere summary of the issues, one appropriate to the objectives stated in our preface. More detailed information is readily available from the references cited. Of particular value and broad interest are the reports of the NATO conferences on software engineering [NATO68, NATO70] ; the proceedings of SIGOPS Symposia on Operating System Principles in 1967, 1969, and 1971 [SIG67, SIG71, SIG72] ; and the proceedings of COINS (*Co*mputer and *In*formation *S*ciences) International symposia in 1969 and 1972 ([Tou70], [Tou71b], [Tou73]).

QUESTIONS

1. Categorize each of the following as (1) survey response, (2) requirement, or (3) objective:
    a. 2-second response for a typical interaction when system is dedicated to 25 interactive users writing COBOL programs.

b. 1.5-second retrieval of indexed data from 2-million-byte file.
c. Fast enough for an airline reservation system.
d. High-level languages compatible with system it replaces.
e. Data never seen by unauthorized user.
f. No more than two unscheduled interruptions per month.
g. Runs FORTRAN benchmark job stream as fast as some other system.
h. Never loses working space of interactive user due to line-drop.

2. Speculate as to the fault(s) most likely to be observed in operating systems designed only in the following ways:
   a. Levels.
   b. Top-down.
   c. Nucleus-extension.
   d. Modules-interface.
   e. Deadline (Note: While "all of the above" may be an answer, you should be more specific.)

3. Prepare an organization chart for the development of an operating system of four major and two minor, highly integrated components. Account for the development of tools and documentation. Show support groups and their organization. It will not be possible to have every group in close organizational proximity to all those with which it must deal. Show where proximity has been sacrificed and explain why.

4. Consider the problems involved in simulating each of the stores described below in a store matching the other description. Discuss the relative merits of three possible mappings for the case where (*a*) describes the simulated system and (*b*) the host.
   a. 6 bits per character and 6 characters (36 bits) per word. (IBM 7090/ 7094, and others)
   b. 4 bits per arithmetically manipulable unit (digit), two digits per printable character, 4 characters per word (which can also be manipulated arithmetically, but as a binary quantity with no "digits"). (IBM System/360-370)

5. Comment on the simulation of the instructions described by the following table showing operations and operation codes:

Operation	Operation code (octal)
Add fixed	20
Subtract fixed	22
Multiply fixed	21
Divide fixed	23
Add floating (short)	40
Subtract floating (short)	42
Multiply floating (short)	41
Divide floating (short)	43
Add floating (long)	50
Subtract floating (long)	52
Multiply floating (long)	51
Divide floating (long)	53

6. Make analogies between the use of a prototype in developing an operating system and in developing some other product, such as an automobile. List similarities, differences, and aspects of each which seem to have no analog with respect to the other.

7. Formulate some standards for systems programming. Comment on the applicability of your standards, and of the ones used as examples in the text, to (*a*) assembly language and (*b*) higher-level language implementations.

8. Explain your own reasons for preferring flow charts or HIPO diagrams to the other.

9. Describe a good set of test cases for the processor of the following statement:

SCRATCH FILE = (filename, filename . . .)

where a filename is an alphabetic character followed by zero to seven (inclusive) alphabetic or numeric characters, no more than five filenames can appear on a single statement, one or more blanks must appear on either side of "SCRATCH," and the statement can appear anywhere within an eighty-character input record.

10. Obtain a user's guide and evaluate it employing the list of suggested contents in Section 7.3. Criticize this list based on your own experience.

11. The matrix below describes the ordering of objectives (1 = most important consideration) for three hypothetical operating systems. Suggest a primary implementation language for each.

	Sys. X	Sys. Y	Sys. Z
Elapsed time for development	4	4	1
Ease of maintenance	1	5	3
Cost of implementation	3	3	2
Efficiency of code	2	1	5
Utilization of unique hardware facilities	5	2	4

12. Match measurement techniques and objectives:

A. Hardware monitor   a. Choose system
B. Software monitor   b. Predict performance over load conditions
C. Analytical model   c. Configure hardware
D. Simulative model   d. Improve design
E. Benchmarks   e. Perform accounting

13. Suggest objective criteria for the decision as to whether a module to be modified should be entirely recoded or patched.

Answers

CHAPTER 1

1. monitor, executive, supervisor, operating system
2. d, f, e, c, b, a
3. higher-density tape, overlapping of I/O with computation, new accessing techniques for directly accessible media, larger main storage, changing requirements of storage media for error recovery procedures.
4. b
   e; data conversion, resource specification
   a; file-search, time-sharing, teleprocessing
   d; more detailed job-description, archival storage
   c; load-balancing, geometric graphic display

CHAPTER 4

10. (a) If a page has long been unused, it is likely to remain unused for awhile.
    (b) A program which often makes reference to precisely the number of pages in its working set before making a consecutive reference to a given page.
11. THRASHING
13. *Criterion:*   *1 2 3 4 5 6 7 8 9 10*
    Subgoal: *1 2 2 5 3 3 2 2 − 2*

CHAPTER 5

1. a. paper, for human readability; b. magnetic tape, because no deletions or insertions are likely to be needed; c. magnetic strip, because of the huge volume of data and activity against the file; d, disk or drum, because rapid random access is needed; e. disk, because of high activity and rapid random access requirements.
2. a. sequential, because records are never retrieved by the system; b. sequential, same reason; c. indexed, for rapid access without the wasted space of direct; d. partitioned, for programs; e. direct, for most rapid access.
3. a. P: Part Number, because most access will be on this unambiguous basis; S: Part name, because human-originated queries will use this field.
   b. P: Employee Number, same reason as P for a; S: Employee Name, same reason as S for a.
   c. P: Charge Number, same as a; S: Customer Name, same as a.
   d. P: Flight Number, same as a, again, the unique identifier of the record; S: Destination, Stops, for queries on these items.
5. Inventory of parts, personnel, customer, vendor, students, flights, volumes in a library, articles from scientific journals, social security, Internal Revenue Service, vehicle registration.

6. User error due to use by unskilled individuals; mass destruction of data due to size of file; inconsistency of data due to redundancy in the file.
7. Tactile-response, telepathic entry, odoriferous response, Intensive Care Unit control, electroshock response: the first three require voluminous data, the fourth rapid interaction, and the fifth high reliability.

CHAPTER 6

1. a. value, b. value, c. value, d. location, e. location, f. value, g. value.
2. OS/360 Assembly Language:
   a. X   NOP
   b. X   DSECT
   c.   DC   A(X)
   d.   ENTRY X
   e. Y   DC   A(X–Y)
       X   DS   F
   FORTRAN:
   a. 10   CONTINUE
   b.   COMMON   X
   c.   CALL X
   d.   SUBROUTINE MAIN   X
   e.   N(X,Y)=1
   PL/1:
   a. X:
   b. DECLARE X AUTOMATIC
   c. CALL X or DECLARE X
   d. PROCEDURE X
   e. A(X,Y)=1
4. a. program translation
   b. program translation, OSCL, dynamic
   c. program translation, OSCL, dynamic
   d. Sysgen, IPL, OCL, OSCL
   e. Sysgen, OCL, dynamic
5. (a) optimization, (b) necessary, (c) necessary, (d) superfluous, (e) necessary, (f) optimization, (g) necessary, (h) necessary, (i) optimization, (j) necessary.
6. a. FILENAME or FN better; data set is jargon, ambiguous
   b. INcomprehensible
   c. excellent
   d. meaningless jargon
   e. acceptable
   f. good
   g. abbreviation likely to be ambiguous
7. (i) (a) easily keyed, natural, but often entered by mistake, consecutive delimiters must not be significant
   (b) not difficult to key, fairly natural, consecutive delimiters may denote an omitted parameter
   (c) hard to key, fairly natural where many subparameters occur
   (ii) disadvantage of semicolon as lower case magnified, else as (i).
9. a. meaningless to operator
   b. as in 6

c. good word if one is needed in OCL
d. meaningless to operator
e. good
f. good
g. as in 6

10. a. of no use under any conceivable circumstance
b. useful if operator can/must select alternate drive for currently mounted volume
c. may signal card jam; ability to vary off-line may be needed
d. same as a
e. of use if operator can learn why overhead is excessive and eliminate some causes

11. a. M 293 528
b. L 00D 3876X
c. 183 FAILING
d. X WAITING FOR Y, Z, TO END

12. a. ii, v; b. vii, xi; c. i, ix, xi; d. iii, vi, x; e. iv, x, xi; f. vii

CHAPTER 7

1. a. (2), b. (3), c. (1), d. (2) or (1), f. (3), g. (2), h. (3).

2. a. Inefficiency due to cascade effect.
b. Inefficiency due to lack of opportunity for global optimization.
c. Excessive amounts of code due to the constant addition of code to modules which should have been rewritten.
d. High redundancy of information as each component, subcomponent, and module defines a unique interface (table or control block) to contain only those data it needs.

4. Mappings of (a) in (b):
i. character-by-character
ii. one word of (a) in two of (b) right-adjusted
iii. use all bits [8 words of (a) in 9 of (b)]

11. X: PL 360 or the like; Y: assembly language; Z: PL/1 or ALGOL.

12. A,c; B,e; C,b; D,d; E,a.

13. Recode if over n% of statements have been added since first release of module.
Recode if number of branch instructions has doubled since initial release.
Recode if cost-justifiable.
Recode if nth derivative of bug rate is positive.
Recode if no present employee understands module.
Recode if no original coder of module is still on project.

Appendix A
Operating System Glossary

Many of the specialized or technical terms used by operating system designers may not be found in a dictionary, even a technical one. We have provided definitions of such terms as we feel need defining to read this book. We provide only the specialized meanings of these terms as we use them. A more complete glossary was prepared by Sayers [Say71] and many of the present definitions were adapted from there.

—A—

abnormal termination Termination of a job or task due to an error condition (contrasted with *normal termination*).

absolute program A program which must occupy the same area of main storage each time it is loaded.

access Ability to *use* a *resource*.

access control Granting suitably *authorized* requests for access to sensitive *resources*, denying all other requests, and precluding *access* in the absence of a request. Access control is *physical access control, programmed access control,* or *cryptography. Programmed access control* is either *individual-based* or *resource-based.*

access method Any of the data management techniques available to the user for transferring data between main storage and an I/O device (e.g., *direct, indexed, keyed, queued* or *sequential* access).

access time The time required to position the mechanism of a storage unit or device to receive or transmit data after the instruction to do so is given.

address (1) A label, name, or number identifying a register, location, or unit where information is stored. (2) The operand part of an instruction.

address constant A constant whose value is equivalent to the machine location assigned to a particular symbolic address.

address translator A software or hardware feature which dynamically translates virtual addresses to real addresses in main storage. (See **virtual address; real address.**)

allocation Assigning a resource, e.g., allocating an area of main storage to a task or allocating an I/O device to a job.

assembler A language processor which translates symbolic instructions into a machine language.

asynchronous Without regular time relationships (opposite of **synchronous**); hence, as applied to program execution, unpredictable with respect to time or instruction sequence.

attack An attempt to effect un*authorized access.*

audit Use a *reduced log* in determining whether *access* is controlled in accordance with management policy and generally accepted accounting practice. ("Audit" embraces far more, but the present definition is restricted to the context provided by the rest of the glossary.)

authenticate Determine accuracy, for example, of a user's claim of identity, claim of *authorization*, or of a message's embedded assertion of its time or place of origin.

authorize Permit a *use* of a sensitive *resource*.

availability A system attribute which means the system will function even though some of its components may malfunction.

–B–

basic access A access method in which each input/output macroinstruction causes a corresponding machine operation to be executed.

benchmark A standard program used to evaluate the performance of computers relative to preselected criteria.

binding Combining one or more program segments into a composite program which is acceptable for execution; also called *collecting* (UNIVAC), and *linkage editing* (IBM and RCA).

block (records) (*v.*) To group records for the purpose of conserving storage space or increasing the efficiency of access of processing. (*n.*) Such a group of records.

bootstrap (*v.*) To bring a machine into a desired state by means of its own action. (*n.*) A machine routine whose first instructions are sufficient to bring the rest of itself into the computer from an input device.

byte A generic term used to indicate a measurable portion of consecutive binary digits (e.g., and 8-bit or a 6-bit byte). A byte is frequently coded so as to hold one character.

–C–

capacity A system attribute which causes the system to appear as large as possible within its physical constraints.

catalog A directory to locations of files and libraries; a mechanism for pairing symbols and addresses.

cataloged procedure A set of job control statements which has been placed in a special file and which may be used for job control by being named on a special control card.

channel A device that connects input and output units to the main part of the computer or to each other, that is, a data path.

common page A page allocated to more than one program, usually used for passing data between separate programs.

command language A source language consisting primarily of procedural operators, each capable of invoking a function to be executed; an interpreted control language.

compiler A language processor which translates a problem-oriented language into a machine language.

compiler interfaces (operating system) Operating system functions which are oriented to providing supporting services to the system language compilers.

contention Rivalry for use of a system resource.

control block A storage area through which a particular type of information required for control of the operating system is communicated.

control program A collective or general term for all routines or programs which are part of the operating system supervisor.

CPU (central processing unit) The portion of a computer which directs the sequence of operations, interprets the coded instructions, and initiates the proper commands to the computer circuits for execution.

create Bring a *resource* into being and associate it with an *identifier,* a type of *use.*

cryptography A form of *access control* applicable to sensitive *resources* that are beyond the scopes of both *programmed access control* and *physical access control* (for example, portable media or communication lines). Cryptography prevents un*authorized read*ing of a sensitive *resource.*

cylinder For a direct-access device, a set of records that can be accessed without moving the access mechanism.

—D—

data management Comprehensive facilities which provide support for programmed access to the data files within the system. These facilities may be of two forms: routines supporting application program access to the data base, and the independent data management system supporting user access to the data base.

data management system A group of integrated routines for creating and maintaining a large, organized, and structured collection of related data (known as the data base) and for interrogating the data base and producing various types of formatted reports.

data manipulation functions The components of the operating system which permit the user to access and process data. These functions may be independent utility programs or subroutines incorporated within a user program.

data set (1) A term used in IBM documentation for a file. See **file.** (2) A device used to connect terminals to a communications line.

deallocation Restoring the availability of a system resource. See **allocation.**

deblocking The decomposition of a data block into its constituent records for processing. See **block.**

default option An option which will automatically be assumed if not overridden by a parameter specification.

destroy Cause a *resource* to cease to exist, a type of *use.*

device A term used to refer to a computer component.

direct access A method of accessing data records directly, without regard for the sequence in which they are recorded.

dispatching Allocation of processor time by the supervisor to a specific task.

dynamic allocation Providing resources (storage space, I/O devices, etc.) to a program or task in response to an actual demand by the program or task.

dynamic buffering A buffering technique which provides buffers to a program or task in response to an actual demand for buffers by the program or task.

dynamic program loading The process of loading a program module into main storage upon the demand for that program module by an executing program.

dynamic program relocation Moving or relocating a program to another part of storage without modifying it, before it has completed execution, and still permitting subsequent execution.

dynamic storage allocation Method of assigning main storage such that the location of programs and data is determined at the moment of need.

—E—

efficiency A system attribute which forces the system to make optimum use of its resources.

event An occurrence of significance to a task; typically, the completion of an asynchronous operation, such as input/output.

event synchronization Delaying task execution until some specified event occurs or triggering a task upon the occurrence of a specified event.

exchange buffering A buffering technique which eliminates the need to move data in main storage by exchanging a system buffer area for a user buffer area.

exhaustion An *attack* carried out by providing all possible values (for example, for a *password* or for a *cryptograph*ic key) in trying to supply a secret quantity one is not supposed to know (and, in fact, does not know).

extensibility A system quality which allows addition of new functions desired by its users.

—F—

fault analysis The analysis of hardware or software malfunctions by the system for purposes of error recovery.

file A collection of related records treated as a unit (synonymous with *data set* in IBM systems). The records in a file may or may not be sequenced according to a key contained in each record.

file management routines The collection of operating system routines which are used to accomplish all the various file services provided by the system, such as file control, cataloging, file protection, and the like.

file protection Preventing unauthorized access to a file. The protection may extend to read access, write access, or both.

firmware Hardware and software integrated in such a fashion that only the combination realizes the functions intended to be provided.

flexibility A system attribute that allows modification of the system in response to the needs of its users.

—G—

generality A system attribute which forces the system to do what its users want it to do.

generated code The executable programs or subroutines produced from a set of specifications or commands.

—H—

hardware Physical equipment, e.g., mechanical, electrical, or electronic devices. (see **software; firmware**)

hashing Calculation of the address of data from its value.

—I—

identifier A value uniquely associated with one user (or *group* of users) or one sensitive *resource*.

indexed file structure A file structure in which the records can be accessed by the contents of one or more fields within the records. In addition to containing the individual records, indexed files may include a directory of the values of indexed fields and the corresponding locations of all records containing each value.

individual-based (Of *access control*) permitting or denying *access* to *authentic* users according to previously recorded *authorization* without interaction accompanying a *request* for *access;* safer and more convenient for users than *resource-based*.

input/output control system A collection of computer routines designed to perform input/output operations and control other functions such as label processing, error correction, checkpoint, and restart.

input stream The sequence of control statements and data submitted to the operating system on an input unit especially designated for this purpose at system generation time, or by the operator.

inquiry A technique whereby interrogation of a data base or file may be initiated from a keyboard.

integrity An attribute of a system which protects itself and its users from each other's errors.

interface (1) The place at which two different systems (or subsystems) meet and interact with each other. (2) The linkage and conventions established for communication between two independent elements, usually between a program and another program, computer operator, terminal user, etc.

interleave To arrange parts of one sequence of things or events so that they alternate with parts of one or more other sequences of things or events and so that each sequence retains its identity.

interrupt Suspension of the normal sequencing of operations such that later resumption is possible. Usually accompanied by a transfer to one of a small number of fixed locations to process the situation causing the suspension.

interrupt stacking Recording the occurrence of one or more interrupts and allowing them to remain pending while processing continues.

—J—

job control language The language used to provide job specifications to the job scheduler.

job scheduler The control program function which controls input job streams, obtains input/output resources for jobs and job steps, and otherwise regulates the use of the computing system by jobs.

—K—

key A data item which serves to identify a data record.

keyed file structure A file structure in which a data item is used to identify each data record. The search for a specific record by using the record key can be implemented by hardware or by software.

—L—

language processor A compiler, assembler, or program generator which transforms source modules into object modules.

library support (compiler interface) Support provided to maintain compiler-oriented libraries. These libraries may be compiler source program libraries, macro statement libraries, or compiler subroutine libraries. See also **compiler interfaces**.

list file structure A file structure in which each data element incorporates links to successor or predecessor elements.

load module A program in a format suitable for loading into main storage for execution.

—M—

main storage A digital computer's principal working storage, from which instructions can be executed or operands fetched for data manipulation. Also frequently referred to as memory or core storage, since magnetic cores sometimes serve as the storage device. See also **secondary storage**.

mask (interrupt) To suspend recognition of a type of interrupt.

multiprocessing The employment of multiple interconnected processing units to execute two or more different programs or tasks simultaneously.

multiprogramming A technique for handling numerous routines or programs simultaneously by overlapping or interleaving their execution, that is, by permitting more than one program to time-share machine components.

—N—

normal termination Termination of a job or a task upon successful completion of processing.
nucleus That portion of the control program which remains resident in main storage at all times.

—O—

object module A machine language program produced by a language processor; relocation and external attribute information may be included.
opacity A system attribute that keeps its users ignorant of its properties beneath the interface.
overlay program A segmented program in which the segment currently being executed may use the same core storage area occupied by a previously executed segment.

—P—

paging The division of the program and the data into small fixed-size blocks, or pages, usually 1 to 4K. Individual pages may be loaded into main memory only as required.
partition A subdivision of main storage which is allocated to a job or a system task for job or task execution. A partition may be fixed or variable in size.
password Loosely, any data a user provides for purposes of *authentication*.
penetration Un*authorized access* that gives one effective control of the system, a type of *attack*.
peripheral A term referring to devices that are not a part of the central processor (e.g., card reader/punch, printer, tape, disk).
physical (Of *access control*) concerning anything other than magnetically recorded data to which the system can control *access;* concerns portable media in libraries or elsewhere, and rooms such as computer centers and libraries.
polling A technique by which each of the terminals sharing a communications line is periodically interrogated to determine if it requires servicing.
priority queue A queue maintained in priority sequence.
privileged instruction An instruction which can be executed only in supervisor mode.
problem mode A state of the central processor in which certain critical instructions cannot be executed. Also called problem state, normal state, slave mode, standard mode, nonprivileged mode, guard mode. See also **supervisor mode**.
processor (1) A hardware component which performs some activity (see **CPU**). (2) A program which transforms some input data into a form desired for output.
programmed (Of *access control*) concerning magnetically recorded data to which the system can control *access*.

—Q—

query A *request* for information from a data base; specifically, one for data collected from a number of records and presented as a sum, average, or the like (because, in such a case, the *resource* involved is the specially constructed response, one for which no *authoriza*tion could have been established previously in any conventional sense).

queue An ordered list of items. With no other specification, a queue is assumed to be ordered on a first-in, first-out basis (as contrasted with a **priority queue**).

–R–

read Acquire data, a type of *use*.

real address An actual location in main or secondary storage. See also **virtual address**.

real-time operation Concurrent operations for data processing and physical processing performed in such a way that the results of the computing operations are available whenever needed by the physical processing operations.

record A collection of related items or data, treated as a unit.

reduce Process a *log* so as to extract from it only the data needed for *audit*ing purposes.

reliability An attribute of a system which fails as little as possible with as little effect as possible on the users.

relocation (1) Loading a program into main storage at an address other than that specified at assembly or compilation time. (2) Moving a program module from one area of main storage to another. (3) The modification of a program module required to effect relocation as defined above.

request An application for the right to effect *access* to a sensitive *resource*.

resident routine A routine which executes from and remains permanently in main storage. See also **transient routine**.

residue Data left after a process is completed; undestroyed residue to subject to *attack* by a *browser*.

resource Any facility of the computing system or operating system required by a job or task. These include main storage, input/output devices, the central processing unit, files, and control and processing programs. Any service, capacity, device, or data *access*ible via a system.

resource allocation Assigning a system resource for the use of a partition, job, job step, or task. See **allocation**.

resource-based (Of *access control*) permitting or denying *access* to users according to their ability to provide *authenticat*ing data in association with a *request*.

ring file structure A circular list structure in which the last data element points back to the first. See also **list structure**.

round-robin scheduling A technique for allocating CPU time to a number of contending programs. The technique involves establishing a circular list of users and allocating a fixed amount of time to each user in turn without regard to priority. See also **time slicing**.

–S–

salami (From the way that salami is sliced, of an *attack*) involving very many small amounts; for example, a misappropriation of very many, very small sums; the mythical "round-off" fraud is of this type.

scavenge Conduct an *attack* by *brows*ing through discarded material.

secondary storage The storage facilities not an integral part of the computer but directly connected to and controlled by the computer e.g., magnetic drum and magnetic tapes. See also **main storage**.

security A system attribute by which the system protects against unauthorized access to information entrusted to it.

sequential file structure A file structure in which elements are stored and accessed serially.

service program Any of the class of standard routines or programs which assist in the use of a computing system and in the successful execution of problem programs, without contributing directly to control of the system or production of results; includes utilities, simulators, test and debugging routines, etc.

software The collection of programs and routines associated with the computer. See also **hardware; firmware.**

source module A series of statements in the symbolic language of a language processor which constitutes the entire input to a single execution of the processor.

spooling A technique by which slow input/output operations (card reading, printing) are accomplished by an intermediate transfer to a faster secondary storage device so that input/output may be asynchronous with program execution. See **symbiont.**

stack A list of items ordered on a last-in, first-out basis.

stand-alone utilities Routines which are not under operating system control during execution.

supervisor mode A state of the central processor in which all instructions may be executed. Also called control state, monitor state, master mode, supervisor state, privileged state. See also **problem mode.**

swapping The process of storing low-priority or suspended programs on secondary storage in order to obtain main storage for another program.

symbiont A data transfer routine or program which executes concurrently with user and system programs.

synchronous Occurring concurrently, and with a regular or predictable time relationship (opposite of **asynchronous.**)

system integrity The extent to which a system resists *penetration.*

system generation A process which creates a particular and uniquely specified operating system. System generation combines user-specified options and parameters with manufacturer-supplied general-purpose or nonspecialized program subsections to produce an operating system (or other complex software) of the desired form and capacity.

–T–

task A program subdivision which is treated as the basic unit of work by the supervisor.

teleprocessing A general term expressing data transmission between a computing system and remotely located devices via a unit which performs the necessary format conversion and controls the rate of transmission.

throughput Measure of system efficiency – the rate at which work can be handled by a computing system (e.g., jobs per day).

ticket An *authoriz*ation that is associated with an individual; not to be confused with a *list.* Sometimes called a "capability," a term used to mean a particular mechanism by which the notion of a ticket can be implemented.

time bomb A routine that, for the coder's nefarious purposes, executes at a particular time (for example, to destroy data of the coder's now-former employer); a mechanism used in an *attack.*

time sharing A technique or system for furnishing computing services to multiple users simultaneously, while providing rapid responses to each of the users.

time slicing The allocation of limited intervals of time (quanta) to programs in contention for use of the CPU. See also **round-robin scheduling.**

time stamp *Authenticat*ing data indicative of the time that an event took place (for example, the sending of a message).

TOCTTOU (Time of Check to Time of Use). Failing to protect data upon whose accuracy the system depends for *integrity* between the time that the system validates the data and the time that the system uses the data; a flaw that permits *penetration.*

track The portion of a moving storage medium, such as a drum, tape, or disk, which is accessible to a given reading head in a given position.

tracker A *query* or set of *queries* designed to make it possible for a user of a data base to deduce information without proper authorization.

transient area An area of main storage reserved for transient routines.

transient routines Routines permanently stored on the system resident device and loaded into a transient area when needed for execution. Generally, they accomplish selected supervisory functions but are not executed often enough to merit inclusion in the nucleus.

trap-door A *Trojan horse* that executes only under particular circumstances, a mechanism used in an *attack*.

Trojan horse A routine that does not contribute to the documented function of the program that contains it but, instead, does something the program's caller would prevent if possible; typically, a routine that either copies passed data that the coder is not *authorized* to *read* or takes advantage of the caller's *authorization* to effect some un-*authorized access;* a mechanism used in an *attack.*

—U—

usability An attribute of a system whose interfaces are convenient for the user.

use *Access* to a *resource* for the purpose of *read*ing, *writ*ing, *creat*ing, or *destroy*ing it; also, to effect such *access.*

—V—

virtual address A relative or imaginary location in main or secondary storage. A virtual address must be converted to a real address before use. See also **real address.**

visibility A system attribute which allows the user to learn about the system properties.

volume All that portion of a single unit or storage media which is accessible to a single read/write mechanism, e.g., a reel of tape or a removable disk pack.

—W—

waiting state The state of a program which is idle pending the occurrence of some event, e.g., completion of an I/O operation or allocation of a resource.

write Modify data, a type of *use.*

—Z—

zap *Write* data in a program so as to modify it for subsequent execution; specifically refers to un*authorized* modification of a program that runs with a privilege the user does not have *authoriz*ation to use; a mechanism used in an *attack.*

Appendix B
Operating System Functions

One of the difficulties in trying to standardize operating system functions lies in the wide variations in the conception of and documentation of these functions by different manufacturers. ANSI committees have started to work on the problem of standards for operating system control languages by which some operating system functions are specified. The outline which follows is an attempt to describe functions systematically. The goal of standardization in this field is the ability to make a machine-independent operating system control language so that routine operations, such as compiling a COBOL program or copying a tape, could be done with the same control language on any machine. The outline as presented should provide a useful basis for comparing different systems in a consistent way, although this use goes beyond the original intent of the outline.

1. Control System Characteristics
   1.1. Hardware Architectural Features
        1.1.01 Processor configuration
               1.1.01.01 Single CPU
               1.1.01.02 Internally connected multiple processors
               1.1.01.03 Externally connected multiple processors
        1.1.02 Memory configuration
               1.1.02.01 Single level – modular units
               1.1.02.02 Hierarchical
               1.1.02.03 Virtual
               1.1.02.04 Associative
        1.1.03 Execution control unit
               1.1.03.01 Execution stack hardware
               1.1.03.02 Single register set
               1.1.03.03 Multiple sets of registers
               1.1.03.04 Interrupts handled via hardware
               1.1.03.05 Microprogrammable control memory
               1.1.03.06 Array-processing via hardware
   1.2 Executive Software Characteristics
        1.2.01 Software configurability
               1.2.01.01 Modular system generation
               1.2.01.02 System editing (dynamic reconfiguration)
        1.2.02 Control features
               1.2.02.01 Facility for soft stop (depletion of job queues)
               1.2.02.02 Facility for warm restart
               1.2.02.03 Facility for cold restart
               1.2.02.04 Facility for multiprogramming
               1.2.02.05 Facility for remote entry of jobs

          1.2.03 System input/output features
                1.2.03.01 Multiple input streams
                1.2.03.02 Concurrent peripheral operations
                1.2.03.03 Simultaneous multiple assignment of system output
                1.2.03.04 Ability to accept audio input
                1.2.03.05 Optical character recognition
                1.2.03.06 Ability for audio response
          1.2.04 Language processors
                1.2.04.01 Assembler
                1.2.04.02 Macro
                1.2.04.03 COBOL
                1.2.04.04 FORTRAN
                1.2.04.05 ALGOL
                1.2.04.06 PL/1
                1.2.04.07 SNOBOL
                1.2.04.08 JOVIAL
                1.2.04.09 BASIC
          1.2.05 System utilities
                1.2.05.01 Sort/merge
                1.2.05.02 File update
                1.2.05.03 File copy
                1.2.05.04 File compare
                1.2.05.05 File position
                1.2.05.06 File list
                1.2.05.07 File restructure
                1.2.05.08 Core dump user area
                1.2.05.09 Core dump system area
                1.2.05.10 Clear user core
   1.3   Modes of Operation
       1.3.01 Batch
       1.3.02 Critical time (real-time)
       1.3.03 Transaction
       1.3.04 Conversational
       1.3.05 Time-sharing
       1.3.06 Concurrent modes
              1.3.06.01 Real-time/batch
              1.3.06.02 Transaction/batch
              1.3.06.03 Conversational/batch
2. System Operating Facilities
   2.1   Operator Control of Executive Functions
       2.1.01 Ability to suspend system
       2.1.02 Ability to enter control data
       2.1.03 Ability to set date/time
       2.1.04 Ability to set system logging attributes
       2.1.05 Ability to establish or alter core partitions
   2.2   Ability to Display System Information
       2.2.01 Display system configuration
       2.2.02 Display job queue
       2.2.03 Display file status
       2.2.04 Display volume status

2.2.05 Display outstanding messages
2.2.06 Display job status
2.3 Job Queue Management
2.3.01 Ability to change job priorities
2.3.02 Ability to hold/release jobs
2.3.03 Ability to cancel jobs
2.4 Control of System Configuration
2.4.01 Ability to specify mounting location
2.4.02 Ability to unload volumes
2.4.03 Ability to start devices
2.4.04 Ability to set devices off-line
3. System Administration Facilities
3.1 User Administration
3.1.01 Ability to declare authorized users of the system
3.1.01.01 User name
3.1.01.02 User aliases
3.1.01.03 User privilege level
3.1.01.04 User priority
3.1.01.05 User charge code
3.1.02 Ability to establish user resource limits
3.1.02.01 By single run time
3.1.02.02 By accumulated run time
3.1.02.03 By accumulated file space
3.1.02.04 By number of files
3.1.02.05 By core space
3.1.02.06 By accumulated charges
3.2 Job Administration
3.2.01 Job cataloging
3.2.01.01 Ability to define a self-contained unit of work
3.2.01.02 Ability to catalog job resource requirements
3.2.01.03 Ability to assign job priorities
3.2.01.04 Ability to edit job catalog
3.2.02 Job scheduling based upon
3.2.02.01 Time/date
3.2.02.02 Demand
3.2.02.03 Completion of other jobs(s)
3.2.02.04 Combination of conditions
3.3 System Accounting
3.3.01 Ability to specify accounting basis
3.3.01.01 By user
3.3.01.02 By job
3.3.01.03 By file
3.3.01.04 By terminal
3.3.02.05 By program
3.3.02 Ability to establish parameters of performance measurement
3.3.02.01 Elapsed processor time
3.3.02.02 Processor idle time
3.3.02.03 Job queue time per job
3.3.02.04 Terminal active time
3.3.02.05 Terminal idle time

5. Job Entry and Job Control Facilities
   5.1   Interactive Control Facilities
         5.1.01 Ability to logically connect a terminal
               5.1.01.01 Dial-in facility
               5.1.01.02 Log-in facility
               5.1.01.03 Ability to communicate with system operator
         5.1.02 Command facilities
               5.1.02.01 Ability to enter interactive mode
               5.1.02.02 Ability to initiate background processing
               5.1.02.03 Ability to interrupt job activity (attention, halt)
               5.1.02.04 Ability to cancel background processing
               5.1.02.05 Ability to edit commands (delete char, line, etc)
               5.1.02.06 Ability to engage tutorials
               5.1.02.07 Ability to checkpoint/restart jobs
               5.1.02.08 Ability to initiate job recovery
   5.2   Resource Management (Interactive and/or Noninteractive)
         5.2.01 Ability to specify core allocation
               5.2.01.01 At job initiation
               5.2.01.02 During execution
         5.2.02 Ability to specify file space allocation
               5.2.02.01 At job initiation
               5.2.02.02 During execution
         5.2.03 Ability to specify device allocation
               5.2.03.01 At job initiation
               5.2.03.02 During execution
         5.2.04 Ability to specify processor allocation
               5.2.04.01 Select among multiprocessors
               5.2.04.02 Specify processor time slice
               5.2.04.03 Specify elapsed time limit
         5.2.05 Ability to specify aging algorithm for roll-out
         5.2.06 Ability to assign memory protection limits
   5.3   Program Control (Interactive and/or Noninteractive)
         5.3.01 Ability to breakpoint/resume a program
         5.3.02 Ability to revert n levels in the control hierarchy
         5.3.03 Ability to checkpoint/restart a program
         5.3.04 Ability to modify object code during a break
         5.3.05 Ability to cause dynamic loading of subprograms
         5.3.06 Ability to invoke dynamic overlays
         5.3.07 Ability to specify segmentation parameters
         5.3.08 Binding of load modules
               5.3.08.01 Prior to loading
               5.3.08.02 During execution
         5.3.09 Dynamic linking facilities
               5.3.09.01 Between separately compiled modules
               5.3.09.02 Ability to pass data between modules
               5.3.09.03 Ability to activate asynchronous routines
6. User Data Facilities
   6.1   File Management
         6.1.01 Ability to assign files to physical devices

6.1.02 Ability to associate symbolic names with physical devices
6.1.03 Ability to specify access rights
6.1.04 Ability to specify data storing strategy
    6.1.04.01 Sequential
    6.1.04.02 Index sequential
    6.1.04.03 Partitioned sequential
    6.1.04.04 Random
6.1.05 Ability to concurrently share files
6.1.06 Ability to specify record protection
    6.1.06.01 Via file lockout
    6.1.06.02 Via read-only mode
    6.1.06.03 Via record lockout
6.1.07 Ability to specify device type for a file
6.1.08 Ability to catalog file descriptions
6.1.09 Ability to select type of file destruction
    6.1.09.01 By deleting catalog entry
    6.1.09.02 By deleting volume directory entries
    6.1.09.03 By zeroing the file contents
  6.2 Logical Data Management
    6.2.01 Availability of logical structures
        6.2.01.01 Sequential
        6.2.01.02 Hierarchical
        6.2.01.03 Lists
        6.2.01.04 Rings
        6.2.01.05 Plex (directed graph)
    6.2.02 Automatic garbage collection for list structures
    6.2.03 Ability to organized data into pages
        6.2.03.01 Control over page size
        6.2.03.02 Control over page aging algorithm
    6.2.04 Ability to specify retrieval algorithm
        6.2.04.01 Sequential
        6.2.04.02 Index sequential
        6.2.04.03 Random with actual key
        6.2.04.04 Random with relative key
        6.2.04.05 Random with calculated key
        6.2.04.06 Via logical restructures
7. Control Language Characteristics
  7.1 Metalanguage Facilities
    7.1.01 Ability to define synonyms
    7.1.02 Ability to define new commands
    7.1.03 Ability to define levels of verbosity
    7.1.04 Ability to establish levels of privilege
    7.1.05 Ability to establish default attributes
  7.2 Language Syntax
    7.2.01 Field delimiters
        7.2.01.01 Comma
        7.2.01.02 Blank
        7.2.01.03 Parenthesis
        7.2.01.04 Other

7.2.02 Assignment character
 7.2.02.01 Equal sign
 7.2.02.02 Parenthesis
 7.2.02.03 Other
7.2.03 Continuation character
7.2.04 Stream delimiters
 7.2.04.01 For end of statement
 7.2.04.02 For beginning of data
 7.2.04.03 For end of data
7.2.05 Ability to write comments in command stream
7.2.06 Ability for multilevel data-name qualification
7.2.07 Statement identification
 7.2.07.01 By name
 7.2.07.02 By sequence number
7.2.08 Appearance of keywords
 7.2.08.01 Random order
 7.2.08.02 Positional
7.2.09 Syntactic type
 7.2.09.01 Fixed format
 7.2.09.02 Free form
7.2.10 Number of syntactic levels
7.2.11 Significance of levels
 7.2.11.01 Level one
 7.2.11.02 Level two
 7.2.11.03 Level three
7.3 Control stream facilities
7.3.01 Ability to catalog control streams
7.3.02 Ability to edit control streams
7.3.03 Ability to select level of verbosity

Appendix C
Sample Control Block

The task control block (TCB) is used as the basic representation of a task by IBM operating systems. The version described here is for an MFT system [IBM8]. Task control blocks may be located by two methods: (*a*) They are part of a queue whose head is pointed to by a field in the communications vector table (CVT). (*b*) The current TCB and old TCB are also pointed to by another pair of words whose address is in the CVT. The CVT address is located at absolute address 16 and is thus always locatable. The TCB contains data fields as given in the following table. The data fields consist generally of addresses, flags, and save areas. The addresses are used to locate additional control blocks for the task. The flags record the status of the task and describe some of the task attributes. The save areas are used to save the contents of general and floating-point registers so that a suspended task can be restored to its former state. The dispatcher searches the TCB queue to determine what action should be taken for each task desiring resources.

FIELD NAME	RELATIVE ADDRESS	VALUE	USE OF DATA OR DATA POINTED TO BY ADDRESS
TCBFRS	−32	Save Area	Save floating-point registers
TCBRBP	0	A(Request block queue)	Describe executing program
TCBPIE	4	A(Program interrupt element)	Control program interrupt processing
TCBDEB	8	A(Data extent block queue)	Describe data set characteristics and location
TCBTIO	12	A(Task I/O table)	Link device data and DD card data
TCBCMP	16	Task completion code	Flags, system code, user code
TCBTRN	20	Flags	Special processing required
	21	A(Control core table)	Used for TESTRAN
TCBMSS	25	A(Boundary box)	Describe partition limits
TCBPKF	28	Storage protection key	Record key for this task
TCBFLGS	29	Flags	Record task status and dispatching
TCBLMP	34	Number of resource queues	Describe task resource demands
TCBDSP	35	Dispatching priority	Record task priority
TCBLLS	36	A(Most recent request block)	Describe loaded program
TCBJLB	40	A(JOBLIB data control block)	Locate library of load modules for task

FIELD NAME	RELATIVE ADDRESS	VALUE	USE OF DATA OR DATA POINTED TO BY ADDRESS
TCBFTJST	44	A(Job step TCB)	Locate TCB for step from a subtask
TCBGRS	48	Save area	Save general registers
TCBIDF	112	Identifier	Describe TCB
TCBFSA	113	A(Problem program save area)	Save general registers
TCBTCB	116	A(Next TCB)	Find lower priority TCB
TCBTME	120	A(Timer element)	Used for task timing
TCBPIB	124	Flags	Partition type
	125	A(Partition information block)	Record partition data
TCBNTC	128	A(Previous TCB)	Establish subtask chaining
TCBOTC	132	A(Attaching TCB)	Establish subtask chaining
TCBLTC	136	A(Attached TCB)	Establish subtask chaining
TCBIQE	140	A(Interrupt queue element)	Schedule ETXR routine
TCBECB	144	A(Event control block)	Record task termination
TCBFTLMP	152	Task limit priority	Highest possible subtask priority
TCBFTFLG	153	Flags	Task termination status
TCBNSTAE	160	Flags	Used by STAE routine
	161	A(STAE control block)	Intercept abnormal termination
TCBTCT	164	A(Timing control table)	Data used by SMF
TCBUSER	168	Arbitrary	Can be set by user
TCBDAR	172	Flags	Record damage assessment status
TCBNDSP	173	Flags	Secondary dispatchability status flags
TCBRECDE	180	Flags	Used by ABEND routines
TCBJSCB	181	A(Job step control block)	Used to locate JSCB

Appendix D
Data Security Considerations

The goals, objectives, of operating systems introduced in Section 1.2 are all worthy ones in themselves and almost all of them are well-understood, even if the means of attaining them are not. Also, technology has not reached the point where designers know so well how to attain these goals that they sacrifice other worthy goals in the process. The exceptions to the characterization of the preceding two sentences are probably generality, security, and integrity. The two topics, because of the similarity of their motivations, are here combined under the heading "data security."

The common misconceptions that cloud many people's perception of the value of data security are that:

1. Losses that occur as a result of phenomena related to operating systems are either small or unavoidable, leading to undervaluation of security.
2. Most loss of this type results from malicious, rather than honest but misdirected, acts.

Increasing media attention to the subject should leave few concerned individuals with an underappreciation of the potential for loss. How to avoid loss is another matter. Our Sections 3.7 and 4.5 should have served to alert the reader to the folly of such a view. A remaining concern, however, is the perception of the nature of the threat to data.

Every sober view of the subject [Cou75] leads to the same conclusion: flawed well-intentioned individuals are far more dangerous than dishonest ones.

Consider an inventory control system that, like most, provides for the automatic reorder of an understocked part. Imagine that some part is no longer needed by a firm, so the firm sells as surplus and at a loss all of its stock of that part. The mere failure to prevent reorders of the part could cost the firm huge sums, far more than anyone has ever stolen from one victim.

Even when restricting one's view to malice, one can easily fall into grievous error. Think of your defenses against malice as a fence [McP78]. Any adversary will attack only the weakest portion of your fence, so that is the (only) portion you must strengthen at any one time. Because authorized employees and their foibles are usually any establishment's Achilles' heel, most of what establishments do to strengthen their operating systems' resistance to deliberate attack is often wasted. And one can waste a lot of money on efforts to make systems impregnable [Ame79].

The thrust of the above is that designers of operating systems are best advised, when considering security, to concern themselves with prevention, through improved usability, and detection, through auditing facilities, of error, not so much with defense against hostile acts. In fact, if one effectively prevents people from doing what they are not authorized to do, one will probably have provided adequate defenses against deliberate opponents.

Bibliography

In the following bibliography, indicators after certain entries help the reader to assess the value of a work for his purposes. The first indicator cites the section of this text to which the work is most relevant. Other indicators classify the work as follows:

INDICATOR   SIGNIFICANCE

S   A survey of the field or some portion of it.
I   A particularly important work in its field.
M   A familiarity with higher mathematics will help the reader to appreciate this work.
P   A particularly practical work devoid of viating assumptions of ideal worlds.

Indicators are omitted for manufacturers' publications.

All works are listed alphabetically by author and chronologically within the works of a single author, as is customary. Where a normal bibliographic reference in the text — the first three characters of the author's last name followed by the last two digits of the year of publication — would be ambiguous, a lower case letter has been appended to the text reference to identify which of the possible works is intended: a for the first, b for the second, and so on. Exceptions are manufacturers' publications. In this case, digits in the reference correspond to the number of the item appearing in the list under that manufacturer's name in the alphabetical listing.

Abate, J., and Dubner, H.: "Optimizing the performance of a drum-like storage," *IEEE Trans. on Computers* 18, No. 11 (Nov. 1969), 992–997.

Abbott, R.P., et al.: "A bibliography on computer operating systems security," Lawrence Livermore Laboratory, University of California, The RISOS Project, Report UCRL-51555 (April 1974). *4.5.*

Abel, V.A., Rosen, S., and Wagner, R.E.: "Scheduling in a general purpose operating system," *Proc. AFIPS 1970 Fall Joint Computer Conference,* Vol. 37, AFIPS Press, Montvale, N.J., 89–96.

Abernathy, D.H., et al.: "Survey of design goals for operating systems," *Operating System Review* 7, (1973), 29–48. *1.2, 2.2; P*

Abrams, M.D.: "A comparative sampling of systems for producing computer drawn flow-charts." *Proc. 1968 ACM Conference,* Brandon Systems Press, Princeton, 1968, 743–750. *7.3; S*

ACM: *Workshop on System Performance Evaluation* (April 1971), ACM, New York. *7.5; M*

ACM Curriculum Committee on Computer Science: "Curriculum 68," *J. ACM* 11, No. 3 (March 1968), 151–197.*I.*

Adiri, I.: "A dynamic time-sharing priority queue," *J. ACM* 18, No. 4 (Oct. 1971), 603–610.

Adiri, I.: "A note on some mathematical models of time-sharing systems," *J. ACM* 18, No. 4 (Oct. 1971), 611–615. *7.5; M*

Adiri, I., and Avi-Itzhak, B.: "A time-sharing queue," *Management Sciences* 15, No. 11 (July 1969), 639–657.

Aho, A., et al.: "Principles of optimal page replacement," *J. ACM* 18, (Jan. 1971), 80–93. *4.1; M*

Alsberg, P.A.: "Extensible data features in the operating system language OSL/2," *Proc. Third ACM Symposium on Operating Systems Principles* (Oct. 1971), 31–34.

Alsberg, P.A., and Mills, C.R.: "The structure of the ILLIAC IV operating system," *Proc. Second ACM Symposium on Operating Systems Principles* (Oct. 1969), 92–96.

Ames, S.R., Jr.: "Security kernels: are they the answer to the computer security problem?," *Proceedings Western Electronic Show and Convention (WESCON)*, Western Periodicals Co., North Hollywood, California (1979). *4.5; P*

Andersen, R.E.: "EDP auditing in the 1980's, or, the vanishing paper trail," *ACM SIGSAC Review* 1, No. 1 (Winter 1981-1982), 6–13. Reprinted from Harold J. Highland (Ed.), *Proceedings of the Sixteenth Meeting of the Computer Performance Evaluation Users Group*, National Bureau of Standards Publication 500-65 (1980).

Anderson, M.A., and Sargent, R.G.: "Modeling, evaluation, and performance measurements of time-sharing computer systems," *Computing Reviews* 13, No. 12, ACM 1972, 603–608.

Anonymous: "How to find bottlenecks in computer traffic," *Computer Decisions* 2, No. 4 (1972), 44–48. *7.5; P*

ANSI Committee X3.4.2f: *Report to SPARC from Ad Hoc Committee on Operating System Control Language*, 1971, pp. 155–195. *1.3; P*

Anthony, A.: "Techniques for developing analytical models," *IBM Systems J.* 11, (1972), 316–328. *7.5; M*

Arden, B., and Boettner, D.: "Measurement and performance of a multiprogramming system," *Proc. Second ACM Symposium on Operating Systems Principles* (Oct. 1969), 130–146. *7.5; M*

Arden, B.W., et al.: "Program and addressing structure in a time-sharing environment," *J. ACM* 13, No. 1 (Jan. 1966), 1–16.

Aron, J.D.: "Estimating resources for large programming systems," in [NATO68]. *7.1; P*

Arora, S.R., and Gallo, A.: "Optimization of static loading and sizing of multilevel memory systems," *J. ACM* 20, No. 2 (April 1973), 307–320.

Aschenbrenner, R.A., et al.: "The neurotron monitor system," *Proc. Fall Joint Computer Conference* (Nov. 1971), 31–37.

Atkinson, M.P., Lister, A.M., and Colin, A.J.T.: "Multi-access facilities in a single stream batch processing system," *Computer Bulletin* 14, No. 3 (March 1970), 75–78.

Attanasio, C.R., Markstein, P.W., and Phillips, R.J.: "Penetrating an operating system: a study of VM/370 integrity," *IBM Systems J.* 15, No. 1 (1976), 102–116. *4.5; I*

Auroux, A., and Hans, C.: "The virtual machine concept," *Revue Francaise d'Informatique et de Recherche Operationelle* 15, B3 (1968), 45–51.

Badger, G.F., Jr., Johnson, E.A., and Philips, R.W.: "The Pitt time-sharing system for the IBM System/360: two years' experience," *Proc. AFIPS 1968 Fall Joint Computer Conference*, Vol. 33, AFIPS Press, Montvale, N.J., 1–6.

Baecker, H.D.: "The impact of multi-access," *Computer Bulletin* 11, No. 4 (March 1968), 270–275, 281.

Baecker, H.D.: "Garbage collection for virtual memory systems," *Comm. ACM* 15, No. 11 (Nov. 1972), 981–986. *P*

Baer, J.L.: "A survey of some theoretical aspects of multiprocessing," *Computing Surveys* 5, No. 1 (March 1973), 31–80. *2.4*

Bahler, R.C.: "Steps toward a compiler for BLISS 360," MS Thesis, Naval Postgraduate School, Monterey, Calif. (1972), Document AD-747530. *7.4*

Bairstow, J.N.: "A review of systems evaluation packages," *Computer Decisions* 2, No. 6 (June 1970), 20. *7.5; S, P*

Baker, F.T.: "Chief programmer team management of production programming," *IBM Systems J.* 11, No. 1 (1972), 56–73. *7.3; I, P*

Balzer, R.M.: "EXDAMS — extendable debugging and monitoring system," *Proc. AFIPS 1969 Spring Joint Computer Conference,* AFIPS Press, Montvale, N.J. *7.5*

Balzer, R.M.: "An overview of the ISPL computer system design," *Comm. ACM* 16, No. 2 (Feb. 1973), 117–122.

Balzer, R.M.: "PORTS — A method for dynamic interprogram communication and job control," *Proc. AFIPS 1971 Spring Joint Computer Conference,* Vol. 38 AFIPS Press, Montvale, N.J., 485–489. *4.4; I, P*

Bard, Y.: "Performance criteria and measurement in a time-sharing system," *IBM Systems J.* 10, No. 3 (1971), 193–216. *7.5; M*

Barron, D.W.: *Assemblers and Loaders,* American Elsevier, New York, 1969. *6.2*

Barron, D.W.: *Computer Operating Systems,* Chapman and Hall, London, 1971. *1.1*

Barron, D.W., and Jackson, I.R.: "The evolution of job control languages," *Software — Practice and Experiences* 2, (1972), 143–164. *6.2; P*

Baskett, F., Frowne, J.C., and Raike, W.M.: "The management of a multi-level non-paged memory system," *Proc. AFIPS 1970 Spring Joint Computer Conference,* Vol. 36, AFIPS Press, Montvale, N.J., 459–465.

Batson, A., Ju Shy-Ming, and Wood, D.C.: "Measurements of segment size," *Comm. ACM* 13, No. 3 (March 1970), 155–159.

Beizer, B.: *The Architecture and Engineering of Digital Computer Complexes,* 2 vols., Plenum Press, New York, 1972.

Belady, L.A.: "A study of replacement algorithms for a virtual storage computer," *IBM Systems J.* 5, No. 2 (1966), 78–101. *4.3; M*

Belady, L.A., and Kuhner, C.J." "Dynamic space-sharing in computer systems," *Comm. ACM* 12, No. 5 (May 1969), 282–288. *M*

Belady, L.A., Nelson, R.A., and Shedler, G.S.: "An anomaly in space-time characteristics of certain programs running in a paging environment," *Comm. ACM* 12, No. 6 (June 1969), 349–353. *M*

Bell, C.G., and Newell, A.: *Computer Structures: Readings and Examples,* McGraw-Hill, New York, 1971. *3.1; I*

Bell, D.E., and LaPadula, L.J.: "Computer security model: unified exposition and multics interpretation," THE MITRE CORP., ESD-TR-75-306, HQ Electronic Systems Division, Hanscom AFB, Ma. (June 1975) (NTIS*AD A023588). *4.5; I*

Bell, J.R.: "The quadratic quotient method: a hash code eliminating secondary clustering," *Comm. ACM* 13, No. 2 (Feb. 1970), 107–109. *1.4, 5.2; I, M, P*

Bell, J.R., and Kaman, C.H.: "The linear quotient hash code," *Comm. ACM* 13, No. 11 (Nov. 1970), 675–677. *1.4, 5.2; M*

Benjamin, R.I.: "The Spectra 70/45 emulator for the RCA 301," *Comm. ACM* 8, No. 12 (1965), 748–752. *7.2*

Bensoussan, A., Clingen, C.T., and Daley, R.C.: "The MULTICS virtual memory," *Proc. Second ACM Symposium on Operating Systems Principles* Oct. 1969, ACM, New York, 30–42. *7.1, 5.6; I*

Bernstein, A.J., Detlefsen, G.D., and Kerr, R.H.: "Process control and communication," *Proc. Second ACM Symposium on Operating Systems Principles* (Oct. 1969), 60–66.

Bernstein, A.J., and Sharp, J.C.: "A policy-driven scheduler for a time-sharing system," *Comm. ACM* 14, No. 2 (Feb. 1971), 74–78.

Betourne, C., et al.: "Process management and resource sharing in the multiaccess system ESOPE," *Proc. Second ACM Symposium on Operating Systems Principles* (Oct. 1969), ACM, New York, 67–75.

Bhat, U.N., and Nance, R.E.: "Busy period analysis of a time-sharing system modeled as a semi-Markov process," *J. ACM* 18, No. 2 (April 1971), 221–238.

Bisbey, Richard L., II, and Popek, Gerald J.: "Encapsulation: an approach to operating system security," *Proceedings, 1973 ACM Conference,* San Diego, Cal. Also AD-771-758 (October 1973) (ARPA). *4.5; I*

Bjork, L.A., and Davies, C.T.: "Semantics of the preservation and recovery of integrity in a data system," IBM Technical Report TR 02.540 (Dec. 22, 1972). *3.3*

Blatny, J., et al.: "On the optimization of performance of time-sharing systems by simulation," *Comm. ACM* 15, No. 6 (June 1972), 411–420.

Bloom, B.H.: "Space/time tradeoffs in hash coding with allowable errors," *Comm. ACM* 13, No. 7 (July 1970), 422–426.

Bobrow, D.G., et al.: "TENEX-A paged time-sharing system for the PDP-10," *Comm. ACM* 15, No. 3 (March 1972), 135–144. *Chap. 2*

Boettner, D.W.: "Command (job control) languages for general purpose computing systems," *Advanced Topics in Systems Programming,* Univ. of Mich., 1969. *6.2; P*

Boettner, D.W., and Alexander, M.T.: "MTS," *Operating Systems Review* 4, No. 4 (Dec. 1970), 15. *3.6; P*

Böhm, C., and Jacopini, G.: "Flowcharts, Turing machines, and languages with only two formation rules," *Comm. ACM* 9, No. 5 (May 1966), 366–371. *7.3; I, M*

Bonner, A.J.: "Using system monitor output to improve performance," *IBM Systems J.* 8, No. 4 (1969), 290–298. *7.5; P*

Bonyun, David: "The role of a well defined auditing process in the enforcement of privacy policy and data security," I.P. Sharp Associates Limited, Ottawa, Ontario, Canada (1981). *3.7; P*

Botterill, J.H.: "The design rationale of the system/38 user interface," *IBM Systems J.* 21, No. 4 (1982), 384–423. *6.2*

Bouvard, J.: "Perspective on operating systems," in *Comparative Operating Systems: A Symposium,* Brandon Systems Press, Princeton, N.J., 1969, pp. 43–56. *1.2*

Bowdon, E.K.: "Priority assignment in a network of computers," *IEEE Trans. Computers* C-18, No. 11 (Nov. 1969), 1012–1016.

Braddock, D.M., et al.: *SIMTRAN Manual,* IBM Poughkeepsie, N.Y., 1965. *7.5*

Branstad, Dennis, Gait, Jason, and Katzke, Stuart: "Report of the workshop on cryptography in support of computer security," NBSIR 77-1291 (September 1977). *5.5; P*

Branstad, Dennis: "Computer security and the data encryption standard," NBS Spec. Pub 500-27 (February 1978). *5.5*

Brawn, B.S., and Gustavson, F.G.: "Program behavior in a paging environment," *Proc. AFIPS 1968 Fall Joint Computer Conference,* Vol. 33, Part II, AFIPS Press, Montvale, N.J., 1019–1032. *I, M, P*

Brawn, B.S., Gustavson, F.G., and Mankin, E.S.: "Sorting in a paging environment," *Comm. ACM* 13, No. 8 (Aug. 1970), 483–494. *I, M, P*

Brewer, S.: "Data base or data maze . . . ," *23rd ACM National Conf.,* Brandon Systems Princeton, N.J., (1968), 623–630. *5.4*

Brinch Hansen, P.: "Short-term scheduling in multiprogramming systems," *Proc. Third ACM Symposium on Operating Systems Principles* (Oct. 1971), 101–105. *M*

Brinch Hansen, P., (ed.): *RC4000 Software Multiprogramming System,* RESL No. 55-D140, A/S Regnecentralen, Copenhagen, 1971. *Chap. 2*

Brinch Hansen, P.: "Structured multiprogramming," *Comm. ACM* 15, No. 7 (July 1972), 574-578. *Chap. 2*

Brinch Hansen, P.: "The nucleus of a multiprogramming system," *Comm. ACM* 13, No. 13, No. 4 (April 1970), 238-241, 250.

Broderick, W.R., and Barker, P.J.: "An operating system for the Elliott 903 computer," *Computer Bulletin* 13, No. 7 (July 1969), 228-230.

Brown, G.D.: *System/360 Job Control Language,* Wiley, New York, 1970. *6.2*

Brown, P.J.: "A survey of macro processors," *Annual Review In Automatic Programming,* Vol. 6, Part 2, (1969), 37-87.

Brown, W.S.: "Software portability," *NATO Conference on Software Engineering* (Rome, 1969), 80-84. *7.4; I*

Bruno, J., et al.: "Scheduling independent tasks to reduce mean finishing time," *Operating Systems Review* 7, No. 4 (1973), 102 (abstract only, paper in press). *4.4; I, M*

Buchholz, W.: "A synthetic job for measuring system performance," *IBM Systems J.* 8, (1969), 309-318. *7.5; P*

Buchholz, W.: "File organization and addressing," *IBM Systems J.* 2, No. 2 (1963), 86-111. *5.2; S*

BUR (Burroughs Corp., Detroit)
1. "Narrative Description of B5500" 1023579 (1969).
2. "B5500 MCP Reference Manual" 1042462 (1969).
3. "B5500 Reference Manual" 1021326 (1968).
4. "B6700 MCP Information Manual" 5000086 (1970).
5. "B6700 Program Binder" 5000045 (1970).
6. "B6700 ESPOL Language" 5000094 (1970).
7. "B6700 DC ALGOL" 5000052 (1971).
8. "B6700 Makeuser Program" 5000227 (1971).
9. "B6700 Input/Output Subsystem" 5000185 (1971).
10. "B6700 Sort Program" 5000144 (1971).

Burge, W.H., and Konheim, A.G.: "An accessing model," *J. ACM* 18, No. 3 (July 1971), 400-404.

Burkinshaw, P.: A comment in [NATO70], p. 24. *7.3*

Cadow, H.W.: *OS/360 Job Control Language,* Prentice-Hall, Englewood Cliffs, N.J., 1970. *6.2*

Calingaert, P.: "System performance evaluation: survey and appraisal," *Comm. ACM* 10, No. 1 (Jan. 1967), 12-18. *7.5; S, I*

Campbell, D.J., Cook, W., and Heffner, W.J.: "Three dimensional operating system," in *Comparative Operating Systems: A Symposium,* Brandon Systems Press, Princeton, N.J., 1969, 71-84.

Campbell, D.J., and Heffner, W.J.: "Measurement and analysis of large operating systems during system development," *Proc. AFIPS 1968 Fall Joint Computer Conference,* Vol. 33, AFIPS Press, Montvale, N.J., 903-914. *7.3*

Cantrell, H.N., and Ellison, A.L.: "Multiprogramming system performance measurement and analysis," *Proc. AFIPS 1968 Spring Joint Computer Conference,* AFIPS Press, Montvale, N.J., 213-221. *7.5*

Carlstedt, J.: "Protection errors in operating systems: a selected annotated bibliography and index to terminology," ISI/St-78-10 (1978). *4.5*

CDC (Control Data Corp., Minneapolis, Minn.)
1. "3300/3500 Computer Systems-MASTER Reference Manual" 60213600 (1968).
2. "CYBER 70, Model 74-Reference Manual" Vols. 1,2,3 60347400, 60347300, 60347100 (1971).
3. "CYBER 70, Models 72,73,74, SCOPE Reference Manual" 60307200 (1971).

Chamberlin, D.D., et al.: "A page allocation strategy for multiprogramming systems with virtual memory," *Operating Systems Review* 7, No. 4 (1973), 66–72. *4.2; M*

Chandy, K.M.: "Optimization of information storage systems," *Information and Control* 13, No. 6 (Dec. 1968), 509–526.

Chapin, N.: "An introduction to decision tables," *Data Processing Management Quarterly* 3, No. 3 (1967), 2–23. *7.3*

Chapin, N.: "Program documentation: the valuable burden," *Software Age* 2, No. 4 (1968), 24–26, 28–30. *7.3; I*

Chapin, N.: "Common file organization techniques compared," *Proc. AFIPS 1969*, Fall Joint Computer Conference, AFIPS Press, Montvale, N.J., 413–422. *5.2*

Chapin, N.: "A comparison of file organization techniques," *Proc. 24th ACM National Conference*, ACM, New York (1969), 273–283. *5.2*

Chapin N.: "Flow charting with the ANSI standard," *Computing Surveys* 2, No. 2 (1970), 119–146. *7.3; P*

Chapin, N.: *Flowcharts*, Auerbach, Princeton, J.J., 1971. *7.3*

Chapin, N.: "Flowchart packages and the ANSI standard," *Datamation*, 18, No. 9 (1972), 48–53. *7.3; S, P*

Chapin, N.: "Operating systems," in *Computers*, Van Nostrand-Reinhold, New York, 1971, 460–483.

Cheng, P.S.: "Trace-driven system modelling," *IBM Systems J.* 8, (1969), 280–289. *7.5*

Christensen, C., and Hause, A.D.: "A multiprogramming virtual memory system for a small computer," *Proc. AFIPS 1970 Spring Joint Computer Conference*, Vol. 36, AFIPS Press, Montvale, N.J., 683–690.

Clark, D.D., et al.: *The Classroom Information and Computing Service*, Project MAC TR-80, MIT (Jan. 1971). *3.1, 3.4; P*

Clarke, K.E., and Johnson, C.B.C.: "A comparison of time-sharing languages," *Proc. of the Conference on Man-Computer Interaction: IEE Conferences, Publication Number 68*, Inst. for Elec. Eng., London, 1970. *6.2; 5*

CODASYL Systems Committee: "Introduction to feature analysis of generalized data base management systems," *Comm. ACM* 14, 5 (May 1971), 308–318. *5.4; I*

CODASYL: *Data Base Task Group Report* (1971). *5.4; I*

Coffman, E.G., Jr., Elphick, M., and Shoshani, A.: "System deadlocks," *Computing Surveys* 3, No. 2 (June 1971), 67–78. *2.2; S, M*

Coffman, E.G., Jr., and Kleinrock, L.: "Computer scheduling measures and their counter-measures," *Proc. AFIPS 1968 Spring Joint Computer Conference*, Vol. 32, AFIPS Press, Montvale, N.J., 11–21.

Coffman, E.G., Jr., Muntz, R.R., and Trotter, H.: "Waiting time distributions for processor-sharing systems," *J. ACM*, 17, No. 1 (Jan. 1970), 123–130.

Coffman, E.G., Jr., and Muntz, R.R.: "Models of pure time-sharing disciplines for resource allocation," *Proc. 24th ACM National Conference*, Vol. 33 (San Francisco, Aug. 1969), 217–228.

Coffman, E.G., Jr., and Ryan, T.A., Jr.: "A study of storage partitioning using a mathematical model of locality," *Comm. ACM* 15, No. 3 (March 1972), 185–190.

Coffman, E.G., Jr., and Varian, L.C.: "Further experimental data on the behavior of programs in a paging environment," *Comm. ACM* 11, No. 7 (July, 1968), 471–474.

Coffman, E.G., Jr.: "Feedback queueing models for time-shared systems," *J. ACM* 15, No. 4 (Oct. 1968), 549–576.

Coffman, E.G., Jr., and Denning, P.J.: *Operating Systems Theory*, Prentice-Hall, Englewood Cliffs, N.J., 1973. *Chap. 4; I, M*

Cohen, D.: "A parallel process definition and control system," *Proc. AFIPS 1968 Fall Joint Computer Conference*, Vol. 33, Part II, AFIPS Press, Montvale, N.J., 1043–1050.

Cohen, L.J.: "S3, the system and software simulator," *Digest of Second Conference on Applications of Simulation,* New York, 1968.

Cohen, L.J.: *Operating System Analysis and Design,* Spartan Books, New York, 1970. *5.3, 7.1; P*

Coleman, D.: "Operating systems: development for a computer family," in *Comparative Operating Systems: a Symposium,* Brandon Systems Press, Princeton, N.J., 1969, 57–70. *Chap. 2*

Colin, A.: *Introduction to Operating Systems,* American Elsevier, New York, 1971. *1.1*

Collier, W.W.: *System Deadlocks,* IBM Technical Report TR00.1756, Poughkeepsie, N.Y. 1968. *2.2; M*

Conrow, K., and Smith, R.G.: "NEATER 2: a PL/1 source statement reformatter," *Comm. ACM* 13, No. 11 (Nov. 1970), 669–675. *7.4*

Consiglio, W.C.: *Defensive Coding Techniques in the Generalized Trace Facility,* IBM Technical Report TR00.2324, Poughkeepsie, N.Y. 1972. *7.3; P*

Conway, M.E.: "How committees invent," *Datamation* 14, No. 4 (April 1968). *Chap. 7*

Corbató, F.J., et al.: "MULTICS, the first seven years," *Proc. 1972 Spring Joint Computer Conference,* AFIPS Press, Montvale, N.J. *Chap. 2; I*

Corbató, F.J.: "PL/1 as a tool for system programming," *Datamation* 15, No. 5 (May 1969), 68–76. *7.4; I*

Corbató, F.J., and Saltzer, J.H.: "Some considerations of supervisor program design for multiplexed computer systems," *Proc. IFIP Congress 1968,* Thompson, Washington, D.C., 66–71.

Corbató, F.J., and Vyssotsky, R.A.: "Introduction and overview of the MULTICS system," *Proc. AFIPS 1965 Fall Joint Computer Conference,* Vol. 27 AFIPS Press, Montvale, N.J., 185–196. *1.1, Chap. 2*

COSINE Committee: "An undergraduate course on operating system principles," National Academy of Engineering, (June 1971). *7.7; S, I*

Courtney, R.H., Jr.: "Security risk assessment in electronic data processing systems," IBM TR-21.700, SCD Kingston, New York (December 1975). *Ap. D; I, P*

Courtois, P.J., et al.: "Concurrent control with readers and writers," *Comm. ACM* 14, No. 10 (Oct. 1971), 667–668.

Crisman, P.A.: *The Compatible Time-Sharing System: A Programmers Guide,* MIT Press, Cambridge, Mass., 1965. *1.1*

Cuttle, G., and Robinson, P.B.: *Executive Programs and Operating Systems,* American Elsevier, New York, 1970. *1.1*

Dahl, O.J., Dijkstra, E.W., and Hoare, C.A.R., *Structured Programming.* Academic Press, New York, 1972.

Daley, R.C., and Dennis, J.B.: "Virtual memory, processes, and sharing in MULTICS," *Comm. ACM* 11, No. 5 (May 1968), 306–312.

Darga, K.: "On-line inquiry under a small-system operating system," *IBM Systems J.* 9, No. 1 (1970), 2–11.

David, E.E., Jr., in [NATO68]. *7.3*

Dean, A.L., Jr.: "Development of the Logicon 2+2 system," *Proc. AFIPS 1970 Fall Joint Computer Conference,* Vol. 37, AFIPS Press, Montvale, N.J., 169–180.

DEC (Digital Equipment Corp., Maynard, Mass.)
  1. "PDP-18 Batch Processing" (1968).
  2. "PDP-10 Reference Handbook" (1969).
  3. "PDP-8 User's Handbook" 5037 (1965).
  4. "Small Computer Handbook" C-800 (1968).

DeFiore, C.R., and Berra, P.B.: "A quantitative analysis of the utilization of associative memories in data management," Rome Air Development Center, Rome, N.Y., (1972). *5.2; M*

Delbrouck, L.E.N.: "A feedback queuing system with batch arrivals, bulk service, and queue-dependent service time," *J. ACM* 17, (April 1970), 314–323.

DeMillo, R.A., Lipton, R.J., and Perlis, A.J.: "Social processes and proofs of theorems and programs," *Communications of the ACM* 22, No. 5 (May 1979), 271–280. *7.3; P*

Denning, Dorothy E.: "Secure statistical databases with random sample queries," *ACM Transactions on Database Systems* 5, No. 3 (September 1980), 291–315. *5.4; I*

Denning, P.J.: *Queuing Models for File Memory Operation,* Project MAC-TR-21, MIT (Oct. 1965).

Denning, P.J.: "A note on paging drum efficiency," *Computing Surveys* 4, (March 1972), 1–4. *S, M*

Denning, P.J.: "A statistical model for console behavior in multiuser computers," *Comm. ACM* 11, No. 9 (Sept. 1968), 605–612. *M*

Denning, P.J.: "Equipment configuration in balanced computer systems," *IEEE Trans. Computers* C-18, No. 11 (Nov. 1969), 1008–1012. *M*

Denning, P.J.: "The working set model for program behavior," *Comm. ACM* 11, No. 5 (May 1968), 323–333. *Chap. 4; I, M*

Denning, P.J.: "Trashing: Its causes and prevention," *Proc. AFIPS 1968 Fall Joint Computer Conference,* Vol. 33, AFIPS Press, Montvale, N.J., 915–922. *I, M*

Denning, P.J.: "Virtual memory," *Computing Surveys* 2, No. 3 (Sept. 1970), 153–189. *4.2; S, I, M*

Denning, P.J.: "Resource allocation in multiprocess computer systems," PhD Thesis, MIT, Cambridge, Mass., MAC-TR-50, May 1968.

Denning, P.J., and Schwartz, S.C.: "Properties of the working set model," *Comm. ACM* 15, No. 3 (March 1972), 191–198; *corrigendum,* 16, (Feb. 1973), 122. *M*

Dennis, J.B.: "Segmentation and the design of multi-programmed computer systems," in *Programming Systems and Languages,* McGraw-Hill, New York, 1967, 699–713. *I*

Dennis, J.B.: "Segmentation and the design of multi-programmed computer systems," *J. ACM* 12, No. 4 (Oct. 1965), 589–602. *I*

Dennis, J.B.: "Programming generality, parallelism and computer architecture," *Proc. IFIP Congress 1968,* North-Holland, Amsterdam, 1969, 484–492.

Dennis, J.B., and Van Horn, E.C.: "Programming semantics for multiprogrammed computations," *Comm. ACM* 9, No. 3 (Mar. 1966), 143–155.

Denver, J.L.: *System Using Control Libraries as a Management Tool,* IBM Technical Report TR00.1515, IBM, Poughkeepsie, N.Y. 1966. *7.2*

Dijkstra, E.W.: "Cooperating sequential processes," in *Programming Languages* (F. Genuys, ed.), Academic Press, New York, 1968, pp. 43–112. *2.2; I, M*

Dijkstra, E.W.: "The structure of the THE multiprogramming system," *Comm. ACM* 11, No. 5 (May 1968), 341–346. *2.2, Chap. 7; I*

Dijkstra, E.W.: "Complexity controlled by hierarchical ordering of function and variability," *NATO Conference On Software Engineering* (Garmisch, Germany, Oct. 1968), 181–185.

Dijkstra, E.W.: Letter to the editor, *Comm. ACM* 11, No. 3 (March 1968), 147–148. *7.3*

Dodd, G.G.: "Elements of data management systems," *Computing Surveys* 1, No. 2 (June 1969), 117–132. *5.2*

Dodds, W.R.: "Multiprogramming in a medium-sized hybrid environment," *Proc. AFIPS 1970 Fall Joint Computer Conference,* Vol. 37, AFIPS Press, Montvale, N.J., (Nov. 1970). 363–368.

Doherty, W.J.: "Scheduling TSS/360 for responsiveness," *Proc. AFIPS 1970 Fall Joint Computer Conference,* Vol. 37, AFIPS Press, Montvale, N.J., 97–112. *P*

Donovan, J.J.: *Systems Programming,* McGraw-Hill, New York, 1972.

Drummond, M.E., Jr.: "A perspective on system performance evaluation," *IBM Systems J.* 8, (1969), 252–263. *7.5*

Earl, D.P., and Bugely, F.L.: "Basic time-sharing: a system of computing principles," *Proc. Second ACM Symposium On Operating Systems Principles* (Oct. 1969), 75–79.

Easton, W.B.: "Process synchronization without long-term interlock," *Proc. Third ACM Symposium On Operating Systems Principles* (Oct. 1971), 95–100.

Ellis, T.O., and Sibley, W.L.: "On the problem of directness in computer graphics," in *Engineering Concepts in Computer Graphics,* W.A. Benjamin, New York, 1968. *5.5*

Elmendorf, W.R.: *Controlling the Functional Testing of an Operating System,* IBM Technical Report TR00.1729, IBM, Poughkeepsie, N.Y., 1969. *7.3*

Engles, R.W.: *A Tutorial on Data Base Organization,* IBM Technical Report TR00.2004, IBM, Poughkeepsie, N.Y., 1970. *5.5; I*

Engles, R.W.: "An analysis of the April 1971 data base task group report," IBM (1971). *5.4; I*

Estrin, G., and Kleinrock, L.: "Measures, models, and measurements for time-shared computer utilities," *Proc. ACM Conference 1967,* 85–96. *7.5*

Evans, T.G., and Darley, D.L.: "On-line debugging techniques: a survey," *Proc. Fall Joint Computer Conference 1966,* Spartan, Montvale, N.J. (1966), 37–50. *7.3; S*

Fabry, R.S.: "The case for capability-based computers," *Operating Systems Review* 7, No. 4 (1973), 120 (abstract only, paper in press). *4.1; I*

Falkoff, A.V.: "Criteria for a system design language," in [NATO70], 88–93. *7.4*

Farina, M.V.: *Flowcharting,* Prentice-Hall, Englewood Cliffs, N.J., 1970. *7.3*

Faust, R.S.: *Multiprogramming on Small Computers,* Moore School of Electrical Engineering, Univ. of Pennsylvania, Philadelphia, 1969.

Fenichel, R.R., and Grossman, A.J.: "An analytic model of multiprogrammed computing," *Proc. 24th ACM National Conference* (San Francisco, Aug. 1969), 717–721. *7.5*

Ferdinand, A.E.: *Quality in Programming,* IBM Technical Report TR 21.485, IBM, Kingston N.Y., 1972. *7.1; M*

Fernandez, E.B., Summers, R.C., and Wood, C.: *Data Base Security and Integrity,* Addison-Wesley, Reading, Mass., 1981. *5.4; I, P*

Fine, G.H., Jackson, C.W., and McIsaac, P.V.: "Dynamic program behavior under paging," *Proc. 21st ACM National Conference, 1966,* MDI Publications, Wayne, Pa., 223–228.

Fischer, J.A.: "B 6500/B7500 MCP design concepts," in *Comparative Operating Systems: a Symposium.* Brandon Systems Press, Princeton, N.J., 1969, pp. 95–105.

Fitzsimmons, R.M.: "TRIDENT-a new maintenance weapon," *Proc AFIPS 1972, Fall Joint Computer Conference,* AFIPS Press, Montvale N.J. (1972), 255–262. *7.5*

Flaks, M., and White, G.L.: *Introduction to PERT/CPM,* Booz, Allen, and Hamilton, New York, 1967.

Flores, I.: *Computer Sorting,* Prentice-Hall, Englewood Cliffs, N.J., 1969. *3.5; M*

Flores, I.: "Intraprogram documentation," *Software – Practice and Experience* 2, No. 4 (1972), 353–358.

Fontao, R.O.: "A concurrent algorithm for avoiding deadlocks," *Proc. Third ACM Symposium On Operating Systems Principles* (Oct. 1971), 72–79. *2.2; M*

Forsdick, H.C., and Reed D.P.: "Patterns of security violations: multiple references to arguments," MIT (1975). *4.5*

Foster, C.C.: "An unclever time-sharing system," *Computing Surveys* 3, No. 1 (March 1971), 23–48. *Chap. 2*

Foster, C.L.: "Operating system 360," in *Comparative Operating Systems: a Symposium,* Brandon Systems Press, Princeton, N.J., 1969, 85–94. *Chap. 2*

Frailey, D.J.: "A practical approach to managing resources and avoiding deadlocks," *Comm. ACM* 16, No. 5 (May 1973), 323–329. *2.2*

Frank, H.: "Analysis and optimization of disk storage devices for time-sharing systems." *J. ACM* 16, No. 4 (Oct. 1969), 602–620. *M*

Franta, W.R.: "A note on storage allocation for CDC 6600," *Computer Bulletin* 14, No. 1 (Jan. 1970), 10-12.

Fraser, A.G.: "User control in a multi access system," *Computer J.* 2, No. 1 (May 1968), 12-16.

Fraser, A.G.: "On the meaning of names in programming systems," *Comm. ACM* 14, No. 6 (June 1971) 409-416. *6.1*

Freiberger, W., (ed.): *Statistical Computer Performance Evaluation*, Academic Press, New York, 1972.

Friertag, R.J., and Organick, E.J.: "The MULTICS input/output system," *Proc. Third ACM Symposium On Operating Systems Principles* (Oct. 1971), 35-41. *3.2*

Fuchi, K., et al.: "A program simulator by partial interpretation," *Proc. Second ACM Symposium On Operating Systems Principles* (Princeton, N.J., Oct. 1969), 97-104.

Fuchs, E., and Jackson, P.E.: "Estimates of distributions of random variables for certain computer communications traffic models," *Comm. ACM* 13, No. 12 (Dec. 1970), 752-757. *M*

Fuller, S.H.: "Random arrival and control of commands," *Operating Systems Review* 7, No. 4 (1973), 54-57. *4.2; I; M*

Gaines, R.S.: "An operating system based on the concept of a supervisory computer," *Proc. Third ACM Symposium On Operating Systems Principles* (Oct. 1971), 17-23.

Gaver, D.P.: "Analysis of remote terminal backlogs under heavy demand conditions," *J. ACM* 18 (July 1971), 405-415.

GEN (General Electric Corp., now HIS)
    1.   "General Electric GECOS III Reference Manual" (1969).

Gerhart, Susan L.: "Program verification in the 1980's: problems, perspectives and opportunities," ISI Report SR-78-71 (1978). *7.3; I, P*

Ghosh, S.P., and Senko, M.E.: "File organization: on the selection of random access points for sequential files," *J. ACM* 16, No. 4 (1969), 569-579. *5.2*

Gilbert, P., and Chandler, W.J.: "Interference between communicating parallel processes," *Comm. ACM* 15, No. 6 (June 1972), 427-437.

Gillette, H.C.: "Aids in the production of maintainable software," in [NATO68], 111. *7.3*

Glein, G.A.: *Program Flowcharting*, Holt, Reinhart, Winston, New York, 1970. *7.3*

Goldstein, A., et al.: *TMGP-Test Matrix Generating Program*, IBM Technical Report TR00.2353, 1972. *7.3*

Gottlieb, C.E., and MacEwen, S.: "System evaluation tools," in [NATO70], 93-99. *7.5*

Gracon, T.J., et al.: "A high performance computing system for time critical applications," *Proc. AFIPS 1971 Fall Joint Computer Conference*, AFIPS Press, Montvale, N.J., 549-560. *Chap. 2*

Graham, G.S., and Denning, P.J.: "Protection – principles and practice," *AFIPS Spring Joint Computer Conference, 1972*, AFIPS Press, Montvale, N.J., 417-429. *Chap. 1*

Graham, R.L.: "Bounds on multiprocessing timing anomalies," *SIAM J. Appl. Math.* 17, No. 2 (March 1969), 416-429. *M*

Graham, R.M., et al.: "A software design and evaluation system," *Comm. ACM* 16, No. 2 (Feb. 1973), 110-116. *7.1*

Graham, R.M.: "Protection in an information processing utility," *Comm. ACM* 11, No. 5 (May 1968), 365-369. *3.1, 4.1; S, I, P*

Gries, D.: *Compiler Construction for Digital Computers*, Wiley, New York, 1971. *3.4; I*

Grihalva, Richard A.: "Auditing load libraries," *EDPACS Newsletter* (October 1977), 1-6. *3.7*

Grochow, J.M.: "Real-time graphic display of time-sharing system operating characteristics," *Proc. AFIPS 1969 Fall Joint Computer Conference*, Vol. 35, AFIPS Press, Montvale, N.J., 379-386.

Gruenberger, F.: *Computing Reviews* 11, No. 6 (1970), 329-330. *7.3*

Gunderman, R.E.: "A glimpse into program maintenance," *Datamation* 19, No. 6 (1973), 99-101. *7.5*

Gunton, A.: "Recovery procedures for direct access commercial systems," *Computer J.* 13, No. 2 (May 1970), 123-126.

Habermann, A.N.: "Prevention of system deadlocks," *Comm. ACM* 12, No. 7 (July 1969), 373-377, 385. *2.2; I, M*

Habermann, A.N.: "Synchronization of communicating processes," *Comm. ACM* 15, No. 11 (Nov. 1972), 171-176. *I, M*

Habermann, A.N.: "On the harmonious cooperation of abstract machines," Doctoral Thesis, Technological University of Eindhoven, Eindhoven, Netherlands, 1967. *I, M*

Habermann, A.N.: "Synchronization of communicating processes," *Proc. Third ACM Symposium On Operating Systems Principles* (Oct. 1971), 80-85. *I, M*

Hamlet, R.G.: "Efficient multiprogramming resource allocation and accounting," *CACM* 16, No. 6 (June 1973), 337-342. *2.3, 4.5*

Hammer, C.: "Operating systems and multiprogramming overview," *Data Processing*, Vol. 13, Data Processing Management Association, Park Ridge, Ill., 1968, 19-20.

Hanford, K.V.: "Automatic generation of test cases," *IBM Systems J.* 9 No. 4 (1970), 242-257. *7.3*

Hansen, W.J.: "User engineering principles for interactive systems," *Proc. AFIPS 1971 Fall Joint Computer Conference,* AFIPS Press, Montvale, N.J., (1971), 523-532. *6.2*

Harris, S.J.: *A Comparison of System Commands and Editing Facilities in Conversational Time Sharing Systems,* Univ. of North Carolina, Chapel Hill, N.C., 1970. *6.2*

Hart, L.E.: "The user's guide to evaluation products," *Datamation* 16, (1970), 32-35. *7.5; S, P*

Hartley, D.F., Landy, B., and Needham, R.M.: "The structure of a multiprogramming supervisor," *Computer J.* 11, No. 3 (Nov. 1968), 247-255. *Chap. 2*

Havender, J.W.: "Avoiding deadlock in multitasking systems," *IBM Systems J.* 7, No. 2 (1968), 74-84. *2.2; I, P*

Heacox, H.C., Jr., and Purdom, P.W., Jr.: "Analysis of two time-sharing queuing models," *J. ACM* 19, (Jan. 1972), 70-91.

Hebalkar, P.G. *Deadlock-Free Sharing of Resources in Asynchronous Systems,* Project MAC-TR75 (Sept. 1970). *4.1; M*

Heine, S.: *Über Einege Probleme bei Kommando-Sprachen,* (On Some Problems in Command Languages), 1971), available from the author, IBM Labor, 703 Boblingen, 220 Schonaicher First, W. Germany. *6.2; P*

Hellerman, H.: "Some principles of time-sharing scheduler strategies," *IBM Systems J.* 8, No. 2 (1968), 94-117. *M, P*

Hellerman, H.: *Digital Computer System Principles,* McGraw-Hill, New York, 1967. *5.3; M, P*

Hellerman, H.: "Complementary replacement – a meta scheduling principle," *Proc. Second ACM Symposium On Operating Systems Principles* (Oct. 1969), 43-46.

Hellerman, H., and Smith, H.J., Jr.: "Throughput analysis of some idealized input, output, and compute overlap configurations," *Computing Surveys* 2, (June 1970), 111-118. *5.3; M, P*

Hetzel, W.C. (ed.): *Program Test Methods,* Prentice-Hall, Englewood Cliffs, N.J., 1973. *7.5*

Hill, J.C.: *Priority Structures for Multiaccess Memory Systems,* Oregon State Univ., Corvallis, Oregon, 1969.

HIS (Honeywell Information Systems, Minneapolis, Minn.)
1.   "Honeywell Mod 4 Systems Manual" (1970).
2.   "System 700-Summary Description" 6010 (1972).

Hoare, C.A.R., and Perrott, R.H., (eds.): *Operating Systems Techniques,* Academic Press, New York, 1973.

Hoffman, Lance J.: "Computers and privacy: a survey," *ACM Computing Surveys* 1, No. 2 (June 1969). *Ap. D; S*

Holt, R.C.: "Comments on prevention of system deadlocks," *Comm. ACM* 14, No. 1 (Jan. 1971), 36–38. *2.2; M*

Holt, R.C.: "Some deadlock properties of computer systems," *Computing Surveys* 4, (Sept. 1972), 179–196. *2.2; I, M*

Holt, R.C.: "On deadlock in computer systems," PhD Thesis, Cornell University, Ithaca, N.Y. (1971). *2.2; I, M*

Holt R.C.: "Some deadlock properties of computer systems," *Proc. Third ACM Symposium On Operating Systems Principles* (Oct. 1971), 64–71. *2.2; I, M*

Hopkins, M.E.: Comment in [NATO70], 20. *7.5*

Hopkins, M.E.: "A case for the GOTO," *Proc. 27th ACM National Conference (1972),* 787–790. *7.4*

Hornbuckle, G.D.: "A multiprogramming monitor for small machines," *Comm. ACM* 10, No. 5 (May 1967), 273–278.

Horning, J.J., and Randell, B.: "Structuring complex processes," Report No. RC 2459, T.J. Watson Research Center, IBM, Yorktown Heights, N.Y., 1969.

Horning, J.J., and Randell, B.: "Process structuring," *Computing Surveys,* 5, No. 1 (March 1973), 5–30. *4.4*

Howard, J.H.: "Mixed solutions for the deadlock problem," *Comm. ACM* 16, No. 7 (July 1973), 427–430. *2.2*

Huesman, L.R., and Goldberg, R.P.: "Evaluating systems through simulation," *Computer J.* 10, (1967), 150–155. *7.5*

Hume, J.N.P., and Rolfson, C.B.: "Scheduling for fast turnaround in job-at-a-time processing," *Proc. IFIP Congress 1968* (Edinburgh, Scotland, Aug. 1968), 60–64. *P*

Hume, J.N.P.: "Job-at-a-time processing from multiple remote terminals," *Proc. 5th National Conference of the Computer Society of Canada,* J.L. Pennington, Winnipeg, Manitoba, Canada, 1967, 127–129.

Husson, S.S. *Microprogramming-Principles and Practices,* Prentice-Hall, Englewood Cliffs, N.J., 1970. *7.2; I, P*

IBM (International Business Machines, White Plains, N.Y.)
1. "OS/VS System Generation" GC 26-3790 (1972).
2. "OS/VS Linkage Editor and Loader" GC 28-3813 (1972).
3. "System/360 Time Sharing System Command System-User's Guide" C 28-2001 (1966).
4. "System/360 Operating System Job Control Language" GC28-6704 (1970).
5. "Operator's Library: OS/VS2 Reference" GC 38-0210 (1972).
6. "IBSYS Operating System" C 28-6248 (1963).
7. "OS/VS1 Planning and User's Guide" C 24-5090 (1972).
8. "OS/VS System Control Blocks" GC 28-6628 (1973).
9. "OS/VS Virtual Storage Access Method (VSAM) Planning Guide" GC 26-3799 (1973).
10. "OS-Service Aids" GC 28-6719 (1974).
11. "Introduction to Virtual Storage in System/370" GR 20-4260 (1972).
12. "OS-Data Management Services" GC 26-3746 (1971).
13. "OS-Linkage Editor (F)" GY 28-6667 (1972).
14. "OS-Programmer's Guide to Debugging" GC 28-6670 (1972).
15. "Linkage Editor and Loader" GC 28-6538 (1972).
16. "System/370 Principles of Operation" GA 22-7000 (1972).
17. "System/360 Principles of Operation" GA 22-6821 (1970).
18. "Virtual Machine Facility/370: Introduction" GC 20-1800 (1974).
19. "GPSS V-Introduction" B 200001 (1972).
20. "RTOS User's Guide" Houston (1967).
21. "7090/7094 Support Package for System/360" C 28-6501 (1965).

22. "Chief Programmer Teams: Principles and Procedures" FSC 71-5108 (1971).
23. "OS/VS1 Supervisor Logic" SY 24-5155 (1972).
24. "System/360 TEXT360: Introduction and Reference Manual" C 35-0002 (1969).
25. "I/O Supervisor Logic" GY 28-6616 (1972).
26. "Operators Library OS/VS 2 Display Console" GC 38-0260 (1974).
27. "OS/VS MVS System Management Facilities" 28-1030 (1981).
28. "FORTRAN G Logic" GY 28-6638 (1968).
29. "PL/I F Logic" GY 28-6800 (1971).
30. "HIPO: Design Aid and Documentation Tool" SR 20-9413 (1972).
31. "Data Management for System Programmers" GC 28-0631 (1972).
32. "Data Security Through Cryptography" GC 22-9062 (1977).
33. "OS/VS2 MVS Utilities" GC 26-3902 (1977).
34. "OS/VS2 MVS Resource Access Control Facility (RACF) General Information Manual" GC 28-0722 (1980).
35. "OS/VS Mass Storage System (MSS) Services: Reference Information" GC 35-0017 (1980).
36. "OS/VS2 MVS Hierarchical Storage Manager: User's Guide" SH 35-0024 (1981).
37. "IBM 8100 Information System Principles of Operation" GA 23-0031 (1981).
38. "System/38 Introduction" GC 26-3829 (1978).
39. "Introducing the IBM 3800 Printing Subsystem and its Programming" GC 26-3829 (1979).
40. "System Modification Program" GC 28-0673 (1980).

Iliffe, J.K., and Jodeit, J.G.: "A dynamic storage allocation scheme," *Computer J.* 5, (1962) 200–209. *4.2*

Irons, E.T.: "A rapid-turnaround multiprogramming system," *Comm. ACM* 8, No. 3 (March 1965), 152–157. *Chap. 2*

James, E.B., and Partridge, D.P.: "Adaptive correction of program statements," *Comm. ACM* 16, (1973), 27–37. *6.2; P*

Jamison, F.L., (ed.): *Comparative Operating Systems: a Symposium,* Brandon/Systems Press, Princeton, N.J., 1969. *Chap. 2*

Johnston, J.B.: "Structure of multiple activity algorithms," *Proc. Second ACM Symposium on Operating Systems Principles* (Princeton, N.J., Oct. 1969), 80–83.

Jones, P.D.: "Operating system structures," *Proc. IFIP Congress 1968,* North-Holland Publishing Co. Amsterdam, 1969, 525–530.

Jones, R.M.: "Factors affecting the efficiency of a virtual memory," *IEEE Trans. Computers* C-18, No. 11 (Nov. 1969), 1004–1008.

Judd, R.: "Practical modular programming," *Computer Bulletin* 14, No. 1 (Jan. 1970), 4–7. *7.3*

Kahn, G.: "An approach to systems correctness," *Proc. Third ACM Symposium on Operating Systems Principles* (Oct. 1971), 86–94. *7.3*

Karafin, B.J.: "A sampled-data system simulation language," in *System Analysis by Digital Computer,* (F.F. Kuo, ed.), Wiley, New York, 1955. *7.2*

Karger, P.A., and Shell, R.R.: "Multics security evaluation: vulnerability analysis," ESD-TR74-193, Vol. 11, HQ Electronic Systems Division, Hanscom AFB, Ma. (June 1974) (NTIS AD A001120). *4.5*

Karp, R.M., and Miller, R.E.: "Parallel program schemata," *J. Computer and System Sciences* 3, No. 2 (May 1969), 147–195.

Karush, A.D.: "Two approaches for measuring the performance of time-sharing systems," *Proc. Second ACM Symposium on Operating Systems Principles* (Oct. 1969), 159–166. *7.5*

Karush, A.D.: "Two approaches for measuring the performance of time-sharing systems," *Software Age* (March 1970), 10–13. *7.5*

Karush, A.D.: "Evaluating time-sharing systems using the benchmark method," *Data Processing Magazine* (May 1970), 42–44. *7.5*

Katzan, H. Jr.: *Advanced Programming,* Van Nostrand-Reinhold, New York, 1970.

Katzan, H. Jr.: *Operating Systems: A Pragmatic Approach,* Van Nostrand-Reinhold, New York, 1973.

Katzan, H., Jr.: "Operating systems architecture," *Proc. AFIPS 1970 Spring Joint Computer Conference,* Vol. 36, AFIPS Press, Montvale, N.J., 109–119. *7.1*

Keefe, D.D.: "Hierarchical control programs for systems evaluation," *IBM Systems J.* 7, No. 2 (1968), 123–133. *7.5*

Keister. W., et al.: "No. 1 ESS: system organization and objectives." *Bell System Technical J.* 43, No. 5 (1964), 1831–1844.

Kellington, M.R., (ed.): *Proc. Second ACM Symposium on Operating System Principles,* ACM, New York, (Oct. 1969). *Chap. 1*

Kennedy, P.R.: "ADEPT-50 time sharing user's guide: user/executive interface and summary of ADEPT-50 executive functions," System Development Corp., Santa Monica, Calif., 1969. *6.1*

Kent, S.T.: "A comparison of some aspects of public-key and conventional cryptosystems," *Proceedings of the International Conference on Communications,* IEEE, Boston, Mass. (1979), 431–435. *5.5; P*

Kernigham, B.W.: "Optimal segmentation points for programs," *Proc. Second ACM Symposium on Operating Systems Principles,* Princeton, N.J., (Oct. 1969), 47–53.

Keyser, S.J.: "Linguistic theory and system design," *Information System Science* (1965), 495–504. *6.2*

Kho, J.W., and Pinkerton, T.B.: "Optimal I/O buffer size for multiprogramming," Univ. of Wisconsin Computer Science Dept. Report 107, (Jan. 1971).

Kilburn, T., Payne, R.B., and Howarth, D.J.: "The Atlas supervisor," in *Programming Systems and Languages,* McGraw-Hill, New York, 1967, 661–682. *1.1, Chap. 2*

Kimbleton, S.R.: "The role of models in performance evaluation," *Comm. ACM* 15, No. 7 (July 1972), 586–590. *7.5*

Kleinrock, L.: "A continuum of time-sharing scheduling algorithms," *Proc. AFIPS 1970 Spring Joint Computer Conference,* Vol. 36, AFIPS Press, Montvale, N.J., 453–459.

Kleinrock, L., and Muntz, R.R.: "Processor sharing queuing models of mixed scheduling disciplines for time-shared systems," *J. ACM* 19, (July 1972), 463–482.

Kline, Charles S., and Popek, Gerald J.: "Public key vs. conventional key encryption," *Proceedings National Computer Conference 1979,* 831–838. *5.5*

Knopp, H.: "Testverfahren (Testing)," in *Systemprogrammierung (Systems Programming),* (K. Ganzhorn et al., ed.), Oldenbourg, Munich, 1972. *7.3; P*

Knuth, D.E.: *The Art of Computer Programming Fundamental Algorithms,* Vol. 1, Addison Wesley, Reading, Mass., 1968. *1.4, 5.3; I, M*

Knuth, D.E., and McNeely, J.L.: "SOL-a symbolic language for general purpose systems simulation," *IEEE Trans. on Computers* 13 (1964), 401–408. *7.5*

Kobayashi, R.: "Some recent progress in analytical models," RC 3990, IBM, 1972. *7.5*

Konheim, A.G., and Meister, B.: "Service in a loop system," *J. ACM* 19, (Jan. 1972), 92–108.

Kosaraju, S.R.: "Limitations of Dijkstra's semaphore primitives and petri nets," *Operating Systems Review* 7, No. 4 (1973), 122–126. *4.4; I, M*

Kuck, D.J., and Lawrie, D.H.: "The use and performance of memory hierarchies: a survey," *Report No. 363,* Univ. of Illinois, Urbana, Dec. 1969. *S*

Kuck, D.J., and Lawrie, D.H.: "The use and performance of memory hierarchies: a survey," in *Software Engineering* (J.T. Tou, ed.) Vol. 1, Academic Press, New York, 1970, 45–78. *S*

Kuehner, C.J., and Randell, B.: "Demand paging in perspective," *Proc. AFIPS 1968 Fall Joint Computer Conference,* AFIPS Press, Montvale, N.J., 1011–1018.

Kurzban, S.A.: "The future of secure electronic data processing," *Proceedings of the Third U.S. Army Automation Security Workshop,* Williamsburg, Va. (December 1980). *Ap. D; P*

Kurzban, S.A.: "A selective, briefly annotated bibliography of works on data security and privacy," *Computers and Security,* 1, No. 1 (1982), 57–64. *P*

Kurzban, S.A.: "Programming for Data Security," *Proceedings of the First Annual IACSS Conference and Exhibition,* Orlando, Fla. (May 1982). *3.7*

Kurzban, S.A.: *Computers and Reason: A Sociobiological View of Technology and Society,* (forthcoming), 1983. *6.3*

Lampson, B.W.: "A scheduling philosophy for multiprocessing systems," *Comm. ACM* 11, No. 5 (May 1968), 347–360.

Lampson, B.W.: "Dynamic protection structures," *Proc. AFIPS 1969 Fall Joint Computer Conference,* Vol. 35, AFIPS Press, Montvale, N.J., 27–38. *I*

Lampson, B.W.: "Protection," *Proc. 5th Princeton Conference on Information Sciences and Systems* (1971), 437–443. *4.1; S, I, P*

Landeck, B.W.: "MPX – an operating system for process control," *Advances in Instrumentation* 23, *Proceedings of 23rd ISA Conference* (Oct. 1968), 68–709. *Chap. 2*

Landy, B., and Needham, R.M.: "Software engineering techniques used in the development of the Cambridge multiple-access system," *Software – Practice and Experience* 1 (1971), 167–173. *7.3*

Lang, C.A.: "Languages for writing systems programs," in [NATO70], pp. 101–106. *7.4; S, I*

Lang, C.A.: "SAL-systems assembly languages," *Proc. AFIPS 1969 Spring Joint Computer Conference,* AFIPS Press, Montvale, N.J. (1969), 543–555. *7.4*

Lanzano, B.C.: "Loader standardization for overlay programs," *Comm. ACM* 12, No. 7 (July 1969), 541–550. *6.1*

Laschenski, J.P.: *Three Tools for the Management of a Programming Project,* IBM Technical Report TR00.2111, IBM, Poughkeepsie N.Y., 1970. *7.3*

Lasser, D.J.: "Productivity of multiprogrammed computers – progress in developing an analytic prediction method," *Comm. ACM* 12, No. 12 (Dec. 1969), 678–684. *M*

Lazarus, R., Wells, M., and Wooten, J., Jr.: "The Maniac II system," *Proc. ACM Symposium on Interactive Systems for Experimental Applied Mathematics* (Washington, D.C., Aug. 1967), 38–43.

Leavenworth, B.M.: "Programming with(out) the GOTO," *Proc. 27th ACM Conference,* 1972, ACM, New York (1972), 782–786. *7.4*

Lefkowitz, D.: *File Structures for On-Line Systems,* Spartan Books, New York, 1969. *5.2*

Lett, A.S., and Konigsford, W.L.: "TSS/360: a time-shared operating system," *Proc. AFIPS 1968 Fall Joint Computer Conference,* Vol. 33, AFIPS Press, Montvale, N.J., 15–28. *Chap. 2*

Lewis, P.A.W., and Schedler, G.S.: "A cyclic-queue model of system overhead in multiprogrammed computer systems," *J. ACM* 18, No. 2 (April 1971), 199–220. *M*

Licklider, J.C.R.: "Languages for specialization and application of prepared procedures," in *Information Systems Science,* Spartan Books, Washington, D.C. 1965, 177–187. *6.2*

Linde, R.R.: "The ADEPT-50 Time-Sharing System," *Proc. AFIPS 1969 Fall Joint Computer Conference,* Vol 35, AFIPS Press, Montvale, N.J., 39–50. *Chap. 2*

Liptay, J.S.: "Structural aspects of the System/360 Model 85: II – The Cache," *IBM Systems J.* 7, No. 1 (1968), 15–21.

Liskov, B.H.: "The design of the Venus operating system," *Proc. Third ACM Symposium on Operating Systems Principles* (Oct. 1971), 11–16, *7.1*

Liu, C.L., and Coffman, E.G., Jr.: "Scheduling algorithms for multiprogramming in a hard-real-time environment," *J. ACM* 20, (Jan. 1973), 46–61.

Llewelyn, A.I., and Wickens, R.F.: "The testing of computer software," in [NATO68], pp. 189–199. *7.3*

London, K.R.: *Decision Tables,* Auerbach, Philadelphia, 1972. *7.3*

London, R.L.: "Bibliography on proving the correctness of computer programs," TR No. 68, Computer Science Dept., Univ. of Wisconsin (1969). *7.3*

Lorin, H.: *Parallelism in Hardware and Software – Real and Apparent Concurrency,* Prentice-Hall, Englewood Cliffs, N.J., 1972.

Lowe, T.C.: "Analysis of Boolean program models for time-shared, paged environments," *Comm. ACM* 12, No. 4 (April 1969), 199–205.

Lucas, H.C., Jr.: "Performance evaluation and monitoring," *Computing Surveys* 3, (Sept. 1971), 79–92. *7.5; S, I*

Luccio, F.: "Optimal variable allocation in multiple working positions," *Second International Conference on Computing Methods in Optimization Problems* (San Remo, Italy, Sept. 1968), 213–222. *M*

Luconi, F.L.: "Asynchronous computational structures," PhD Thesis, MIT, Cambridge, Mass., MAC-TR-49 (1968). *M*

Lum, V.Y., and Ling, H.: "An optimization procedure on the selection of secondary keys," *Proc. 1971 ACM Conference,* ACM, New York (1971), 349–356. *5.4*

Lum, V.Y., et al.: "Key-to-address transform techniques: a fundamental performance study," *Comm. ACM* 14, No. 4 (April 1971), 228–239. *1.4; S, M, P*

Lynch, W.C.: "Operating system performance," *Comm. ACM* 15, No. 7 (July 1972), 579–586. *7.5*

MacDougall, M.H.: "Computer system simulation: an introduction," *ACM Computing Surveys* 2, No. 3 (Sept. 1970), 191–209. *7.2*

Madnik, S.E., and Alsop, J.W.: "A modular approach to file system design," *Proc. AFIPS 1969 Spring Joint Computer Conference,* Vol. 34, AFIPS Press, Montvale, N.J. (1969), 1–14.

Maisel, H., and Gnugnoli, G.: *Simulation of discrete stochastic systems,* Science Research Associates (1972), 317–341.

Mamelak, J.S.: "Multiprogram scheduling," *Proc. 5th National Conference of the Computer Society of Canada* (J.L. Pennington, ed.), Winnipeg, Manitoba, 1967, 213–217.

Margolin, B.H., et al.: "Analysis of free-storage algorithms," *IBM Systems J.* 10, No. 4 (1971), 283–304. *4.2; M*

Marine, G.: "The engineering mentality," *Playboy,* (Sept. 1970), 120–1, 128, 266–9. *1.1; P*

Markowitz, H.M., and Dimsdale, B.: "A description of the SIMSCRIPT language," *IBM Systems J.* 3, (1964), 57–67. *7.5*

Martin, J.: *Programming Real-Time Computing Systems,* Prentice-Hall, Englewood Cliffs, N.J., 1965. *5.5*

Martin, J.: *Design of Real-Time Computer Systems,* Prentice-Hall, Englewood Cliffs, N.J., 1967. *5.5*

Martin, J.: *Telecommunications and the Computer,* Prentice-Hall, Englewood Cliffs, N.J., 1969. *5.5*

Martin, J.: *Introduction to Teleprocessing,* Prentice-Hall, Englewood Cliffs, N.J., 1972. *5.5*

Martin, W.A.: "Sorting," *Computing Surveys* 3, No. 4 (Dec. 1971), 147–174. *3.5; S*

Mattson, R., Gecsei, J, Slutz, D., and Traiger, I.: "Evaluation techniques for storage hierarchies," *IBM Systems J.* 9, No. 2 (1970), 78–117. *M*

Maurer, W.D.: "An improved hash code for scatter storage," *Comm. ACM* 11, No. 1 (Jan. 1968), 35–38. *1.4; M*

Mayer, D.B., and Stalmaker, A.W.: "Selection and evaluation of computer personnel," *Proc. 23rd ACM National Conference,* Brandon Systems Press, Princeton, N.J., 1968, 657–670. *7.1; S, I, P*

McCarthy, J., et al.: "The linking segment subprogram linkage and linking loader," *Comm. ACM* 6, No. 7 (July 1963), 391–395. *6.1; I*

McGowan, C.L.: *Structural Programming,* Petrocelli/Charter, New York, 1974. *7.3*

McGrath, M.: "Virtual machine computing in an engineering environment," *IBM Systems J.* 11, No. 2 (1972). *7.1*

McIlroy, M.D.: "Mass produced software components," NATO Conference on Software Engineering (Garmisch, Germany, Oct. 1968), 138–155. *7.3*

McKee, P.A.: *Analysis of Job Management Functions in Multiprogramming Computer Operating Systems,* Univ. of North Carolina, Chapel Hill, 1970.

McKeehan, J.V.: "An analysis of the TSS/360 command system II," *SDD Technical Report,* TR53.0002, IBM Systems Development Division, Mohansic Laboratory (Oct. 28, 1968). *6.2*

McKeeman, W.M., et al.: *A Compiler Generator,* Prentice-Hall, Englewood Cliffs, N.J., 1970. *3.4; P*

McKinney, J.M.: "A survey of analytical time-sharing models," *Computing Surveys* 1, No. 2 (June 1969), 105–116. *7.5; M*

McLain, T.G., and Trice, A.R.: "The MINIMOP multi-access operating system," *Computer J.* 13, No. 3 (Aug. 1970), 237–242. *Chap. 2*

McPhee, W.S.: "Operating system integrity in OS/VS2," *IBM Systems J.* 13, No. 3 (1974), 230–252. *4.5*

McPhee, W.S.: "Perspective on system security and system integrity," *Proceedings of SHARE European Association (SEAS),* Stresa, Italy (1978), 264–280. *4.5*

Mealy, G.H.: "The system design cycle," *Proc. Second ACM Symposium on Operating Systems Principles* (Oct. 1969), 1–7. *7.1; I, P*

Mealy, G.H.: "A generalized assembly system," in *Programming Systems and Languages,* McGraw-Hill, New York, 1967, 535–559.

Mealy, G.H.: "Operating systems," in *Programming Systems and Languages,* McGraw-Hill, New York, 1967, 516–534. *1.2*

Mealy, G.H., et al.: "Program transferability study," Rome Air Development Center, Technical Report No. RADC-TR-68-341 (Nov. 1968). *7.4*

Mealy, G.H., Witt, B.I. and Clark, W.A.: "The functional structure of OS/360," *IBM Systems J.* 5, No. 1 (1966), 2–51. *Chap. 2*

Meeker, J.W., et al.: "OS-3: the Oregon State open shop operating system," *Proc. AFIPS 1969 Spring Joint Computer Conference,* Vol. 34, AFIPS Press, Montvale, N.J., 241–248. *Chap. 2*

Meinstein, L.S.: "RCA's time-sharing operating system," in *Comparative Operating Systems: a Symposium,* Brandon Systems Press, Princeton, N.J., 1969, pp. 1–10. *Chap. 2*

Meissner, Paul: "Evaluation of techniques for verifying personal identity," PB-255-200, National Bureau of Standards (1976). *5.5*

Merten, A., and Teichroew, D., "The Impact of Problem Statement Languages on Evaluating and Improving Software Performance," *Proc. AFIPS 1972 Joint Computer Conference,* AFIPS Press, Montvale, N.J., 1972, pp. 849–857.

Meyer, C.H., and Matyas, S.M.: *Cryptography, A New Dimension in Data Security,* John Wiley and Sons, New York, 1982. *5.5; P*

Michigan Computing Center Staff: *University of Michigan Executive System,* Univ. of Michigan Computing Center, Ann Arbor, 1963. *1.1*

Mills, D.L.: "Multiprogramming in a small systems environment," *Second ACM Symposium on Operating Systems Principles* (Oct. 1969), ACM, New York, 112–119.

Mills, H.D.: "Syntax-directed documentation for PL/360," *Comm. ACM* 13, No. 4 (April 1970), 216–222. *7.3*

Mills, H.D.: "Mathematical foundations for structured programming," Report FSC 72-6012, IBM, Gaithersburg, Md., 1972. *7.3; I, M*

Minker, J.: "An overview of associative or content addressable memory systems and a KWIC index to the literature: 1956–1970," *Computing Reviews* 12, No. 10 (1971), 453–504.

Minker, J., and Sable, J.: "File organization and data management," *Annual Review of Information Science and Technology* 2, Interscience, New York, (1968), 123–60. *5.2*

Minsky, N.: "Rotating storage devices as partially associative memories," *Proc. AFIPS 1972 Fall Joint Computer Conference,* Vol. 41, Part I, AFIPS Press, Montvale, N.J., 587–595. *5.2*

MIT, Clark, O.C., Ed.: *Ancillary Reports: Kernel Design Project,* MIT/LCS/TM-87. *4.5*

Mitrani, I.: "Nonpriority multiprogramming systems under heavy demand conditions, customers viewpoint," *J. ACM* 19, (July 1972), 445–452.

MITRE, "A random word generator for pronounceable passwords," ESD-TR-75-97 (November 1975). *5.5*

Molho, L.: "Hardware aspects of securing computing," *Proc. AFIPS 1970 Spring Joint Computer Conference,* Vol. 36, AFIPS Press, Montvale, N.J., 135–141.

Moore, C.G. and Manor, R.P.: "Cypher text: an extensible composing and typesetting language," *Proc. AFIPS 1970 Fall Joint Computer Conference,* AFIPS Press, Montvale, N.J. (1970), 555–561. *Chap. 7*

Morenoff, E. and McLean, J.B.: "An approach to standardizing computer systems," *Proc. 22nd ACM National Conference* (1967), 527–536.

Morgan, H.L.: "Spelling correction in system programs," *Comm. ACM* 13, No. 2 (Feb. 1970), 90–94. *6.2; P*

Morris, J.B.: "Demand paging through utilization of the working sets on the MANIAC II," *Comm. ACM* 15, No. 10 (Oct. 1972), 867–872.

Morris, M., and Pomerantz, A.: "Shapes highlight strains as performance plotted," *Computerworld* (Oct. 3, 1973), 13. *7.5*

Morris, R.: "Scatter storage techniques," *Comm. ACM* 11, No. 1 (January 1968), 38–44.

Morrison, R.L.: *An Approach to Performance Measurement,* IBM Technical Report TR00.2272, IBM, Poughkeepsie, N.Y., 1972. *7.5*

Motobayashi, S., et al.: "The HITAC 5020 time-sharing system," *Proc. 24th ACM National Conference* (San Francisco, Aug, 1969), 419–529.

Mullery, A.P., and Driscoll, G.C.: "A processor allocation method for time-sharing," *Comm. ACM* 13, No. 1 (Jan. 1970), 10–14. *M*

Muntz, R.R., and Coffman, E.G., Jr.: "Optimal pre-emptive scheduling on two-processor systems," *IEEE Trans. Computers* C-18, No. 11 (Nov. 1969), 1014–1020. *M*

Muntz, R.R., and Coffman, E.G., Jr.: "Preemptive scheduling of real-time tasks on multiprocessor systems," *J. ACM* 17, No. 2 (April 1970), 324–338. *M*

Murphy, J.E.: "Resource allocation with interlock detection in a multi-task system," *Proc. AFIPS 1968 Fall Joint Computer Conference,* Vol. 33, Part 2, AFIPS Press, Montvale, N.J., 1169–1176.

Nakamura, G.: "A feedback queuing model for an interactive computer system," *Proc. AFIPS 1971 Fall Joint Computer Conference,* AFIPS Press, Montvale, N.J., 57–64. *M*

National Bureau of Standards: "Computer security guidelines for implementing the privacy act of 1974," Department of Commerce, National Bureau of Standards, FIPS PUB 41 (September 1975). *3.7*

National Bureau of Standards: "Data encryption standards," Department of Commerce, National Bureau of Standards, FIPS PUB 46 (January 1977). *5.5*

National Bureau of Standards: "Evaluation of techniques for automated personal identification," Department of Commerce, National Bureau of Standards, FIPS PUB 48 (April 1977). *5.5*

NATO68 – Naur, P. and Randell, B., (eds.): *Software Engineering,* NATO, Bruxelles, 1968. *7.1; I, P*

NATO70 – Buxton, J. N., and Randell, B., (eds.): *Software Engineering Techniques,* NATO, Bruxelles, 1970. *7.1; I, P*

NCR (National Cash Register Corp., Dayton, Ohio)
1. "300 Multiprogramming Operating System" SP-1889 (1970).
2. "300 System" SP-1884 (1970).
3. "Software" SP-1874 (1971).
4. "Utility Routines" 189400 (1970).
5. "NCR Century Operating System B1" ST-9453 (1970).

Needham, R.M.: "Handling difficult faults in operating systems," *Proc. Third ACM Symposium on Operating Systems Principles* (Oct. 1971), 55–57. *3.3*

Needham, R.M., and Hartley, D.F.: "Theory and practice in operating system design," *Proc. Second ACM Symposium on Operating Systems Principles* (Princeton, N.J., Oct, 1969), ACM, New York, 8–12. *7.1; P*

Nelson, E.R.: *Management Handbook for the Estimation of Computer Programming Costs,* TM-3225/000/00, System Development Corp., Santa Monica, Calif. 1966. *7.1*

Nemeth, A.G., and Rovner, P.D.: "User program measurement in a time-shared environment," *Comm. ACM* 14, No. 10 (Oct. 1971), 661–667.

Neumann, P.G.: "The role of motherhood in the pop art of system programming," *Proc. Second ACM Symposium on Operating Systems Principles* (Princeton, N.J., Oct. 1969), 13–18. *1.2; I*

Newton, G.: "Deadlock prevention, detection, and resolution: an annotated bibliography," *Operating Systems Review* 13, No. 2 (April 1979), 33–44. *2.2*

Nickerson, R.S., et al.: "Human factors and the design of time-sharing systems," *Human Factors* 2, (April 1968), 127–134. *6.2; P*

Nielsen, N.R.: "The simulation of time-sharing systems," *Comm. ACM* 10, No. 7 (July 1967), 397–412.

Nielsen, N.R.: "An analysis of time-sharing techniques," *Comm. ACM* 14, No. 2 (February 1971), 79–90.

Northcote, R.S.: "Some software considerations in utilization of a network of computers," *Document No. 232,* Univ. of Illinois, Urbana (Nov. 1969).

Oden, P.H., and Shedler, G.S.: "A model of memory contention in a paging machine," *Comm. ACM* 15, No. 8 (August 1972), 761–771. *M*

Ohlgren, E.: "6000 SCOPE operating systems," in *Comparative Operating Systems: a Symposium,* Brandon Systems Press, Princeton, N.J., 1969, pp. 106–124. *Chap. 2, 3.2*

Oppenheimer, G., and Weizer, N.: "Resource management for a medium scale time-sharing operating system," *Comm. ACM* 11, No. 5 (May 1968), 313–322.

Opler, A.: "Acceptance testing of large programming systems," in [NATO68], pp. 113–114. *7.3*

Orceyre, Michael J., and Courtney, Robert H. Jr., Edited by Gloria R. Boltosky: "Considerations in the selection of security measures for automatic data processing systems," NBS Spec. Pub. 500-33 (June 1978). *Ap. D*

Pankhurst, R.J.: "Program overlay techniques," *Comm. ACM* 11, No. 2 (Feb. 1968), 119-125. *6.1*

Parmalee, R.P., et al.: "Virtual storage and virtual machine concepts," *IBM System J.* 11, (1972), 99-130. *Chap. 4; S, I, P*

Parnas, D.L.: "On the use of transition diagrams in the design of a user interface for an interactive computer system," *Proc. 24th ACM National Conference* (San Francisco, Aug. 1969), 378-385. *6.2*

Parnas, D.L.: "On simulating networks of parallel processes, on which simultaneous events may occur," *Comm. ACM* 12, No. 9 (Sept. 1969), 519-531.

Parnas, D.L.: "On the criteria to be used in decomposing systems into modules," *Comm. ACM* 15, No. 12, (Dec. 1972), 1053-1058. *7.1; P*

Parnas, D.L., and Darringer, J.A.: "SODAS and a methodology for system design," *Proc. AFIPS 1967 Fall Joint Computer Conference,* Vol. 31, AFIPS Press, Montvale, N.J., 449-474. *7.1*

Parsons, H.N.: "The scope of human factors in computer-based data-processing systems," *Human Factors* 12, (April 1970), 165-175. *6.2*

Patel, R.M.: "Basic I/O handling on Burroughs B 6500," *Proc. Second ACM Symposium on Operating Systems Principles* (Princeton, N.J., Oct. 1969), ACM, New York, 120-123. *3.2*

Patil, S.S.: "Coordination of asynchronous events," *Project MAC TR-72,* Cambridge Mass. (June 1970). *4.4; M*

Perry, W.E.: "Computer audit practices," *EDPACS Newsletter* (July 1977), 1-9. *3.7*

Pietrasanta, A.M.: *Management Control in Program Testing,* IBM Technical Report TR00.1474, IBM, 1966. *7.3*

Pietrasanta, A.M.: "Resource analysis of computer program system development," in *On The Management of Computer Programming,* Auerbach, Princeton, N.J., 1970. *7.1*

Pinkerton, T.B.: "Performance monitoring in a time-sharing system," *Comm. ACM* 12, No. 11 (Nov. 1969), 608-610. *7.5*

Pollack, S.L., et al.: *Decision Tables: Theory and Practice,* Wiley, New York, 1971. *7.3*

Pomeroy, J.W.: "A guide to programming tools and techniques," *IBM Systems J.* 3, (1972), 234-254. *7.2*

Poole, P.C.: "Some aspects of the EGDON 3 operating system for the KDF9," *Proc. IFIP Congress 1968* (Edinburgh, Scotland, Aug. 1968), 43-47.

Poole, P.C., and Waite, W.M.: "Machine independent software," *Proc. Second ACM Symposium on Operating Systems Principles* (Princeton, N.J., Oct. 1969), 19-24. *7.4*

Popek, G.J., and Kline, C.S.: "The PDP-11 virtual machine architecture: a case study," *Operating Systems Review* 9, No. 5 (November 1975), 97-105. *2.2*

Presser, L., and White, J.R.: "Linkers and loaders," *Computing Surveys* 4, No. 3 (Sept. 1972), 149-167. *6.1; S*

Price, C.E.: "Table lookup techniques," *Computing Surveys* 3, No. 2 (June 1971), 49-65.

Pullen, E.W., and Shuttee, D.F.: "MUSE: A tool for testing and debugging a multiprogramming system," *Proc. AFIPS 1968 Spring Joint Computer Conference,* AFIPS Press, Montvale, N.J. (1968). *7.3; I, P*

Purdom, P.W., Jr., and Stigler, S.M.: "Statistical properties of the buddy system," *J. ACM* 17, No. 4 (Oct. 1970), 682-697. *M*

Radke, C.E.: "The use of quadratic residue search," *J. ACM* 13, No. 2 (Feb. 1970), 103-105. *1.4, 5.2; M*

Ramamoorthy, C.V., and Tsuchiya, M.: "A study of user-microprogrammable computers," *Proc. AFIPS 1970 Spring Joint Computer Conference,* AFIPS Press, Montvale, N.J., 165–181. *7.3*

Randell, B.: "Towards a methodology of computing system design," *NATO Conference On Software Engineering* (Garmisch, Germany, Oct. 1968), 204–208. *7.1; I*

Randell, B.: "A note on storage fragmentation and program segmentation," *Comm. ACM* 12, No. 7 (July 1969), 365–369, 372.

Randell, B., (ed.): "Proceedings of the ACM symposium on operating system principles (the 'Gatlinburg Symposium')," *Comm. ACM* 11, No. 5 (May 1968), 295–377.

Randell, B., and Kuehner, C.J.: "Dynamic storage allocation systems," *Comm. ACM* 11, No. 5 (May 1968), 297–306.

Rasch, P.J.: "A queueing theory study of round-robin scheduling of time-shared computer systems," *J. ACM* 17, No. 1 (Jan. 1970), 131–145.

Reed, Susan K., and Gray, Martha: "Controlled accessibility bibliography," NBS Technical Note 780 (June 1973). *3.7*

Reed, Susan K.: "Automatic data processing risk assessment," NBSTR 77-1228 (March 1977). *Ap. D*

Reiter, R.: "Scheduling parallel computations," *J. ACM* 15, No. 4 (Oct. 1968), 590–599. *M*

Rembert, A.J.: *A Multiprocessing Control System,* Moore School of Electrical Engineering, Univ. of Pa., Philadelphia, 19.

Rettus, R.C., and Smith, R.A.: "Accounting control of data processing," *IBM Systems J.* 11, No. 1, (Jan. 1972), 74–92. *3.6; P*

Rice, J.R.: "Letter to the editor," *Comm. ACM* 11, No. 8 (Aug. 1968), 538–541. *7.3*

Richards, M.: "BCPL: A tool for compiler writing and system programming," *Proc. AFIPS 1969 Spring Joint Computer Conference,* AFIPS Press, Montvale (1969), 557–566. *7.4*

Robson, J.M.: "An estimate of the store size for dynamic storage allocation," *J. ACM* 18, No. 3 (July 1971), 416–423.

Rodriguez, J.E.: "A graph model for parallel computation," PhD Thesis, MIT, Cambridge, Mass., MAC-TR-46, (Sept. 1967). *M*

Rosen, S., (ed.): *Programming Systems and Languages,* McGraw-Hill, New York, 1967.

Rosen, S.: "Programming languages and systems," *Comm. ACM* 15, No. 7 (July 1972), 591–600. *S*

Rosin, R.F.: "Supervisory and monitor systems," *Computing Surveys* 1, No. 1, (March 1969), 37–54. *1.1; S, I*

Rosin, R.F.: "Contemporary concepts of microprogramming and emulation," *Computing Surveys* 1, No. 4, (Dec. 1969), 197–212. *7.2; S, I*

Rutledge, R.M., et al.: "An interactive network of time-sharing computer," *Proc. 24th ACM National Conference* (San Francisco, Aug. 1969) 431–441.

Ryder, K.D.: "A heuristic approach to task dispatching." *IBM Systems J.* 9, (1970), 189–198.

Sackman, H.: "Time sharing versus batch processing: the experimental evidence," *Proc. AFIPS 1968 Spring Joint Computer Conference,* Vol. 32, AFIPS Press, Montvale, N.J., 1–10.

Saltzer, J.H.: "Traffic control in a multiplexed computer system," ScD Thesis, MIT, Cambridge, Mass., MAC-TR-30, 1966.

Saltzer, J.H., and Gintell, J.W.: "The instrumentation of MULTICS," *Comm. ACM* 13, No. 8 (Aug. 1970), 495–500. *7.5; I*

Saltzer, J.H.: "Protection and the control of information sharing in MULTICS," *Operating Systems Review* 7, No. 4 (1973), 119 (abstract only). *4.1; I, P*

Sammet, J.E.: *Programming Languages: History and Fundamentals,* Prentice-Hall, Englewood Cliffs, N.J., 1969. *7.4; S, I*

Sammet, J.E.: "Perspective on methods of improving software development," in *Software Engineering,* COINS VII, Vol. I (J.T. Tou, ed.), Academic Press, New York, 1970, 103–119. *7.3; P*

Sammet, J.E.: "Brief survey of languages used in systems implementation," *SIGPLAN Notices* 6, No. 9 (1971), 2–19. *7.4; S, I*

Sayers, A.P., and the Comtre Corp.: *Operating System Survey,* Auerbach, Princeton, N.J., 1971. *1.1; S, I*

Sayre, D.: "Is automatic 'folding' of programs efficient enough to replace manual?" *Comm. ACM* 12, No. 12 (Dec. 1969), 656–660. *6.1; I*

Scheffler, L.J.: "Optimal folding of a paging drum in a three level memory system," *Operating Systems Review* 7, No. 4 (1973). *4.2; M*

Schneider, M.L., Wexelblat, R.L., and Jende, M.S.: "Designing control languages from the user's perspective," *Proceedings of the IFIP TC 2.7 Working Conference on Command Languages,* Berchtesgaden, West Germany, (D. Beech, Ed.), North-Holland, Inc., New York, 1980, 181–200. *6.2*

Schoen, T.A., and Belsole, M.R., Jr.: "A Burroughs 220 emulator for the IBM 360/25," *IEEE Trans on Computers* C-20, No. 7 (1971), 795–797. *7.2*

Schoenberg, R.L.: "The philosophy of the Univac 1108 operating system," in *Comparative Operating Systems: a Symposium,* Brandon Systems Press, Princeton, N.J., 1969, 11–42. *Chap. 2*

Schöneborn, K.: "Dokumentation von Systemprogrammen," (Documentation of Systems Programming), in *Systemprogrammierung* (K. Ganzhorn et al., eds.), Oldenbourg, Munich, 1972, 129–135. *7.3; I, P*

Schorr, H.: "Compiler writing techniques and problems," in [NATO70], 114–122. *7.4*

Schrage, L.: "Analysis and optimization of a queueing model of a real-time computer control system," *IEEE Trans. Computers* C-18, No. 11 (Nov. 1969), 997–1003.

Schriber, T.: *Fundamentals of Flowcharting,* Wiley, New York, 1969. *7.3*

Schroeder, M.D., and Saltzer, J.H.: "A hardware architecture for implementing protection rings," *Comm. ACM* 15, No. 3 (1972), 157–170. *3.1; I, P*

Schubert, R.F.: "Basic concepts in data base management systems," *Datamation* 18, No. 7 (1972), 42–47. *5.4; S*

Schussel, George: "The role of the data dictionary," *EDPACS Newsletter* (August 1977), 12–13. *5.4*

Schwartz, J.I.: "Interactive systems – promises, present and future," *Proc. AFIPS 1968 Fall Joint Computer Conference,* Vol. 33, AFIPS Press, Montvale, N.J. 89–98. *Chap. 2*

Schwetman, H.D., and Deline, J.R.: "An operational analysis of a remote console system," *Proc. AFIPS 1969 Spring Joint Computer Conference,* Vol. 34, AFIPS Press, Montvale, N.J., Boston, 1969, 257–264.

Seaman, P.H., Lind, R.A., and Wilson, T.L.: "An analysis of auxiliary storage activity," *IBM Systems J.* 5, No. 3 (1966), 158–170. *M*

Seaman, P.H., and Soucy, R.C.: "Simulating operating systems," *IBM Systems J.* 8, No. 2 (1969), 64–279. *7.2*

Sedgewick, R., et al.: "SPY-a program to monitor OS/360," *Proc. AFIPS 1970 Fall Joint Computer Conference,* AFIPS Press, Montvale, N.J., 119–128. *7.5*

Self, S.B., Jr.: "Logic Flow Table," *J. Data Mgt,* 5, No. 12 (1967), 30–36. *7.3*

Selig, F.: "Documentation standards," in [NATO68], pp. 209–211. *7.3; I*

Selwyn, L.: "Computer resource accounting in a time sharing environment," *Proc. AFIPS 1970 Spring Joint Computer Conference,* Vol. 36, AFIPS Press Montvale, N.J., 119–130. *3.6; P*

Senko, M.E.: "File organization and management information systems," *Annual Rev. of Information Science and Technology 4,* Encyclopedia Britannica, Chicago (1969).

Sevcik, K.C.: "The use of service time distributions in scheduling," PhD Thesis, Institute For Computer Research, Univ. of Chicago, 1971. *M*

Sevcik, K.C., et al.: "Project SUE as a learning experience," *Proc. AFIPS 1972 Fall Joint Computer Conference,* AFIPS Press, Montvale, N.J. (1972), 331-338. *Chap. 2*

Shedler, G.S., and Yang, S.C.: "Simulation of a model of paging system performance," *IBM Systems J.* 10, No. 2 (1971), 113-128. *M*

Shedler, G.S.: "A queuing model of a multiprogrammed computer with a two-level storage system," *Comm. ACM* 16, No. 1 (Jan. 1973), 3-10. *M*

Shemer, J.E., and Heying, D.W.: "Performance modeling and empirical measurements in a system designed for batch and time-sharing users," *Proc. AFIPS 1969 Fall Joint Computer Conference,* Vol. 35, AFIPS Press, Montvale, N.J., 17-26. *7.5; M*

Sherman, S., Browne, J.C., and Baskett, F.: "Trace driven modeling and analysis of CPU scheduling in a multiprogramming system," *Proc. ACM Workshop On System Performance Evaluation* (April 1971), 178-199. *M*

Shoshani, A., and Bernstein, A.J.: "Synchronization in a parallel-accessed data base" *Comm. ACM* 12, No. 11 (1969), 604-607. *4.1; M*

Shoshani, A., and Coffman, E.G., Jr.: "Sequencing tasks in multiprocess, multiple resource systems to avoid deadlocks," *Proc. 11th Annual Symposium on Switching and Automata Theory* (1970), 225-233. *4.1; M*

SIGOPS: "Proc. ACM Symposium on Operating System Principles," ACM, New York (1967). *I*

SIGOPS: "Proc. Second Symposium on Operating System Principles," (Oct. 1969), Brandon Systems Press, Princeton, N.J. *I*

SIGOPS: "Proc. of the Third Symposium on Operating System Principles," *Operating Systems Review* 6, No. 1, (Oct. 1971). *I*

SIGOPS: "Proc. Fourth Symposium on Operating System Principles," *Operating Systems Review* 7, No. 4 (1973). *I*

Simmons, G.J.: "Symmetric and asymmetric encryption," *ACM Computing Surveys* 11, No. 4 (December 1979), 305-330. *5.5; S*

Slutz, D.R.: "The flow graph model of parallel computation," PhD Thesis, MIT, Cambridge, Mass., MAC-TR-53, 1968. *M*

Smith, C.L.: "Digital control of industrial processes," *Computing Surveys* 2, No. 3 (Sept. 1970), 211-241. *2.5; S*

Smith, J.L.: "Multiprogramming under a page on demand strategy," *Comm. ACM* 10, No. 10 (Oct. 1967), 636-646. *M*

Snyderman, M., and Kline, R.A.: "Job costing a multiprogramming computer," *Data Management* 7, No. 1 (Jan. 1969), 19, 20, 42. *3.6; P*

Standeven, J., Bowden, K.F., and Edwards, D.B.G.: "An operating system for a small computer providing time shared data collection, computing, and control functions," *Proc. IFIP Congress 1968* (Edinburgh, Scotland, August 1968), 55-59. *Chap. 2*

Stanley, W.L.: "Measurement of system operational statistics," *IBM Systems J.* 8, (1969), 299-308. *7.5*

Stanley, W.L., and Hertel, H.F.: "The performance measurement and analysis of System/360 multiprogrammed systems," IBM Federal Systems Division, Houston (1966). *7.5*

Staudhammer, J., et al.: "Analysis of computer peripheral interference," *Proc. 22nd ACM National Conference* (1967), 97-101.

Steadman, H.L., and Sugar, G.R.: "Some ways of providing communication facilities for time shared computing," *Proc. AFIPS 1968 Spring Joint Computer Conference,* Vol. 32, AFIPS Press, Montvale, N.J., 23-29.

Steel, T.B., Jr.: "Multiprogramming – promise, performance, and prospect," *Proc. AFIPS 1968 Fall Joint Computer Conference,* Vol. 33, AFIPS Press, Montvale, N.J., 99–103.

Steinard, R.J.: "IBM System/370 maintenance," *Proc. 32nd Guide International,* DC8: 1–10 (1971). *7.5*

Stephenson, C.J.: "On the structure and control of commands," *Operating Systems Review* 7, No. 4 (1973), 127–136. *6.2; I*

Stimler, S.: *Real Time Data-Processing Systems,* McGraw-Hill, New York, 1969.

Stimler, S.: "Some criteria for time-sharing system performance," *Comm. ACM* 12, No. 1 (Jan. 1969), 47–53. *7.5*

Stowe, H.B.: *Uncle Tom's Cabin,* Cassell, London, 1892. *7.1*

Strachey, C.: In [NATO70], 29. *7.1*

Strauss, J.C.: "A simple thruput and response model of EXEC8 under swapping saturation," *Proc. AFIPS 1971 Fall Joint Computer Conference,* AFIPS Press, Montvale, N.J., 39–49. *M*

Sutherland, W.T.: "On-line graphical specification of computer procedures," TR 405 Lincoln Laboratory, MIT Document AD639, 1966. *7.3*

Taber, J.K.: "A survey of computer crime studies," *Computer Law Journal* 2, No. 2 (Spring 1980), 275–327. *Ap. D*

Takacs, L.: *Introduction To The Theory of Queues,* Oxford University Press, New York, 1962. *M*

Taylor, A.: "Must management replace DP in billing quandary," *Computerworld* 11, (Dec. 8, 1971). *3.6; P*

Teichroew, D., and Lubin, J.F.: "Computer simulation – discussion of the technique and comparison of languages," *Comm. ACM* 9, No. 10 (Oct. 1966), 723–741. *7.2; S*

Teorey, T.J., and Pinkerton, T.B.: "A comparative analysis of disk scheduling policies," *Proc. Third ACM Symposium on Operating Systems Principles* (Oct. 1971), 114–121. *S, M*

Thompson, R.N., and Wilkinson, J.S.: "The D824 automatic operating and scheduling program," in *Programming Systems and Languages,* McGraw-Hill, New York, 1967, 647–660. *Chap. 2*

Tou, J.T., and Wegner, P., (eds.): "Proc. Symposium on data structures in programming languages," *SIGPLAN Notices* 6, No. 2 (Feb. 1971).

Tou, J.T., (ed.): *Software Engineering COINS,* Vol. I, Academic Press, New York, 1971.

Tou, J.T., (ed.): *Software Engineering COINS III,* Vol. II, Academic Press, New York, 1971.

Tou, J.T., (ed.): *Software Engineering COINS IV,* 1973.

Trapnell, F.M.: "A systems approach to the development of systems programs," *Proc. AFIPS 1969 Spring Joint Computer Conference,* AFIPS Press, Montvale, N.J. (1969). *7.1; P*

Trimble, G.R., Jr.: "A time sharing bibliography," *Computing Reviews* 9, No. 5 (May 1968), 291–301. *Chap. 2*

Tucker, A.B., and Flynn, M.J.: "Dynamic microprogramming: processor organization and programming," *Comm. ACM* 14, No. 4 (April 1971), 240–250.

Tucker, S.G.: "Emulation of large systems," *Comm. ACM* 8, No. 12 (Dec. 1965), 753–761. *7.2*

Tucker, S.G.: "Microprogram control for system/360," *IBM Systems J.* 6, (1967), 222–241. *7.2*

Tung, C.: "On the apparent continuity of processing in a paging environment," *IEEE Trans. Computers* C-19, No. 11 (Nov. 1970), 1047–1057. *M*

Turn, Rein, and Shapiro, Norman Z.: "Privacy and security in databank systems: measures of effectiveness, costs and protector-intruder interactions," The Rand Corporation, Santa Monica, Ca., P-4871 (July 1972). Also in *Proceedings, Fall Joint Computer Conference 1972,* AFIPS Press, Montvale, N.J. (1972). *5.4; I*

Turn, Rein: "Privacy and security in personal information," The Rand Corporation, Santa Monica, Cal., R-1044 NSF (March 1974). *5.4*

Turn, Rein: "Classification of personal information for privacy protection purposes," *Proceedings National Computer Conference 1976*, AFIPS, Vol. 45, AFIPS Press, Montvale, N.J. (1976), 301–307. *5.4*

UNI (UNIVAC Division of Sperry-Rand Corp., Blue Bell, Pa.)
1. "EXEC VIII Programmer's Reference" UP 4144 Rev 1 (1968).
2. "Sort-Merge in 1108 Executive, Programmer's Reference" UP 7621 (1968).
3. "1108 Multiprocessor System" UP 4046 Rev 3 (1970).

Van de Goor, A., Bell, C.G., and Witcratt, D.A.: "Design and behavior of TSS/8: a PDP-8 based time-sharing system," *IEEE Trans. Computers* C-18, No. 11 (Nov. 1969), 1038–1043.

Van Fleet, D., and Bornn, J.A.: "HIPO: A new program documentation technique," *Proc. GUIDE* 36, 1973. *7.3; I*

Van Horn, E.C.: "Three criteria for designing computing systems to facilitate debugging," *Comm. ACM* 11, No. 5 (May 1968), 360–365. *7.3*

Vareha, A.L., Rutledge, R.M., and Gold, M.M.: "Strategies for structuring two level memories in a paging environment," *Proc. Second ACM Symposium on Operating System Principles* (Princeton, N.J., Oct. 1969), ACM, New York, 54–59. *M*

Varney, R.C.: "Process selection in a hierarchical operating system," *Proc. Third ACM Symposium on Operating Systems Principles* (Oct. 1971), 106–108. *M*

Verhelst, M.: "Conversion of limited-entry decision tables to optimal and near-optimal flowcharts: two new algorithms," *Comm. ACM* 15, No. 11 (Nov. 1972), 974–980. *7.3*

Walden, D.C.: "A system for interprocess communication in a resource sharing computer network," *Comm. ACM* 15, No. 4 (April 1972), 221–230.

Walsh, D.A.: *A Guide for Software Documentation*, Interact Corp., New York, 1969. *7.3; P*

Walther, W.: "Multiprocessor self diagnosis, surgery, and recovery in air terminal traffic control," *Operating Systems Review* 7, No. 4 (Oct. 1973), 38–44. *2.5*

Watson, R.W.: *Time Sharing System Design Concepts*, McGraw-Hill, New York, 1970. *5.6*

Webb, D.A: "The development and application of an evaluation model for hash coding systems," Syracuse University, Syracuse, N.Y. (1972). *5.2; M*

Wegner, P.: "Communication between independently translated blocks," *Comm. ACM* 5, (1962) 376–381. *6.1; I*

Wegner, P.: "Machine organization for multiprogramming," *Proc. 22nd ACM National Conference* (1967), 135–150.

Wegner, P.: *Programming Languages, Information Structures and Machine Organization*, McGraw-Hill, New York, 1967

Weinberg, G.M.: *The Psychology of Computer Programming*, Van Nostrand-Reinhold, New York, 1971. *7.3; I*

Weinberg, G.M. "The psychology of improved programming performance," *Datamation* 18, (Nov. 1972), 82–83, 85. *7.3; I*

Weinberg, G.M., *Structured Programming in PL/C: An Abcedarian*, Wiley, New York, 1973. *7.3*

Weinwurm, G.F., (ed.): *On The Management of Computer Programming*, Auerbach, Princeton, N.J., 1970. *7.3; P*

Weissman, C.: "Security controls in the ADEPT-50 time-sharing system," *Proc. AFIPS 1969 Fall Joint Computer Conference*, Vol. 35, AFIPS Press, Montvale, N.J., 119–133.

Weissman, Clark: "System security analysis/certification methodology and results," System Development Corporation, Santa Monica, Cal., SP-3728 (October 1973). *7.3*

Weizer, N., and Oppenheimer, G.: "Virtual memory management in a paging environment," *Proc. AFIPS 1969 Spring Joint Computer Conference*, Vol. 34, AFIPS Press, Montvale, N.J., 249–256.

Wichmann, B.A.: "A modular operating system," *Proc. IFIP Congress 1968* (Edinburgh, Scotland, Aug, 1968), 48–54.

Wilkes, M.V.: *Time-sharing Computer Systems,* American Elsevier, New York, 1968.

Wilkes, M.V.: "A model for core space allocation in a time-sharing system," *Proc. AFIPS 1969 Spring Joint Computer Conference,* Vol. 34, AFIPS Press, Montvale, N.J., 265–271. *M*

Wilkes, M.V.: "Slave memories and dynamic storage allocation," *IEEE Trans. Computers* 14, No. 4 (April 1965), 270–271. *M*

Wilkes, M.V.: "The growth of interest in microprogramming: a literature survey," *Computing Surveys* 1, (Sept. 1969), 139–145. *7.2; S*

Wilkes, M.V.: "The dynamics of paging," *Computer J.* 16, No. 1 (1973), 4–9. *4.2; I, P*

Winick, R.M.: "QTAM: control and processing in a tele-communication environment," *Proc. 24th ACM National Conference* (San Francisco, Aug. 1969), 611–618.

Winitz, H.E. Herriman, and Belleross, B.: "Long-term recall of speech sounds as a function of pronounceability," *Language and Speech* 18, (1/75), 74–82. *5.5*

Winograd, J., Morganstein, S.J., and Herman, R.: "Simulation studies of a virtual memory time-shared demand paging operating system," *Proc. Third ACM Symposium on Operating Systems Principles* (Oct. 1971), 149–155.

Wirth, N.: "PL360 – A programming language for the 360 computers," *J. ACM* 15, No. 1 (Jan. 1968), 37–74. *7.4*

Wirth, N.: "On multiprogramming, machine coding and computer organization," *Comm. ACM* 12, No. 9 (Sept. 1969), 489–498.

Wood, D.C.M.: "An example in synchronization of cooperating processes: theory and practice," *Operating Systems Review* 7, (July 1973), 10–18. *5.3; P*

Wood, D.C.M., and Forman, E.H.: "Throughput measurement using a synthetic job stream," *Proc. AFIPS 1971 Fall Joint Computer Conference* (Nov. 1971), 51–56. *7.5*

Wood, Helen M.: "The use of passwords for controlled access to computer resources," NBS Special Publication 500-9 (May 1977). *3.7*

Woon, P.Y.: *Private communication* (1972). *6.3*

Wulf, W.A., et al.: "BLISS – A language for systems programming," *Comm. ACM* 14, No. 12 (Dec. 1971), 780–790. *7.4*

Wulf, W.A.: "Performance monitors for multiprogramming systems," *Proc. Second ACM Symposium on Operating Systems Principles* (Princeton, N.J., Oct. 1969), 175–181. *7.5*

Wulf, W.A. et al.: "The kernel of a multiprocessor operating system," *Comm. ACM* 17, No. 6 (June 1974), 337–344.

XDS (Xerox Data Systems, El Segundo,)
1. "Sigma 6 Computer-Reference Manual" 90-17-113B (1971).
2. "Sigma 9 Computer Reference Manual" 90-17-33C (1972).
3. "XOS-Batch Processing Reference Manual" 90-17-65A.
4. UTS-Time Sharing Reference Manual" 90-09-07C (1971).
5. "UTS-System Management Reference Manual" 90-16-74C (1972).

Yale Computer Center Staff: *7044/7040 Operating Systems Guide,* Yale University Computing Center, New Haven, Conn., 1963.

Yourdan, E.: "Reliability of real-time systems," *Modern Data.,* (Jan. 1972), 37–41; (Feb.), 50–55; (Mar.), 36–41; (April), 52–57; (May), 38–53; (June), 38–46.

Zimmerman, N.A.: "System integration as a programming function," *Proc. 24th ACM National Conference,* (San Francisco, Aug, 1969), 459–465. *7.3*

Zurcher, F.W., and Randell, B.: "Iterative multi-level modeling – a methodology for computer system design," *Proc. IFIP Congress 1968,* North-Holland, Amsterdam, 1969, 867-871. *7.2*

Index

409